ANNUAL REPORT

OF THE

ARCHAEOLOGICAL SURVEY OF INDIA

1921-22

ANNUAL REPORT
OF THE
ARCHAEOLOGICAL SURVEY OF INDIA
1921-22

EDITED BY

D. BRAINERD SPOONER, O.B.E., Ph.D., F.A.S.B.,

Officiating Director-General of Archaeology in India.

GYAN

Published by

Gyan Publishing House
5, Ansari Road
Daryaganj, New Delhi-110002
Phone: 011-47034999, 9811692060
E-mail: books@gyanbooks.com

Distribution Network
gyanbooks.com
India, USA, Canada, UK, Australia, France

ISBN : 978-81-212-2642-4 (HB)
First Published, 1924

2nd Impression 2021

Printed at: Gyan Press, Delhi.

Annual Report
of the
Archaeological Survey of India
Author: D. Brainerd Spooner

ANNUAL REPORT

OF THE

ARCHÆOLOGICAL SURVEY OF INDIA

1921-22

EDITED BY

D. BRAINERD SPOONER, O.B.E., PH.D., F.A.S.B.,

Officiating Director-General of Archæology in India.

SIMLA
GOVERNMENT OF INDIA PRESS
1924

Price Rupees Twenty-four and Annas Eight

ANNUAL REPORT
OF THE
ARCHÆOLOGICAL SURVEY OF INDIA

1921-22.

PREFACE.

IT is unfortunate that the editing of this Report should have devolved, owing to the absence on leave of Sir John Marshall, Director General of Archæology in India, upon the present writer, as it is the first of the new consolidated reports. Sir John was able to revise practically all the contributions sent in for the Conservation Section of the Report, and to arrange the plates; but otherwise the editorial responsibility rests upon the undersigned and Mr. Blakiston, though all concerned would have preferred that Sir John's riper experience should have moulded the new form throughout.

Ever since the re-organization of the Department in 1902, it has been the rule for each Provincial Superintendent to issue an independent Annual Progress Report for the Circle of which he is in charge, the Director General's Report then summarising the year's work as a whole, and recording particulars of his own activities. So long as each Province bore the cost of its own Archæological work, this arrangement was inevitable, but it necessarily involved a considerable amount of repetition and duplication of effort. Now that Archæology is centralised under the Reforms, and the entire cost is borne by the Imperial Government, it has seemed best to do away with the Provincial Reports, and to issue instead one joint or consolidated Report for the Archæological Survey as a whole. This joint Report is naturally made up of the contributions received from the several Circles, put together under the editorship of the Director General, who, in normal years, will also contribute a record of his own work during the year. The method is one from which a certain unevenness is inseparable, but it is the only one permitting the officers of the Department to express their individuality. To emphasize this aspect of the Report the fullest possible use has been made of inverted commas, so that each officer's contribution may, so far as possible, stand alone, and rest visibly upon his own authority.

Simla, 6th June 1923.

TABLE OF CONTENTS.

LIST OF PLATES.

ANNUAL REPORT

OF THE

ARCHÆOLOGICAL SURVEY OF INDIA

FOR THE YEAR

1921-22.

SECTION I.

CONSERVATION OF MONUMENTS.

Northern Circle.
Muhammadan and British Monuments.
United Provinces.

AS a consequence of the changes arising out of the Reforms, a certain dislocation of work was inevitable. Thus Mr. Blakiston, Superintendent of Muhammadan and British Monuments in the Northern Circle, reports that: "In the United Provinces, owing to the late submission by the Provincial Government of the revised Programme of Conservation works, funds could not be allotted till January, and on funds being so allotted there was almost a rush to submit 'lapse statements' under one pretext or another, Public Works officers finding it difficult, if not impossible, to utilise funds placed at their disposal so late in the year. In some cases estimates were found to be out of date and work in consequence could not be proceeded with. In others, the Public Works' Code rules were quoted which forbid a 'special work' being commenced in the month of March. In some cases it was discovered that no arrangements had been made for the acquisition of land. As a result, in the United Provinces alone out of a total of Rs. 1,13,645 *plus* Rs. 21,593 for Departmental charges allotted to conservation, Rs. 31,137 were allowed to lapse.

"In the Punjab affairs were conducted with more success. Rs. 82,885 including Departmental charges were allotted by the Government of India for conservation, and of this sum, although also received rather late in the year, only about Rs. 3,700 were permitted to lapse. In the Province of Delhi out of Rs. 1,19,915 *plus* Rs. 14,085 for Departmental charges received for conservation and maintenance of gardens, only a few rupees were relinquished."

Northern Circle.
Agra Office.
United Provinces.

In compiling the statements of expenditure given in Appendix A (1) Mr. Blakiston says some difficulty has been experienced. "Funds are allotted for the financial year (April 1st to March 31st) but in two of the Provinces in this Circle annual repairs are continued up to June 30th in the case of the Punjab and July 31st in the Delhi Province. In consequence it will be seen that many annual repair works are shown as 'in progress'. It has been the custom of Superintending Engineers in these Provinces when submitting their statements of expenditure on Conservation to account for only that sum which has been expended out of the year's allotment, ignoring the sum that was expended from the previous year's allotment during the period from April 1st to June 30th (or July 31st) with the result that the annual reports of this Circle have never accounted for the expenditure in those three or four months. This year endeavours have been made to obtain correct figures for expenditure during the whole financial year under report and, as a consequence, the expenditure in some instances appears greater than the allotment, owing to the fact that a large sum had been spent from the previous year's grant during the early months of the financial year. It is hoped that in future arrangements may be made whereby grants must be expended during the financial year in which they are allotted, so that complications in compiling the expenditure statement may be avoided.

Agra.

"But notwithstanding the failure of the Local Government to take full advantage of the allotment made to it, and despite other set-backs, the excellent work executed by the Public Works Department in Agra must not be overlooked. Khan Bahadur Hira Khan, the Executive Engineer, and his subordinates have earned the gratitude of the Archæological Department for the manner and rapidity in which they completed the restoration of the colonnade along the south side of the Taj forecourt. Although orders to continue the estimate were not received until late in the year, they managed by putting their best into the work to finish it in time for H. R. H. the Prince of Wales' visit on 13th February at an outlay of Rs. 28,261. This now completes the restoration of the *dalans* (colonnades) which have already taken their place in the general picture as though they had never been missing (Plate I*a*). The work of restoration on the east causeway at Akbar's Tomb at Sikandara, Agra, is another important work which was continued from last year and is still in progress, and which it is hoped to complete during the ensuing year if sufficient funds can be made available. In conjunction with this work repairs to the large well attached to the causeway on the south have also been taken in hand. Several large trees that were growing up against it have been removed besides much earth and accumulated debris. The interior, too, has been cleaned out and pointed and the brickwork has been repaired down to the bottom; so that the only item now remaining to be done is the repair of the surrounding passage and exterior. At Mariam's Tomb (she was the wife of Akbar) a small red stone *jali* was set up to prevent visitors falling down a dangerous flight of steps. Conservation of the little mosque known as Itbari Khan's on the road to Sikandara, interesting chiefly on account of a long and well-executed inscription, was taken in hand and completed, and, at the same time, Akbar's Horse which stood on the opposite side of the railway embankment from the road (Plate II*d*) and could not be seen, was removed from its pedestal and placed on a new one provided for it near the mosque mentioned above. The construction of bridle paths to the tombs of Itbari Khan, Sadiq Khan and Salabat Khan, nobles of the time of Akbar, which are in the vicinity of the little mosque, was also put in hand and nearly finished except for a portion of the pathway to Itbari Khan's Tomb, which had to be postponed pending certain proceedings in connection with the acquisition of land. Four red sandstone seats

Northern Circle.

Agra Office.

United Provinces.

Agra.

for Akbar's Tomb and four for Itimad-ud-Daulah's Tomb, intended for the convenience of visitors, were made from designs supplied by the Archæological Superintendent. In the Fort at Agra special repairs to the marble *chajja* in the Moti Masjid were carried out. The stones had in some instances become loose or broken on account of the iron dowels and cramps being eaten away by rust. The Delhi Gate in the Fort also received attention, the work there comprising, among other things, the renewal of broken or decayed stone, pointing and cleaning. At the Kanch Mahal at Sikandara a commencement was made in the construction of a tube well and engine house with pumping plant. This work is being undertaken by the Sanitary Department and is designed to supply water for the area outside the main entrance to Akbar's Tomb, which, when water is made available, is to be planted with grass and trees. The only other works of importance in the United Provinces were at Lucknow where certain repairs were undertaken both at the Chhatar Manzil and at the Residency. At the latter monument *surkhi* was spread on the roadways and marble tablets with inscriptions describing the position of certain historical spots were erected and some extensions were made to the iron railings partly surrounding the grounds.

Lucknow.

The Punjab.

Lahore.

" In the Punjab Lahore was the centre round and about which most conservation of Muhammadan monuments was undertaken during the year. A very considerable amount of work was executed at Shalamar against the visit of the Prince of Wales in March. The white marble work of the water courses was repaired and cleaned, and the floors and ceilings of the *baradaris* were also repaired and their walls distempered ivory white. Improvements were made to some of the fountains by increasing the size of the jets from ⅜ inch to ¾ inch, and silt deposited by the canal was dug away from the irrigation channel in front of the main entrance gate. A pair of handsome new doors designed in the office of the Superintendent, Muhammadan and British Monuments, was constructed and hung in position in place of the old rotten ones in the entrance gateway. The bronze studs and bolts for it were made in the Mayo School of Art under the personal supervision of the Principal, who is always most obliging in undertaking works of this description for the Archæological Department. In addition, a new counter has been purchased for the pumping engine and will shortly be fixed. The foot path from the Grand Trunk Road through the Gulabi Bagh Gateway to Dai Anga's Tomb was completed, and also the special repairs to the Chauburji Gateway which were in progress from the previous year. The chief item at the latter was the erection of a fence round the buildings. At Shahdara, the roadways in the Akbari Sarai have been remetalled and a new notice board provided at the tomb of Nur Jahan. The works in connection with the conservation of Asaf Khan's Tomb adjoining the Akbari Sarai are now almost completed. The estimate for this improvement amounted to Rs. 38,549 and this has been gradually dealt with during the past three years. During the year under review work has been confined chiefly to repairs to the old brick causeways, which after removing the earth with which they had become almost completely covered, were found to be badly dilapidated. Certain levelling and grassing was also done. Arrangements for irrigating the grass have yet to be made and the fixing of a pump for that purpose is in hand. The conservation of the gateways, *dalans* and walls around the Akbari Sarai has been in progress. Work here consisted for the most part of underpinning brickwork and repairing, pointing and edging plaster, while some marble inlay-work on the gateway leading to Jahangir's Tomb requires yet to be attended to. At Nawakot, a village a couple of miles outside Lahore, repairs were commenced and works executed on the outsides of walls and to the two remaining corner pavilions. Much remains to be done here as the gateway and pavilions, which are

Northern Circle.
Agra Office.
The Punjab.
Lahore.

decorated with coloured tiles, have for many years been occupied by the villagers as habitations, with the result that they have got into a very bad state of repair. In the centre of the village is a tomb ascribed locally to Zeb-un-Nissa, the learned daughter of Aurangzeb, but since it is known that she was buried in Delhi, the identity of the person buried in this tomb remains a mystery.

Hissar.

"Outside the Lahore area the chief work in progress was the conservation of Firoz Shah's palace at Hissar, where tons of earth have had to be removed in order to expose the ancient walls and *dalans*; part of the roof too has been concreted and some of the walls secured. In the Phillaur and Nakodar Tahsils in the Jallandar District all the Kos Minars along the old Mughal highway have been repaired, and at Rohtas, Sher Shah Sur's ancient stronghold in the Jhelum District, special repairs have just commenced on some of the gateways and walls. Much of the walling of this large Fort is far too ruined to justify repair, and attention is therefore being concentrated on those parts which are still fairly intact or of special interest. Among other monuments in the Punjab which were under repair were Sheikh Chilli's Tomb and the small stone mosque at Thanesar in the Karnal District. Work at the former had only just commenced when the financial year closed, but at the latter repairs, which for the most part consisted of laying stone paving in the courtyard, providing a new stone *jali* screen and odds and ends of repairs to walling, were completed. The sarcophagus from Lala Rukh's Tomb at Hasan Abdal has been brought from the site to Agra for repairs by a firm of stone masons. Most of the funds provided for this work were expended in quarrying the *abri* stone which is only obtainable at Jaisalmer in the centre of Rajputana, and bringing it thence over 100 miles across desert country by camel to the railway. Special repairs which had been started in the previous year to the memorial obelisk on the battlefield of Chillianwala were completed."

Rohtas.

Thanesar.

Hasan Abdal.

Chillianwala.

Delhi Province.

"In the Delhi Province" Mr. Blakiston reports, "the conservation of various structures in Firoz Shah's Kotla, which had been in progress for some time past, has now been practically completed, the chief task still remaining to be done being the grassing of the newly levelled areas. The principal items of work executed during the year were underpinning of enclosure walls and bastions, and of the main entrance gateway, *dalans*, *baoli*, mosque and buildings in the elevated courtyard (Plate I*b*); the removal of earth and debris from along part of the enclosure wall, the roof of the *baoli*, the *dalans* and the elevated courtyard to the south of the mosque, and the levelling of a large area at the southern end of the Kotla from which a large amount of earth had to be excavated. Besides these measures, buildings were made watertight, old plaster was edged and various walls and remains of buildings exposed. At Tughlaqabad the conservation of Ghiyas-ud-din's Fort was also continued, the main tasks achieved being the underpinning and strengthening of crumbling pillars on the inside of the fort, the waterproofing of wall tops, the reconstruction of the flight of steps up to the front gateway (Plate III *a* and *b*), and the purchase and demolition of some huts which encroached on the walls. Another useful improvement taken in hand this year was the conservation of the walls of Qadam Sharif, a building of Firoz Shah's period, where earth and débris were removed from the outside walls, and the walls themselves were underpinned, while repairs were also carried out to the terrace floors behind the parapets, to the *kanguras*, andportions of the walls (Plate III *c* and *d*). Besides many graves there is a village in the interior of this enclosure, so that at present it is quite impossible to attend to the inner sides of the walls, but it is hoped that later on this work also can be taken up. At Sher Shah's Gateway and at the Khair-ul-Manazil opposite the Purana Qila a good start was made in the removal of accumulated débris, the roadway leading through the gate and *dalans* on both sides being cleared as well as part of the northern side of the gateway. The courtyard of the Khair-ul-Manazil, which is a mosque built by Maham Angah, the foster mother of the Emperor Akbar, was entirely cleared of débris and earth, and underpinning and repairs were begun on the *dalans* on the north and south sides. At the mosque at Khirki earth to the extent of some eight feet in depth and fifteen feet in width has been excavated from the four sides of the structure, and the cells around, previously hidden to view, have been exposed. Special repairs were undertaken at the palace of Bahadur Shah II, the last king of Delhi, known as the Zaffar Mahal, in the village of Mehrauli. The building is of no great architectural value, being interesting only on account of its historical associations. Repairs mainly consisted of the removal of earth and débris from the courtyard and rooms, underpinning in patches, relaying one roof and removing another which was past repair, edging plaster, making the tops of broken walls watertight and clearing up the palace generally. An item of great utility was the provision of an electric pump at the tomb of Safdar Jang for irrigating the grass on either side of the approach, the necessary feeder and pipe lines also being laid down. Among the smaller works undertaken during the year may be mentioned a pair of new teak doors provided for the Tah-Khana beneath the Rang Mahal in the Fort and the construction of a stable for the bullocks used in the Fort gardens, and a small godown. Some small repairs were also undertaken at the rear of the Diwan-i-Amm, and an inlaid black marble panel at the back of the throne was repaired. At Purana Qila the small Devi Temple inside the Fort was put into a proper state of repair. Certain badly undermined places that had appeared in the north-west wall of the Begumpuri Mosque were underpinned at short notice to save that portion from possible collapse; and repairs of a petty nature were undertaken at the Chauburji and Wazirabad Mosques. Finally a commencement was made on an approach roadway 7-8ths of a mile in length from the Qutb Road to Hauz Khas to take the place of the footpath now in use. When completed the road should be a great convenience to visitors wishing to see the historic and interesting buildings there.

Northern Circle.
Agra Office.
Delhi Province.

Gardens in Delhi.

" With the Protected Monuments the Government of India have also assumed charge of the gardens connected with them, where such have been laid out. The Northern Circle possesses some exceedingly good gardens, mostly of the Mughal type designed on formal lines, such for example as those of the Taj Mahal and Itimad-ud-Daulah's Tomb at Agra, Safdar Jang's and Humayun's Tombs at Delhi and Jahangir's Tomb and the Shalimar Garden at Lahore. The Qutb and Delhi Fort Gardens are also formal in the main, but an attempt has been made to show the positions of ancient buildings no longer in existence by means of additional shrubberies. With the exception of those at Delhi, funds for the upkeep of all these gardens have this year been provided by the Provincial Government of the Province in which they are situated, as Budget arrangements had already been made. The expenditure in connection with these has therefore been shown separately in the Appendix. It is by no means an inconsiderable sum. We hope, however, that the cost of maintaining these gardens can be gradually reduced by developing their revenue-producing possibilities. Although none can be said to be self-supporting at the present time, some at any rate do bring in some small income to Government through the sale of grass or dead trees, plants and flowers, etc., while at the Taj Mahal a fairly substantial sum is realised from licences to vendors for the sale of photographs and curios. At the Delhi Fort, where a small fee of two annas is charged, the handsome sum of Rs. 13,792-6-0 was realised against an expenditure of Rs. 6,839

Northern Circle.
Agra Office.
Delhi Province.

for the pay of the Caretaker and his staff. The specially severe heat during the summer of 1921 did great damage to all our gardens and many shrubs and trees died. The question of water supply is a very difficult one everywhere and nearly all the Superintendents of Gardens have something to say on that subject in their reports. At Delhi the lack of sufficient good water is seriously felt and several schemes for the improvement of the gardens are held up on that account. This is specially true in the case of Humayun's Tomb, where hardly any fresh water is available and it is necessary to use the salt-impregnated water from the wells, which is practically useless for shrubs and flowers. At the Qutb, although there are two good wells worked by bullocks and another worked by an engine, there is an insufficiency of water to keep the gardens in as high a state of efficiency as is desired. The little garden at Hauz Khas, to which a roadway from the main road is now in course of construction, is an exception and always looks green and well attended to. At Purana Qila over 16 acres of land had to be regrassed during the monsoon and trees were kept alive throughout the summer with water brought from outside. Firoz Shah's Kotla sadly needs a better water supply. There is a quantity of grassing to be done there, but it is useless to do anything until better watering arrangements are available. The Delhi Fort is always green, though here, too, the great heat of the summer of 1921 killed off nearly half the Grevillea trees. But the Superintendent of the garden is to be congratulated on the excellence of his shrubberies, which afford a beautiful setting to the palaces and other buildings. The garden was looking at its best at the time of H. R. H. the Prince of Wales' visit in February. Conditions at Safdar Jang have improved since the introduction of two electrically driven pumping plants provided during the previous year, and in consequence the new scheme for the layout can now be proceeded with.

Gardens in the United Provinces.

"In the United Provinces the garden at the Taj is, of course, the most important. This is fed by canal water, which though nearly always available also introduces a considerable amount of undesirable mud and silt and on that account is not without its objections. A scheme for pumping clean water from a large well in the Bagh Khan-i-Alam for the fountains and water channels was commenced two years ago, but on the assumption of the charge of archæological buildings by the Central Government the work, which had been started by the Provincial Government, was stopped and no funds for its resumption have since been forthcoming. In parts of the garden the shrubberies have become somewhat thin and ragged-looking, but steps are being taken to plant a quantity of new flowering shrubs of various descriptions. At the Ram Bagh the scarcity of water is very seriously felt. There are two wells in use but they are insufficient for the needs of the garden, which is an old Mughal one chiefly planted out with fruit trees. The garden has been sadly neglected of late and whereas, if properly looked after in spite of the shortage of water, it should have shown a profit, it has come to entail an annual loss to Government of several thousand rupees. The new Superintendent of Gardens is paying particular attention to the Ram Bagh with a view to making it both more presentable and more paying. The garden connected with the Tomb of Itimad-ud-Daulah also lacks water, an oil-engined pump in one corner being the sole means for supplying water. It may be remarked also that the price of oil has risen considerably of late and that this extra expenditure is rather seriously affecting the limited financial resources of all gardens dependent on oil engines. A scheme has been prepared for improving the shrubberies at the Tomb of Itimad-ud-Daulah, which are by no means good, and incidentally restoring the old causeway around the edge of the garden.

Northern Circle.
Agra Office.
Gardens in the United Provinces.

Likewise at Akbar's Tomb at Sikandara steps are being taken for the improvement of the shrubberies, for which many flowering plants have already been struck in the nurseries, and for restoring the whole of the south-east quarter of the garden more or less to its original state, by removing winding roadways and earthen water channels and in their place providing pathways with proper water channels according to the Mughal principles of garden design. However, the question of water again arises and much work will have to stand over till arrangements can be made for a regular and sufficient supply. Work has already been taken in hand on a large well near the Kanch Mahal outside the Tomb compound, but this well will only be used for the lawns outside the main south entrance, which will be laid out when the well is in working order. It should be mentioned here that proposals have been submitted to Government for the separation of the budgets of Provincial and Archæological Gardens at Agra but providing that the Garden Superintendent and his headquarters staff shall be common to both. The garden known as the Khusru Bagh at Allahabad, in which are situated the Tombs of Khusru, the son of Jahangir, and of his mother, is still under the control of the Provincial Government. If it is decided to take it over as an archæological garden, it is evident from the statement showing expenditure and income that something radical will have to be done, as we should hardly be prepared to face an annual loss of some Rs. 10,000. The only other garden of note in the United Provinces is that of the Residency at Lucknow. This, like the other archæological gardens, is looked after by the local Superintendent of Gardens. It is fairly well kept, but it is considered that with a little more attention it could be made more tidy and the flowers be improved. The caretakers here are very untidy, not having been provided with uniforms for the past three or four years, and it is hoped that steps will be taken to rectify the omission as soon as possible since without official uniform their efficiency is much reduced.

Gardens in the Punjab.

"In the Punjab the gardens at Jahangir's Tomb, Shalimar and Hazuri Bagh are the most important. These are all quite well looked after but the grass is of a poor nature, there being, it seems, considerable difficulty in making the good *dūb* grass grow properly in Lahore. Funds for the upkeep of these gardens were provided by the local Government in 1921-22, but it is presumed that in future the Central Government will take over the responsibility as the monuments connected with them are already in that Government's charge."

Northern Circle.
(Hindu and Buddhist Monuments).
Punjab.
Amb.

Of the Hindu and Buddhist monuments in the Punjab Rai Bahadur Daya Ram Sahni says eight only came under special repairs. "At the temple at Amb the principal item was the partial reconstruction of the core of the massive basement, which had been brought to light in the preceding year. The new masonry has been executed in old blocks obtained from the site similar in all respects to those used in the original structure; and pathways have been provided from both temples up to the walls of the fort. I found that the excavation provided for in the original estimate fell short of the actual requirements as the original floor lies about three feet below the level reached in the previous year's operations. A fresh estimate amounting to Rs. 2,601 had therefore to be framed providing for the completion of the excavations, besides the construction of a concrete floor on the top of the basement and the drainage of the precinct.

Kangra.

The work undertaken in the hill fort at Kangra consisted mostly of petty measures, such as the removal of undergrowth, repairs to the entrance gate and the making of an approach way to the temple. A small temple was also excavated and freed from debris. At the Baijnath temple in the same district further progress was made with the scraping

Northern Circle.
Lahore Office.
Punjab.

off of the whitewash which concealed valuable carvings in the main sanctuary, and one of the pilasters in the entrance to the mandapa was also taken out and re-set in its original position. Shrine No. 4 in the northern portion of the enclosure which had been badly damaged in the earthquake of 1905 was dismantled and rebuilt with the old material, while the Dharmasala attached to the main temple underwent further repairs. At the ancient temple in the Nurpur Fort the large basement which was buried under enormous masses of débris was completely laid open on the east, south and west sides. The retaining wall is composed of small chisel-dressed blocks of stone in lime mortar, but it is much decayed and will have to be reconstructed at many places. It should be observed that the excavation along the south side disclosed the original flight of steps behind the broad staircase constructed in modern times. The temple itself does not stand in need of repairs, but the floor of the Jagmohan, which had sunk in part, was taken up and relaid in its original position."

United Provinces.
Sarnath.

Among Hindu and Buddhist monuments in the United Provinces attention focussed on the Buddhist remains at Sarnath. on the ancient pillar at Kosam, and on certain monuments at Mahoba in the Hamirpur District. The total expenditure on these works amounted to Rs. 9,383-8-4 of which Rs. 8,114-13-4 was devoted to the conservation and excavation work at Sarnath, Rs. 861-8-0 to Kosam, and the balance to Mahoba. The operations at the first two places were carried out under the personal supervision of Rai Bahadur Daya Ram Sahni, who says :—" At Sarnath the Public Works Department completed the construction of the stone pavilion over the stump of the Asoka Pillar at a cost of Rs. 1,189 (see Plate IV*a*). The repairs executed by the Archæological Superintendent pertain chiefly to the mediaeval monastery brought to light in 1917-18 to the west of Kittoe's monastery, to a number of stupas round about the Jagat Singh stupa and north-west of the Main Shrine (Plate IV*b*) and to various structures excavated by me during the course of the year in the extensive fore-court of the Main Shrine. For want of bricks of the old patterns it was not possible to undertake large measures of conservation in the northern or monastery area, where much work still remains to be done. I succeeded, however, in carrying out some urgently needed works at monastery No. I which I propose to identify with the Dharmachakrajinavihara built by Kumaradevi, the Buddhist queen of King Govindachandra of Kanauj. The area in front of the entrance to the principal block of this building, which is composed of accumulated earth and other débris, was in a very precarious condition, and to prevent further erosion a solid retaining wall fifty-four feet in length and twelve feet high has been provided. The new wall is built throughout with old bricks of the Gupta period collected from the site and is not obtrusive (Plate V*a*). The area between this building and the earlier monastery No. III stood sorely in need of drainage, as did also the interior of the latter building ; for though it had its usual outlet, rain water could not escape on account of high foundations on three sides and a bank of unexcavated earth on the side of the *jhil*. In ancient times the drain of monastery No. III referred to above continued in a westerly direction where the monastery No. I was erected in later times. The only course open, therefore, was to provide a new channel along the entire length of the west wall of monastery No. III right up to the edge of the lake. Another improvement has been made in this area by filling up the large pit about sixteen feet in depth which disfigured the south-west corner of the first forecourt of monastery No. I. The filling comes up to the level of the floor in the forecourt referred to and has been consolidated and levelled up. Time was also found to complete the clearance of the long subterranean passage to the west of monastery No. I, the greater part of which had been excavated in the year 1918-19. The difficulty of draining the area to the east of the Main Shrine was luckily solved by the discovery this year of the original drain several hundred feet in length which has been cleared in its entirety. All conservation work on this site has hitherto been carried out with old bricks found in the excavations. They are, however, now completely used up and arrangements are being made for the manufacture of new bricks of the various dimensions required." **Northern Circle.** *Lahore Office.* **United Provinces.**

At Kosam, Mr. Sahni took up the task of excavating and re-erecting the famous old pillar which must have been lying in its present inclined position at least since before the days of Akbar. "From the excavation made around its base it now appears that the existing portion of the pillar is 34 feet 6 inches in length of which the base, 1 foot 9 inches in height, was meant to be buried in the ground and therefore neither smoothed nor polished like the upper portion (Plate XI*a*). The excavation also brought to light two broken pieces measuring 4'-6" and 2'-3" respectively, which constituted the upper end of the column and which though noticed by General Cunningham about the year 1862 had again become buried. Another fact disclosed by the excavation is that the pillar has sustained somewhat serious injury by the separation, from its lower portion, of a piece 10'-8" in length with a segment of 2'-9", which must have occurred when the pillar fell down. What strikes one as so surprising about this pillar is the *kachcha* nature of its foundations, clearly the cause of its downfall; for whereas the other ancient pillars such as those at Rampurva, Sarnath, Sanchi, etc., were erected on strong stone slabs or on the natural rock and imbedded to a depth of some six feet or more in a heavy mass of solid masonry, this one at Kosam was set up direct on the soil, with a thin brick platform around it, which was bound to give way the moment the pillar began to subside. *Kosam.*

"As to the re-erection of the pillar, two courses are open, either to re-erect it on its original site or to lift it out of the trench and set it up on the present ground level. After careful consideration it has been decided to adopt the former alternative, mainly because it will be less expensive. The separated portion at the lower end will, of course, have to be securely fastened by means of strong iron collars, and a strong masonry platform about ten feet square be constructed around the pillar. The new platform will be high enough to conceal the lower damaged portion of the pillar but will leave about twenty-four feet of the shaft exposed to view. The area around the pillar will then be levelled up flush with the top of the platform. A search will also be made for the capital of the pillar which presumably lies hidden on the south side where no excavation has so far been attempted." *

In addition to the works summarized above the budget of this circle for the past year included a provision of Rs. 2.000 for the exploration and preservation of the Gupta relics at Bilsar in the Etah District. This project was to have been executed under the direct supervision of the Superintendent, but, as the land required for the purpose could not be acquired up to the end of the year, the money was reappropriated for work at Sarnath. *Bilsar.*

The programme of works in the Frontier Circle provided for various measures of conservation at Bilot in the Dera Ismail Khan District, at Takht-i-Bahi and Jamalgarhi in the Peshawar District, and at Jaulian in the Hazara District. Work at the two first mentioned sites was to be undertaken by the Public Works Department and at the other two under the direct control of the Superintendent, Mr. Hargreaves, whose report follows. **Frontier Circle.**

* *See* further page 45 below.

Frontier Circle. " A grant of Rs. 13,900 was placed by the Government of India at the disposal of the Superintendent, Frontier Circle, for the conservation and maintenance of monuments, and of this sum Rs. 11,943-15-5 was expended as well as Rs. 1,003-13-6 from the special grant for excavation. Rupees 6,900 was also allotted to the Public Works Department for works under their control, but of this sum only Rs. 1,987 was spent. The cost of the paths to the two Kafirkots was met from the Public Works Department funds, and not from the Archæological budget.

Bilot. " A revised conservation note for work at the Bilot monument was issued, but it was impossible to give effect to the recommendations of the note as the Secretary to the Chief Commissioner, North-West Frontier Province, Public Works Department, recommended that no work should be started at Bilot in 1921-22 in view of the condition of affairs in the Dera Ismail Khan District, which rendered the execution of civil works a very difficult matter. As works here have been continuously postponed for many years, it is all the more regrettable that when money was available it should have been found impossible to carry out conservation. A necessary preliminary to conservation at the Bilot Kafirkot and its counterpart, the Northern Kafirkot, is the construction of good paths to the sites, for without these, material for conservation cannot be brought to the monuments. When it was realized that the conservation of the Bilot Temples could not be attempted, enquiries were made of the Deputy Assistant Director, Military Works, Dera Ismail Khan, whether he could at least do something to improve the pathways leading to the two Kafirkots from the bank of the river Indus, and as he was of opinion that it could be undertaken, details of the proposed paths were forwarded to him with a request that estimates might be drawn up and submitted for approval. The Personal Assistant went to Bilot on the 19th November to meet the Garrison Engineer, Dera Ismail Khan, and to accompany him to the two monuments, but the latter officer saw only the one more readily accessible, and did not visit the Northern Kafirkot, stating that pressure of work necessitated his presence at headquarters, and he could not spare the time. The Deputy Assistant Director, Military Works, Dera Ismail Khan, reports that he has carried out improvements to the pathways at Bilot and the Northern Kafirkot at a cost of Rs. 1,001-14-0 and Rs. 500-8-0 respectively, but it is not known how far these conform with the proposals submitted, for no estimates were sent for countersignature, and the work was carried out without any information being sent to the Superintendent. The sites will be visited during the coming touring season, but until the Frontier is more settled it seems unlikely that any serious attempt at conservation can be made in the Dera Ismail Khan District.

Northern Kafirkot.

"The plan of the Northern Kafirkot referred to in paragraph 2 of the last report of the Frontier Circle is illustrated in Plate XXVI of this report.

Takht-i-Bahi. "The Deputy Assistant Director, Military Works, Nowshera, forwarded an estimate for Rs. 2,721 for conservation of the Takht-i-Bahi Monuments. Of the various items detailed in the estimate only one was completed at a cost of Rs. 1,987-0-0, this being the restoration of a large revetment on the west of Court XX, *i.e.*, the high retaining wall of the courtyard which contains the three preserved stupas. This wall had collapsed on account of the excessive winter rains. The engineers report that the original foundations were mere rubble, and that the filling behind the wall was loose, and required consolidation. The revetment has been inspected since its restoration, and appears to have been most successfully restored. The remaining items of the estimate are to be executed during the year 1922-23.

"The wall in Court T XIX, which had been dismantled and re-erected in 1920-21, fell in a violent storm of wind and rain. There is a conflict of opinion as to the cause of the collapse. It is not proposed to restore this wall immediately, and in any future restoration some courses at least should be set in lime mortar. **Frontier Circle.**

"Conservation at Jaulian in the Hazara District was started on the 8th December 1921, and was carried on continuously under my personal direction until the 1st March 1922. Interruptions were numerous, the weather being unusually wet rendering outdoor work impossible for several days every week. My only assistant was the office draftsman, to whose intelligent interest I desire to express my indebtedness for the successful execution of the work. Masons were obtained principally from the village of Mora Maliar, about four miles away, close to the ancient city of Sirkap, and many of them were intelligent and clever workmen, taking a lively interest in the work, and able to meet successfully the various difficulties that arose. Conservation proper was limited to the monastery area, to the west and south walls, and to certain of the cells, the west wall being out of plumb, with part of it missing, and the long south wall being in a similar condition (Plate V*a*). *Jaulian.*

"The stones were numbered with chalk, and the walls photographed in sections before being dismantled. After dismantling, the back of each stone was numbered with coal-tar, and the stones arranged in order, ready for replacement. By means of the photographs the restoration of the stones to their original positions was rendered comparatively easy. The top course of the walls was set in lime mortar to render them watertight. The condition of the walls after conservation may be seen from figure *b* of Plate V.

"Several of the dividing walls of the cells received attention, and many of the small infilling stones of the diaper masonry were restored, being set in invisible lime mortar.

"All the stone for conservation was obtained from the spoil of the previous excavation. The woodwork of the various chapels was given two coats of Solignum and certain portions of the woodwork protecting the stupas and sculptures were coal-tarred.

"While dismantling a portion of the south wall the following were found in the débris :—One copper bell, diameter 3", one copper ornament, a five petalled flower, diameter 2½", and the copper base of a lamp-stand 5½"-- 5½". These were sent to the Archæological Museum, Taxila.

"A good path, nowhere less than 6' wide, was made from the terminus of the motor road across the *nala* up the hill to the entrance of the Stupa Court, and will prove of great convenience to the numerous visitors to this site.

"The total cost of conservation at this monument, including the path, was Rs. 5,827-13-6.

"It is regrettable to have to report that on the evening of the 11th of April 1921 some ill-disposed persons forced open the doors protecting the little chapel on the left of the entrance to the monastery at Jaulian, and deliberately smashed the beautiful stucco Buddha image which had so miraculously escaped the destruction which overtook this religious establishment about the fifth century. The offence was immediately reported to the authorities and the Chief Commissioner, North-West Frontier Province, personally interested himself in the matter. The Deputy Commissioner, Hazara, took up the investigation but despite the offer of a reward of Rs. 1,000 for information which would lead to the discovery of the perpetrators of the outrage and the endeavours of the police, the culprits have not yet been brought to justice.

Frontier Circle. "The very numerous fragments of the broken image were carefully collected and, under the personal direction of Sir John Marshall, who was then at Taxila, the image was restored. In consequence of this outrage it has been necessary to increase the number of chowkidars at the site and to strengthen the doors of this chapel and those of the three other small shrines within the monastery.

Jamalgarhi. "It had been hoped that conservation at Jamalgarhi would be started early in January, but the interruptions to the work at Jaulian due to bad weather rendered this impossible. The Personal Assistant who was to have begun clearance there, unfortunately fell while on tour and broke his left arm, so that there was no one to start and supervise the work until February 6th, when he began work on the still uncleared areas.

"Conservation properly speaking has been limited to a very few of the structures, for, unlike Jaulian, Jamalgarhi is remote from any large village which can supply competent masons. A few were obtained from Sawaldher, but they came very irregularly and the work made little progress. The inconvenience was not very greatly felt this year as clearance could proceed without masons, and, indeed, is an essential preliminary to conservation of the remains, as well as equally necessary for the preparation of the complete plan of the site which is now progressing satisfactorily. Conservation proper was carried out in the Conference Hall, and the four-roomed structure east of the Main Stupa. As the operations for want of necessary masons resolved themselves into clearance rather than conservation they are described at length below under the head Exploration."

Western Circle. Mr. Rakhal Das Banerji, Archæological Superintendent in the Western Circle, reports that, "During the year under review one lakh and ten thousand rupees were allotted for the conservation of ancient monuments in the Bombay Presidency. This figure compares favourably with the sums granted in the previous year, when eighty thousand rupees were received from the Government of Bombay and eighteen thousand from the Government of India. But since 23 % on estimates had to be paid to the Public Works Department of Bombay for current repair and special repair works undertaken by that Department, the actual amount available for expenditure was reduced from Rs. 1,10,000 to Rs. 98,252. Out of the total grant, Rs. 31,600 were placed at the disposal of the Archæological Superintendent, for certain urgent special repair works which were considered to be too technical to be placed in the hands of the Public Works Department. These were—the excavations for ancient Nizamshahi Buildings in the fort at Ahmadnagar, the excavation of the Caves at Elephanta, special repairs to the Portuguese monuments in Bassein Fort, the conservation of the Faria Bagh water-palace at Ahmadnagar and the excavations at and special repairs to the Peshwa's Palace in Poona. The balance Rs. 78,400 was placed at the disposal of the Public Works Department of the Government of Bombay for both special repairs and current repairs and maintenance. The total expenditure on conservation during the year thus amounted to Rs. 97,334, out of which Rs. 67,545 were utilised in special repairs, and Rs. 29,789 for current repairs and maintenance.

Elephanta. "The largest amount of work was at Elephanta, where Rs. 14,000 were spent in carrying out preliminary special repairs to the Caves on this Island. The Caves fall into two distinct groups. The first group consists of Cave No. 1 only, which is the largest, and generally known as the large Cave of Elephanta. The second group consists of six smaller excavations belonging to the same period, but which were totally neglected in the past and had become covered with jungle at the time of their excavation in the

Western Circle. Elephanta.

beginning of this year. In Cave No. 1 or the large cave the two wings were cleared of jungle and débris and the ancient drains for the drainage of rain water were exposed. During these excavations the original courtyard of the left wing with a large circular *Nandivedi*, only portion of which had been visible before the excavations, was brought to light. Jungle was cut up to a radius of 50′ from the ends of this cave and all loose stones and débris were removed to a distance. The removal of débris from the left and right wings of Cave No. 1 has enhanced their beauty considerably. Four ugly steps built by the Executive Engineer, Presidency District, Bombay, in 1921, on four sides of the temple of Siva in the main hall of Cave No. 1, which were objected to by the Director General of Archæology, were taken down and rebuilt. In the second group débris was removed from the Caves Nos. 2, 3 and 4 (Plate XII*a*) and during the removal a new cave was discovered by the side of Cave No. 4. The removal of jungle and débris in front of these caves has now made it possible for visitors to go and examine them closely. Cave No. 2 was a small shrine by the side of the left wing of Cave No. 1 which does not appear to have been completed. Caves Nos. 3 and 4 are excavations on a very large scale and were Saiva shrines; the *arghapatta*, and in one case the huge *linga* is still in position in spite of two centuries of Portuguese possession, when most of the other images were broken to pieces and desecrated. Fragments of these images were discovered during the excavations (Plate XII*c*). In order to make these caves easily accessible to the public, a roadway was constructed from the existing roadway in front of Cave No. 1 to the front of Cave No. 4. Two other caves of the same group are to be found on the adjoining hill, which were never easily accessible to the public. A footpath was constructed from the military road on Elephanta Island to Caves Nos. 5 and 6. Débris was excavated from the interior of Cave No. 5 and its original plinth-lines exposed. This cave, like Cave No. 4, was originally a Saiva shrine, but was appropriated to the use of the Christian Church during the rule of the Portuguese in Bombay. The accumulation of water in the main hall of Cave No. 5 was drained off and the interior cleared (Plate XII*b* and *d*).

Poona.

"At Shanwar Wada in Poona City His Excellency the Governor of Bombay paved the way for effecting certain urgently needed restorations and repairs by raising subscriptions. The Delhi Gate, or the main entrance to the palace of the Peshwas, was being used by the Department of Land Records as one of its attached offices (Plate XIII). These offices were removed according to the orders of His Excellency, and the old Naqqarkhana on the top was restored to its former condition by paving it with stone, removing modern additions and alterations and clearing whitewash. The railing on the southern face of this fine Naqqarkhana had been demolished when the Land Records Office was placed in it and could not be found, but this difficulty was rectified by removing a portion of a similar carved wooden railing from a palace nearby, called Konkar's Wada, which belonged to one of the nobles of the Peshwas. The removal of this carved wooden railing from Konkar's palace to the Naqqarkhana of the Shanwar Wada Palace was kindly approved by His Excellency. The pavement of the ground floor inside the gateway was renewed at places, and a fine series of fresco paintings on the walls of the ground floor was revealed after the removal of coats of whitewash applied over these paintings. These frescoes belong to the early eighteenth century and possess a marked affinity to the Rajput School of painting. The subjects depicted can be recognised even now. On the northern wall of the southern portion of the main gate we find Vishnu lying on Sesha, Ganesa and Brahma, and on the side walls the ten incarnations of Vishnu and some incidents from the life of Krishna. From the money raised by His Excellency from the Ruling

Western Circle. Chiefs of India the northern part of the garden in the interior of the walled enclosure of the palace was repaired and restored. The ancient stone paved way from the Delhi Gate to the terrace in front of the main building was repaved. The retaining wall on the northern, eastern and western sides of this terrace was rebuilt up to its original height, and the area turned into a grass plot. This terrace contained two cisterns with copper fountains in it. The copper fountains could not be restored in time for the Prince of Wales' visit though the water supply is still adequate to make them run. The main staircase leading from this terrace to the first court of the palace was repaired by renewing missing treads, and the plinth of the interior of the first court was repaired wherever stones were found to be missing (Plate XIV). Similarly a small court to the west of the first court of the palace was also repaired, enabling people to go through the first court to the small court, and then to the court of the thousand fountains, discovered during the previous year. The terrace-garden along the eastern wall was partly repaired. An ancient staircase leading from the first terrace in this area to the second was rebuilt, and portions of the stone fountains in the second terrace were replaced in position. In all Rs. 18,000 were spent from the funds raised by His Excellency the Governor, by subscriptions among the Ruling Chiefs for repairs to this portion of the Shanwar Wada palace, and Rs. 10,800 spent on urgently needed repairs to the inner walls of this fortress. The walls had collapsed at certain places and at other places were on the verge of collapsing. All of these portions were repaired on the lines of the old construction. All of these repairs were carried out before the visit of H. R. H. the Prince of Wales to the Shanwar Palace on the 19th November 1921. Expenditure on current repairs and maintenance to the Shanwar Wada, including the pay of the Police guard, amounted to Rs. 1,665.

Bassein. "The principal Portuguese remains inside the fort at Bassein lie to the south of a road running east to west through this fort. Nearly one-third of the area enclosed by the old fort is in the charge of the Revenue Department of the Government of Bombay, and is cultivated. The remaining area is covered with dense jungle and the ruins of the principal buildings of the Portuguese in India. In 1917 the remains inside the fort were so thickly overgrown with jungle that it was impossible to examine them at close quarters. In 1919 the Executive Engineer, Thana District, was provided with funds to remove this jungle in order to make the preparation of conservation notes possible. The work of jungle cutting was done very carelessly at that time, only the branches of trees being cut off. The trees grew rapidly again, and at the beginning of this year the jungle was almost as thick as it had been in 1917. Attention had to be devoted, therefore, in the first instance to the removal of large and small trees with their roots from both the citadel and the fort walls. During the year unde review more than half of the length of the fort walls, both inside and outside, was cleared of large and small trees. The roots of big banian and pipal trees enveloping the fort walls at places had hid more than 40′ to 50′ from view. These roots had to be chiselled out from cracks and joints of the masonry. As an experimental measure, small ends of roots were treated with a mixture of asaphœtida, lime and molasses in order to prevent future growth. The platform on the top of the rampart had swelled up at places on account of the ingress of water and the penetration of very long and thick roots of pipal and banian trees. These swollen patches were dug up and the roots were extracted from the interior. The work was in progress throughout the year.

"The fine barrel vault of the Dominican Church, which had partly collapsed on account of continued neglect, was demolished, as no suitable means could be found for its preservation. The only course left was to dismantle the vault entirely and to rebuild.

"The total expenditure on special repairs in Bassein fort amounted to Rs. 4,000." **Western Circle.**

Ahmadnagar. Mr. Banerji further reports that "The Water Palace of The Nizamshahi kings of Ahmadnagar, now called Faria Bagh, is a two-storied octagonal structure neatly planned and built on an elevation inside a square tank. The tank itself is surrounded by a terraced garden on all four sides. Formerly this tank was fed by water brought into it through channels from reservoirs on the higher plateaux which surround the depression in the centre of which the City of Ahmadnagar had been built. This water supply is at present utilised to irrigate the fields of the Army Remount Department at Ahmadnagar, and consequently the tank is always dry. The bed of the tank as well as the terrace was paved with lime concrete which is still remarkably well preserved at places, and if the cracks in the bed of the tank are repaired then even the scanty rainfall of Ahmadnagar would prove sufficient to keep the tank of the Faria Bagh palace full throughout the year. Unsightly modern additions and alterations made in this palace by the Army Remount Department were removed, and the top of the platform on which the palace stands was excavated revealing nine ornamental tanks and cisterns which formed part of the lay-out of the ground floor four hundred years ago. The continued use of this building as a cattle-shed had made this once gorgeous palace extremely dirty and evil smelling. Marks of cow-dung and other dirt and squalor were removed as far as possible. Trees growing in the bed of the tank and on the sides were removed to prevent further damage to the concrete terraces on the outer side of the tank. Some years ago the arched roof on the top collapsed at four different places, and stones and debris from it were lying on the domes just below it. These domes were relieved of this extra weight by the removal of this debris. The urgently required underpinning of the jambs of doors and arched openings was undertaken and some missing stone steps of the staircases leading to the second floor of the palace were replaced. In all Rs. 2,800 were spent on special repairs to the Faria Bagh palace.

Bijapur. "In Bijapur the work of erecting a compound wall around the open space surrounding the Gol Gumbaz, which was taken up in 1919-20, was almost entirely completed, the sum of Rs. 6,353 having been spent on it. The work could not be entirely completed because the Revenue Department has not as yet acquired the land in private possession which lies in this open area. Until these plots of land are acquired and the houses on it demolished it will not be possible to complete this compound wall. The breach in the city wall to the east of the Gol Gumbaz, through which the modern road to the Station used to pass, was completely closed, as this road has been diverted through another gap in the city wall; and the bridge over the moat was also dismantled to prevent people passing through the gap.

"Special repairs to the Gagan Mahal, an ancient durbar hall of the Adilshahi Sultans of Bijapur, were undertaken during the current year. The Gagan Mahal palace consists of a large hall in the centre with two small side rooms and a larger open verandah in front. The royal seat was placed in the large hall in the centre over which was a structure supported by four massive pillars of wood. The ladies of the court used to sit in the upper balconies. In front of the main hall was a verandah running along the entire length of the building where the nobles and other court attendants were accommodated. The Gagan Mahal and the Sangit Mahal are the only two remaining examples of the durbar halls of the Adilshahi Sultans. The hall of the Gagan Mahal was taken up for special repairs according to the directions of Sir John Marshall, who had inspected it in February 1921. A large amount of underpinning and pointing was

Western Circle. *Bijapur.* carried out in the main building. The open chases in the masonry, formerly occupied by wooden beams, posts and brackets, were filled in with stone and lime concrete. Reinforced concrete lintels were provided to the heads of door openings. Cracks in the walls of the building were properly grouted with cement and finished with lime pointing. At certain places the ancient plaster was repaired and in all Rs. 5,100 were spent on the Gagan Mahal.

"Two separate pillars of stone were built under the verandah in front of the main hall of the Sangit Mahal at Navaraspur to support the overhanging roof of this verandah. Stone and debris were removed from the main hall and the verandah, exposing the former floor to view. The tops of walls were also made watertight. The Sangit Mahal, after the Gagan Mahal, is the second existing instance of the palaces of the Adilshahi kings. It consisted of a huge octagonal enclosure surrounded by a high wall of stone in the centre of which stood a palace partly two-storied and partly three-storied. In plan the palace consists of a large open verandah with a huge arch in front, running along the entire length of the building. Behind the verandah is a large hall with another huge arched opening in front. The floor of this hall was higher than the floor of the verandah, and on each side of it were two small rooms of the same height as the main durbar hall. Behind the hall were a net-work of chambers connecting the durbar hall with another large hall as long as the palace itself. On the top of the durbar hall and of the second hall as well there were a net-work of small rooms most probably used as living rooms. After the downfall of the Adilshahis this palace fell into decay, and during the British period the land inside was farmed to a Deccani Brahmin who diverted the waters of a small *nala* to the interior of this building. The water of this *nala* annually conveys a huge amount of silt and has buried the fine garden with tanks and fountains which once surrounded this noble structure. Trial pits were dug at places proving that there were huge paved cisterns with fountains both in front and at the back of the palace. Proposals have been submitted for the acquisition of this area, which is now cultivated, so that the silt may be excavated and the original garden exposed to view.

"Among miscellaneous special repairs undertaken during the year at Bijapur may be mentioned the reconstruction of a section of the fort wall near the Malik-i-Maidan bastion which was rebuilt in order to keep this monster gun from sinking. Similarly the rear part of the first water pavilion at Kumatgi, which lies at a distance of ten miles from Bijapur City, was rebuilt. Rupees 1,433 were spent in acquiring the land for the extension of the compound of the tomb of Ibrahim Adilshah II, popularly known as Ibrahim Rauza, and Rs. 759 for acquiring land for the diversion of the public road to the Station, it having originally passed through the area of the Gol Gumbaz. The Inspector employed to keep the ancient monuments in Bijapur City clean, succeeded in removing prickly-pear for a length of more than two and a half miles from the city walls without incurring any additional expenditure. This work was done by the caretakers under the supervision of the Inspector. Less than one-fourth of a mile of the city wall now remains to be cleared of prickly-pear, as some work was done in 1920-21. The charges for current repairs and maintenance in the District of Bijapur amounted to Rs. 8,204.

Champaner. "The dome of the porch of the Lila-Gumbaz-ki-Masjid and the Minars attached to the Bohra-ki-Masjid or Shahar-ki-Masjid were partly repaired. Special repairs to the seven-storied palace of the Sultans of Gujrat, in front of a waterfall on Pavagadh Hill, were begun during this year. On account of continued neglect and want of funds this building collapsed in 1918 leaving only the basement. This basement, which provides a fine view of the waterfall, stood in need of very urgent repairs which consisted

Western Circle.

in providing a buttress along the narrow rock face in order to prevent the heavy weight of the basement from pressing it down into the pit below, providing tie-rods to the room on the basement, repairs to the steps and removal of débris. Rs. 3,486 were spent on repairs to the Lila-Gumbaz, Bohra-ki-Masjid and the seven-storied palace on Pavagadh Hill. The plinths of the Kevda Masjid, Lila-Gumbaz, Khajuri Masjid, Nagina Masjid, Kamani Masjid and Baba Man's Masjid, which had been buried out of sight, were exposed at a cost of Rs. 2,399. The cost of current repairs and maintenance at Champaner and Pavagadh amounted to Rs. 1,810.

Ahmedabad and Dholka.

"At Ahmedabad the special repairs to Rani Sipri's Masjid and tomb were completed at a cost of Rs. 605. The pillars of the gateway of the compound wall were properly rebuilt and a collapsible gate was provided. At Dholka in the same district repairs to the minaret on the south pylon of the Khan Masjid, which possesses the distinction of being the highest masjid in the whole of Gujrat, were begun. A reinforced concrete platform was built to support the weight of the minaret on one side and the two missing pillars were rebuilt. Rupees 2,797 were spent on this monument. The Khan Masjid at Dholka stands on the bank of an ancient tank the sides of which are covered with stone steps, and lies within a stone's throw of Dholka Railway Station. The masjid originally consisted of a large portico in front supported by three tall arches about 50′ in height from the ground level. This portico collapsed during an earthquake. Behind it are three large separate chambers with three huge domes of brick all of which were more or less on the point of collapsing when repairs were commenced. The dangerous portion of the masonry of the original portico has been dismantled and the front part of the main masjid (*i.e.*, the rear wall of the portico) has been rebuilt and made perfectly safe. The cost of current repairs and maintenance in the Ahmedabad District amounted to Rs. 2,267.

Sholapur.

"At Sholapur finishing touches were put to the sides of the pit from which the Chalukyan temple was excavated in the rampart of the inner fort wall (Plate XV). The earthen ramp temporarily built for workmen was removed, and a dry rubble wall with stone pitching on the slope above it was built all round. Steps were provided at the end of the old rampart just in front of the ancient temple for the convenience of visitors. The fort wall near the north-eastern corner of the Chalukyan temple was underpinned. The breach in the fort wall made by the British in order to allow transport wagons to enter the fort was closed up entirely, and all modern buildings in the fort were demolished and their remains carted away.

Bhaja.

"The work of special repairs to the caves at Bhaja was almost entirely completed during the year, including the dry-stone compound wall of the rampart and a self-closing gate was provided in front. The votive stupas exposed to the destructive influence of the weather were covered with a roofing of stone-slabs in iron frames. A flight of dressed stone steps was provided to the north side of the main chaitya cave in order to enable people to gain easy excess to the first floor. Support pillars were built under the overhanging portions of the roof in order to prevent it from collapsing. The cost of these measures came to Rs. 843.

Ahmadnagar Fort.

"Inside the Ahmadnagar Fort excavations were carried out in front of the Brigade Office as well as behind it in search of ancient remains of the Nizamshahi period, and a sum of Rs. 1,353 was spent for this purpose. Continuous stone steps were exposed behind the Brigade Office and in front of them there was a small square tank probably

Western Circle. intended for a fountain. The ancient plinth of the old gate (*vide* plate No. III, Annual Progress Report of the Archæological Survey of India, Western Circle, for the year ending 31st March 1920) was exposed. In the area outside the Brigade Office, the old arched drain, which was broken at different places, was repaired and the excavated areas both inside and outside the old gate were filled in as required by the Military authorities.

Satyan-jo-Than. " At Rohri in the Sukkur District of Sind special repairs to the Satyan-jo-Than were completed at a cost of Rs. 1,349. The modern huts near the oldest masjid in Sindh were removed and the old residential quarters of the Mujawar built in an angle of the old platform were repaired. The plaster of the tombs and the platforms round them was repaired by filling in cracks and grouting. Tiles and bricks damaged by alkaloids were replaced. The north wall of the platform of the tombs had collapsed at places. This portion was entirely rebuilt with old bricks and made safe. The Satyan-jo-Than was once an island in the bed of the river Indus but has now ceased to be so. On it stands an ancient Nathapanthi temple, the upper part of which has been utilised for the tombs of Muhammadans. The eternal light (*ananta-jyotih*) of the Nathapanthis is still kept burning in the underground chambers of this temple by the Muhammadan Mujawars who have forgotten everything about Nathism and now tell an absurd story regarding seven sisters. The upper part of this temple was converted into an open platform on which some old tombs stand. Some of these tombs belong to the reigns of Akbar and Jahangir. The tombs are made of yellow Jungshahi stones or covered with enamelled tiles and on the whole present a very pleasing appearance to the visitor. To the west of this island stand the majestic ruins of the once impregnable fort of Bhakkar and the sister shrines of Sadhubela and Zindapir, and between these and the Satyan-jo-Than flows the river the current of which is always very swift between Sukkur and Rohri gauge. Males are not allowed to visit the shrine in the underground room where the eternal light is kept burning. Such Nathapanthi shrines are common in Sindh, *e.g.*, the Lal Shahbaz in the Larkana District and Uderolal in the Hyderabad District, and at all of these places the attendants of the light are Muhammadans. Kanphata yogis of the Nathapanthi sect are not seen in Sindh though they still come as far as Jeysulmer from Nepal."

Indian States in Western India. Junagadh and Kolhapur. The Political Agent, Sorath Prant, Kathiawar, reports that the Junagadh State spent Rs. 2,215 in conserving the Uparkote Masjid during 1921-22 ; while the Resident at Kolhapur states that Ambabai's temple at Kolhapur as well as Nurkhan's Dargah at Shirol were conserved and maintained in good order by the Kolhapur State, but more detailed information is not available.

Central Circle. Mr. Page reports that in the Central Circle a sum of Rs. 33,084 in all was expended on the Conservation of Ancient Monuments. Of this amount Rs. 13,475 were spent in the Province of Bihar and Orissa, *viz.*, Rs. 9,215 on Special Repairs (non-recurring expenditure) and Rs. 4,260* on Annual Repairs and maintenance (recurring expenditure) ; and a sum of Rs. 19,607 in the Central Provinces and Berar, where Rs. 13,080 were devoted to Special Repairs and the remainder Rs. 6,527 to Annual Repairs.

With the exception of the operations at Nalanda, which were carried out by the Archæological Superintendent direct, all conservation work was done through the agency of the Public Works Department of the Local Government concerned ; an additional charge of 23 % on the estimated cost of the works being paid for this service.

On his recent winter tour in the Central Provinces it was apparent to Mr. Page that " In many cases the special considerations demanded in the conservation of an old fabric

* Includes the expenditure on Nalanda detailed in Appendix.

are not adequately appreciated by the Public Works Department subordinate in immediate charge of the work, such as the suitable treatment of pointing, when applied to the open joints of an old structure, to make it harmonize with the weathered appearance of the old work ; the treatment of broken patches of plaster on an old surface ; and the need of maintaining the distinctive character of old rubble masonry in any new repair. Such items may, perhaps, be deemed negligible in themselves, but are, indeed, very far from negligible in their disastrous effect on an old structure when badly carried out ; for the preservation of the natural beauty and mellow charm of an old monument is of equal importance to ensuring its structural security. However, with the appointment of a number of Conservation Assistants (which it is hoped will be sanctioned shortly) actively to assist in the work of conservation while in progress, a considerable improvement in this respect should become manifest—an improvement which will increase with their experience in this special branch of building work ; for the men appointed will require to be specially trained before satisfactory results can be expected of them." **Central Circle.**

Bihar and Orissa Province.

The only "special repair" works executed by the Public Works Department in Bihar which call for notice were those carried out in the Orissa Circle. Here a sum of Rs. 966 was spent on the conservation of the Black Pagoda at Konarak, in the Puri District, a structure dating from the 13th century. "The work," Mr. Page says, "involved the removal of sand heaps accumulated to the west of the temple and on the paving and platforms of the shrines ; the collection and arrangement of scattered sculptures in the vicinity and the removal of others to the adjacent Museum ; while damaged corbels and lintels in the Mahadevi shrine were supported on iron rails and dry-ashlar piers. The work, which was commenced in the previous year, has now been completed. At Jajpur, in the same district, the repair of the old Mahratta bridge known as the Tentulimul bridge—reputed to have been erected by the early sovereigns of Orissa, before the Mughal conquest of that province, was completed at a total cost of Rs. 975. This work, which had been commenced in the previous year, included the dismantling and rebuilding of disturbed pier and arch masonry, and the replacement of missing portions of the face walls ; earthwork in making up hollows near the bridge ; the removal of pipal trees in its vicinity and of jungle growth from the structure itself ; the erection of parapets formed of laterite posts connected by galvanised iron tubing for the security of traffic over the bridge, and the provision of wheel guards to prevent damage to the old structure." *Konarak.* *Jajpur.*

The work done at Nalanda by the Archæological Superintendent during the cold season of 1921-22 did not commence until late in December after Mr. Page had taken over charge of the Central Circle, and in consequence has been somewhat limited in its extent. "Activities were principally confined," Mr. Page says, "to the conservation of the fragmentary remains already disclosed, such excavation as was attempted being merely incidental to this conservation work, and limited to the clearance of débris-strewn areas and the sinking of foundations for new piers, etc., to support the old structure. Nevertheless, the clearance effected was instrumental in bringing to light the remains of an early brick pavement, and a curious plastered *chabutra*-like feature projecting into the courtyard of Monastery No. 1 from its south side. In the *chabutra* was found inset a couple of long low duplicate panels carved in basso-relievo with a representation of bird-bodied human figures revering a lotus plant, dating from the 6th or 7th century A. D. (Plate VII*a*.). This brick-paving is some 3′ 6″ below the level of the courtyard which, from the evidence afforded by the copper plate inscription discovered by Pandit Hirananda Sastri last year, may be assigned with some probability to the early 9th century. The accumulation of earth between these two levels may not unreasonably be *Nalanda.*

Central Circle. *Nalanda.*

assumed to account for a period of some two to three hundred years, thus indicating the 6th or 7th century A. D. as the approximate date of the brick paving now come to light.

"Since the highest level attained by the subsoil water in the rains, as indicated in the original well in the N.-W. corner of the courtyard in the monastery, comes only some 4' below the level of this paving, the probability of earlier structures existing at a still lower level is discounted. However, trial pits will be sunk next year with a view to exhaust the possibilities of the site in this direction.

"Yuan Chwang in speaking of the succession of princes who founded monasteries at Nalanda, makes mention of the names Baladitya and Buddhagupta [1]; and if these personages are to be identified with the Gupta rulers of those names who are recorded to have been reigning in the years 490 and 484 A. D., respectively, it is conceivable that the lowest brick paving now disclosed is to be associated with them, and may thus be considered to date from about the end of the 5th century A. D. Certain it is that no fewer than eight different levels [2] and distinct periods occur at the Monastery site No. 1; and in conserving these fragmentary remains the Superintendent is making it his aim to preserve a definite portion of each stratum. The fact that each succeeding monastery adheres to one and the same plan necessarily restricts the area of each stratum that can be maintained as such, and increases the difficulties in the carrying out of requisite measures of repair. However, by dealing with the different periods systematically it is hoped to make them intelligible to the interested visitor, and to preserve intact the internal evidence which each of them contributes to the history of the Nalanda site. With this purpose in view, it is intended to preserve, as far as possible, the stratigraphic evidence afforded by the earth through which the excavations have been sunk; and a substantial mound of earth left undisturbed by Dr. Spooner to this end in the S.-W. corner of the courtyard of Monastery No. 1 has been cut back cleanly to a slight batter (photo. No. 2166) preparatory to erecting around it a permanent shelter to protect it from erosion by the weather. The stratigraphic evidence contained in this feature is of unusual interest, as it discloses with extraordinary clearness the vicissitudes through which the successive structures have passed from the period of the original foundation of the monastery. Layers of ashes, potsherds, heavy brick débris, more ashes, and finally natural earth accumulation are most clearly defined, and serve at once as an indisputable record of fire and destruction, and of the abandonment and subsequent reoccupation of the site.

"As to the structures that have been under repair during the year, the principal work done was in Monastery No. 1, where the ruined north wall of the main west entrance-vestibule (Plate VII*b.* and VIII*a.*) was built up to match its fellow on the south with its simple brick niche. The shattered portions of the brick façades in the N.-W. corner of the courtyard here were also rebuilt in conformity with the old remains, and an original concrete parapet, of which a few traces fortunately remained, was reconstructed to protect the tops of the enclosing walls of this courtyard from the weather.

"The ruined central stupa-feature previously disclosed in the courtyard was supported at its base on an earthen ramp, with a view to revealing the high level of its foundations in relation to the lower level of the earlier courtyard around it. The exposed brick face of an inner stupa contained within this one was also provided with necessary support on a frankly modern wall in which weep-holes have been left, both for structural reasons and to proclaim at once its modern origin in distinction to the old work above.

---

(1) *Vide* Cunningham, *A. S. R.*, Volume I (1861-62), pages 28—30; Watter's *Yuan Chwang*, Volume II, page 164 *et seq.* Duff's *Chronology*, page 288 and V. A. Smith's *Early History of India*, page 281.

(2) Two of these are illustrated in the small central stupa in the quadrangle.

" The plain dressed-brick facing along the eastern exterior façade of the monastery was also built up in accordance with the indications of the old work *in situ* approximately to the level of the remaining hearting of the wall ; while the full height of this external wall was opened up to view in front of the central projecting bay, and a uniform slope formed in front of it to negociate the difference between the level of the earlier foundations and the general level of the ground along this front. A feature of interest here is the way in which a later brick casing has been applied to an earlier one. In order to support the former in position after the earth had been reduced below the level of its bottom course, recourse was had to the temporary expedient of strutting it with wooden poles. This temporary wooden construction will eventually be replaced by rail-iron cantilever supports which will be more enduring and less conspicuous. Difficulties created by the recent railway strike prevented this method being adopted in the first place.

" A similar temporary arrangement has also been erected to support the overhanging brickwork of a third and still later facing of the ruined stupa in the internal courtyard previously mentioned, which will also be replaced by the neater rail-iron cantilevers when these can be obtained.

" The upper half of an original brick stair (Plate VI*a*.) leading down from the lowest of the three separate pavements at the top of the monastery is being built up again to give access, as originally, to the courtyard below. By repairing and making use of this original feature it will be possible to remove the modern stair-descent built in the width of the inner verandah on the south side of the monastery which, though at present a most necessary addition in the absence of the original stair, is inevitably misleading in any attempt to visualise the old plan.

" In clearing the interior courtyard of this monastery my aim has been as stated above to maintain intact a definite portion of each successive level as disclosed by the excavations. Thus, the ground about the foot of the original stair-descent above referred to has been maintained at this level over approximately a quarter of the court yard, in which area is also located the upper structure of the well in the north-west corner, the cave-like structure contiguous to the north wall of the court, and the brick facing of its high enclosing wall ; all of which would appear to be contemporary. In the N.-E. quarter of the courtyard the level has been reduced some 3′ 6″ below this last down to that of the bottom course of the projecting *chabutra* of an earlier open-colonnaded verandah (Plate VI*b*.) assumed to be contemporary with the copper plate inscription of Devapaladeva referred to above. On the ruined remains of this verandah the high brick wall previously mentioned was afterwards erected. Along the south side of the courtyard, between its enclosing wall and the central stupa, the still earlier brick paving, 3′ 6″ lower and 22′ 0″ below the topmost parapet, has been left open to view.

" In the extreme S.-W. corner of the same courtyard is the mound of earth referred to on page 20, which it is proposed to shelter from the weather and maintain intact, in view of the important stratigraphical evidence it affords and the three separate upper pavements which it supports.

" The only other structure which was under repair was the monastery denominated No. 1-A, situate to the immediate S.-W. of Monastery No. 1. Here the concrete parapet of a low verandah wall enclosing the courtyard was reconstructed between the rough

Central Circle. base-stones still *in situ*, which formerly supported the pillars of an open colonnade (Plate VIII*b*.). By carefully recording in plan the precise positions of such few of these rough stone-bases as still remain, it has been possible to work out the intervals originally separating the columns, thus enabling the positions of the missing pillars to be indicated on the site.

" The ruined remains of the western wall of the north entrance vestibule of this monastery were built up to the level of the corresponding and better preserved wall on the opposite side, the lower portion of the simple brick niche extant here being repeated in the new work. Some excavation was also necessitated along the external edge of the south enclosing wall of this building to disclose the position of the outer wall-face, which was recovered some 6 feet or more beneath the surface of the ground.

" Conservation work on the site has up to the present been impeded by the necessity of utilising such of the larger fragments of the old bricks as could be recovered from the excavated débris, which have necessarily to be dressed to an even face to conform with the old work *in situ*. This operation of cutting and dressing old bricks has been a very slow process, owing to the scarcity of suitable labour in the locality. It is, however, hoped to experiment in the manufacture and burning of new bricks locally, with a view to obtaining the large sizes averaging 15″×9″×3″ used by the Gupta builders, and so necessary for the appropriate repair of the old walls. There is some doubt as to the possibility of matching the exact colour of the old bricks, but unless suitable new bricks are forthcoming in sufficient quantities it is obviously impossible to push on with the work of conservation."

The cost of the works above described was Rs. 2,859, of which amount Rs. 1,000 were spent from funds placed at the Archæological Superintendent's credit with the Local Government, and the remainder from a separate grant received from the Director General of Archæology in India direct. An additional sum of Rs. 560 was spent on the upkeep of the Nalanda monuments—a recurring charge; while other incidental disbursements made in connexion with this site will be found detailed in Appendix A (page 159) of this report. A list of finds made at Nalanda during the year is given on pages 259 and 260.

Central Provinces and Berar. In the Central Provinces and Berar, the principal conservation works undertaken were those enumerated below :

Pali. " In the Bilaspur District, on the Mahadeo Temple at Pali, an elaborately ornamented shrine of the mediæval period, a sum of Rs. 92 was spent in the correction of certain defects due to a former repair; blocked-up windows in the *Mandapa* were opened up and the precarious masonry of the jambs and head supported on new ashlar piers and iron joists. The removal of mortar once promiscuously smeared over the old structure and the general tidying up of the site are further items in this work still remaining to be done, the estimated cost of which amounts to Rs. 121.

Arbhar Temple. " On the preservation of the Arbhar Temple in the same district (another mediæval structure, of which however practically only the sculptured door jambs and lintels now exist) a sum of Rs. 240 was spent; the sculptural fragments of the ruin being considered of sufficient interest in themselves to warrant it. The works in progress comprise the erection of neat masonry buttresses behind the old piers and the underpinning of two columns near the entrance, as well as the jambs of the doorway. Holes in the existing concrete are to be filled and the floor of the interior laid with paving stones. Earth accumulation will be removed and jungle growth eradicated. The estimate for the work amounts to Rs. 365. **Central Circle.** **Central Provinces.**

"The Kanthi Dewal Temple at Ratanpur in the same district, a late mediæval structure reputed to have been built by the Haihaya kings, was also under repair, a sum of Rs. 219 being spent against an estimate of Rs. 349. The work embraces the dismantling and re-erection, with the old stones, of the balcony windows projecting on the south and west sides of the structure; the filling of cracks in the domed ceiling internally, and the weatherproofing of the top with concrete; the grouting of hollows and open joints in the walls, and the repair of the floor. The surrounding platform is also to be made good, and jungle growth, both on the shrine and in its immediate vicinity, eradicated. *Ratanpur.*

"The needs of the old Fort of Rajnagar, in the Damoh District, which is ascribed to the Gonds, were also attended to, and a sum of Rs. 102 spent on the clearance of dense jungle growth from the walls. *Rajnagar.*

"The Fort at Rahatgarh, in the Saugor District, built by the Sultan Muhammad Khan of Bhopal in the 18th century, was also taken in hand. Here, again, the work principally consisted of the removal of trees and heavy jungle from the walls and the structures in the interior; though the conservation of these latter was not undertaken as the Public Works Department considered them past repair. In this connexion it may be noted that Mr. Blakiston in a memorandum on the fort, dated 1913, remarks that most of these buildings are not more than 150 years old, and that the walls and bastions are the most interesting feature of the place. A sum of Rs. 1,258 was spent on this work, which is reported to have been completed. *Rahatgarh.*

"On the conservation of the old monuments at Khimlassa in the same district, a sum of Rs. 1,000 was spent. This group comprises the Dargah of the Panch Pirs, the Nagina Mahal, and an old well, all inside the Fort, as well as the entrance gateway thereof; and the Idgah and a three-domed mosque outside the village walls, these two last dating from Jahangir's reign. The estimate for this work amounts to Rs. 2,436 in all and the principal items are those for the Panch Pirs Dargah, the walls of which are formed of beautifully perforated screen work. The work on this tomb, which was badly damaged by lightning a number of years ago, when the dome covering it collapsed, included the replacement of the broken pieces of chajja on all four sides, the renewal of a broken jali panel, as well as a couple of fractured lintels; and the removal of modern rubble walling above the eaves of the structure, and substitution of plain ashlar stone to match the original. The broken top of the tomb was made watertight with concrete, and jungle growth removed. *Khimlassa.*

"The Nagina Mahal is reported by the Public Works Department to be past repair; and work on other monuments of this group will be limited to the clearance of jungle growth and the erection of notice boards warning the public of the penalties under the Ancient Monuments Preservation Act, for damage to the remains.

"On the repair of the Jami Masjid, Asirgarh, in the Nimar District a structure erected in the reign of Shah Jahan, a sum of Rs. 839, on a revised estimate of Rs. 9,792, has been spent. The mosque had formerly been used as a barrack during the military occupation of the Fort by the British, and the works in hand aim at the reclamation of the structure to its former state. The work involved the dismantling of a modern structure erected on the roof; the removal of alien window frames from the mihrab *Asirgarh.*

Central Circle. **Central Provinces.** recesses in the west wall, and the making good of damaged plaster, as well as the dismantling and rebuilding to the old design of the southern minar, which was in a very precarious condition (Plate IX*b*.) ; all of which items had been practically completed in the previous year. In the year under report the replacement of fallen chajja stones and their supporting brackets, both along the east front and in the flanking minars, was taken in hand at the cost already stated. A further sum of Rs. 864 was also spent on the initial removal of the dense jungle growth from the walls of the Asirgarh Fort, for which a special repair estimate of Rs. 1,551 has been sanctioned ; while the repair of the compound wall of the Tomb of Shah Gohar in the vicinity was completed at a cost of Rs. 118.

Burhanpur. "At Burhanpur, in the same district, a sum of Rs. 507 on an estimate of Rs. 1,680 was spent on the execution of the more urgent works required to preserve the remaining fragments of the ruined old fort ; undermined walls along the river front being underpinned and missing wooden lintels replaced by new ones of reinforced concrete. A low breast wall to enclose the dangerously ruined portions of the terrace along this front was also erected. In the same town, work on the Tomb of Nadir Shah (? Nasir Khan 1399—1437) of the Faruqi dynasty of Khandesh, was continued, and a sum of Rs. 858 expended on a revised estimate totalling Rs. 9,775. The conservation of this monument involved the re-facing with coursed rubble of the high chabutra platform on which the tomb is raised, and the paving of its top surface with stone to match the old fragments still remaining *in situ*. The re-facing with plain dressed ashlar masonry of the ruined exterior walls of the tomb was also taken in hand ; while the interior will be re-paved with dressed stone. No new carved decoration will be executed in the re-facing of this tomb, the work being strictly limited to the provision of plain ashlar masonry, in which the main offsets and projections alone will be repeated (Plate X*b*.).

Deogarh. "On the conservation of the old buildings in the Fort at Deogarh in the Chhindwara District a sum of Rs. 978 was spent out of a total estimate of Rs. 1,841. The structures affected were the Naqqarkhana and its entrance gate, the royal seat in the ruined throne room, and the Badal Mahal,—buildings which are attributed to a Gond Chief, Bakht Buland, who was converted to the Moslem faith about the beginning of the 18th century. The work here was practically confined to the removal of the dense jungle growth covering the fort walls and the buildings contained within them ; roofs were made water-tight with concrete, simple underpinning executed, and, in the case of the Naqqarkhana, certain of the missing cornice stones were renewed to match the old ones *in situ*, the loose masonry being secured, and broken plaster protected with a fillet of mortar run around the edges.

Gawilgarh. "On the conservation of the Fort at Gawilgarh (photo. No. 610-c.) in the Amraoti District, a stronghold, the present structure of which is recorded by Firishta to have been built in the year 1425 by Ahmad Shah Wali, ninth king of the Bahmani Dynasty, a sum of Rs. 332 was spent, principally on petty repairs designed to keep the old remains *Lasur.* weather-proof ; while at Lasur, in the same district, the conservation of the ruined Temple of Anandeshwar (Plate IX*a*.), a structure reputed to have been built by Hemadpanth, the 13th century Brahmin counsellor of the Yadava kings of Deogir (after whom the Hemadpanthi architectural style is named), was continued, a sum of Rs. 875 being expended. The work consisted chiefly in the replacement of the missing upper course of a high stepped chabutra on which the triple-shrined temple is elevated, the main work of reconstructing the fallen external facing of the ruined shrine itself, for which an estimate of Rs. 12,851 was sanctioned in 1914, having been carried out in previous years.

"The Narnalla Fort, in the Akola District, the present fortifications of which also probably date from the time of the Bahmani king Ahmad Shah Wali, who is stated by Firishta to have repaired them in 1425, also received attention during the year, Rs. 1,777 being spent on its conservation out of a total estimate of Rs. 3,111. The works undertaken comprised the clearance of dense jungle from the several more important gates of the Fort, as well as from a small mosque in the interior, where whitewash has also to be removed. A couple of platforms previously built to support old guns have also been stripped of their obtrusively modern cement-plastering, and the joints in the exposed masonry have been suitably treated. A bulging parapet on the Shah Nur Gate is to be dismantled and rebuilt with the old stones, and some loose masonry of the interior vaulting made good.

Central Circle.
Central Provinces.
Narnalla Fort

"The following monuments omitted from the Public Works Department's report are also said to have received attention during 1921-22 :—

Ghogra-Khapa.

"The Mahadeo Temple at Ghogra-Khapa, in the Nagpur District, where a sum of Rs. 388 was spent on completing the repairs for which an estimate of Rs. 911 had been sanctioned. This temple, an early mediæval type, and attributed to Hemadpanth, is a plain structure of massive stones and devoid of any sculptural ornament. The work on it consisted chiefly in securing disturbed facing masonry, in building up fallen quoins, replacing missing roof slabs, and repairing the paving in the interior. The existing iron-post and stretched wire railing was also strengthened and a new gate fitted to it, the immediate vicinity of the temple being cleared of loose stones and débris on the completion of the work.

Sirpur.

"At Sirpur, in the Raipur District, a sum of Rs. 2,539 was spent on finishing the work of constructing a shelter for the protection of the sculptures, Buddhist, Saivite, Vaishnavite, some 200 in all, recovered from the surrounding jungles and collected in the vicinity of the Lakshman Temple there, the latter being an early structure of finely cut bricks reputed to date from the 9th century. The shelter is a structure of brick piers roofed with concrete on brick jack-arches between R. S. beams, and has been erected on an old *pakka* platform measuring some 70 feet by 35 feet. The total cost of the work, which was commenced in the previous year, amounted to Rs. 4,249."

Eastern Circle.
Bengal.
Vishnupur.

In Bengal Mr. Dikshit reports that "The most important enterprise undertaken was the special repair of the temples at Vishnupur, a work which was executed directly under the supervision of the Archæological Department, at a cost of Rs. 4,000. The temples at Vishnupur form a fine group ranging in date from the sixteenth to the eighteenth century, and represent a distinctive type of architecture developed in Bengal along with the rise of Vaishnavism, under the royal patronage of the Rajas of Mallabhum. The more ornate and better preserved of the Vishnupur temples were taken in hand several years ago, but there were some which though protected had not had their share of attention. Pre-eminent among these stands the Ras Mancha, a dilapidated structure but one of great historical and architectural interest. It is reputed to have been built by Bir Hambira, a contemporary of the Emperor Akbar and the first among the Vishnupur Rajas to embrace the faith of the Vaishnavas which later on became the State religion of Mallabhum. The building was intended for use at the Rasa festival, when all the idols of the Vishnupur temples used to be brought here. In plan the temple is unique, its design being due perhaps to the necessity of accommodating an unusually large concourse of people attending the festival. It takes the form of a square shrine quite small in itself, (9 ft. sq.), but surrounded on all sides by

Eastern Circle.
Bengal.
Vishnupur.

three galleries with an open verandah, and with a sloping pyramidal roof, culminating in a squat dome over the shrine and a Bengali curvilinear roof over the façade arches. The soundness of a building of such dimensions (plinth area 100 ft. sq.) necessarily depends upon the strength of the supporting pillars. Unfortunately the hearting of the pillars in the Ras Mancha consists of nothing but mud and rubble and is so weak that one wonders why any part of the building has survived at all. As a result, some of the pillars had collapsed, cracked, or bulged out ; the roof had fallen in at several places, notably in the northern and western galleries and in the ante-chamber, and was leaking seriously, especially in the eastern galleries. The main task that confronted the Department here was to strengthen the pillars as they stood and water-proof the roof without adding extra weight. All disintegrated and bulged out surfaces of pillars and walls were renewed after dismantling, wherever necessary, an operation which necessitated the temporary insertion of brick piers to support the adjoining roof. A large amount of grouting was also done to the cracked surfaces of the pillars and walls ; the decayed plaster and débris from the top of the roof were picked up and the roof was thoroughly repaired, the brickwork of the pyramidal portion of the roof, which rises in tiers or steps, being renewed in cement mortar ; the part between the pyramidal and the curvilinear cornice portions of the roof, which drains the roof, was terraced with 3" concrete ; the tops of pillars and walls exposed to the weather were made water-tight by bedding the upper courses in lime mortar ; and the stucco facing of the arches in the façade of the eastern gallery was properly secured to the body of the pillars, wherever it had begun to flake off. On the whole, a new lease of life has been given to the Ras Mancha and it is hoped that apart from annual maintenance, little will be needed at least for some years to come for the preservation of the structure.

" The Radha Vinod Temple in the Khar Bangla quarter of the town of Vishnupur was another monument taken in hand during the year. It derives special interest from its beautifully moulded brickwork as well as from the fact that it illustrates a transitional type of temple architecture evolved in Vishnupur, standing midway between the single-cell type represented by the Mallesvar Temple and the fully developed four-verandah type of the Madan Mohan and other temples. The monument was added to the list of protected monuments in 1911 at the instance of Dr. Spooner, but it was not found possible to include it in the curtailed programme of works during the last few years. The condition of this building which was far from satisfactory, has now been considerably improved. Débris that had accumulated for years in front of the temple owing to the collapse of the eastern half of the spire and the verandah roof has been cleared away, and the eastern or main entrance has been thrown open to the public for the first time since the building fell into disrepair. The southern entrance, which had been blocked up by the *pujari*, has been reopened and the improvised opening in the western wall has been duly closed and the original face of the wall restored. A particularly difficult undertaking in connection with these repairs was the dismantling and rebuilding of the south-western corner, which had uneven cracks from top to bottom. The exposed hearting of the spire was treated with cement pointing to prevent water from penetrating into the masonry and the sloping roof on the sides was terraced with fresh concrete. The bare walls of the verandah were strengthened by grouting the cracks and decayed bricks in the walls were replaced by new ones. The platform round the temple has now been renewed and proposals have been made to acquire more land on the north and east so as to permit of the erection of a wire fence. It is a matter for congratulation that the repairs to this monument were practically finished during the cold weather of 1921-22; otherwise the exceptionally heavy rains of June 1922 must inevitably have added to the ruin. **Eastern Circle. Bengal.**

"The third temple at Vishnupur where work was carried on this year was the Murali Mohan temple in the town of Vishnupur. It is built in laterite and its architectural interest, as noticed by Dr. Spooner, lies in the fact that unlike the majority of Vishnupur temples, it has no rooms at the corners of the verandah, the shrine being surrounded by a continuous arcaded verandah with four columns on each side. The most urgent and difficult item here was the dismantling and rebuilding of the south-east corner of the verandah. The ground at this point having settled, the corner pillar has sunk, threatening to bring down with it the stones forming the roof and lintels on either side. Great care was taken in rebuilding to ensure that every stone was set in its original position. Flat iron bars used in the original building for supporting the stone lintels were found broken and were replaced by new ones. All cracks were grouted and missing stones in the spire were reset. The plinth on which the temple stands, which was damaged beyond recognition, has also been repaired. When the wire fencing now in hand is completed, stray cattle will be effectually kept out. Repairs to other temples at Vishnupur are included in the programme for 1922-23, and it is hoped that the whole of this remarkable group of Hindu monuments will soon be restored to a structurally sound condition.

Gaur. "Among the monuments conserved through the agency of the Public Works Department, the Gumti Gate and Darasbari and Chamkatti Mosques at Gaur deserve prominent mention. The Gumti Gate is a beautifully ornamented little gateway in the south-east corner of the citadel at Gaur, built by the early independent Sultans of Bengal about the 15th century. In the seventeenth century, this gate was superseded by the Lukachuri gateway, a short distance to the north, and subsequently fell into neglect and disrepair. It is now proposed to remove all the débris from the building, grout the cracks in the dome, reset missing bricks and coloured tiles wherever possible, water-proof the top and enclose the whole within a wire fence. An allotment of Rs. 2,000 was provided for completing this work during 1921-22, on the basis of a prewar estimate, but the revision of the estimate necessitated by the present high rates as well as the difficulty of obtaining fencing material from Calcutta, owing to the East Indian Railway strike, made a partial postponement of the work necessary.

"The Darashari Mosque is situated near Mehdipur in the midst of thick bamboo jungle at a distance of about a mile to the west of the main road passing through Gaur. It is believed to have been built by the independent Sultan Yusuf Shah in 884 A. H. (1479 A. D.). It measures 112′ × 66′ and must at one time have been a rather imposing structure somewhat similar to the small golden mosque at Gaur. It had a central chamber with a row of three pyramidal or 'barrel vaulted' domes, and two side rooms, each with three bays and nine domes in three rows, supported on stone pillars. It has now completely lost its roof, but the walls are still standing and the beautifully moulded brick-work in the western *mihrabs* richly deserves preservation. Out of an estimate of Rs. 2,175, a sum of Rs. 855 has been spent during the year. The inside of the mosque has been cleared of débris, and bamboo clumps that had encroached on the structure have been destroyed, while such of the stone pillars as are still *in situ* in a reclining or recumbent position have been re-erected. The walls have been completely cleared of all vegetation and the top courses have been bedded in cement mortar to prevent the penetration of water to the hearting of the masonry. Other measures,

Eastern Circle. Bengal.

including repairs to cracks, demarcation of boundaries, erection of a wire fence and construction of an approach road, are still in progress.

"The Chamkatti Mosque, situated on the main road near the 10th mile post, is another monument ascribed to the reign of Yusuf Shah, but differing widely from the Darasbari Mosque both in plan and in construction. It is a neat little mosque consisting of only one room roofed by a dome and provided with a verandah and three doors in the front and one on each of the sides, in these respects resembling the well-known Lattan Masjid, the most lavishly decorated mosque in Gaur. The main items provided for in the estimate are the renewal of the concrete and the grouting of cracks in the dome, underpinning the disturbed stone-work of pillars, filling gaps in the brick-work of the arches and relaying the floor, besides the usual jungle clearance, wire fencing, etc. This estimate has only been partially dealt with during the year under review.

Katra.

"The mosque at Katra near Murshidabad, is the oldest extant monument at the last capital of Bengal, its construction being ascribed to the founder of that city, Nawab Murshid Kuli Khan, who lies buried below the entrance to the mosque. The mosque is a simple five-domed structure with little ornamentation, but the surrounding cloisters with the towers at the south-west and north-west corners add to the dignity and impressiveness of the building. Repairs here were urgently needed to the cracked arches of the tower entrances, and to the cloisters which were in a sorry state of dilapidation. These and other repairs, such as the edging of existing plaster with lime fillets, filling cracks in the body of the main building, clearing and levelling the compound, etc., were undertaken during the current year, and were still in progress when the year came to its close, the expenditure incurred being Rs. 573.

Masjidbari Mosque.

"The only other special works in Bengal were certain additional repairs to the Masjidbari Mosque in Bakarganj District, conserved in 1918, and a few minor works at the Math at Rajbari in Dacca District The latter monument (Plate XI*b*) is typical of a class of monuments found mostly in Deltaic Bengal, which consist of a single cell with a high tower, built in commemoration of a deceased relative. The Rajbari Math is ascribed to Chand Ray and Kedar Ray, two local potentates who lived in the 16th century, and serves as a valuable landmark for miles round owing to its situation at the junction of the great rivers Meghna and Padma."

Assam.

As regards the programme of works in Assam, Mr. Dikshit reports a striking improvement, thanks to the Local Government having deputed a specially selected subordinate of the Public Works Department for archæological works. "One of the main difficulties in the repair of ancient buildings in Assam," Mr. Dikshit says, "is the absence of intelligent and competent artisans. In modern house-building in Assam masonry work has practically been eliminated, the roofs being either thatched or corrugated and the walls made of '*ikra*' and plastered with mud, owing to the frequency of seismic disturbances and the heavy rainfall. In the old days the Ahom kings and their nobles, who were great temple builders, depended mostly on masons imported from the Gangetic Valley. This deficiency of good local masons and contractors has retarded the completion of the special repairs to the Bardole temple at Bishnath in Darrang District which had been begun in the previous year. The work was estimated to cost Rs. 1,912 and the whole of it would easily have been completed within the year, but for the fact that, in spite of frequent and careful instructions, the contractor (reported to be the best man locally available) failed completely over the plaster and stucco work. It is hoped that the defects will be remedied as far as is now possible during the current year. The lesson learnt at Bishnath will not be forgotten when the more

Bishnath.

extensive works on the monuments at Sibsagar come to be taken in hand. At the latter site a small beginning has already been made toward what will eventually develop into a comprehensive campaign at this important centre, by the erection of concrete platforms for seven pieces of old Ahom cannon in the Kutchery Compound, and the execution of some special repairs to the Ahom palace at Garhgaon, the grounds of which have been levelled and dressed, the hollows in the ground floor filled up, the flights of steps leading to the upper stories repaired and the terraced floors relaid, so as to prevent the percolation of water into the interior. Parenthetically it may be noted that this is the first time that chaukidars have been employed to look after the monuments in Sibsagar. **Eastern Circle.** **Assam.** *Sibsagar.*

" The scheme of collecting at the Municipal park all the sculptures lying about the town of Tezpur, which had been postponed during the war, has also been put in hand a sum of Rs. 814 being expended on building the platform on which the sculptures are to be placed. *Tezpur.*

" The only other undertaking of note during the year was at the ruins of the last capital of the Kachari Rajas at Khaspur, near Silchar in the Surma Valley. The estimate for this work had also been sanctioned before the war, but was postponed for want of funds. The monuments conserved at Khaspur are three temples of Ranachandi, the tutelary goddess of the Kachari king, a *Baradwari* or audience hall, a *Singh Darwaza* or lion gate and a bathing pavilion. The chief task at each of these buildings was the clearance of jungle and removal of roots, water-proofing the roof, grouting cracks and preserving the existing plaster of walls. The luxuriant growth of vegetation over these monuments, only a little more than a century old, has been very destructive and in one case, *viz.*, that of the Baradwari, it has been thought safest to leave the existing structure as it is and not to attempt to remove the giant roots of the trees which hold the building in their embrace. *Khaspur.*

" No reports about the conservation of monuments in the Indian States connected with the Eastern Circle have been received. It may be mentioned, however, that at the Unakoti hill in the Koilashahar division of the Tripura State, the rock-cut sculptures and stone images are known to have been cleared of jungle and made accessible during the year ". A conservation note on the monuments in the Udaypur and Koilashahar divisions in the Tripura State, which were visited by Mr. Dikshit, is now in preparation. *Indian States, (Bengal).*

During the absence of Mr. Longhurst on long leave out of India, Pandit Hirananda Shastri has been officiating as Superintendent in the Southern Circle, and the following account of the maintenance and repair of monuments in the Madras Presidency is from his pen. **Southern Circle.**

" In the Southern Circle Rs. 28,574-14-10 were devoted to conservation of which Rs. 17,931-13-0 went to Special and the residue to Annual repairs. In the Kistna District the Bandar Fort at Masulipatam came in for its share of conservation, and substantial progress has been made during the year in carrying out Mr. Longhurst's instructions. This fort is connected with the early struggles of the Dutch, the French and the British in India and contains some of the last memorials of the former greatness of Masulipatam. As described by Captain Albert Harvey in his *Ten Years in India* the fort had an Arsenal which was the entrepot of stores supplied to the troops in the Hyderabad and Nagpur subsidiary forces, as well as the whole of the Northern Division of the army. It contained necessaries of every *Masulipatam.*

Southern Circle.

description and was kept in first rate order by the Commissariat and the many warrant officers attached to the establishment. The curious old records kept in it gave an idea of how things were managed in those times. Owing to neglect it fell into decay. The Dutch magazine and some of the old European barracks passed into private hands. The old hospital, which is now roofless, is said to belong to the Nizam. The St. John's Church had been ruthlessly pulled down and the Belfry was very much neglected. Mr. Longhurst inspected the fort and drew up a note suggesting necessary repairs. At his recommendation, all the three important structures in the fort were taken up for conservation, namely, the Armoury including the Arsenal; the Belfry, Plate XVII (*b*), and the Powder Magazine. The Armoury, which is now used as Customs and Port Office, consists of a quadrangular enclosure with rooms and godowns built round it, and a large gateway. The enclosure is divided into two open courts by a narrow block of buildings in the centre. Mr. Longhurst during his subsequent inspection found that the measures he had proposed, had been executed satisfactorily. In the Armoury some of the walls which were broken have been rebuilt, the old and damaged lintels of the doors have been renewed and the terrace, which leaked badly, has been repaired. At the Belfry, the damaged parts of the compound wall were renovated, plastering done where necessary, and general clearance effected. At the Powder Magazine similar measures were taken to arrest decay.

Penukonda.

"Penukonda, the headquarters of the Taluk of the same name in the Anantapur District, is famous for having been the residence of the Vijayanagar kings within an easy reach of the capital at Hampi, and for its fort, which gave shelter to Sadasiva and his court after the disastrous battle of Talikōta in 1565. The citadel of this fort and the remains of other structures in it, including the northern gateway with its interesting inscriptions, and the watch-tower (which is a quaint old structure built upon a square bastion in the Indo-Saracenic style adopted by the later Vijayanagar kings), have all been under repair during the year and have been provided with doors and windows where necessary and generally tidied up. At Chandragiri, to which place Ranga, the son and successor of Tirumala, who murdered Sadasiva, the puppet king of the Vijayanagar Dynasty, transferred his capital shortly after 1575, both the Fort and the Palace received attention, and much has been done to clear the surroundings and effect general tidiness. Both these buildings are remarkable for the excellent quality and wonderful tenacity of the cement and mortar used in their construction, particularly in the highly interesting series of flat arches and coffered ceilings. At several other forts, such as Gingee, Gurramkonda, Sankaridrug, the Vellore Fort, which is one of the most beautiful specimens of military architecture in Southern India, and the well-known fortress of Dansborg at Tranquebar, founded by Ovo Gedde on behalf of the Danish East India Company in 1620, much has been done to remedy structural defects and clear away exuberant vegetation. Yet another fort which came in for repair is that at Anjengo which was built in 1695 on a sandy piece of land first acquired by the East India Company in 1684 from the Rani of Attengal for the purpose of trade in pepper and spices. During the Carnatic wars this fort was used as a depôt for military stores and was the first signalling station for vessels arriving from England. Over two centuries ago it was equipped with a council and a garrison subordinate to Bombay. It is associated with several historical personages. Robert Orme, the historian, who was the earliest chronicler of the story of Anglo-Indian progress, was born here in 1728. This monument, of so great historical interest and value, was crumbling into ruins when

Chandragiri.

Gingee, etc.

Anjengo.

Mr. Longhurst first inspected it in 1918. Much has been done this year towards its preservation; the tops of the parapets and gun embrasures have been repaired; a new flight of steps has been built in the north-east corner of the enclosure for the convenience of visitors, and sundry other measures have been taken. The palace at Tanjore, which came into existence about 1550 A. D., contains a bewildering series of large and rambling buildings, one of which is an eight-storeyed tower, about 190 feet high and designed like a temple *gopuram*. On the east side of the inner quadrangle in the palace is the Telugu Durbar Hall of the Nayakkar kings called the Statue Hall on account of the fine marble statue of Saraboji, the last but one Raja of Tanjore, which it contains. Both these structures and the Schwartz Church in the Little Fort with its memorial, (representing Saraboji's visit to Schwartz, the founder of the Church, a very fine work of art that any church might be proud of), have all undergone a variety of structural repairs.

Southern Circle.

Tanjore.

"Another important monument in the Southern Presidency which received attention this year is the Chola Temple of Virabhadra standing at Mottupalle in the Guntur District. Though an ordinary village shrine of the usual type, Plate XVI (*b*), it is of a special historical value on account of the inscriptions it contains. The most important of these records is an epigraph engraved on one of the pillars of the *mandapa*, forming an *abbayasasana* issued by the Kakatiya King Ganapatideva-Maharaja in the Saka year 1166, which granted immunity, excepting the usual customs duty, to all foreign traders whose vessels might be wrecked on the coast; as theretofore, the whole cargo of such ships had been forfeited to the state. This epigraph further shows the extent of Kakatiya power in the Telugu land and refers to taxes on articles of export and import at the harbour of Motupulle *alias* Desyuyyakkondapattana. The north-western wall of this sanctuary has been rebuilt, a damaged part of the terrace renovated, the flooring mended and much grouting carried out to the *gopuram* and other parts of the structure.

Mottupalle.

"Among monuments noted particularly for their architectural importance, several came in for their share of conservation during the year. The village of Undavalli in the Guntur District, which may easily be reached by crossing the Kistna from Bezwada, possesses some rock-cut temples of the early Pallava period. Of these the one which lies around the hill in a recess towards the south and faces north is the largest and the best. It is a five-storeyed excavation having all the upper storeys set back one above the other. As is shown by the colossal image of the reclining Vishnu, about 17 feet long, which is cut out of the rock in the third-storey, and by representations of some of the *avatāras*, it must have had a Brahmanical origin. The excavation belongs to about the 7th century A. D. and furnishes an interesting example of early Pallava architecture. It stood in need of urgent repairs which have been effected during the year by renovating certain much dilapidated pillars, filling crevices in the roof, pointing where necessary, and general clearance. A flight of steps has also been added to the monument to give access to the south end of its first floor.

Undavalli.

"In the Hospet sub-division of the Bellary District further headway has been made in the campaign of work that has been going on for many years among the famous group of monuments at Vijayanagar. In the Vitthala Temple, which is the most splendid building at Hampi, the two cracked pillars in the Kalyana *mandapa* were supported by iron straps, the flooring was relaid and pointed where it had been disturbed, stone buttresses were provided and a new approach road constructed; the

Vijayanagar (Hampi).

Southern Circle.

entrance of the Sarasvati Temple has had its facing reset in plumb and a new stone lintel inserted ; in the Ranga Temple the top of the main *mandapa* and the two small *mandapas*, standing close by, have been plastered, voids grouted and pointed and the main entrance provided with fresh lintel stones in place of the broken ones. The Hazara Rama Temple, which is one of the most perfect specimens of Hindu temple architecture of the Vijayanagar period, had the top of its verandah waterproofed, the fallen compound wall at the south side reconstructed, a masonry pillar provided to support a broken architrave in the west verandah, and displaced

Mahabalipuram. stones reset where necessary. At Mahabalipuram in the Chingleput District, so very famous for its fascinating group of rock-cut temples, measures were taken to keep the monuments tidy, repair the approach roads and plant avenue trees. Yet another sanctuary which has been an object of care during the year in this District is the old

Conjeeveram. Matangesvara Temple at Conjeeveram, standing in a field at a distance of a few furlongs to the south-west of the Kailasanātha Temple. In style it belongs to the later period of Pallava architecture which was started by Rajasimha about the beginning of the 8th century A. D. Temples of this style are built in stone with sometimes a brick superstructure covered in plaster and decorated in stucco. On plan the shrine is a small square cella surrounded by a circumambulatory passage and faces the east. Externally, the lofty tower, rising in tiers which diminish in size as they approach the summit, is built over the central shrine in front of which is a small porch leading into a large pillared hall or *mandapa*. The bases of the pillars are decorated with conventional lions with their tails curved up. Over the lion is to be seen an ornamented band with polygonal necking, a large projecting capital and a square abacus above. The back of the porch has pilasters with figured panels on each side. This temple has been repaired by filling the cracks and pointing the joints in the *gopuram* as well as the terrace, and exuberant vegetation has been removed, especially from its *gopuram*.

Coorg.

" In Coorg the Fort and Raja's seat at Mercara and the Palace at Nalknād, though comparatively modern, are the only monuments possessing any feature of architectural interest. The Mercara Fort is small but picturesque and contains the palace, the Commissioner's residence, and a group of modern out-houses as well as a church. The palace is a barrack-like structure built in the form of a quadrangle enclosing an open paved courtyard, with a pair of lifesize brick and plaster elephants set up by one of the old Rajas of Coorg. At both these monuments some measures though not of any special magnitude were taken to repair the walls, approach roads, doors and windows, to waterproof the roofs and repair the elephant figures."

Burma Circle.

The Superintendent in Burma, Mr. Charles Duroiselle, sends me the following résumé of his year's work in the field of conservation, a more detailed account having appeared in the Annual Report of the Burma Circle issued separately by that Government. " The total amount spent this year on the conservation of monuments in Burma was Rs. 56,363 (excluding the Public Works Department charges) which is slightly in excess of the amount funded last year for the same purpose, *viz.*, Rs. 53,120. The two principal items of work during the year were (*i*) the continuation of the construction of the gardens on the platform of the palace at Mandalay ; and (*ii*) the continuation of the special repairs to the Tilominlo Temple at Pagan. On the garden Rs. 10,998 was expended and Rs. 12,192 on the Tilominlo.

Burma Circle.
Mandalay.

"The palace at Mandalay is unique of its kind in Burma, for though it was built on the traditional plan of former palaces in this Province, it is the only one now in existence, the others built at the numerous capitals having long completely disappeared. The buildings on the platform were very numerous, and divided into two distinct parts. The eastern half of the platform contained the Royal apartments, throne-rooms and other appurtenances. These were the most beautiful and full of a distinctive historical interest; and it is these buildings which form the palace now being conserved by this Department. The western half was covered with numerous small buildings of no particular historical or architectural interest which were the abodes of lesser queens, their retinues, etc. When the preservation of the palace was decided upon, practically all the latter buildings, of no intrinsic interest whatever, were dismantled, thus leaving the whole western half of the platform an arid and unsightly waste. It was at last decided to do away with this eye-sore by constructing a garden over it. The work was begun in 1920-21, and Rs. 8,013 were spent upon it; as already said above, Rs. 10,998 was spent on the work this year and it is now practically completed. The lawns, shrubs and flowers make now a thing of beauty of what was but lately desolate ground. But two items of work still remain to be done in this connection; first the construction of a balustrade round the enclosure and, most important in a climate so dry as Mandalay, the provision of water supply. This last item has received earnest consideration from the Garden Committee for several years past, and it has been now decided that in consideration of expense a pump should be located near the North Wall of the Palace Garden to pump water direct on to the lawns from the canals close at hand, and also for use in case of fire. The Committee have also come to the conclusion that, when all the works have been completed, they should also take over charge of the gardens outside the palace platform, which have up to now been in charge of the Cantonment Committee, with a view to extending the area around the palace, and to preserving the whole as palace precincts.

"Besides the Palace Garden, there were no works of any moment in the Mandalay Division calling for special attention. There were the usual petty repairs necessary to a wooden building such as the palace and the minor monuments within the Fort. The much needed repairs to King Mindon's Tomb and to those of the Laungshe and Medawgyi queens near the palace have now been completed. Plate XVIII (*b*) shows the north view of Fort Dufferin, in the centre of which stands the palace. Fort Dufferin is a perfect square, surrounded beyond the moat by a crenelated wall one mile and a quarter long on each side. On the top of the walls, which are reinforced by a glacis on the inside, are twelve *pyatthats* or bastions on each face, that is, forty-eight in all. These bastions are very graceful wooden structures and very good examples of a distinctive feature of Burmese architecture. Each wall is pierced in the middle by a large gate through which the king and royal family only had access. Other smaller gates were for the use of the citizens living outside the walls. The bastions on those four principal gates and at the corners of the walls are considerably larger than the others. Besides the outer crenelated walls above mentioned, the palace was further protected by two other enclosures, not far from the palace itself. The first consisted of a palisade made of huge teak logs, access within which was gained by a small gate in each of the four faces; and about seventy feet beyond this again, was the third enclosure, consisting of a brick wall slightly lower than the palisade and through which access was also had by a small gate in each face. It was in the middle of this third and last enclosure that the palace was situated; within it also were to be found the

Burma Circle. *Mandalay.* principal buildings necessary to the life of an eastern capital; the Supreme Court of Law, guard-houses, elephant sheds, stables, the mint, etc., etc., most of which have by now disappeared. It is also within this enclosure, and facing the palace on the east, that are situated the tombs mentioned above. The bricks of the outer walls are set in mud mortar which is not conducive to strength and durability; they have, as a consequence, shown signs of deterioration in many places; but considering their great length, a scheme of repairs to them in their entirety must necessarily be spread over several years. The *pyatthats* or bastions on those walls being of wood require constant attention; this year, the bastion over the eastern gate and bastion No. 6 have been thoroughly repaired while that on the south-east gate, which showed signs of weakness, has been propped up and stiffened.

"Plate XVIII (*a*) shews the three royal tombs in Fort Dufferin, which have been repaired during the year under review. They stand close to one another a few hundred feet to the north-east of the palace. Figure 2 is the resting place of King Mindon, the last king but one of the Alaungpra dynasty. He abandoned the previous capital, Amarapura, in 1856 and founded the City of Mandalay, which was completed in 1859. He died in 1878, only partly aware of the bloody intrigues which were being set on foot during his illness to procure the succession to the prince who became King Thibaw. Contrary to Burmese customs, the body of Mindon was not cremated and his ashes thrown into the river, but was buried at the spot where his tomb now stands. This monument had been in a rather bad state and the repairs to it, carried out during a period of three years, were completed this year. Some of the plaster carvings with mosaic work on the several roofs of the Pyatthat above the basement, were damaged, while in other cases they had fallen down; these were carefully repaired and replaced adhering strictly to the original models. The beautiful glass mosaics which cover the basement, which had in some places fallen off, were replaced. The railing round the edge of the plinth, which was crumbling here and there, leaving hideous gaps, has been replaced by railings of reinforced concrete. The staircases were rebuilt, and the finial above the *pyatthat* as well as the *hti* crowning it were repaired and strengthened. Figure 1 is the tomb of the Laungshe Queen; she was one of the queens of King Mindon, and the mother of King Thibaw, the last king of Burma; and died in 1881. The tomb commemorates the spot where she was cremated. Figure 3 is the monument raised on the place where the remains of the Medawgyi Queen were cremated. She had been the wife of King Shwebomin, and was the mother of Pagan Min (Mindon's predecessor) as well as the mother-in-law of Mindon, the latter having married her daughter. Nos. 2 and 3 are wooden buildings consisting of a multiple roof *pyatthat* supported by four posts, the space between these posts being closed in by fine filigree work ornamented with pieces of coloured glass forming a kind of mosaic. Some of the sculptures at the corners and the middle of the roofs had become loose or were broken and some had disappeared; all these have now been repaired, or strengthened, and new wood carving substituted where necessary. The filigree work was repaired and the coloured glass replaced wherever it had fallen off.

Shwebo Division. "Monuments are comparatively few in the Shwebo Division, but a sum of Rs. 823 was spent on repairs to some of them. The two main gates of the Sinbyume Pagoda at Mingun were found to be loose and on the point of falling; they were strengthened and refixed, the other gates being provided with wickets and turn-stile gates to prevent the ingress of cattle, one of the banes of old monuments in Burma. In the same locality, the flooring of the building wherein hangs the great Mingun Bell was repaired. Repairs also were made to the revetment wall protecting the small but fine Pondawpya pagoda from the annual flood of the Irrawaddy River. The Pondawpya was erected as the model of the enormous pagoda not far from the Mingun Bell, known as the Mingun pagoda, and shows what the latter would have looked like had it ever been completed, which it never was. **Burma Circle.**

"At Old Prome (Srikshetra) in the Tharrawaddy Division, petty repairs were carried out at a cost of Rs. 295 to the Bawbawgyi pagoda, one of the oldest monuments in Burma, and also to the Bebe and Lemyethna pagodas which probably antedate the buildings at Pagan. At the Bebe, the arch over the west corridor was in a rather bad state; it is now supported with timber work. At the Lemyethna, cow-herds had dug into the walls, which have now been repaired. *Old Prome.*

"On Hainggyi Island, in the Bassein Division, are the remains of a factory built by the Agents of the Old East India Company. It was sometime ago decided to erect on the spot a marble tablet with an inscription for perpetuating the memory of these old remains; this has been effected at the cost of Rs. 674. *Hainggyi Island.*

"Pagan, owing to its numerous monuments spread over a comparatively small area, is the principal centre of conservation work in Burma. Special repairs are executed from time to time, and annual repairs to temples already conserved. At the Tilominlo Temple, one of the most imposing among the larger monuments, special repairs to the octagonal terrace below the *sikhara* have been completed, as well as repairs to the stair-cases leading up to the *sikhara* on each of the four sides, and to all the terraces on the second storey. The scrolls and flamboyant ornaments of the pediments over three of the principal porches have been carefully repaired, and cracks in the arches over the vaulted corridors have been thoroughly grouted and made watertight. During the year under review a further expenditure of Rs. 12,192 was incurred on the above temple. A great part of the work on the second storey and the repairs to the two circuit walls still remain to be carried out, and it is estimated that this will cost a further sum of Rs. 25,000. The special repairs to the Sulamani Temple were continued, and necessitated the expenditure of Rs. 3,815; this sum, however, was too small, and just allowed repairs to be undertaken to battlements, the subsidiary small stupas at the corners, and to the steps on the second storey leading to the *sikhara*. The ugly cement caps on the battlements, which were not an original feature of the monument, were removed and replaced by brickwork in conformity with the old. *Pagan.*

"The Min-O-Chantha pagoda at Pagan, near the great Ananda Temple, is of unpretentious size but of fine proportions. It is of the type which became later so familiar in Burma, that is, a solid building conical in shape. It was built during the reign of King Kyanzittha (1084-1112) by, tradition has it, his own son Rajakumar for the restoration of his old father's health, hence its name. Though it is not a protected monument, it is one of those in the charge of the Pagoda Durwans. This pagoda is seen in Plate XIX, fig. (*a*). It is built on two terraces, and the only access to it is by a flight of steps on the south face, protected by roofs ornamented with wood carvings. The wooden building with three superposed roofs on the upper terrace, is a prayer hall, wherein the villagers assemble from time to time to recite prayers in the evening. The walls of the two terraces, and the floors are in several places in a bad

Burma Circle. state of repair. The pagoda itself is still very strong, but cracks are showing here and there and the facing plaster has fallen off in some places. A Buddhist monk of Pagan, U Sittara, has asked for permission to carry out the necessary repairs ; and permission was granted on the understanding that he would take advice from the Archæological Superintendent, and carry out the repairs in consultation with the overseer in charge of the Pagodas at Pagan, so as to preserve the character of the old work. The work has already been begun. It is pleasant to record that, in recent years in Burma, private enterprise has a tendency to participate increasingly in the repair of old monuments, the people in each instance proving perfectly willing to consult the Archæological Department as to the best methods to follow. Such was not the case a few years ago.

Arakan. " Arakan remains to the fore in the matter of private enterprise. Some of the monuments at Mrohaung are unique of their kind, and a few Arakanese gentlemen have earnestly taken in hand the repairs to some of the most important, always in consultation and under the guidance of this Department. Thus, with the Rs. 5,000 generously contributed by the Local Government, and the further help of Rs. 3,000 contributed by the people themselves, it was possible to begin the special repair works to the Shitthaung Temple, one of the most interesting monuments in Burma, which had fallen into a lamentable state of disrepair. The Public Works Department carried on the work for the people. Large portions of the vaulted roof over the southern corridor had fallen in ; but as it was found impossible to restore it efficiently the corridor was strengthened and covered by a supporting arch built from inside. The roof over the whole building, which leaked badly, was made watertight. A portion of the northwest angle of the outer corridor, which had crumbled away and during the rains allowed streams of water to flow in, is now being repaired. The Public Works Department having, after a time, withdrawn their help, the work has now been taken up and carried on by the Trustees themselves who are personally superintending it. The collection of funds is prosecuted with commendable energy, and it is gratifying to learn that a further sum of Rs. 2,000 is now at the disposal of the Trustees, to whose energy and public spirit all lovers of the ancient arts of Burma are indebted.

" In Plate XIX, fig. (*b*), may be seen the Ratanaman-aung Pagoda, which is also being repaired by a public spirited gentleman of Mrohaung in Arakan, according to the instructions given by me when I visited the place in 1920. This pagoda is said to have been built by King Candasuddhamma (A. D. 1652—1684). It is a solid structure entirely built of stone blocks, and octagonal from the base to the top. It is completely devoid of any ornamental designs, thus acquiring an air of austere majesty not to be seen in other buildings of this type found in Burma proper. Rs. 3,000 have already been spent by Shwe Tha U, the gentleman mentioned above, solely on repairs to the main structure, from which a certain number of stones had fallen down ; others were dangerously loose ; and thick roots were growing out of the joints loosening many more. The triple enclosing walls which had suffered severely, are now under repair. When these repairs have been completed, Shwe Tha U intends preserving several other beautiful little monuments erected within the pagoda enclosure."

Indian States. *Chhattarpur.* At Khajuraho in the Chhattarpur State the work of conservation and restoration among the famous monuments of the Chandel Rajputs continues under the supervision of Mr. B. L. Dhama. The work at present is confined to the two dilapidated temples of

Duladeo and Jatkari. At the Duladeo Temple the fallen corner dados in alto-relievo, and the missing portions of the north and south projecting balconies of the Maha-Mandapa have been restored in outline. The precariously hanging core of the Maha-Mandapa roof which was a great menace to visitors has been dismantled ; and a broken lintel over the south bay of the Maha-Mandapa carrying part of the recessed circular ceiling has been supported by a suitable ashlar pillar. Besides these measures several other structural repairs of importance have been carried out. The work of restoring the Sikhara or Great Spire over the Sanctum is in progress. **Indian States.** *Chhattarpur.*

At the Jatkari Temple the fallen portions of the south and north projecting balconies have been restored in outline and other structural repairs and restoration works are in progress.

The expenditure on these works, which will be described more in detail in next year's Report, is being met by joint contributions from the Government of India and the Chhattarpur Darbar.

Gwalior State. In a résumé of his Annual Report for 1921-22, Mr. Garde, the State Archæologist in Gwalior, after recording the appreciation of the Darbar for the assistance rendered them by Sir John Marshall and Mr. Sana Ullah, writes as follows of the conservation work carried out by the State during the period in question.

" The conservation campaign started in such good earnest last year was pushed on with the same vigour during 1921-22. By order of the Finance Member, Rs. 7,000 was transferred from the Budget of the Archæological Department to that of the Education Department, to be handed over to the *Panditāsrama Sabhā* of Ujjain, which is entrusted with the work of restoring and preserving the old Astronomical Observatory built at Ujjain by Raja Sawai Jaisingh of Jaipur. The work is being carried out under the direct supervision of Pandit Gokulchandji, an astronomer of Jaipur, who has taken a prominent part in repairing Jaisingh's observatories located elsewhere in India.

" The Central *Mazhabi Auqāf* Committee transferred Rs. 6,482-9-10 to this Department for conserving (1) the Bijayamandal Mosque at Bhilsa, and (2) the Khokai Monastery at Ranod, two archæological monuments which are still being used for religious purposes and with which therefore both the *Mazhabi Auqāf* Committee and the Archæological Department are concerned.

" Apart from the annual upkeep of monuments conserved in past years at Gwalior, Bhilsa, Udaygiri and Surwaya, initial repairs were executed to the nine groups of monuments detailed below, at a total cost of Rs. 13,074-2-9 excluding the Rs. 7,000 transferred to the *Panditāsrama Sabhā*, but including the Rs. 6,482-9-10 received from the *Mazhabi Auqāf* Committee.

" I. *Tomb of Muhammad Ghaus at Gwalior.*—The major portion of the repairs to the principal tomb, the minor tombs, the mosques and the surrounding graveyards had been carried out in the previous year. The items which remained to be attended to in the year under report were as follows :—

(*a*) Good teak wood shutters were provided for the entrance into the shrine proper.

(*b*) Pigeons and bats entered through the *jali* work and infested the interior of the hall. To prevent these pests all the *jali* arches were fitted with wire screens from inside.

Gwalior State.

(c) An ugly *kaccha* hut built in modern times in close vicinity to the stately building, and which disfigured the appearance of the latter, was removed.

(d) Two small rooms touching the west compound wall, known as the *musafir-khana* or shelter for pilgrims were totally in ruins. The roof had disappeared altogether and the walls were also dilapidated. This structure was thoroughly renewed for the use of pilgrims. One of these rooms is intended for use as a kitchen in place of the old hut referred to in (c) above.

(e) The gateway in the west compound wall known as the *Naubat-khana* was in a half ruined state. This was repaired.

(f) The western compound wall was continued for about 250 feet to the north beyond the *musafir-khana,* to screen the unsightly view of certain heaps of ruins in that direction.

(g) An iron bar gate was provided for the compound of the large mosque.

(h) Cracks in the roofs of the verandahs of the main tomb and in that of the small mosque near Tansen's tomb were grouted with cement so as to prevent leaking in the rains.

(i) Two of the larger trees in the compound had their roots exposed. Platforms of dry rubble masonry were therefore provided for them.

(j) Last year's new filling had sunken in places owing to the first rains. The pits thus caused were refilled and rammed.

"II. *Gujari-mahal (Gwalior Fort).*—The additions and alterations which had been started last year with a view to adapt this building to the requirements of the Archæological Museum, were completed in the year of report. The following work was done this year :—

(a) The underground cellar in the court-yard, which consists of a massively built hall with galleries on all four sides, was full of débris. As many visitors wish to see the cellar it was freed from débris and thoroughly cleaned. Three of its doorways were repaired and iron bars were provided for openings between the pillars of the galleries to guard against visitors falling down, the danger being all the more serious as the place is dark. To prevent the pest of bats the three entrances and a window opening were furnished with half teak-wood and half wire-gauze doors.

(b) There are some dark cells in the building which could be of no use for exhibiting sculptures but which only served as shelters for bats. The door openings of these cells were therefore closed up with masonry.

(c) Narrow platforms touching the walls were built in the exhibition rooms to serve as pedestals for sculptures.

(d) Cracked lintels and slabs in the ceiling of one of the rooms were supported on rails so as to render the ceiling safe.

(e) The inclined ramp constructed last year for carrying up sculptures proved to be too steep. It was therefore remodelled into a more gradual slope.

(f) A *pucca* hut was constructed within the compound of the building to serve as quarters for the Chowkidar of the Museum. Gwalior State.

(g) An awkward corner in the passage leading to the entrance was rectified so that carts, etc., now have ample turning room.

(h) To conceal from view the unsightly uneven ground on the south of the passage to the proper entrance of the Mahal, a row of *mendi* shrubs was planted.

"III. The Garuda pillar at Besnagar (District Bhilsa), locally known as *Khamb Baba*, received further attention, in that a fence consisting of iron bars passed through stone posts was erected in order to protect the platform and inscriptions from the *Gosai's* cattle which pass by them every morning and evening.

"IV. *Udaygiri Caves (District Bhilsa)*.—The fair-weather road laid out last year at the foot of the excavated face of the hill was washed away by the rains in some places during the last monsoon. To prevent similar damage in future, a small retaining wall was constructed near Cave No. 7, the causeway near the tank in front of Cave No. 5 was improved, and a few drains were provided to let the water from the hill slope pass away without damaging the road.

"The Archæological Chemist to the Government of India was invited to inspect on the spot some of the decaying carvings and inscriptions in the caves and to suggest measures for their preservation. His recommendations have reached this office and are receiving attention.

"V. *Buddhist Caves at Bagh (District Amjhera)*.—The work of freeing important caves in the series from débris was started last year, and it is intended to push on with the work slowly but steadily year after year until we have reclaimed all that is worth preserving in the remnants of these vast caves. The work is a huge one and it will naturally take a number of years to finish. Cave No. 2 was cleared last year. This year the work of clearance was extended to Cave No. 3 and part of the débris with which the entrance of the cave is choked up was removed. The débris is being utilised to form a spacious platform in front of this cave in continuation of the platform of the last preceding cave. A few decorative carvings originally belonging to the façade of the cave, which has now collapsed, were unearthed from the débris in the course of the cleaning work. These have been carefully taken out and are preserved on the site.

"VI. *Koshak-mahal at Fatehabad near Chanderi (District Esagarh)*.—A brief description of this, the noblest and most important of the buildings now surviving at or around the town of Chanderi, was given in my last year's report. The conservation of this building had been nominally commenced that year, but the work was pushed through and all the items covered by the original estimate were carried out this year. The original estimate was framed at a time when the building was full of débris, but clearance has revealed further defects which it is proposed to remedy by certain supplementary measures next year.

"The following items were carried out this year :—

(a) Of the four floors which make up the building, the lower two had already been freed from débris. The two remaining floors have now been cleared. There were many big stones among this débris, and the work of carrying these down four storeys without injuring the building was not easy. The bigger stones were let down with the help of strong ropes and pulley blocks. Some good carvings exposed in the clearance have been stacked neatly on the tops of walls.

(*b*) The original top of the building having disappeared, rain water found its way into the inner core of the masonry and caused serious damage. As a provision against this source of trouble, the uppermost floors and some of the tops of walls exposed to the sky were rendered water tight with concrete in good lime spread over them and rammed thoroughly.

(*c*) Two of the eight large radiating archways over the cross-shaped passage which divides the building into four quadrants had been weakened owing to the falling away of the masonry filling, the weight of which provided the pressure necessary to hold the components together. The missing masonry filling has therefore been supplied so as to render the arches safe.

(*d*) The staircases and the cut stone facing masonry were repaired in places where absolutely necessary for the safety both of the building and of visitors.

(*e*) Jungle was cleared to a distance of 50 feet all round the monument.

" VII. *Miscellaneous Monuments at Chanderi* (*District Esagarh*).—There are quite a number of old tombs, mosques and finely built *baodis*, large and small, scattered all round Chanderi which testify to the bygone vastness and prosperity of the place. It is neither possible nor necessary to preserve all these structures, but a few of them that are architecturally or historically important have been selected for preservation. These are : (1) the larger *Madrasa* Tomb, (2) the Battisi *Bāodi*, (3) the smaller *Madrasa*, which is supposed to be the tomb of an Emperor's daughter (*Shāhzādī kā Rauzā*), (4) the mosque known as *Panch Madhi*, (5) the *Rājā kā Maqbara*, (6) the *Rānī kā Maqbara*, (7) the tomb of Nizamuddin's family, (8) the *Bādal mahal* gate, (9) the *Akolke Bāgh kā gumbaz*, (10) the *Badhaiyon kā gumbaz*, (11) the Chaklā *Bāodi*, (12) the *Gol Bāodi*, (13) the Kati-ghati, and (14) the *Kurbani chabutra* near Fatehabad. All these have been freed from jungle, which is one of the most destructive of agencies where ancient monuments are concerned.

" The larger Madrasa tomb was further repaired as follows :—

(*a*) Part of the masonry of the north-east corner of the plinth had fallen. This was made good with old stone.

(*b*) Some of the *dasa* or coping stones over the retaining wall of the plinth were missing. These were supplied.

(*c*) New steps were constructed giving access to the plinth.

(*d*) There were large pits in the floor of the tomb. These were filled up. The dome having disappeared, rain-water descended directly into the interior. The floor was therefore made *pucca* by ramming concrete in lime and sloping it so as to carry off rain-water through a drain which was provided in the west wall. The grave-stones which had been displaced were reset properly.

(*e*) Part of the roof of the north verandah which was hanging dangerously, was taken down. The tops of the walls still need to be rendered water-tight, and the surrounding ground requires to be cleaned and fenced. This work will be done next year if possible.

" The other monuments will be taken up for repairs at some later date.

" VIII. *Bijayamandal Mosque at Bhilsa.*—This mosque is built on the site of, and in the main with the materials of a large old Hindu temple. The plinth of the temple is still to be seen underneath the mosque. Most of the numerous pillars, pilasters and lintels used in the building are carved in the Hindu and Jaina style of the mediæval period, and some also bear Sanskrit inscriptions. No doubt is thus left that the major portion of the materials with which the mosque is constructed were taken from one or more older temples. An inscription on one of the pillars mentions a temple of the goddess Charchikā, which was perhaps identical with the demolished temple on the site of which the mosque now stands. The old temple, it is said, was built by Vijayā, a Baniya lady. This perhaps explains the reason why the mosque still goes by the Hindu name of Bijay mandal, which is nothing but a corrupt form of *Vijayā-mandira.*

" This is the largest mosque at Bhilsa ; but until recently it was in disuse and was neglected. It appears that the Musalman community have now begun to take some interest in the building and to say their prayers there occasionally. Probably at their request the Central *Mazhabi Auqāf* Committee consulted this Department regarding repairs to this monument and made a contribution of Rs. 4,377 to meet the cost of the repairs suggested. They were carried out under the supervision of the Archæological Department, in the year under report, the more important items being :—

(*a*) Jungle was cleared to a distance of 25 feet all round.

(*b*) Some of the upper courses of the massive back wall of the hall had disappeared altogether. The missing portion was restored and the dislocated portion was dismantled and reset.

(*c*) The pilasters touching this wall were out of plumb. They were all restored to their upright position.

(*d*) Some of the old beams and slabs of the ceiling had either broken or were missing. New ones were substituted for them.

(*e*) The old concrete roof had badly cracked. The cracks were first grouted with cement and then a three-inch layer of good brick concrete was spread over the whole existing roof. A part of the roof which was altogether missing was renewed.

(*f*) The corner minarets, composed of heavy blocks of stone piled one over another, were leaning westwards and had become a menace to passers by and also to the structure below. These were pushed back into their proper position and are now quite safe.

(*g*) The compound wall at the north-west corner of the court-yard which had collapsed, was restored, and the damaged tops of walls were rendered waterproof with a layer of concrete.

(*h*) The pits and depressions in the floor, especially of the hall of the mosque. were repaired so as to render the floor fit for use during prayers.

(*i*) An iron gate was provided for the entrance to the courtyard so as to keep out cattle.

Gwalior State.

(j) The ceiling and roof of the portico had disappeared. They were restored as the portico is used by visitors to keep such things in as are not admitted into the mosque, and also to store water, etc., for ablutions before prayers.

(k) The massive flight of steps was repaired where it had been damaged.

(l) Immediately at the back of the *masjid* there was a large sink in the ground where rain-water used to accumulate. This pool of water being close to the foundations of the building was probably responsible for the movement in the back wall, which had to be dismantled and rebuilt. As a protective measure against similar danger hereafter, the depression was filled and a sloping bank of earth was provided at the back of the foundations of the plinth so as to drain away all rain-water to a distance from the monument.

(m) A few unsightly platforms on both sides of the entrance to the mosque were slightly repaired so as to make them neat and tidy.

"IX. *Khokhai Monastery at Ranod* (*District Narwar*).—This monument bears a long Sanskrit inscription from which it is seen that it is a *matha* or monastic residence of Saiva monks originally built in the 9th century, and extended about a century later. It is a two-storeyed edifice built with heavy blocks of stone laid without any kind of mortar. The roof is made up of huge stone slabs also laid dry. The three-storeyed tower which shelters the stair-case at the north-west corner of the main building, is covered by a single slab measuring about 14 feet long by 14 feet wide by 8 inches thick, which excites admiration for the builders as such an achievement is not easy even with the use of modern mechanical appliances. The monument is famous in the locality for its uncommonly massive architecture, and has in modern times become a religious centre, the central hall of the monastery being at present used as a temple to a goddess and a religious fair being held on the eleventh lunar day of every fortnight. It is thus a monument of importance both to the Archæological Department and to the Religious Aucaph Committee, and the two departments have therefore agreed to repair it with joint funds.

"As the necessary sanction to the revised estimate for the work was received in this office late, the work was only nominally begun this year. Details are therefore reserved for next year's report."

Kashmir.

In the note sent to me by Mr. Kak, State Superintendent of Archæology in Kashmir, it is recorded that the conservation of the Bandi Temple, commonly known as *Dhatha-mandir*, or "the ruined temple", which was taken in hand in 1920-21, has now been almost completed. "All that remains to be done", Mr. Kak writes, "is to clear the site and carry out a few minor repairs by way of improving the appearance of the buildings." The temple at Pandrethan, as is well known, stands at present in the middle of a marsh which not only prevents access to the monument for a great part of the year, but also floods the cella. Mr. Kak reports that to remove this defect a drain is under construction which it is hoped to complete before the end of the financial year.

SECTION II.

EXCAVATION AND EXPLORATION.

Sarnath.

In the Northern Circle excavations were carried out by Mr. Daya Ram Sahni at three different places, namely at Sarnath and at Kosam in the United Provinces, and at

Kurukshetra in the Punjab. The operations at Sarnath which entailed a total outlay *Sarnath.* of Rs. 8,114-13-4 including the cost of conservation works, were of a comprehensive character and resulted in useful additions being made to our knowledge of the history of these remains. The biggest item of the year's work was the final clearance of large unexcavated portions of the extensive open court attached to the Main Shrine [Plate XX (*a*)] the real character of which was ascertaind in the year 1919-20. This court-yard measures two hundred and seventy-one feet in length from east to west and a hundred and twelve in width. The boundary wall, which is constructed mostly with brick-bats of the Gupta period obtained from ruined buildings on the site, is in a very dilapidated condition and the greater part of it on the north and south sides has disappeared. The structures brought to light in this court during the recent and previous excavations are varied in character, and belong to different periods. Some of them situated in the western portion of the court will be found illustrated in Sir John Marshall's Annual Report for the years 1906-07 and 1907-08, while a group of remarkably well preserved stupas built in stone which was brought to light in 1919-20 is figured in the Annual Report for that year. The remains laid bare during the operations of 1921-22 are, as was to be expected, for the most part stupas in the usual design and material. "The most striking of these", Mr. Sahni says, "are two long rows running parallel to each other and built upon a common platform in the northern portion of the court. Some of these have niches meant for the reception of images, all of which have disappeared with the exception of a single pedestal bearing the feet of a goddess which has survived in stupa No. 90. Two masonry platforms also occur along the southern wall of the enclosure, but they have lost most of the structures which they originally supported. A noteworthy feature of this enclosure is a raised causeway which ran along its centre and which has survived for a length of 164 feet. It rests upon the original paved approach which stretches from the flight of steps by which the court was entered up to the eastern entrance to the Main Shrine, and was manifestly constructed at the latest period in the history of the Deer Park, when water collected in the courtyard and made access to the Main Shrine inconvenient.

"The most interesting structure brought to light inside this enclosure during the operations of the year 1921-22 is a fascinating stupa plinth (No. 136) built entirely in brick and faced with elegant carvings which in beauty of decorative detail far excel any other structure yet brought to light at Sarnath. The plinth is 8′-6″ square and 4′-7″ high excluding smaller square plinths which project from the corners of the central structure. The stupa itself which rested on this plinth has entirely perished. At the time of its discovery, the structure lay hidden under a terraced floor which was removed. Some of the carvings including panels, niches, pilasters and brackets which beautify the several faces of the structure are illustrated in Plate XX (*b*). They are in typical Gupta style and display a variety of motifs remarkable in so small a structure. Yet with all this decoration there is no lack of symmetry or appearance of overcrowding. The niches which occur in the middle of each face must have contained Buddhist images, but none of these were found.

"The floor that originally surrounded this stupa is solidly constructed in lime and brick concrete which has suffered little deterioration during the many centuries that have elapsed since it was first made. It occurs at a depth of only 1′-3″ below the later floor level of the enclosure, and shows how small was the accumulation of débris on this

Sarnath. part of the site between the Gupta and the mediaeval periods to which the majority of the structures inside the courtyard belong.

"Close to the stupa plinth (No. 136) was found a somewhat later chapel (No. 137) 37 ft. in length and 27′—10″ wide containing two standing Buddha images with broken heads and bases, which were lying face downwards near the entrance. Worthy of note also is a plastered brick-lined reservoir or *kunda* with sloping sides about seven feet square and five feet in depth, which came to light on the outside of this court adjacent to the flight of steps. Such tanks are sometimes met with on ancient Buddhist sites as for example in some of the monasteries unearthed at Kasia. They would appear to have been kept filled with water with which monks and nuns could purify their hands and feet before entering the sacred precinct, more especially on occasions of the *uposatha* ceremony.

"An important outcome of the last year's work in this area was the discovery of a well built drain 1′—9″ to 2′—7″ in width and three feet in depth which carried off rain water from this court. It is composed of brick-bats and covered with hammer dressed stone slabs including architectural stones of sorts, such as fragments of lintels, posts of railings, umbrella tops and the like. It starts from the north-east corner of the courtyard and has been completely exposed for the whole of its length which measures two hundred and fifty-nine feet. At the distance of two hundred and forty-two feet from the starting point the drain runs underneath the foundation of the second gateway of the Monastery No. 1, thus showing that the latter building must be a good deal posterior to the Main Shrine.

"Only a few inscriptions were found inside the enclosure. They are short dedicatory records of no special interest and will be found referred to in the epigraphical résumé published in this report. Among sculptures found in the same area, special mention may be made of a pot-bellied figure carved on a brick tile; a female chauri-bearer without head and feet, carved in the round [Plate XXI (*b*)] which might be a *yakshi*, an incomplete image of Tara with the Dhyanibuddha Amoghasiddhi in her head-dress, an inscribed headless image of Buddha seated in *vyākhhyāna-mudrā*, a figure of Brahma which must have been installed in one of the Buddhist shrines after the abandonment of the site by the Buddhists, and the head of an image of Avalokitesvara [Plate XXI (*a*)].

"Among the buildings brought to light in other parts of the site, there is one which deserves special mention. It was disclosed to the east of the spot where the excavations of 1908 had revealed a set of railing posts of the Sunga period and proves to be a shrine of the late Gupta period containing a narrow rectangular chamber with entrances on the east and west sides. Both the entrances were provided with stone doors of which the jambs only have survived. In front of the eastern entrance and to the north and south of the shrine, my excavations laid bare pedestals of images once protected with stone umbrellas. One of these pedestals bears an inscription in Gupta characters stating that the image to which it belonged was the gift of a Buddhist monk named Nanala. The shrine was restored at some later date which is approximately determined by a terra-cotta tablet inscribed in characters of the 8th or 9th century A.D., found near the floor on the north side. The interior of the shrine yielded nothing except a curiously shaped *kunda* in the floor, which to judge by the heaps of ashes in front of the entrance may have been an *agni-kunda* erected by the adherents of the Brahmanical faith in the late mediæval period."

During his stay at Sarnath for the operations detailed above, Mr. Sahni took the opportunity of re-examining the generally accepted view as to the nature of the building designated Monastery No. I. He arrives at the conclusion that it cannot have been a monastery at all, first because its plan is entirely different from that of other monasteries which are invariably *chatuhsāla*, whereas this building is quite open on one side ; secondly, because the structural arrangement is such as to afford little room for actual residential cells ; thirdly because no other monastery known to us is preceded by such extensive courts with massive gateways as occur in this building ; and fourthly, because builders of monasteries seldom lavished so much ornament on their work as this edifice displays. Mr. Sahni infers, therefore, that this building was a temple, and suggests that it was the one which Kumaradevi, the Buddhist queen of King Govindachandra of Kanauj erected at Sarnath. The construction of this temple under the name of 'Dharmachakrajinavihāra' is mentioned in the stone inscription of Kumaradevi found to the south of the second gateway of this building, but which might well have been fixed in the gateway itself. The building so far designated as monastery I on account of its decoration and boldness of design fully accords with the high sounding description of the *vihāra* built by Kumaradevi which was "an ornament to the earth" and "like to the palaces of the gods." It is true that none of the images that were presumably installed in this temple by Kumaradevi, have so far been found, but as Mr. Sahni says, "much weight ought not to be attached to negative evidence of this kind."

As indicated above in the section relating to conservation, the main object of the little excavation carried out at Kosam, District Allahabad, was to ascertain the condition of the ancient pillar that stood half buried in the ancient ruined city at that place and which it is proposed to re-erect in a vertical position. A small area one hundred feet square was acquired around the pillar and excavated by Mr. Daya Ram Sahni, as far as the exigencies of the case would permit. The data obtained by him about the pillar itself have already been described (*vide* page 9 above). The only spot where it was possible to penetrate to the original level was immediately to the north of the column, but as this portion had already been opened by Mr. Nesbitt in the year 1870, no fresh objects of the earliest period were found, though it is manifest that some of the terracottas to be referred to presently must have been left here by him. The rest of the acquired area could only be examined to a depth of a few feet below the present ground level, as it was necessary to leave hard, undisturbed ground round about the pillar for setting the tackle necessary for hoisting it. It will be understood, therefore, that the remains uncovered during the year are relatively late as compared with the pillar itself, but among these remains two strata are clearly distinguishable one at a depth of 5½ ft. and the other of 9 ft. below the surface. The only well preserved structure is a well 5′-3″ in diameter, its steaning wall being only one brick thick and composed of wedge-shaped bricks. The other remains comprise portions of rooms, which yield no regular plan, and—on the northern side—a brick built drain, fifteen feet in length. *Kosam.*

The minor antiquities found by Mr. Sahni in this excavation consist mostly of terracotta objects, earthen vessels, earthen weights and a few stone objects. "In fabric and workmanship these objects resemble the antiquities unearthed by Sir John Marshall at Bhitā. The following are typical examples :—

(1) Terracotta tablet (height 5¼″ ; width 2½″) representing a female figure standing facing with her right arm hanging down, while her left hand rests on the

hip. She wears the usual *dhotī*, a short bodice, and several ornaments. A similar relief was found at Bhitā (see the Director General's Annual Report Part II for 1911-12, Plate XXII, No. 18).

(2) Terracotta toy cart similar to those found at Bhitā and other sites.

(3) Bust of a male figure with hands clasped before the breast the whole mounted on wheels in the form of a tricycle. Sunga period.

(4) A dwarfish male figure (ht. 5½") in good preservation; wears a high conical head dress, a cord over the left shoulder in the manner of a *yajnopavīta*, a necklace, girdle and other ornaments. As is usual with objects of this kind the figure was cast in halves which were afterwards joined together.

(5) Base of a terracotta figure (width 6½") on which only the right foot of the image remains with the head of a buffalo lying flat on the top of the base. The fragment may have belonged to a representation of Durga slaying the buffalo demon, but this is a mere conjecture. Gupta period.

(6) A coarsely made male figure seated on a stool (ht. 5½") of which the head and feet are missing. Coarse buff clay, without slip or colour. Gupta period.

(7) A well fashioned terracotta monkey (ht. 4½") wearing a conical cap and holding a round object in its hands.

(8) Bust of a female figure (ht. 5½") wearing heavy earrings and necklace. Gupta period.

(9) Lower half of a steatite box with a flat base (ht. 1¼").

(10) Oval shaped steatite bowl, 2¼" by 2" at the mouth, with two holes cut in the sides which suggest that it is a pan of a weighing scale.

(11) Stone figure without head and feet, probably a *yaksha*. Plate XXI."

These excavations did not yield any inscriptions but in the neighbouring villages Mr. Sahni succeeded in discovering a number of valuable epigraphs, the contents of which will be found summarised in the Epigraphical Section of this report. Here, I need only notice that the Nāgarī inscription (page 120 below) of the year Samvat 1245 confirms General Cunningham's identification of Kosam with the ancient city of Kausāmbī.

Kurukshetra.

The third excavation which Mr. Sahni carried out this year was on the site of Kurukshetra, the scene of the Great War fought between the Kauravas and the Pāndavas and now a celebrated place of Hindu pilgrimage. "The ancient history of Kurukshetra, as far as it is known from literary and other sources, is given in detail in General Cunningham's Archaeological Survey Reports, Vols. II and XIV, and in his Ancient Geography of India. The earliest references to this holy land are to be found in the Satapatha and the Aitareya Brāhmanas which go back to a period long before the composition of the Mahabharata. It is also frequently alluded to in the Buddhist Jatakas, the most prominent reference to it being in the Mahasutasoma-jataka.

"In the Bhagavadgita," says Mr. Sahni, "the region of Kurukshetra is designated Dharmakshetra while in Manu's Dharmasāstra it appears as Brahmāvarta and in the

Mahabharata as Samantapanchaka. All these works unanimously define it as the area lying between the rivers Sarasvati and Drishadvati. The former river, though dry for the greater part of the year, is well known. The latter is identified by General Cunningham with a stream now called Rākshasī, while Smith recognizes it in the Ghaggar. General Cunningham's view appears more plausible as, according to the great epic named above, the Sarasvati flowed to the north of the land of the Kurus. The Mahatmyas of Kurukshetra contain long lists of *tirthas* and places connected with the great war. According to popular belief there are fully 360 such sites within the circuit of Kurukshetra, some of which do actually contain high mounds and brick ruins. When the Chinese pilgrim Hiuen-Thsang visited Sthanvisvara in A. D. 634 he found here only three Buddhist monasteries containing 700 monks while the Brahmanical temples numbered 100. About a mile to the north-west of the town he also saw a brick stupa of Asoka 200 ft. in height, which was said to contain a portion of the Buddha's relics. *Kurukshetra.*

" None of these mounds have yet been explored and it is impossible to say whether they contain any relics of such high antiquity as is claimed for the Mahabharata War. A careful preliminary survey of these remains is urgently needed. The most prominent of the sites are the lofty eminence of Amīn, situated about six miles south-east of Thanesar, the Theh Polar mound on the Sarasvati, seven miles north-west of Kaithal, one or two mounds in the neighbourhood of Thanesar, which General Cunningham proposed to identify as the *stupa* of Asoka, the Visvamitra-kā tila at Pehoa, and the mound known as Raja Karn ka Kila distant two miles from the town of Thanesar. The large *tila* at Amīn is said to represent the remains of the Chakraٖvyūha castle which was constructed with seven miraculous gates by Dronāchārya when he was in command of the Kaurava forces from the 11th to the 15th day of the great battle, and it was here that Abhimanyu, the son of Arjuna was slain by Jayadratha, the brother-in-law of Duryodhana. Although no excavations have ever been carried out at Amīn two inscribed stone pillars have been turned up here by the peasants and are now lying in the shrine of Thākurjī on the west bank of the tank known as Sūrajkund. They are carved on all four sides and have no sockets for cross bars. They would thus appear to have supported some sort of a platform. The inscriptions on them are in characters of the Kushan period, but are quite short and merely supply the names of their donors. The mound near Siwan which is explained by the people as a contraction of Sītāban or Sivaban, the forest home of Sitā or Siva, is stated to be the site of a very ancient village destroyed before the war of the Mahabharata. Very ancient coins are said to have been found in this mound but no record of them is traceable. Pehoa (ancient *Prithūdaka*) where a great bathing fair is held in March or April every year, has yielded two important inscriptions of the time of the kings Bhoja and Mahendrapala of Kanauj, and one may also see fragments of mediæval sculptures lying about this village. The mound known as Visvāmitra kā Tīla situated about a mile above Pehoa on the bank of the Sarasvati is a fairly large eminence, which contains the ruins of a mediæval temple partly constructed in stone. The sculptured stone doorway now employed in the shrine of Sarasvati at Pehoa originally formed part of this temple and the threshold and a few other slabs are still lying on the mound. Half a mile higher up the bank of the stream stood another temple, which, to judge from the existing portion of its doorway, must have been dedicated to Vishnu. The site is now occupied by a modern temple with a subterranean chamber. General Cunningham obtained at Pehoa some excellent terracotta reliefs and he also mentions bricks of large size."

Kurukshetra. The mound that was selected by Mr. Sahni for tentative exploration during the past year is the one known as Raja Karn ka Kila and situated upwards of a mile to the south-west of the holy tank at Thanesar. "It is 500 ft. square at top and about 800 feet square at the base with a height of 30 to 40 feet. By the side of the mound on the west is a large *baoli* of the Muhammadan period, and to the same period must be assigned a large dry well, 13 ft. in diameter and 53 feet deep, sunk into the summit of the mound. The only other remains on the mound are a platform and two separate dwellings in *lakhauri* bricks which are said to have been constructed about fifty years ago. The mound was covered with densely growing brushwood and when it was being cleared, several minor antiquities were picked up on the surface. They consist of ancient pottery, copper coins, terracotta figurines and pieces of glazed pottery of the Mughal period. Among the terracotta objects is a small mould (height 2" ; width 2") which was used for the making of metal images of the goddess Sri. The back half of the mould was not found. The goddess is seated on a full blown lotus with a flower in her right hand. The elephants standing on both sides are pouring water over her. The image dates from the early mediæval period. Another terracotta object is a well-preserved male figure (height 3¾") without any clothing and portrayed, presumably in the act of dancing.

"Seven different trenches" writes Mr. Sahni, "designated below as A to G were sunk in this mound. Those lettered A and E are near the dry well referred to above and revealed a wall more than 40 feet in length and composed of brickbats obtained from the site. The trenches B and C [Plate XXII (*a*)] embraced an area 124 feet by 70 feet at the eastern end of the mound. Several feet of earth and other débris had to be shifted before the operations reached brick remains. The latter are mere fragments of what appear to be temporal buildings and they occur on three different levels. The uppermost stratum contains a fairly large house, part of which is built in sun-dried mud bricks and the rest in burnt bricks measuring 14½"× 9"×3" which appears to be the size of all bricks so far noticed at this mound. The northern portion of the house includes parts of half a dozen rooms, the partition walls being only one brick thick. These rooms are so small that it is difficult to conceive for what purpose they were intended. The portion built in unburnt brick appears to be a large hall 35 ft. in length by 16 ft. in width. The greater part of this room was filled with earthen bowls containing ashes lying face downwards which appear to have been funerary urns. Several small objects were found in this building. One of them is the lower half of a terracotta relief (height 2¾", width 2½"). It represents the lower portions of a man and a woman standing side by side, the woman occupying, as usual, the left position. Both of them wear loin cloths. The upper portion of the tablet was not found and it is difficult to say what the figures represent. We may next notice a votive terracotta tank of which five pieces were recovered (No. 609) similar to those found at Taxila and other sites. Each corner of the tank contained a figure of a musician elevated on a platform. Of the musicians one is playing on a pair of cymbals, while two others are playing on a flute and a tabor respectively. The fourth was a female but the musical instrument on which she played is not certain.

"The next stratum in this trench is some three feet lower than the portion described above, while the earliest structure which has been brought to light on the eastern slope of the mound is a room 24 ft. in length by 8'–5" in width. The walls which are standing to a height of about three feet are composed of a single thickness of bricks of the same size as those mentioned above. The interior of this room was cleared and yielded a small iron bell and a ladle and a tiny earthen bottle (No. 549) for antimony. *Kurukshetra.*

"Among the minor objects found in the middle stratum alluded to above is a round stone ball (diameter 1⅞"; No. 509) which would appear to have been used as a weight. The ball has been rubbed on one side and now weighs about 7 tolas. It bears, sketched on it, a number of sacred symbols, including a pair of fish joined by a piece of string, a *svastika*, a *nandipada* similar to the symbol which begins the Kharavela inscription, a rectangle with diagonals, a device consisting of two triangles joined at the apex, a circle, a three-pointed star and what appears to be a *svastika* without the fourth arm. The exact purpose of these symbols is not known.

"Trench D [Plate XXII (*b*)] is cut in the southern slope of the mound and yielded portions of two separate rooms at the depth of seven to nine feet. The larger of these two structures is 29'-6" long by 7'-6" in width. These walls are constructed in the same style and their bricks are of the same dimensions as those unearthed in Trenches B. & C. Both these structures and another ruin which occurs a little lower down the slope have still to be followed up; at present it is difficult to say anything about their design or purpose. The smaller antiquities unearthed in this area include a flesh rubber (No. 177), a terracotta reel (No. 456), a mould in the same material for printing cloth (No. 454) and a human head (No. 112).

"Trench F was only 95 ft. in length and 15 ft. wide. The only structure brought to light here is a wall 18 ft. in height. It is composed of the same kind of bricks but has a superior bond as the width consists of a stretcher and a header instead of a single width.

"Trench G covered an area just 50 ft. square and revealed part of an enclosure 27'—6" in width, only one corner of which is preserved. Outside this building there is a small chamber constructed of sun-dried bricks. The following are some of the minor objects recovered in this plot:—

(1) Bronze object flattened at the lower end and decorated with two plain raised bands and a row of leaf patterns. [From the photo. (*vide* Plate XL, Fig. *a*) it appears to be a late derivative of a 'celt' with crescentic edge. J. H. M.]

(2) Earthen *chāṭī* (ht. 1' 1½") with broad mouth and round body; plain save for a line of devices representing the wheel and the trident. At the time of its excavation the vessel was filled with charred or rotted wheat.

(3) Earthen pitcher of the usual shape (ht. 11") ornamented round the shoulder [Plate XXI (*c*)]. This vessel also contained charred wheat.

(4) Earthen jug with a spout (No. 555).

(5) Double inkpot (No. 517).

(6) Hollow rattling terracotta flesh-rubber (No. 436).

(7) Fragment of terracotta votive dish (No. 399). Similar to No. 609 described on page 48."

Almora. During the past year Rai Bahadur Daya Ram Sahni performed an interesting journey through the Almora District on which he reports as follows. "This district is very rich in archæological remains, but had received little or no attention up to the year 1913 when Mr. Hargreaves inspected and prepared detailed conservation notes on the temples at Dwarāhat and Jāgesvar situated at distances of 29 and 16 miles respectively from the town of Almora. The main object of my tour was to make a search for and report on a certain monolithic rock-cut temple about the existence of which somewhere in the northern part of the district Mr. Hargreaves had been informed during his stay at Almora, but which he had no time to inspect. Owing to the prevalence of a severe epidemic of cholera in the villages, I had to abandon my enquiries about this temple, but in the course of a fifteen days' journey across the district, I inspected a number of other monuments which lay directly on my route. These are Dwarāhat, Chaun Kotilī between it and Almora, Katārmal six miles from Almora, Devīdhura, famous for a temple of Varāhīdevī, Khetī Khān about 42 miles east of Almora, and Champāvat. None of these places are mentioned in General Cunningham's Archæological Survey Reports, and Dr. Führer's List of Monumental Antiquities in the North-Western Provinces and Oudh only contains a list of copper-plate inscriptions he examined at Champāvat and in villages around it.

Chaun Kotilī. "Chaun Kotilī is the name of a small hamlet on the Almora-Bānskherā road. Near the village, immediately on the road, is a group of three well preserved *sikhara* temples, two of which face eastward and the third in the opposite direction. None of them contain any images. One of these temples bears a short Nāgarī inscription in which only the name *Sivabhata* is decipherable.

Devīdhura. "Devīdhura is a station on the road from Almora to Champāvat distant twenty-nine miles from the former. Here there is a well-known temple dedicated to the goddess Varāhī at which a fair is held in June and July when goats are sacrificed in honour of the goddess. This temple is quite modern, but not far from it there is a small shrine constructed with dressed stones which is locally attributed to Jagachchandra, a Rājā of Kumaon. The shrine is only 4′ 3″ square externally with a ceiling built in the usual Hindu style. The spire which originally crowned the structure has disappeared, but inside it there is an image of Siva and Pārvatī and another image of Mahishāsuramardinī. It is in honour of this latter image that buffaloes are every year sacrificed on a paved platform in front of the shrine.

Katārmal. "Katārmal is the name of a small village about 6 miles to the north of the town of Almora and is situated on the summit of a lofty hill on the right bank of the Kosi river. The pathway that leads up to this village is rugged and steep and starts from a point about the end of the 8th mile from Almora on the Almora-Ranikhet cart-road. On a clear day the temple is visible from the town of Almora, only a part of it remaining hidden behind two large pipal trees growing in the compound. The temple was inspected by Mr. Hargreaves on the 24th June 1915, but does not appear to have been described anywhere. The temple is in the charge of certain private *Kārindas* or agents, who have refused to enter into an agreement for the maintenance of the monuments. This temple is locally known as the Barā Ādit or the Sun God. Though comparatively late in date it is remarkable for more than one reason. The main temple stands at the west end of a large paved enclosure (Photo. No. 2841) measuring 160 feet from north to south, by about 100 feet from east to west, the rest of the area being occupied by some fifty subsidiary shrines. The surrounding wall of the compound, if any ever existed, must have disappeared long ago, and the sides of the enclosure are now protected by rubble-built retaining walls. The main temple which stands on a raised platform originally consisted of a large cella measuring 12′ 6″ square internally and about 24′ 6″ along each side on the outside, with a projecting portico on the east. The spire or *sikhara* must, at one time, have been an imposing structure, but its upper portion has now fallen in and the central faces on the north and south sides have bulged out under pressure of the heavy superstructure. The ceiling consists of horizontal slabs supported on two massive beams of stone, laid in the style of the modern wooden roof. This is also the type found in some of the temples at Champāvat. The image of the Sun, which must originally have rested on the stone-built platform in the centre of the sanctum, is now lost; but a smaller two-armed seated statue of the deity, manifestly of the same date as the temple, is still lying in the portico. The entrance to the cella is provided with a profusely carved wooden door consisting of two leaves with a strong iron chain and loop. Two pairs of iron rings are also provided to serve as handles in closing and opening the door. The carvings on both halves of the door are arranged in four panels. The subjects delineated on the left leaf, from top downwards are (*a*) Siva and Pārvatī, (*b*) Mahādeva dancing on a prostrate female and attended by a male drummer to his right and an animal-bodied figure to his left; (*c*) a medallion containing a *kīrtimukha* with a leogryph on either side, and (*d*) Nārāyana and Srī standing side by side under a dome. The other leaf contains in the same order ; (*a*) Vishnu and Srī (*b*) Mahādeva and Pārvatī, (*c*) as on the other half, (*d*) Brahmā and Sarasvatī. The raised framework of these panels depicts *devas* playing on pairs of flutes (still in use in the district), Nrisimha, etc. The *mandapa* is a later addition, but when it was added is not known. Originally it must have had a flat roof of stone slabs supported on beams of the same material, as is the case in another temple of the Sun at Kheti Khān situated at mile 42 on the Almora to Champāvat road. The present roof is an ugly restoration. The northern portion of this hall contains a pair of wooden pillars each 1′ 6″ square in section and 5′ 10″ high. Late as these pillars are, their carvings call to mind some of the finest Gupta work at Sarnath and other places. The standing male figure on the left-hand pillar, which wears a conical head-dress and a short sword on the left side, appears to be the god Sun. The *mandapa* also contains a large number of stone sculptures of no special interest. There is, however, one sculpture which deserves more than a passing notice. It is an image in *ashtadhātu*, *i.e.*, the alloy of eight metals, 4′ 6″ in height which like a similar image in the Jāgesvar Temple at Jāgesvar, district Almora, is supposed to represent a certain Paun Rājā. The image is fashioned as a Kshatriya prince, with the usual tuft on the skull and clothed in a short *dhoti* and a scarf thrown over the left shoulder and across the chest. His right hand is raised to the chest and holds the stem of a lotus flower. In the Jammu hills, portraits of donors of religious places are sometimes placed in front of the deity. The Paun Rājā at Katārmal might thus be the builder of this temple. *Katārmal.*

The subsidiary temples are small *sikhara* shrines each consisting, as usual, of a small square cella with a portico on two pillars. The ceilings are constructed either on the square within the square design, or of flat horizontal slabs. The lintels have generally the figure of Ganapati and the jambs figures of the river goddesses. Most of these shrines contain pedestals suited to Vishnu images. The smaller temples are generally well preserved and some inexpensive repairs would prevent decay for many years to come. The principal temple requires larger measures of preservation, and it is much to be regretted that the adverse attitude of the so-called owners should prevent Government from carrying out the repairs which are urgently needed.

Kheti Khan. "Kheti Khan is a small hamlet situated at the end of mile 42 on the Almora-Champāvat road, which is noted for its Normal and Middle schools. At this point the road from Almora to Lohaghat takes off from the Champāvat road, and about a furlong from the division of the roads, there is a plateau crowned with a temple built in the same style as the one at Katārmal, like which it faces the rising sun and must have been dedicated to that deity. The cella which is preceded by a *mandapa*, ten feet square internally is a small chamber five feet square on the inside. The front face of the *sikhara* has fallen down and the blocks are lying in the hollow chamber within it. The *mandapa* which had a flat ceiling, similar to that at Katārmal, was supported on three pairs of plain square pillars. The greater part of the roof and the two pillars in the front have fallen down, but the material is still lying near the temple and can easily be restored. The sanctum must have contained several images of the Sun-god of which no complete statue has survived. The largest fragment is a base 1′ 9″ in height including the tenon by which it was mortised into the *āsana*; this apparently belonged to the principal image. Of the god only the right leg and left foot have remained with a well-preserved deformed figure of Aruna standing to the right. On the front of the base are carved four horses with the solar orb between them.

"The only other monument near Kheti Khān is a covered spring or *naulā* about a furlong below the plateau referred to. As is usual with springs in the Chamba and other hill States, the one at Kheti Khān is also adorned with a figure of *Seshasāyi* Vishnu.

"I did not find any inscriptions on either of the two monuments referred to but was shown an inscribed copper plate by a Brahman of *mauza* Tapnipāl distant two miles from Kheti Khān. The epigraph is dated on Monday the *Amāvasāyā tithi* of Vaisākha in the year Samvat 1469, Saka 1334 (A. D. 1412) in the reign of King Gyān Chand. It does not record the foundation of the temple described above or of any other temple, but, the temple at Kheti Khān is so nearly coeval with the record that a reference to the document here is not considered out of place.

Champāvat. "Champāvat is a small village lying at an elevation of 5,545 ft. above sea level fifty-four miles south-east of Almora. It was the headquarters of the Rājās of Kumaon before they transferred their seat to Almora in the middle of the sixteenth century. These princes belonged to the Chand dynasty of which no complete genealogy has as yet been found. Dr. Führer, however, gives in his Monumental Antiquities of the N.-W. P. & Oudh, pp. 48-49, a list of title deeds engraved on copper plates, etc., in the possession of the people of the villages near Champāvat. They range in date from the Saka year 1293 to 1727 and give the names of the ruling princes. The earliest of these rulers so far known was Abhayachandra whose name occurs in inscriptions engraved on two pillars labelled as a Vīrastambha and a Kīrtistambha, respectively, standing in the enclosure around the Bālīsvara temple. These inscriptions are dated in the Saka year 1293 (A. D. 1371). None of these documents unfortunately supply any information about the temples to be described below, but the style of workmanship displayed on them appears to assign them approximately to the fourteenth century A. D. These monuments which are situated immediately below the town are constructed, with one or two exceptions, in the same uniform style. They are the temples of Bālīsvara mentioned above with a few subordinate shrines, a ruined pavilion now known as Kotvāl kā Chautarā and two *naulās* or covered springs. A local tradition attributes the erection of the Bālīsvara temple to Bāli, the brother of Sugrīva, the monkey comrade of Rama.

"The temple of Bālīsvara stands in a spacious enclosure, but the wall which once surrounded it has fallen down and its material been utilized in the construction of modern buildings. Only a small portion of this wall remains on the south side together with a portion of a gateway. What is more, the copious rains to which Champāvat is exposed, have washed down into the enclosure large quantities of earth which conceal the original floor and the plinths of the temples. The principal temple occupies the southern portion of the compound, the smaller temples being those of Ratnesvara Siva and Champāvatī Durgā standing to the north, two others facing east and west and the plinth of a fifth shrine to the north of the western half of the main temple. There is also a modern shrine dedicated to Bhairava. *Champāvat.*

"The Bālīsvara Temple (Photo No. 1597), as far as at present known, appears to be unique, inasmuch as it is a double shrine each half consisting of a sanctum and an audience hall joined by a covered passage. Of the entire building, only the domed *mandapa* of the western shrine has survived. The rest of the structure fell down long ago, leaving only the lower portions of the walls to a height of about four feet. The eastern shrine has been restored in modern times with old material but without any regard to the original design. The stone doorway of the sanctuary is *in situ*, and the central figure on the lintel is Ganapati as would be expected in a Saiva temple. The ceiling would appear to have been built on the principle of intersecting squares and the central slab may still be seen in the *antarāla*. It is beautifully carved with an intricate pattern representing Krishna destroying the serpent Kāliya, whose tail constitutes an elaborate border to the sculpture. The other shrine of this temple had a similar covering slab, which has recently been built into a new house being constructed by the *mahant* in the north-east corner of the enclosure. On the outside the existing portions of the walls are richly ornamented with carvings, among which we notice figures of the goddess Sri and those of Brahmā, Vishnu and Mahesa with their consorts.

"In the western shrine the original Siva-linga still exists in its original position in the centre of the cella and the moulded plinth of the sanctuary is completely visible. The *mandapa* is a square hall with projecting porticoes on the north and south. Originally it was supported on twelve pillars three of which have fallen down. All the existing pillars are erected on a parapet wall 3′—6″ high, with the exception of the two flanking the entrance of the cella, which start from the floor. The dome, as is usually the case in Hindu architecture, is horizontal in construction and with similar bands of ornament. The outer roof of the dome has perished, but it was manifestly of the type of the usual North Indian spire. There is no evidence at present to determine whether this temple stands on any kind of terrace or platform. The modern floor of granite slabs which was built all round the temple by the father of the present Mahant some thirty years ago, should be removed and the hidden portions of the walls brought back to view.

"The Ratnesvara and Champāvatī temples, which stand about thirty-three feet apart, face each other and in all probability formed a pair. like the shrines of the temple described above. That they were also originally connected by a common audience hall is borne out by a corner of the *mandapa* which is partly visible near the temple of the goddess. In general style and technique these temples closely resemble the Bālīsvara Temple and must, as hinted above, have been executed simultaneously with it. The Ratnesvara Temple, which is in all respects similar to that of Champāvatī (Photo No. 1601) is a small cella about six feet square internally, with a hemispherical dome constructed on the lines of that of the existing *mandapa* of the Bālīsvara Temple, and is

Champāvat. preceded by a somewhat smaller portico. The doorway is profusely sculptured and supports a frieze of the nine planets with a row of musicians above it. The decoration on the outside consists of representations of the three principal gods on the different faces, a well-executed band of ornament about half-way up the wall, and a frieze of lions and elephants near the base now hidden under débris.

"The fifth temple of the group, which stands between the eastern half of the Bālīsvara Temple and that of Bhairava, is a re-erection of old material and should be allowed to stand as it is. It is attributed by the people to Kālikā, but this must be a misnomer, as the original pedestal of a *linga* is extant.

"Lastly, there is a small shrine situated to the south-east of the Ratnesvara Temple. It is a tiny structure consisting of a shrine and the usual portico. The lintel bears a figure of Ganapati while the relief above includes one of Mahādeva. The pedestal attached to the back wall shows that the shrine was dedicated to some aspect of the goddess Durgā.

"The *naulā* or covered spring referred to above stands outside the temple enclosure on the south. It is a perennial spring protected with a stone-built reservoir with a rectangular domed chamber over it, manifestly of the same date as the temples described above. The outer walls of the structure, which are now partly hidden under débris, are plain, but there is a mass of ornamental carving on the interior which does not call for any special remarks.

"This was a fairly large stone-built pavilion which stood on a square platform nineteen feet along each side and 2′ 9″ in height. In design, it closely resembled the existing *mandapa* of the Bālīsvara Temple and was crowned with a circular dome with a triangular projection at each corner. Only three of the pillars are standing in their position, and one complete pillar and two capitals, together with the central ceiling slab, are lying close to the platform. The rest of the material has been carried away by the villagers. The terrace is adorned with mouldings on all sides and on the top of it we notice a chess pattern sketched on one of the slabs, which shows the fondness of the people for this game."

Frontier Circle. *Jamālgarhī.* Mr. Hargreaves reports that in connection with conservation at Jamālgarhī, considerable clearance was undertaken which resulted in the disclosure of several interesting structures and the recovery of a number of valuable antiquities. As the Superintendent was detained at Jaulian until March, the operations were started on February 6th, 1922, under the superintendence of the Personal Assistant Khan Sahib Mian Wasi-ud-Din, who was assisted by the office Photographer, Babu Mul Chand. The plan of the site is published as Plate XXIII. Mr. Hargreaves writes :

"The first building to be explored (No. 6 on Plate XXIII) was the one east of the main stupa. The exterior of this structure had been cleared the year before, when it had appeared that the building had had no entrance at ground level. Clearance of the interior confirmed this opinion as it revealed nothing but rough foundation walls tightly packed with débris. In Crompton's plan this building is shown with an entrance to the south, but no such entrance exists at ground level, and it is certain that access to the structure was by a ladder or removable stairway. The north-east and north-west corners which had fallen were restored. No antiquities were recovered in this area during the operations.

"South of the building just described a staircase gives access to a small enclosure which receives a drain from the west. This drain continues southward into Court 7, the courtyard west of the Conference Hall. Conservation was undertaken of the east and south walls of the Conference Hall (No. 10). An extraordinary feature in this building is the non-alignment of the inner and outer faces of both the eastern and the western walls, each of them tapering in thickness from 4' to 2' 9", the eastern wall being 4' thick at the northern end and 2' 9" thick at the southern while in the western wall the dimensions are reversed, so that the interior faces of the walls of the Chapter House are parallel. *Jamalgarhi.*

"In the extreme east of the site, a structure of three rooms (No. 15) with an enclosed verandah facing south has been cleared. It presents no special features but has on the south of its courtyard a rectangular platform which was probably the base of a stupa, as there is a depression in the centre as though it had been deeply excavated. Fragments of *kanjur* lions and elephants found here lend strength to this supposition.

"West of the building with three rooms and a verandah referred to on p. 4 of last year's report (No. 36), and in the same enclosure, further clearance led to the discovery of a structure (No. 37) with one room facing south and a narrow side room to the east opening into a common verandah overlooking a spacious courtyard in which is a small ruined stupa. In the centre of the larger room at a depth of 2 feet below floor level was found a sunk earthen *chatti* 2' in height. This *chatti* contained the carved circular slab of a pedestal. As the *chatti* is 2' below floor level, and has no neat masonry rim above, it would seem to belong to an earlier period.

"Adjoining this building on the west is a pavement in which is another sunk *chatti* with a wide mouth. These *chatti* set in pavements *outside* the various buildings are special features of the site revealed by the operations this year. They are all exterior to buildings, but adjacent to them, and in the courtyards. It is almost certain they were for storing water, as the one referred to above has a raised stone edging of upright slates. Had they been for grain, they would most probably have been inside buildings, not outside, where moisture, rats and insects would be most likely to attack their contents.

"There is an exterior staircase at the back of this building, which was apparently two-storied, and from the south-west corner descend stairs leading towards the entrance of a now much dilapidated vaulted chamber (No. 39) which faces west.

"Further west is a three-roomed structure (No. 41) with a small staircase on the east, and a small verandah at the south-east. It stands like all these structures in its own courtyard, and on the west side are the remains of two small ruined chapels and a stupa (No. 57). This building (No. 41) is superimposed on an earlier one but does not conform to the original plan. It is impossible to describe the various changes without drawings in colour, but these are being prepared for record and later publication. The older construction is of smaller and finer diaper masonry. In the north-west of the court is a vaulted chamber facing west, its corbelled roof broken, and east of it and contiguous, but on a higher level, a single roomed building with verandah (No. 42).

"South-west of Area 5 is a large building with three rooms, two of which open directly on the verandah on the south, the easternmost room having only an inner doorway giving access to the middle room. There is an arch in the exterior of the east wall as though an exterior staircase had been built on that side. The courtyard has not yet been excavated to the original level, and it remains to be seen whether any sunk

Jamalgarhi. waterpots will be found behind this building. There are traces at the south-east of the courtyard which seem to mark the former stupa. In this area were recovered Nos. 2 and 6 of the antiquities recorded below.

" South of Area 6, and across a well marked passage are two buildings in another courtyard. The one to the east (No. 46), has two rooms, facing south, and there are remains of a broad exterior staircase in the west.

" The second building (No. 45) immediately west of the one described has also two rooms and a verandah facing south, and a staircase on the north. The structure is built over an earlier building, the windows of which appear to have been only 9" above floor level. One of these earlier windows is well preserved, and drawings of it have been made for record. West of this building is a low platform with a large sunk *chatti*. The stupa lies on the east of the courtyard.

" South of Area 7 is another courtyard with two buildings. The smaller building (No. 47) has one room and verandah in the south, and must have had a second storey, access to which was, as usual, by way of an exterior staircase on the east. In the south wall of this room, which has a rough pavement of slate slabs, is a neat, well-preserved trefoil arch which must have contained an image. The second building (No. 49) lies to the west and has three rooms with a raised verandah on the south, under which is a small square opening. This building, unlike most of this part of the site, appears to have had no upper storey. Behind this building, *i.e.*, to the north, is an enclosed courtyard with four sunk *chattis*, the upper edge of each surmounted by a rim of fine diaper masonry.

" The line of *chattis* runs parallel to the north wall of the building. At the north-east of the courtyard is a small pit 3½' deep lined with small diaper. [Plate XXIV (*a*)]. It has now no plaster facing, but it would appear to have been likewise a pit for storing water. Owing to the difficulty of procuring water on the site it was impossible to test whether it is now watertight. A stupa and small chapels seem to have existed formerly on the east. There are also rooms (No. 48) at the south-east and south-west corners of the courtyard, the former being built over a vaulted chamber.

" This lies on the extreme south-west of the site and partial clearance has revealed a three-roomed building with verandah (No. 50), lying in a large courtyard. A staircase exists in the west, so the building was probably double storied. The stupa was on the south, but only traces of it exist. In the south-east corner of the revetment is a low-level vaulted chamber (No. 51).

" East of Area 8 and south-west of the main stupa is an enclosure with a three roomed structure (No. 35) having a raised verandah in the south. In front of the verandah are five recesses with flat lintels. The windows are only 15" above the present floor level. In the north of the building are two sunk *chattis* and a rectangular pit of diaper masonry 4'×3' and 4' deep. The stupa was probably in the west of the courtyard.

" Clearance around certain ruined stupas lying outside and to the south of the site resulted in the discovery of many sculptures and reliefs of great importance. These are described in detail below. Nos. 1, 9 and 10 present features of uncommon interest. In one of the small stupas the earthen cinerary urn was discovered firmly embedded in the masonry and, as it was empty, it has been left *in situ*.

" The results of the operations have been most satisfactory. Not only have many valuable sculptures been recovered but clearance has revealed a new form of monastic establishment. At Jamalgarhi is found no monastery of the usual form with cells arranged round a central square courtyard, but in its place a series of small monastic buildings, each in its own courtyard, and having its own little stupa. The common refectory (No. 11) and the Conference Hall (No. 10) lie south-east of the main stupa and quite separate from any of the numerous small monastic buildings, which are such a special feature of the site. *Jamalgarhi.*

" The circular procession path between the main stupa and the surrounding chapels was originally paved with large slabs of dark blue slate, but since its excavation in 1873 the villagers have removed the greater part of this useful material.* Nevertheless, here and there on the southern side and at the top of the stairway traces of this pavement remain. Sir Aurel Stein in 1912 removed a small inscribed slab to Peshawar. These slabs show a large number of shallow circular depressions as, indeed, does also the inscribed fragment referred to above. The number and uniformity of these holes (dia. 1", depth 3-16" to ¼") excited curiosity, but their purpose remained an enigma until this year's clearance provided the solution. *These depressions mark the spots from which have fallen ancient coins formerly inset in the pavement.*

" One fragment has been recovered still containing a copper coin of Vasudeva. † That a large number of coins must have been inset is plain from the fact that one slab alone contains 24 of these depressions.

" The practice of insetting coins in the pavements of shrines still exists and at the Sikh shrine of the Panja Sahib at Hassan Abdal (the tank of the Nāga Elāpatra) both English gold coins and rupees are fixed in the marble flooring, and the modern Visesvara temple at Benares, the Minakshi temple at Madura and the Rameswar temple at Rameshwaram are similarly adorned. The Jamālgarhī pavement carries the practice back with certainty to the second century of our era, and it may well have been such an offering of coins which was made by that king of Swat of whom it is recorded " *Dans le pays du Swat il y avait un roi............une fois il rencontra un stupa et lui fit une offrande de cinq pièces de monnaie*‡ ", for it is hardly probable that the stupa was opened to enable him to deposit his offering therein. There is of course, the further possibility that the five pieces were taken by the officiating monks. Be that as it may, the coin recovered gives proof of a special form of the cult of the stupa, and assists in dating the monument."

Among the antiquities recovered at Jamālgarhī this season may be mentioned the following as being those of largest interest. The complete list of the finds is reserved for publication with the memoir which it is hoped Mr. Hargreaves will prepare on the completion of the work :—

"1. Fragment of relief 9½" × 7¾". In the centre the Bodhi tree the trunk of which springs from a raised, ornamented grass-strewn platform. Standing on this platform and turning right is the tree goddess(?) (shown full length save for the feet) whose clasped hands almost touch the right hand of the Buddha, who is depicted seated in *abhaya-mudra* on a grass strewn throne to the right of the tree. On the left of the Bodhi tree, Māra, his left arm leaning on the right shoulder of his daughter, whose face is turned

* A. R., S. A. S., F. C., 1920-21, page 3.
† Gardner Pl. XXIX, 14.
‡ Foucher *L'art greco-bouddhique du Gandhāra, T. I., p. 62, n. I.*

Jamalgarhi. towards him (Plate XXV*b*). The identification of Māra is determined by an attendant behind him who holds aloft in his left hand a *makara* standard. Except for the seated Buddha the arrangement is that of reliefs depicting the approach to the Bodhi Seat, but the action here is subsequent to that event. *Cf.* 9, *infra*. Area 4.

" 2. Sixty beads, 26 carnelians, 34 bone, and one brass finger ring (dia. ¾) found together in a broken pot. The carnelian beads are mostly circular, but one is barrel-shaped and ornamented with white lines making a pentagonal pattern. White bone beads only roughly shaped. Area 6.

" 3. Fragment of frieze 9″ × 2⅝″. Above a band of moulding of four leaves conventionally arranged three small ogee arches (with saw-tooth ornament) each with bust of a figure, the centre one a female. Between the arches traces of busts of smaller figures, one on left fully preserved. Vaulted chamber. Area 4.

" 4. Relief (8½″ × 8½″) in five pieces. The *Mahāparinirvāna of the Buddha*. On upper edge acanthus moulding. Between two trees of ornate and unidentifiable type the Buddha, head to left on a draped couch with high pillow. No halo. In front of couch Subhadra and water cooler. At the foot of the couch Mahākāsyapa, his hand touching the feet of the Buddha whose robe completely covers them. At the head of the couch Vajrapāni half naked. In background busts of two naked figures with upraised right hands, the one to the left wild and demoniacal in appearance. A fracture in upper centre of relief.

From the ruined stupa south of the site.

" 5. Relief (13″ × 8″) from circular frieze. Sawtooth moulding on upper edge. Between two sunk encased panels where the usual pilaster is replaced by a childish *yaksha* standing on a Persepolitan pillar base, *The Dream of Māyā*. The queen is shown lying on her left side, on a couch with high pillow and in an alcove resembling the section of an angular-roofed *vihāra*. On a raised medallion above the sleeping queen, the little white elephant with trunk downward and projecting slightly over the rim of the medallion. A tall lamp stands at the foot of the couch and outside the alcove to right is a standing *Yavanī* armed with a lance, and in the background the bust of another figure. Well preserved and of good technique. With 4.

" 6. Relief 3½″ × 3½″. *The Bath of the Bodhisattva*. The infant stands on tripod between Indra and Brahma who douche him with water from vessels held high above his head. Preservation fair, technique inferior. Area 6.

" 7. Triangular fragment, (12″ × 7″) depicting the *Dīpankara Jātaka*. On the left, female with flowers, Sumati throwing the flowers and in the foreground the same lying on the ground on his deer-skin garment, his hair under the feet of the Buddha of whom only the right hand and lower part of the body is preserved. To extreme right the feet of Vajrapāni and traces of base of encased Indo-Persepolitan pilaster. Technique good. Area No. 6.

"8. Fragment (10" × 6") of upper curved portion of false niche. Finial on top and seated parrot on edge. Fragment of three panels— *Jamalgarhi.*

(a) The Alms Bowl of the Buddha on canopied throne with adoring winged triton to right,

(b) Buddha seated in *dharmachakra-mudrā* on throne. Kneeling worshipping layman to right,

(c) Head of Buddha between foliage and head of one other figure.

"9. Fragment 24" × 15¾", in three pieces, from rhomboidal lower portion of a false niche. Right side lost. *The approach to the Bodhi Tree.* In the centre the Buddha with halo (face lost) right hand (damaged) in *abhaya-mudrā* advances to left to the Bodhi Tree, which rises from grass-strewn ornamented throne, and from the branches of which hang streamers. The *pipal* foliage is well defined and reveals *à mi-corps* the tree goddess. The throne, or platform around the Bodhi Tree is not shown facing as usual but obliquely, and rising *à mi-corps* from the top of the throne, and completely hiding the trunk of the tree, is a naked corpulent male figure (face damaged) turning towards the advancing Buddha. This figure holds in the left hand a bow (?), the open right hand is upraised, level with the shoulder, and the body is shown so as to expose somewhat his nakedness and the upper portion of his thighs. On the other side of the Bodhi Tree Māra and his daughter, his left arm resting on the shoulder of his companion. *Cf. 1, above.* Following the Buddha a muscular lightly-clad Vajrapani, and adoring layman grasping flowers (?) in both hands. Above the head of the Buddha two flying childish *yakshas* who must have held a now lost crown, and in background traces of four other figures. In upper left of relief two flower-scattering *devas.* [Plate XXIV (c).]

"10. Fragment, 15½×23, in three pieces, from lower rhomboidal portion of a false niche. In one panel two scenes which are not separated in any marked manner.

(a) To right, *Unidentified Scene.* In the centre a standing Bodhisattva facing, right hand in *abhaya-mudrā*, left hand (broken) on hip. Above the head of the Bodhisattva two flying childish *yakshas*, holding a now lost crown over him. To proper right of the Bodhisattva a standing layman turning towards him with hands clasped in adoration and above in background flower-scattering figure. On proper left of Bodhisattva a now headless Vajrapani. Above the worshipping layman and in the air a naked childish figure with dishevelled hair, his face turned towards the Bodhisattva and holding an unidentified object in both hands. He is not one of the crown-bearing *yakshas* and, from his position, might appear to belong to the second scene (b) were not his face turned to right towards the Bodhisattva.

(b) To left. *The nursling of the dead woman.* On the left the Buddha, followed by a youthful Vajrapani advances to right with the right hand extended in a welcoming gesture, towards a naked little child who faces him with clasped hands. Behind this infant is a hut-like structure of ashlar or bricks with a curved roof and rounded finial. This structure is open on one side and out of this opening fall the head.

Jamalgarhi.

and bust of a woman with long hair. The proper left of her body has wasted to a skeleton, the right breast is full, rounded and life-like. The roof of a second similar structure is seen behind that from which the body of the woman projects. In the middle ground facing the Buddha is a layman with clasped hands and in the background two flower-scattering *devas*. The naked little figure with dishevelled hair referred to in (*a*) above is actually above the two hut-like structures and falls into the half of the sculpture which depicts this scene, but his hair is not that of the youthful Sudaya and, as already noted, his face is turned away from the scene under reference. [Plate XXIV (*d*).]

"The technique of the relief is good. The right hand of the Buddha is in two pieces and had been held together by a small iron dowel, marking an ancient repair.

"The presence of Vajrapani with a bejewelled Bodhisattva as in (*a*) is unusual save in the few scenes between the Flight from Kapilavastu and the Exchange of garments with the huntsman. The relief in question does not appear to be one of those scenes, and the Vajrapani here may have resulted from that love of symmetry so marked in this school, and be due to the presence of his counterpart so properly depicted on the opposite edge of the relief.

"11. Relief 12½"×10½". Between two half pilasters supporting acanthus moulding *The First Sermon*. The Buddha, without halo, seated under a tree, on a grass-strewn throne, the right hand in *abhaya-mudrā*, the left grasping the robe near the left knee. In front of the throne a twelve-spoked wheel supported by a dwarf Indo-Corinthian column and flanked on either side by a deer, couchant, regardant. To left two *bhikshus* seated on low thrones, one standing *bhikshu* and *deva* with flowers in background. To right two *bhikshus* similarly seated, Vajrapani by the Buddha's left shoulder and usual *deva*.

"12. Relief 12½" × 8". On upper edge diaper of alternately incised triangles. The Buddha seated on a grass-strewn throne the right hand in *abhaya-mudrā*, the left grasping the robe. In front of the throne a snake with upraised head. On the left of the Buddha a standing princely figure with clasped hands turned towards the Buddha. A large snake-canopy over his head and springing from his shoulders proclaims him a *naga-raja* and seemingly the same who appears in animal form before the throne. To right two standing laymen of importance with a third in background. Conventional tree on right. The scene might be *The visit of Elapatra*, but the absence of monks renders this doubtful. *Cf.* 144 of *App.* V, *A. R., S. A. S., F. C.*, for 1920-21.

"13. Fragment (14"×11") of frieze in four pieces. Saw-tooth moulding on upper edge. The Buddha haloed, seated in *abhaya-mudrā* under a tree on a grass-strewn throne, left hand grasping the robe. On the left a now defaced layman making offering to the Buddha and head of another figure in background. To right a monk, with right hand upraised and first two fingers extended, appears to salute the Buddha. Following the monk two princely figures, one with clasped hands the other in background scattering flowers. Behind left shoulder of the Buddha a bearded Vajrapani. *Jamalgarhi.*

"14. Fragment 12″×10″, in three pieces, from left of a relief depicting the *Adoration of the Naga Kalika.* On upper edge saw-tooth moulding and on left edge an encased panel with a female figure, standing on an Indo-Persepolitan base under a tree, replacing the usual pilaster. In the foreground a tank, ornamented with three rows of alternately incised triangles, and from which water escapes through a lion gargoyle on the right edge. Rising *à mi-corps* from the tank the *naga* Kalika and his wife, both with hands clasped in adoration and turning right to the now lost Buddha. A hooded snake springing from behind the shoulders rises like a canopy over the head of Kalika and his companion. Behind the *naga* a standing adoring layman, and in upper background above the tree three figures, one scattering flowers.

"15. Fragment (11½″×11″) in three pieces from left side of a relief. Saw-tooth moulding on upper edge, encased panel with female figure standing on Indo-Persepolitan base replacing usual pilaster on left edge. The centre and right portion of the scene are lost. The part remaining shows four laymen in the foreground and four similar figures in upper background. The foremost of those in the foreground with princely head-dress advances towards the now missing Buddha or Bodhisattva and with his left hand takes a handful of flowers (?) from a large basket held by an attendant. The attitudes of the assistants vary, one grasps some roundish object on the breast with both hands, another clasps the hands in adoration, while of those in the background one throws flowers like the usual *deva* attendants of the Buddha.

"16. Fragment (13″×11″) from right of a relief. Saw-tooth moulding on upper edge, and on right encased panel with female standing on Indo-Persepolitan base under a tree, the right hand on the hip, left upraised grasping the foliage of the tree ; the part of the scene preserved shows the Buddha, the right hand lost, the left on the thigh. To right of the Buddha, Vajrapani clad in a loin cloth only, *vajra* in right hand, *chauri* in left, and two princely figures with clasped hands. In upper background three similar princely figures. The interlocutor of the Buddha is lost, but on the upper edge of the relief and in front of the Buddha and lower than his head is part of an umbrella, so the scene must have depicted some god or (royal personage), visiting the Buddha.

"17. Fragment (12½″×13″), in five pieces, from right lower side of rhomboidal panel of false niche. Standing Buddha, head slightly to left, both hands lost, followed by a semi-naked Vajrapani and two princely laymen, the nearer one headless, the second with hands clasped in adoration. One figure in background between Vajrapani and the Buddha. Heads of the Buddha and Vajrapani broken, but recovered during clearance.

"18. Fragment (6″×6½″) of lower portion of *Mahaparinirvana* scene. The Buddha (haloed), head to left lying on a draped couch with carved legs, thick mattress and pillow. In front of couch to right Subhadra with back to

Jamalgarhi. spectator and on left edge Vajrapani seated on the ground, the *vajra* in the right hand resting on the ground, the left hand upraised in grief. Between these two figures a water cooler of three rods bound at their centre, from the upper end of one of which hangs a flask-like object. Area 9.

" 19. Stucco bust of female 5½" × 3½", face turned half right. Wears a flat jewelled torque and large circular earrings. A long veil covers the head and falls over the shoulders and upper arms. Bears in right hand a handled jar which is supported by the left hand. A well-modelled figure probably from left of a donation scene.

" 20. Fragment 12" × 9½ (in seven pieces) from right of a relief. On upper edge saw-tooth moulding. The Buddha with right hand raised in *abhaya-mudrā* advances to left followed by a youthful Vajrapani and a monk. In right background a flower-scattering *deva*, in left background bust of a layman."

Notes on places visited by Mr. Hargreaves.

The Superintendent, Frontier Circle, inspected the following sites and monuments: Takht-i-Bahi, Jamalgarhi, Shahbazgarhi, Asota, Chanaka-Dheri, Bala Hissar and Spelani in the Peshawar District; Sirsukh, Jandial, Lal Chak, Badalpur, Jaulian, Chitti, Dobandi, Tarnawa, Tofkian, Haji Bela, Bedadi, Chitti Gatti and Dhamtaur in the Hazara District. Mr. Hargreaves writes:

Khanpur. " On the 27th December 1921 at the invitation of the Chief of the Gakhars I visited Khanpur in the Haro Valley to inspect a '*topi*' which was stated never to have been excavated. It was found on inspection that the so-called '*topi*' was not a monument at all, but the rounded top of a hill where the horizontal stratum had weathered in such a way that it bore a considerable resemblance to a ruined stupa. Information was obtained of several other monuments further up the Haro Valley, including a cave or tunnel, the walls of which were said to be carefully dressed, but a return to Jaulian was imperative and the examination of these monuments must await a more favourable opportunity.

Dhamtaur. " Mr. T. B. Copeland, I.C.S., having sent for inspection some specimens of large but somewhat crude terra-cotta animal figurines which had been obtained close to the *ziarat* of Haji Shah Jamal Ghazi at Dhamtaur, the site was visited on May 18th, 1921. There are two modern tanks, one filled in with earth, and on one side a few large stones which are said to mark the site of an ancient tank which was destroyed to provide material for the modern one. The *ziarat* is built in part of ancient material, but is now merely a walled enclosure of no architectural pretensions whatsoever. The site was, no doubt, from the earliest times, a sacred spot and place of pilgrimage, and would be, in all probability, dedicated to some *nāga*, but the spring which hallowed and beautified the spot failed some years ago after a shock of earthquake. The terra-cotta figurines were found when digging close to the tank and are of considerable age. They are much larger than those found usually at Buddhist sites in the North-West and are coarser in fabric and less skilfully modelled. Horses and elephants seem to have been the favourite models.

" At Dhamtaur it was noticed that modern graves were edged by neatly cut *kanjur* stone, called locally *kaniat*, which is said to be quarried in the neighbourhood. The *kanjur*, it will be recalled, is the material so largely used in the ancient Buddhist monuments of the North-West as the basis of plastered columns, capitals, cornices and pilasters. In Mansehra town modern houses are still built of this *kanjur*.

"Learning from Mr. J. Coatman, Superintendent of Police, Hazara, that ancient remains existed near Shinkiari, eleven miles north of Mansehra, and that coins, seals, inscriptions and other antiquities were occasionally recovered there, an inspection was made on the 21st May 1921. *Shinkiari.*

"The first site visited was about a mile and a quarter from the Shinkiari Rest House and about fifty yards south of the forest path leading to Jaba. There, on a small spur stretching to the south, are the remains of a monastery and stupa of Kushan date, and built of the typical diaper masonry of that period. The stupa is seventeen paces square, but only fragments of the square base, of large diaper masonry, are visible on the east and west, though the greater part of the south wall still exists. Two large pine trees are growing on the stupa mound. A stairway led from the north, *i.e.*, the side facing the monastery, to a circular procession path which ran round the dome, and traces of this path and of the first course of the masonry of the dome are still visible on the north. The stupa mound is now being gradually cut away to extend the surrounding fields. Treasure seekers have destroyed the west side of the stupa and dug very deeply into the centre, but with what result is unknown as nobody was present at the site, and the hut which stands on one corner of the monastery mound was uninhabited, and the few people met in the forest knew nothing of the site save its modern name, Haji Bela. Of the monastery, the only visible remains are fragments of wall at the south-east and north-west corners. The site is a particularly pleasing one and must have provided the monks with that privacy and peace which they so ardently desired. A stream flows by the site about sixty yards away, just below the south-west of the stupa, and at the time of inspection, a season of exceptional drought, would easily have met the needs of even a larger religious establishment than this could ever have been. *Haji Bela.*

"These remains do not figure in any of the lists of ancient monuments, nor are they referred to in the Gazetteer of the district. They are far too ruined to be worth protecting or excavating, but they have been thought worthy of record as throwing light on the position of Buddhism in this region during the time of the Kushans, for they add another to the already growing list of Buddhist monuments in this, as yet little surveyed area.

"About a mile south of the Shinkiari Rest House, on a rocky hill, stand the remains of a stupa which has been excavated on the east side and in the centre. The villagers report that a 'sahib' did this some years ago and that he found a stone box containing 'white gems.' This report is most probably true as a reliquary with crystal ornaments is what might be expected to be recovered in such operations. Part of the east wall of the stupa, of large diaper masonry, still exists. A fragment of ancient wall lying about sixty feet to the east is probably part of the connected monastery. *Bedadi.*

"North of this ruined stupa and about a hundred yards to the north-east across the fields stands a cultivator's hut in front of which some large empty earthen vessels were recovered recently. The occupants of the hut possessed some coins found in the adjoining fields, and these were all Kushan, save one of Soter Megas. An old sepoy who acts as a guide at Bedadi exhibited two silver coins of the Hindu Shahis and one of Azes (elephant and bull type), but as he makes a business of collecting antiquities he may have procured these elsewhere.

Bedadi. "Proceeding a little to the north of this hut, a more or less level plateau is reached. It is some eight acres in extent and the sides to the north and east are very precipitous, but less so on the west, falling away in terraces to join the main hill towards the south. The steep sides of this area are revetted with ancient walls of coarse diaper, the surface is covered with fragments of coarse pottery, and coins are frequently recovered, so that there is no doubt that this was formerly the site of habitations.

"The modern village of Bedadi lies about half a mile south of the area just described, and is likewise built on an ancient site. Many old walls are visible, of a fine type of large diaper, and others very neatly and substantially built of rounded boulders from the River Siran, the interstices filled with small flattish stones, the whole forming a novel form of diaper masonry or modified rubble. Existing walls of the latter type show a very good, smooth, vertical face with the boulders well aligned. The numerous rough stone walls of piled boulders which now form the boundaries of so many of the terraced fields near the village are but the débris of ancient walls of this type and, by their position, give a very correct idea of the limits of the ancient site. The crudely built boulder walls of the modern village mark in unmistakable fashion the inferiority of the present inhabitants in architectural skill and craftmanship. On the south side of the village a considerable stretch of this boulder-diaper still exists and in most places, 3′ 3″ thick, but at the south-east corner it is not less than 6′ in thickness.

"About three quarters of a mile eastward stands a terraced area with a long wall of diaper rising in two terraces, each about 8′ wide, to a level space on which stand the remains of what was in all probability a stupa, but of which no facing remains and into which a large hole has been dug at the south-east side. Of the lowest wall, some 70 feet exists, of the intermediate wall, a few fragments only, and of the uppermost, about 20′.

"About a quarter of a mile further to the east is another mound with a diaper wall about 36′ in length and 4′ in height. The top is more or less level but broken by five small mounds of earth and boulders. These are not, however, the remains of small stupas, but most likely graves.

"Lying outside the main town site the above two monuments mark, seemingly, the sites of former religious establishments.

"East of the village of Bedadi at the end of the path leading up from the sandy ravine is a fragment of very fine ancient wall. It faces east and is of very large diaper, the stones being exceedingly well cut.

"At Bedadi coins of the Indo-Scythian and Kushans have been obtained as well as coins of Menander, and in private possession is a very fine engraved gem depicting a winged Eros playing two pipes, an excellent specimen of later Hellenistic art, which was also obtained from this spot. A stone fragment with two or three Kharoshthi characters, some stone household utensils and the inscribed oil measure referred to below were also recovered at this site. The inscription is said to be in the possession of a private individual in Abbottabad, but the two stone vessels have been presented to the Peshawar Museum by Mr. T. B. Copeland, I.C.S.

"Bedadi is not known from any ancient record, but its position at the entrance to the Bhogarmang Valley and on the high ground immediately on the left bank of the River Siran, whose wide bed is exceedingly fertile and where there is abundant water even in the driest seasons, must from the earliest times, have given it considerable importance. Even to-day it has about twenty water-mills and the adjacent forests supply it with timber, firewood, pasturage and fodder.

"About half way between Dhudial and Mansehra, on the right hand of the road when coming from Dhudial and just before descending into the Ichhar Nala, are the remains of a stupa and monastery. The stupa appears to have lost all its facing; the monastery has 18′ of diaper masonry on the west and traces of walling at the south-east corner. In the centre of the monastery area is a roughly-built square platform surmounted by an octagonal building with flattish dome crowned by a finial. This building, of poor material and technique, must date from Sikh times. The door was found locked but the building, which is said to contain a white stone, the *chitti gatti*, is now a Hindu shrine. People assemble here for worship on the 6th of Phagan, and 1st of Baisakh. We have here another example of an ancient sacred site still retaining its sanctity, though the religion and the object of worship have both changed. *Chitti Gati.*

"On the 5th November 1921 I inspected the stone circle of Asota which is 18 miles from Mardan. To reach it, one travels 16 miles along the road through Shahbazgarhi and then turns due north along a very bad *kachcha* road towards Shiva. An excellent description of the monument as well as an illustration is given by Sir Arthur Phayre in *J. A. S. B.*, Volume XXXIX, 1870, pages 58-59. Many stones then existing are now missing from the circle, the best preserved portion being on the north-west. Of the outer circle of small stones referred to by Sir Arthur Phayre, there are now no surface traces, for since 1870 the adjacent land has been brought into cultivation, and on the north-east is a graveyard so that the smaller stones may have been removed by cultivators or broken up to be used as headstones for graves. There is one isolated stone, however, about 80 feet south of the main circle. It is stated that in 1870 there was in the centre of the circle a pillar, which once upright, was then thrown down and half hidden with earth, and that a hole showed that the pillar had been undermined, probably in search of treasure. There is now no trace of this central monolith above ground. *Asota.*

"All the larger stones incline slightly inwards which may be due to an original inward slope or to subsidence resulting from excavation in the centre of the circle. This inclination of the monoliths is not equal in all cases some sloping as much as one in ten. The people still designate the monument *lakke tigge* (upright stones), but the neighbouring village they call Sota, not Asota. About a quarter of a mile away and south of the village of Sheraghund are two monoliths about 150 yards apart, possibly remains of similar stone circles. The Asota monument was declared protected under Notification 10357-G. of 7th December 1920."

In the garden of the Executive Engineer, Irrigation Department, Peshawar, the Superintendent, Frontier Circle, noticed a well-preserved image of the Buddha with flames on the shoulders. This he obtained permission to photograph (Plate XXV *a*). Images of this type are rare and Mr. Hargreaves states that he has knowledge of four only, *viz.*, one in the Indian Museum emanating from Kabul (*J. A. S. B.*, Volume III, July 1834, p. 363), a headless image in the Central Museum, Lahore, a much damaged one under a *pipal* tree in Nowshera, which is now an object of Hindu worship, and the one in question, which is little inferior to that in Calcutta. An endeavour will be made to obtain this interesting image, which is private property, for the Peshawar Museum. *Buddha image with flames on the shoulders.*

On the 5th November it was reported to Mr. Hargreaves as he was returning from Asota that east of the village of Shahbazgarhi on the south of the main road and opposite milestone 8. the road menders when digging a borrow-pit had disclosed an ancient well. "On examination this was found to be 2′ 3″ in diameter and lined by terracotta rings 9″ high, ¾″ thick and having on the upper edge a projecting lip 1½″. *Ancient well at Shahbazgarhi.*

Frontier Circle. Similar wells or drains have been found at Taxila, and several of these earthen-ware rings are preserved in the Museum there. The Sub-Divisional Officer, P. W. D., Mardan, who was present, was requested to arrange for the filling in of the excavation so that the well might remain undisturbed."

Notes on places visited by Mr. R. D. Banerji.

Western Circle.

Saraspur. "This small masjid was found in the suburban village of Saraspur close to Ahmedabad city. It is a simple structure, built partly of bricks and partly of stone. There are three domes which are supported by walls at the back and sides, and by four pillars in front. Two solid minars rise at each end and there is a *mihrab*, under each arch supporting the domes, in the back wall. An inscription over the central *mihrab* records the erection of the masjid on the 6th of Rabia-us-Sani a Tuesday in the year 922 or 924 A. H. during the reign of Sultan-ul-Azam abu Nasr Muzaffar Shah bin Mahmud Shah bin Muhammad Shah bin Ahmad Shah bin Muhammad Shah bin Muzaffar Shah, *i.e.*, Muzaffar II of Gujarat who reigned from 917 to 932 A. H. The structure measures 36′ 6″ in length and 9′ 11″ in breadth. It is now called Pir-Mancha-ki-Masjid and is occupied by a Fakir (Photograph No. 5581).

Sarai at Kari. "The attention of travellers on the main line of the metre gauge section of the B. B. & C. I. Railway is very often attracted to a brick fort which stands within a stone's throw of the track. It is in reality a fortified camp or Sarai, built during the early Mughal period, which formed the first stage of the journey from the capital of Gujarat to Agra or Delhi. The fortifications were necessary, though the place lies within easy reach of Ahmadabad, on account of the predatory habits of the neighbouring hill tribes, whose outrages are very often recorded by travellers. The camp or Sarai is now included within the limits of the village of Kari in the North Daskrohi (*Dasakrosi*), *i.e.*, the Sadar or Haveli *Taluka* of the district of Ahmadabad. The walls of the enclosure are very high and there is a round tower at each corner with gun platforms and embrasures, as well as loopholes for musketry. Each of these towers is two-storied with a second wall surrounding the inner chamber and with hiding places between the walls for sharpshooters. The main entrance faces the east and the road under it is paved for the passage of wheeled traffic. Over this gate there are one large and two small chambers, access to which can be gained from the ramparts. A large balcony with a small one on each side, projects from the east or front of the main hall, in this second story over the main gate. To the north of the hall there is an open terrace for sleeping on in summer, with steps leading to the roof, the inner ramparts and the ground floor. On the ground floor there is a spacious guardroom on each side. There is a corresponding two-storied building in the middle of the back or west wall [Plate XXXI *a*]. No openings are visible in the north or south walls, the inner faces of which are covered with a network of arches which support the platform on top, 4′ 6″ in width, running along the loopholes in the *kanguras*, three loopholes to each *kangura*. The arches were used as living rooms by common people and the soldiery. A broad platform 12′ 6″ in breadth, runs in front of the arches in the interior, along the entire lengths of the four walls. This platform is wider in front of the building in the centre of the western wall, where it measures 20′. In the centre is a spacious courtyard measuring 305′ × 250′ with the ruins of a central tank and a fountain. Paved platforms were built on each side of the main gate for shops and near the north-eastern corner there is a small masjid. A low wall extended from the bastion in the north-east corner to a well near the railway line.

Maungya Tungya Caves. "To Mr. A. H. A. Simcox, I.C.S., belongs the credit of the discovery of the ancient Jain caves on the Maungya Tungya Hills in the Nasik District, the earliest Jain monuments in this Presidency [Plates XXXI *b* and XXXII]. These caves lie on the western border of the Nasik District, the southern border of the West Khandesh District and very close to the hill fort of Sulher belonging to H. H. the Maharaja Gaikwar of Baroda. The place lies far away from railway lines, in an inaccessible part of the country. The best route is from Manmad Railway Station to Taharabad *viâ* Malegaon and Satana, a distance of seventy-eight miles. The metalled road ceases four miles to the north of Taharabad and the foot of the hills is reached along a cart track. The Digambara Jains have built a Dharamsala at this place and are building steps to go up to the top. At the height of three or four hundred feet are two Jain caves, the oldest at this place, which must be assigned to the eighth or the ninth century A. D. at the latest. This group lies to the west of a waterfall and faces the south. The cave on the right has collapsed partly, as only the stumps of two pillars of the veranda are now visible. This veranda has now been rebuilt by the Jains with modern ashlar masonry, and wooden door and window frames, painted white and black. From the outside nobody would ever suspect that one of the oldest Jain cave-temples lies hidden inside the glaring whitewashed front. The back wall of the veranda is entirely covered with basreliefs [Plate XXXII *a*]. Beginning from the left one finds on the left wall of the veranda the mutilated figure of a seated Jina and below it a standing figure of Parsvanatha. To its left a female with four hands is standing on a lotus, while to her left is the kneeling figurine of a devotee. The following figures are to be found in that portion of the back wall of the veranda which lies to the left of the doorway : in its centre (1) Parsvanatha standing, (2-3) standing female figures, (4) male riding on the back of a bull (Siva ?), (5-6) two kneeling female devotees, (7) a man riding on the back of a lion below two *gandharvas*, (8) a corpulent male riding on the back of an elephant, which stands under a tree (? Indra), (9-11) three Jinas, one over the other (12) a *dvarapala* holding a mace. The sculptures to the right of the doorway begin with (1) a *dvarapala* holding a mace. Then come (2) a female seated on a lion couchant under a tree, with a male attendant standing on each side, (3) Gomatesvara, with creepers entwined round his thigh, (4-5) a male and female devotee, both seated, with a standing female attendant to their left, and a *gandharva*-pair on each side of their heads.

Ma..*ngya Tungya Caves.*

"The following figures are to be found on the right wall of this veranda : (1) a Jina seated in meditation and below him, under a trefoil arch, in a niche, (2) a female (*Sasanadevi*) seated, with four hands, two of which hold lotus flowers, the remaining two being in the postures of blessing (*varada mudrā*) and giving protection (*abhaya*), respectively ; (3) a Jina seated under this and (4-5) two more Jinas and below them again (6-7) two more Jinas all seated.

"Inside the inner cave, a Jina is seated on a pedestal, in front of which a wheel is represented. There is a lion on each side of the wheel and a male attendant standing with a flywhisk on each side. To the left of his head, a *gandharva* is playing on a drum and to the right, another with cymbals. To the left of this figure, on the back wall is a figure of Parsvanath seated and under him a Jina also seated, who is similar to the main figure. On the right of the main figure is another Jina seated on a throne, on which is the wheel and under it two lions. Over this figure four Jinas are seated in a row.

"On the left wall of the chamber the following figures occur : (1) a Jina seated on a lion throne, with a wheel in front, (2) Parsvanatha seated under an umbrella, placed under a tree, (3-5) three flying figures with drum, cymbals and a conch, (6) a Jina standing, (7) a female standing, (8) a female seated with four hands. On the right wall

Maungya Tungya Caves.

there is (1) a Jina standing inside an unfinished niche. Then comes (2) a bigger figure under a tree with two *gandharvas* on each side.

" The other cave is to the left of this one and consists of a veranda, a large *mandapa* and an inner sanctum. The veranda has collapsed and the only remains of it are the stumps of two pillars in front. To the right of the doorway of the *mandapa* are the following figures, (1) a Jina standing followed by some worn out and indistinct figures, (2) a seated figure with four hands. A figure of Ganesa is to be found on the left jamb of the doorway and an unfinished figure of a Jina on the lintel.

" The *mandapa* is a large square chamber covered with basreliefs. Two seated Jinas occur on the front wall, and on the left there are two rows of figures. In the first row are seven seated Jinas on lion thrones, with a wheel in front of each. There are six seated figures in the second row. Between the second and third Jinas, a female is standing on a bracket. There are two rows of figures on the right. In the first row, two Jinas are seated. Then comes a standing nude Jina, followed by four seated Jinas and a female seated on a lion couchant, under a tree, with a child on her lap. In the second row, the first part of the wall is bare. Then comes a large seated figure of a Jina, followed by two small ones. At the end, a male and female are to be found under a tree, in the branches of which is the figure of a Jina seated in meditation.

" Two rows of figures are found to the left of the doorway of the sanctum, *i.e.*, on the left half of the back wall of the *mandapa*. In the first row, there is a small seated Jina and three standing ones, the middle one of which is Parsvanatha. Last of all comes a seated female with four hands, holding a sword (*asi*) and a mirror (*darpana*) in two of them, the remainder being broken. In the second row, the following figures are to be found :—(1) a small seated Jina, (2) a corpulent male, seated on an elephant, under a tree, holding a mango in his right hand and a bag in his left (Kuvera ?), (3) Parsvanatha seated, (4) a male and a female standing under a tree as in the first row, (5-6) two seated Jinas, (7) another seated Jina under No. 6. An unfinished female figure is to be found under the left door jamb, under which is the *dvarapala* holding a mace in his right hand, while the left is in the posture of giving protection. The right door jamb is exactly similar to the left one. On the right of the back wall there are two rows of figures. In the first row four Jinas are seated with one or more attendants, on lion thrones. In the second row there are ten figures of Jinas in all, large and small. To the right of this is a large unfinished figure of a Jina. Inside the sanctum a huge Jina, 5′ 3″ in height is seated on a lion throne with rows of small Jina figurines on each side.

" Leaving this group of caves on the left, an ancient road goes up to the top of the hills, consisting partly of rock-cut steps and partly of galleries hewn out of the rock. Near the top the road bifurcates, the one to the left leading to the Maungya peak, and the one to the right to Tungya. Maungya is the highest peak and a narrow pathway hewn out of the rock, encircles it. There are several cisterns and modern temples along this footpath and the rockside is covered with Jina figurines in small niches. There are four large excavations in this group with several smaller ones, all of which are comparatively modern and still used for worship. Numerous pilgrims' records, many of which are dated, show that the caves were in existence before the fifteenth and sixteenth centuries of the Christian era. There is a narrow and windswept shelf between the two peaks. The ascent to the Tungya is very dangerous because the steps are very high and worn out. The footpath round this peak has collapsed in many places. There are two large excavations one of which has been modernised by the use of marble for the pavement and the benches. On both peaks the walls of the caves are full of standing and seated images, none of which are earlier than the fourteenth century A. D. *Maungya Tungya Caves.*

"The small village of Miri, now a missionary settlement, lies at a distance of twenty-four miles from Ahmadnagar and appears to have been a stronghold of Jainism in later mediæval ages. Numerous Jain images were found in the neighbourhood and a rock-cut cistern, re-excavated recently, in a field nearby, contains two niches, each with the figure of a naked standing Jina, one of whom is Parsvanatha, to be recognised by the serpent-hood over his head. All images discovered at Miri are Digambara images. *Miri.*

"There are two palaces of His Highness the Maharaja Holkar in the Nasik District, one of which is at Lasalgaon near the main line of the G. I. P. Railway and the second at Chandor on the Bombay-Agra Road. The palace at Lasalgaon is a mere heap of ruins and nothing remains except the compound walls and the bastions, but the palace at Chandor is in an excellent state of preservation (Plate XXXIII) and is still occupied by the Maharaja's officers. It is a splendid specimen of a seventeenth century palace, better specimens of which once existed at Nasik and Poona, but both of these have been ruined. The palace at Chandor gives one some idea of the splendour of the Peshwa's palace at Poona, the Shanwar Wada, glimpses only of which are to be obtained from the descriptions of travellers. The palace consists of two courts inside a fortified enclosure. The façade inside the first court is drab and uninteresting, but the second court is a marvel of wood-carving, now a lost art both in the Deccan and in Gujrat. It is surrounded on all sides by double storeyed verandas resting on square pillars in the ground floor, which support massive but wonderfully carved corbels on all four faces. These corbels support an exquisitely beautiful cornice. The pillars in the second floor are tapering towards the top and fluted. They support carved-wood arches and between the pillars of each storey are wooden *jali* railings of marvellous workmanship. *Lasalgaon.* *Chandor.*

"Marai is a small village in the Maihar State four or five miles to the south of the Calcutta-Bombay Road. The village lies at the foot of the Kaimur range and appears to have been a place of considerable importance in the later mediæval age. A tank was created at the foot of the hills by building a dam at a short distance from the hill-side. This tank is triangular in shape, two sides of it having been formed by the dam, the third being covered by the slope of the hill. The sides of the dam are covered with stone steps, which are still in an excellent state of preservation at some places. Three temples stood on the three sides of this dam, the ruins of which lie scattered all round. Among these ruins some pillars with basreliefs were discovered which appear to be unique. The pillars are five in number and all of them are square in section. One of them bears basreliefs on every available inch of space on all four faces. The basreliefs on each face are divided into a number of panels, each bearing a number of divine figures. On the first pillar the twenty-four different forms of Vishnu, the ten incarnations and minor forms of the same deity, have been carved. The second specimen also bears basreliefs on each of its four faces, but on the existing portion of the shaft there is a raised band on each face dividing the basreliefs which are two in number. The surface of the band itself shows two or three sunken panels containing seated figurines. The basreliefs on each face consist of two or three figures, either exclusively males or females. (Photo. No. 5858.) The faces of the three remaining pillars are divided into a number of superimposed niches flanked by round pilasters. These niches contain basreliefs which can be identified in one or two cases only such as :—(1) Krishna taming the Naga Kaliya, (2) A milkmaid of Gokula churning butter (3) Krishna slaying the *Marai in Maihar State.*

Marai in Maihar State. demon Arishta, who being deputed by Kamsa, the King of Mathura, to kill Balarama and Krishna, assumed the form of a bull.

"On the other side of the village of Marai, a ruined temple of Siva was discovered. It stands on a high stone platform measuring about one hundred feet in length and sixty in breadth. The *mandapa* of this temple as well as its *sikhara* has fallen leaving only the *garbhagriha*, which is a plain square chamber. The *antarala* is provided with a beautifully carved stone door-frame, with figures of Ganges and Yamuna on the door-frames and over them four superimposed niches containing amorous couples. The lintel bears the figures of Siva and the seven divine mothers, the nine planets as well as three brackets ; one at each end of the lintel and one in its centre. The bracket at the left end of the lintel bears the figures of Brahma, with four hands, that in the centre that of Siva as Lakulisa with four hands, and the bracket at the right end, Vishnu on Garuda. The *garbhagriha* is built of Kaimur sandstone, the masonry being regularly coursed ashlar. On the body of this *garbhagriha* outside there were niches flanked by square pilasters, one on each face, but the facing on the northern side having collapsed, the niche also has fallen down. There are two rows of divine figures on the exterior of this *garbhagriha*, some of which are mutilated. Interspersed among them are obscene groups of two or three amorous figures, as in some of the Khajuraho temples. Like the temples at Sohagpur and Amarkantak, the trabeate roof of the *garbhagriha* is supported by four pilasters, one in each corner. Inside it is a huge *linga* on a square *arghapatta*, which has been placed on a second *arghapatta*. The temple appears to have been built in the eleventh century A. D.

Manora. "Manora is the name of a village on the top of a high plateau on the Kaimur range. The plateau was at one time thickly populated and well irrigated. The principal approaches were also fortified, remains of the fortifications being still in evidence everywhere. Ruins of three different temples were found on this plateau, all of which belong to the same date as that of the temple of Siva at Bhumara in the Nagode State (*Circa* 5th century A. D.). Numerous images were found among the ruins. One of them, an image of the Man-lion (*Narasimha*) incarnation of Vishnu, deserves special mention. In this image, the figure of the demon Hiranya Kashipu is not placed on the lap of the Man-lion, as usual in North-Indian images, but is found standing on the ground, to the right of the latter.

Doni in Chhattarpur State. "The village of Doni, in the Chhattarpur State, is noted for its large tank. Doni lies about thirteen miles to the east of Nowgong, two miles to the south of the metalled road from the latter place to Banda. The tank is called Drona-sagara by the local Brahmans, and covers an area of 248 local bighas. The dam which retains water in the tank is, at places, twenty to twenty-five feet in height from the surrounding ground level. Near the village there is a stone-paved platform on this dam, oblong in shape, provided with stone steps along three of its sides for descending into the tank. An old temple of Nandin stands on this platform. Three steps from the waterside, built on the platform lead to the level of the ruined porch of this temple. This porch was provided with benches having backrests. Two of the dwarf pillars which once supported the roof of the porch are standing. The main shrine faces west. The pillars which support the benches running along three sides of this temple are taller than the corresponding pillars of the porch. This shrine is really a *mandapa*, opening on all sides, which contained the figure of the bull only ; the *linga* being enshrined in a large but separate temple to the east of it. Similar arrangements are noticeable at the temple of Rajendrachola I at Tanjore and at Parner in the Ahmadnagar District. In addition to the small pillars which rest on the benches, on its sides the roof of the *mandapa* was supported by four tall pillars, at four corners of the chamber. The lintels supported by these pillars are higher than the lintels supported by the smaller ones which rest on the benches. The roof of the *mandapa* is sloping between these parallel but unevenly placed lintels. A similar arrangement is to be found in the ancient temples of the period of the Silahara dynasty of Konkan, around the shrine of *Amba mata* at Kolhapur.

Doni in Chattarpur State.

"To the east of this shrine of Nandin are the ruins of a large mediæval temple which was the main shrine and contained the *linga* of Siva. It is now called the temple of Surajmukhi. The platform on which this temple was built, stands on a high mound of earth. The only portions now remaining of this magnificent shrine, are the base and the core of the *garbhagriha*. The niches on the exterior of the sanctum are now empty. Three stone steps on the west lead from the mound to the platform on which the temple stands. The floor of the ruined *mandapa* is 4′ higher than this platform. A portion of the *antarala* is still existing and it was fitted with a neatly carved stone door-frame. Three steps lead down to the floor of the *garbhagriha* which is now empty. There is a fine niche on its back flanked by pilasters.

"To the north of this temple is a plain temple of Mahadeva on the same mound. There is a very small open porch in front on four pairs of dwarf pillars with benches on each side. The *mandapa* is closed on all sides with the exception of an opening in each of its four walls. The front opening leads to the main entrance and that at the back to the *garbhagriha*. The openings in the centre of its side walls lead to small bays, which are really *ardhamandapas* of the same type and size as the porch in front, but enclosed with benches having backrests. Six pilasters along the back and front walls and two along each of the side walls, together with eight pillars in two rows in the middle, support the heavy weight of the flat roof of the *mandapa*. The sanctum is a very small square chamber, its floor being slightly lower than that of the *mandapa*.

Nagaur in Marwar.

"The old city of Nagaur in Marwar historically known as Nagapur, Nagadurga or Nagagadh, is situated at a distance of about 1½ miles from the Railway station of that name on the Jodhpur-Bikaner Railway. It is 80 miles to the north-east of Jodhpur and 99 miles by rail from it. It is said to have been founded by Rai Visal of Pandrali State, under commands from Prithviraja, the last Chauhan Emperor of Delhi in 1165 A. D. The ancient remains in and around Nagaur City were first visited by Mr. H. B. W. Garrick in the working season of the year 1883-84. Then a preliminary list of antiquarian remains in Rajputana was drawn up by this Department during 1904-10. The monuments of this place were described at some length in the Archæological Survey of India Report, Vol. XXIII. An account of an interesting old monument known by the name of Shams Khan's Masjid situated near Shams Tal or Shamshi Talao, is given on pages 64-69 of the report. The masjid is said to have been built by Shams Khan who was Governor of Nagaur during the reign of Shams-ud-din Altamsh in the beginning of the thirteenth century A.D. It is constructed of stones of different varieties and sizes in lime mortar, and there is no doubt about the fact that the materials used in this building were obtained from Hindu temples. Some sculptures and carvings are still seen at the back of stones built into the drum of the central dome which collapsed long ago. The front façade of the building is pierced by five arch openings, four small ones, two each on either side of a large one in the centre. It is flanked by two tapering minarets and their tops are covered with conical or bullet-shaped domes. They are constructed on top of the terrace instead of building them from the ground level. There are spiral staircases inside them. Two flights of steps built in the thickness of the

Nagaur in Marwar. walls at the ends, lead first to two mezzanine galleries inside the masjid intended for ladies, and thence to the terrace. Mr. Garrick could not account for the use of the galleries and he described them as 'false floors.' Two windows light the stairs to the north and south walls. Access is gained to the top of the front arches by narrow open steps built into the inside face of the front wall and also by covered steps built inside the haunches of the central big arch. Of the three *mihrabs* inside the masjid, the central one is well decorated and there is a corresponding buttress outside, but the other two are very simple and have no buttresses outside them. The roofing is constructed of four small and one large domes, supported by pillars and pilasters. The south end of the masjid collapsed long ago and nothing is now seen on the spot. The walls are all plastered over and finished on top by a neat cornice with fillets and dentils. Just underneath the cornice a fine band of recessed cross decorations adorns the walls, and over it, *kanguras* are built. The plaster has fallen down at several places. The details of the masjid appeared 'curiously Gothic' to Mr. Garrick at the time of his visit. They are not so and can very well be classed as middle Pathan. There are three entrances to the courtyard in front. The compound wall has totally disappeared with the exception of the two gateways to the north and east, and traces of the third one to the south are still visible. There are Arabic inscriptions in this building.

"One old mosque with peculiar features in the rear elevation is situated on the southern bank of the Ginani Tal or Talao. The monument is locally known as Akbari Masjid, and was mentioned on pages 53 & 64 of the A. S. R., Vol. XXIII. One inscription in the masjid records that it was built during the time of Shah Akbar in 985 H. Hamid-ud-din Rehani, one of the two early Muhammadan visitors to Nagaur, converted Rai Visal to the Muhammadan faith. After his conversion from Hinduism to Muhammadanism he built a mosque. The one near the Kotwali is called Visal's Masjid. Mr. Garrick was suspicious about the real name of this masjid. A Hindu after his change of religion to Islam would naturally try to erect a mosque, if at all, with some distinctive features in order to draw the attention of visitors to it. It appears that this masjid which is quite different from usual Muhammadan mosques, was built by Rai Visal and not the one near Kotwali. The walls are constructed of stone in lime mortar and are plastered over with various patterns of lotus flowers. The front façade consists of three arches, two small ones on either side of a large one in the centre. It is flanked by two minarets built from the ground level, instead of from the terrace as in Shams Khan's Masjid. Behind the three outer arches in front, three small ones are built to lead into the three chambers of the mosque. Two spiral staircases lead to the terrace as well as to the top of the minars. The tops of the minars are covered with plain semicircular domes and not with conical domes as in Shams Khan's Masjid. The outer surface of the minars was decorated with blue, yellow and other varieties of tiles arranged in different patterns, traces of them being still visible. The back or rear wall is pierced by five windows, which were probably closed with *jali* screens. One is just over the *mihrab* in the central domed chamber and four others, two in one group are built in the centre line of the two side chambers. The plan of the mosque is divided into three squares. Two cross arches are constructed inside dividing the central chamber from the side ones. The three domes are constructed on four solid walls and not on pillars. The dome over the central square is higher than the two at its sides. Behind the central *mihrab* a projecting two-storied *jharoka* is built just at the sill level of the window above the *mihrab* referred to above. There are four flights of cantilever steps. Access is gained to the lower portion by two flights of steps from the terrace at the lower level, and the other two flights from the central portion lead to the top floor of the *jharoka*. *Nagaur in Marwar.*

"Outside the Maya gate of the city on the north, a beautifully carved lofty gateway stands in the middle of an enclosure containing various tombs of famous Muhammadans. This gateway is known as Atarkin-ka-darwaza. A description of it is given on pages 69-71 of the A. S. R., Vol. XXIII. Atarkin was a very popular Muhammadan Saint and is venerated by Hindus and Muhammadans alike. According to tradition this building was commenced by the Saint Atarkin and finished by his heir, Khwaja Hussein Chisti under the guidance of an able architect, Sheikh Abdul. On the inside face of the wall on top of this gateway there is a Persian inscription dated 630 A. H. which states that it was repaired by the Emperor Muhammad, son of Tughlaq Shah. This magnificent structure measures 53′ 4″ in height from the ground to the top of the corner *chhattri*. Two three-storied square towers with *chhajjas* and *kanguras* and domes are built against the corners of the front façade to the south. The top of the terrace is reached by six flights of steps, three on each side at the east and west ends. The third flight of steps is built outside for want of space. Just below these steps at both ends there are two doors which lead to the projecting balconies, each of which rests on four carved stone brackets. Only the railings on top are missing. Immediately behind the gateway there is a building constructed of yellow and red limestone. The plan of the structure is divided into two small and one large squares, the large one projecting beyond the two adjacent ones. The walls are finished with decorated *chhajjas*, and carved *kanguras* resting on stone brackets. A band of rosettes of different patterns is seen between the string course and the *chhajja*. The roofing is constructed of two small and one large domes, the height of the central one being more than that of the two side ones. There are different Persian inscription-slabs built into the front of the abutments of the arch to the north. A modern parapet wall built on top of the *kanguras* on the inside face of the main gateway looks very ugly.

"While coming from the city towards the fort, visitors come across a three arched gateway locally known as Tin-Darwaza. It is situated near the fort to the south-west of an ancient building now utilised as a District Court and leads to an enclosed area in front of the fort called Jhaveri Bazar. It is a rectangular structure built of red, yellow and grey limestone. There are three arch openings in front and corresponding ones at the back, towards the fort. The middle arch is larger than the two side ones. Four platforms are built inside the gateway for the use of the guards, two at the ends, and two between the two pairs of piers of the central arches. Eight small *jharokas* are built on two long sides of the gateway. Four are in the middle of the piers on both sides and four in the end abutments of the small arches. The roofing is constructed of stone slabs and concrete and no cross arches divide the ceiling inside.

"Of the various buildings inside the fort the elevations of two of them are shewn in Photograph No. 5834. The two-storied structure with three arch openings and a *baithak* or lounge in the centre is known by the name of a Kacheri or law court. There are two doors in front leading up to the first floor. The building to the right with fine *jalis* and projecting *jharokas* with curvilinear *chhajjas* is called 'Ranvas' or the Queen's abode."

Apart from the incidental excavation work carried out at Nalanda in connexion with the conservation of the ancient remains previously exposed (an account of which appears **Central Circle.** *Nalanda.*

Central Circle. earlier in this report, pp. 19-ff.) there is nothing to record under the head of exploration in the Central Circle during the year 1921-22.

Eastern Circle. *Paharpur.* There was no excavation in the Eastern Circle during 1921-22. A sum of Rs. 848-9-8 was, however, spent from the budget of the Circle for the acquisition of land at the Paharpur mound in Rajshahi District where it is hoped that excavations will be undertaken during 1922-23 under the direction of Professor D. R. Bhandarkar of the Calcutta University. The scheme is to be financed partly by the Government of India and partly by Kumar Sarat Kumar Roy of Dighapatiya, who by his munificent donations and active interest in the cause of archæology has set a rare example to his countrymen. An Imperial grant of Rs. 2,000 made during the year to supplement the Kumar Saheb's contribution, was spent in purchasing implements for the impending operations.

Notes on places visited by Mr. Dikshit.

Tamluk. " *Tamluk.*—(Ancient Tamralipti, Damalipta, etc.). This ancient port of Bengal which is mentioned so frequently in early Buddhist and classical literature is rather disappointing to the antiquarian. There are few high mounds now left to mark the position of the ancient city, but the mound on which the Mission house is situated, another on which the temple of Bargabhima stands and the high land close to the river bed, from which a hoard of ancient coins (some of which are described below) was recovered some 40 years ago, must be considered to cover some of the ground occupied by ancient Tamralipta. The antiquity of the Mission Mound has been demonstrated by the find of wood among layers of blue clay extending over several feet at a depth of about 50 feet from the top, during the course of digging a well. The pieces of wood and samples of clay were shown to me by Miss Blake of the Mission house, and I have no doubt that they are entirely similar to the wooden remains discovered in the excavations of Pataliputra, the antiquity of Tamralipta being as great as that of the other city. Of the existing tanks the only ones that can claim a certain antiquity are the Khat Pukur to the east of the Rajbari or the Kaibartta Raja's residence, and the one adjoining the school. The former is nearly square and probably dates from about the 15-16th century. The other tank is oblong and must be more ancient, as a number of old brick walls are reported to have been discovered during its re-excavation a few years ago. The antiquities recovered from the high mound on the river bank referred to above are now preserved, at least partially, at the local High School. A collection of some 350 coins, mostly of the rectangular cast type was examined by me, and also some terracottas, all dating from about the Sunga period or a century or two before the Christian era. Two main types, described below, account for almost all the coins examined, the first represented by some 250, the second by some 100 specimens.

TYPE I.—Rectangular cast (Ref. I. M. C., Vol. I, p. 200, coin 4).

Obv.—Taurine, tree-in-railing, and chaitya with three arches.

Rev.—Square cross, elephant, swastika and triangular-headed symbol.

TYPE II.—Round cast coins (Ref. I. M. C., Vol. I, Pt. XXIII, 3).

Obv.—Three arches with crescent.

Rev.—Elephant.

Of the terracottas, two rams with twisted horns and foliated garlands around the neck remind one of similar toys discovered in the excavations at Bhita (*vide* the Annual Report of the Director-General of Archæology for 1911-12, p. 73) and others acquired at Kosam (ancient Kausambi) in Allahabad District and now in the Provincial Museum, Lucknow.

Another fine terracotta preserved only up to the waist, represents a standing figure with out-stretched arms, the central body line from the navel upwards being clearly visible. Another miniature terracotta plaque, though rather badly broken, has enough of the head-dress preserved to show that the style was similar to the bas-reliefs of Sanchi and Bharhut. The coins and terracotta leave no doubt as to the date of the find, which must be about the 1st-2nd century B. C. *Tamluk.*

" The most famous monument of modern times at Tamluk is the temple of Bargabhīma, standing on the top of a mound in the heart of the town. The place is one of the 52 *pithasthanas* of the Sakta cult, *i.e.*, one of the holy centres, hallowed by the falling of one of the parts of the dead body of Sati, the first wife of Siva. The name Bargabhīma is peculiar to Tamluk and not met with anywhere else. The shrine is small. In the ante-chamber, stone is used between bricks, an unusual mode of construction. The Jagmohan, Nat-mandir, etc., seem to have been thoroughly renewed.

" *Gaganesvar.*—This place is about 18 miles from Khargpur, 15 miles up to Kesiari Thana being metalled and the rest *kutcha.* There is also a *kutcha* road from Contai Road Railway Station, about seven miles distant from Gaganesvar. The name seems to have been derived from a temple of Siva so named, originally built in the middle of the fifteenth century by King Kapilesvara Deva of the Suryavamsi dynasty of Orissa, in whose dominions was included the southern portion of the present district of Midnapore. The temple stood in the centre of a rectangular cloistered stone enclosure, but was destroyed probably during the invasion of Orissa by Hussain Shah, the Sultan of Bengal (*circa* 1509 A. D.) when a part of the building was converted into a mosque. The latter has in its turn fallen into disuse and now the stone enclosure is known to the local people as the 'Karambera' or 'Kurumbera' Garh, though it is doubtful whether it ever served the purpose of a fort. The monument was first brought to public notice by Mr. W. Herschel of the Bengal Civil Service in his article entitled, *Description of a Hindu Temple converted into a Mosque at Gaganesvar, Zila Medinipur* (J. A. S. B., Vol. XXXVII for 1868, pp. 73—76). It was subsequently included in the List of Ancient Monuments in Bengal published under authority in 1895, but no action was taken in regard to its preservation until 1920, when it was declared protected under the Ancient Monuments Preservation Act. On my visit to the place in April 1921, I found that the monument was a particularly interesting and well-preserved Hindu relic earlier than any other extant Hindu building in Bengal proper. The repairs recommended by me in an inspection and conservation note drawn up after my visit, have been sanctioned and are to be executed during 1922-23. In plan the building is oblong, measuring 262 feet in length and 175 feet in breadth externally. The walls are from 12 to 15 feet in height and are constructed of huge laterite blocks, laid dry as in other old Hindu buildings. On the inner side a pillared verandah runs along the entire length of the enclosure wall, excepting the gateway on the north, which is the sole means of access to the interior. The arches of the cloisters are of the corbelled type, springing from squat heavy piers of stone interspaced at a distance of about 8 feet. The ceiling slab of each of the cloisters is carved with a lotus, which is practically the only ornamentation to be found. The number of cloisters is twenty-five each on the longer sides and sixteen each on the shorter. Some of them have been seriously damaged owing to the sinkage of the pillars and the consequent displacement of the corbelled roof. The main wall has been breached for some length at the south-west corner and some of the adjoining cloisters are in a dilapidated condition. The Uriya inscription *Gaganesvar.*

Gaganesvar. recording the building of the 'bera' or enclosure is fixed in the wall in this corner. The sanctum of the original temple which must have faced west is now represented by a well, which Mr. Herschel tells us, was dug by a pious or treasure-seeking Brahman, who had given out that the *linga* had retired there. The superstructure of the main temple and Jagmohan was entirely demolished by the Muhammadans, but the plinth of the Jagmohan, to the west of the sanctum, partly served as the foundation for the mosque. The latter is a small building of simple design, measuring only 23 feet by 14 feet, with three bays surmounted by weak spheroidal domes built of rubble masonry. All the domes have cracked and one has already fallen in. The peculiarities of the mosque, as already noted by Mr. Herschel, are the unusually small size of the door-openings and the existence of a true radiating arch crowning a corbelled one.

Bharat Bhayna. "*The stupa mound at Bharat Bhayna.*—This monument is situated on the southern bank of the old bed of the Bhadra river in the water-logged tract of land to the west of Khulna, at a distance of about 13 miles from Daulatpur on the Satkhira-Daulatpur Road. It still stands to a height of about 40 to 45 feet above the level of the surrounding lands, though the local people say that before the earthquake of 1897 it was still higher. It is fairly circular in shape, its circumference at the base being about 800 to 900 feet. It is full of bricks of large size, many of which have been removed by the inhabitants of neighbouring villages. A modern temple close to the mound is reported to be built almost wholly with materials obtained in this way. Some of the bricks here measure 16″×13″×3″, which bespeaks a high antiquity for the stupa. Comparing with this the dimensions of bricks of known periods found in the excavations at Saheth-Maheth, it can be safely surmised that the stupa at Bharat Bhayna dates back at least to the Gupta period, roughly the fifth century A. D. It is probable that this was one of the 30 Sangharamas mentioned by Hiuen Tsang as existing in his time in the Samatata country, in which modern Khulna must have been comprised at the time. Steps are being taken to bring the mound within the provisions of the Ancient Monuments Preservation Act.

Math at Kodlah. "*Math at Kodlah or Ayodhya.*—This is situated about 2½ miles from Jatrapur Station on the Khulna-Bagerhat Railway. From a fragmentary inscription in Bengali characters over the cornice it seems that the Math was built by some Brahman (the latter part of the donor's name is Sarma) and dedicated to Taraka (the "Saviour," meaning probably Brahma). The building still rises to a height of 45 to 50 feet from the ground level and is a rather pleasing structure with the straight horizontal lines of its corniced spire intersected by the wavy vertical lines of the projections. It is built of fine-chiselled red bricks with thin joints. In plan, it consists of a square cell (measuring inside 10′ 4″ sq.) with 8′ thick walls and 3 entrances, one in each direction except the north, the main door facing the south. The door-way arches are of the overlapping type, but the pendentives have pointed arches, supporting a circular roof. The exterior face is polygonal in plan with five recesses on either side of the central face making 6 planes and 11 recesses. The top of the tower is damaged, and the south-west corner has been undermined by a *pipal* tree, but otherwise the monument is in fair condition, the brick ornamentation being of a singularly high order. The front side must originally have been profusely decorated, but the best work now left is on the north façade where the central band of the frame of the false door-way has some delicate floral designs in moulded brick-work [*vide* Plate XXVII (*a*)]. The date to which the monument can be assigned is about the sixteenth century A. D. When the necessary preliminaries are over, the building will be declared protected, and preserved at the cost of Government.

"*Sibpur.*—This place is situated about 4 miles to the south of Bagerhat and is named after the so-called Siva image (in reality a Buddhist stele), originally found in the excavation of the tank attached to Khan Jehan Ali's tomb at Bagerhat, and now enshrined in a temple. The stele which has a seated figure of the Buddha in the *bhumisparsa* attitude in the centre, surrounded on all sides by representations of various scenes from his life, is believed to be the only one of its kind ever found in Bengal [Plate XXIX *a*]. Together with another stele originally from Bihar and now exhibited in the Indian Museum, with which it can be compared in many particulars, the Sibpur stele can be studied as an illustration of the manner in which the Buddha story was treated in the Eastern school of sculpture. It is 3′ 7″ in height and is made of black basalt. It is regularly worshipped, in course of which milk, oil and other sticky substances are poured on it and have obscured some of the details which might have thrown light on the identity of the incidents depicted. *Sibpur.*

"Unlike the representations of the four or eight great incidents of Buddha's life from Sarnath, where equal space is allotted to all the scenes, the enlightenment of the Buddha is depicted in the present sculpture as the main and pivotal incident and occupies the bulk of the central space, while all the other events preceding or following it, serve to beautify and fill up the space left at the sides.* The central Buddha figure is 1′ in height and is seated in the *vajrâsana*, with his finger pointed towards the earth, under a trefoil arch supported on two pillars and crowned by a spire similar to that of a temple of the familiar Orissa type. The lotus seat is supported by elephants, lions and dwarfs. There are leogryphs by the side and on the spire there is a miniature repetition of the scene itself. The story of Buddha's life begins at the lower half of the proper left, where the birth scene is depicted. Here we see the mother of the Buddha standing under the branch of a tree in the Lumbini garden and the new-born Buddha by her side, the other details being omitted. Below this, at the proper left bottom is the scene of the examination of the horoscope by the sages Asita and Nārada. In the lower of the two panels below the central figure, is represented the Great Renunciation scene; while the upper panel depicts Māra and his wife seated together, with the women forming his army in various attitudes before them. The course of austerities followed by the Buddha and his protection by the Naga Muchalinda are shown in the panels at the right lower end. The first sermon is indicated by the Buddha in the *dharmachakra-mudrā* in the right centre and the top is occupied by the Great Decease. The space between the sikhara of the central temple and the edge of the stone is mostly occupied by various gods, attending the Buddha, prominent among whom may be noticed Indra and his consort, four-handed Vishnu on Garuda, Brahmā, Kārttikeyā, Varuna, etc. Of the minor scenes delineated on the sculpture, the offering of the monkey, the subduing of the elephant Nālāgiri at Rajagriha, the chastening of the robbers and the Great Miracle at Srāvasti can be recognised with more or less certainty. The age to which the present stele can be assigned on the grounds of style is about the 11th-12th century A. D.

"*Bhandirban.*—Bhandirban is about 4 miles to the west of Suri, the headquarters of the Birbhum District. Though the name of the place sounds very ancient, it is reputed to have been a wilderness until Ramnath Bhaduri, the Diwan of the Murshidabad Nawabs, re-discovered it and built the present temple of Bhandisvara [Plate XXVII *b*] in the year 1754 (Sāka 1676) as the inscription fixed in the front wall of the temple informs us. The style of architecture of the laterite stone temple built by Bhaduri is *Bhandirban.*

* This general type of composition is common at Nalanda. [ED.]

Bhandirban. similar to the tall pyramida sikharal type, developed in the Rādha country or south-west Bengal, the Ichai Ghosh Temple in the Burdwan District and the Jatar Deul Temple in the Sunderbans being noteworthy examples, both prior in date to the present example by at least a century. The spire is about 45 feet high. The exterior surface of the temple is quite plain. The floor of the shrine is 5 feet lower than the level of the platform, as is the case with many Saiva shrines. The enshrined *linga* is a natural boulder with the *arghya* built of stone masonry. To the right is a stone image representing a four-handed goddess probably Durga, seated cross-legged, and holding a sword, trisula and lotus respectively in the lower right, lower left and upper left hands. At a short distance from the temple is a stone platform used in the *dol* festival of the neighbouring Gopala Temple. The Bhandirban temple has been recommended to the Government of Bengal for protection, in case the Maharajadhiraj of Burdwan, in whose Zemindary the place is situated, has no objection.

Nannoor. "*Nannoor.*—Nannoor is about 5 miles from Kirnahar Railway Station on the Ahmadpur-Katwa Section of the Burdwan-Katwa Railway. It owes its celebrity to its association with the Bengali poet Chandi Das, whose mound, with the adjoining group of thirteen temples, including that of the goddess Bishalakshi, the poet's favourite deity, are now maintained by Government as protected monuments under agreement with the owners. The temples are mostly of the single-cell pyramidal roof type, not earlier than the seventeenth century, and the temple of Basuli in particular has a very modern appearance. Repairs to these temples are being suggested and will be taken up as soon as funds are available.

Bhadisvar. "*Bhadisvar.*—This place is situated a little to the east of the Railway Station of Murarai. The image of Manasā which is lying in a hut by the side of the road is an excellent example of the representation of the snake-goddess so popular in Bengal. She has a hood of seven cobras, holds a cobra in her left hand, has a breast-band formed by serpents, is attended by a serpent-maid, and the vase (*ghata*) below her seat contains other cobras. The goddess is seated on a double lotus seat in the *līlāsana* pose and wears all the ornaments generally found on images of goddesses. [*Vide* Plate XXVIII (*c*).]

"Another image which lies half-buried in the ground close to the image of Manasā, is that of Hara-gauri, the God Siva seated with his consort Pārvati. The Ūrdhvalinga symbolizing the celibacy of Siva is a peculiarity worth noting in this image.

"At the north end of the village is situated a mound called Shashtitala, which the villagers believe to have been the site of a Raja's palace. It is about 10′ to 12′ in height and 100′×10′ in dimensions. Bricks measuring about $11\frac{1}{2}'' \times 9\frac{1}{2}''$ are scattered all over the mound and the alignment of walls is clearly traceable on all sides. Another smaller mound to the north is supposed by the local people to be the site of a Siva temple. Judging from the remains to be found in the vicinity, the mounds must date back at least to the 10th or 11th century A. D. As a preliminary step it is proposed to bring them within the provision of the Ancient Monuments Preservation Act.

Paikore. "*Paikore.*—The most important epigraphical discovery of late in Bengal is that of the inscribed pillars at Paikore (first noticed in Bengali in the '*Birbhum-Bibaran,*' Vol. II, page 10). The inscriptions refer to the Chedi King Karna [Plate XXVIII *a*] and King Vijayasena, respectively [Plate XXVIII *b*]. The former's invasion of Bengal was before the discovery of this inscription, a mere conjecture based on some expressions found in the Prasastis of the Kalachuris and in the Tibetan life of the Buddhist saint Atīsa Dipankara. The present record of Karnarāja places the event beyond the realm of controversy. It is very probable that Karna following up his victory over Rājyapāla, the Gurjara King of Kanauj, proceeded eastwards and invaded the dominions of the Pālas. His route must have been through south Bihar (ancient Magadha) and Bhagalpur (ancient Anga), till he came to the Rādha country. The situation of Paikore at the north-western limit of the Rādha country suggests that as soon as the invading monarch penetrated so far into the heart of the Pāla domains, the Pāla King must have made peace with the invader. It is easy to assume that the gift of the image must have been made by Karna during his sojourn in Bengal when negotiations were going on between the princes, which probably culminated in peace, strengthened by a matrimonial alliance, whereby Yauvanasri, the daughter of Karna, was given in marriage to the Pāla prince Vigrahapāla III. Paikore is about three miles to the east of the Murarai Station on the Loop Line of the E. I. Railway. The name is supposed to be a corrupted form of Prāchīkot, or the 'Eastern Citadel.' The authors of the Bengali Gazetteer display much ingenuity in speculating about the names of this place and other places in the neighbourhood, such as Nongarh, Mitrapur, etc. They have also recorded certain extraordinary features among the religious usages obtaining at this place, *e.g.*, the existence of a Vaishnavite shrine where animal sacrifices are allowed (contrary to the usual practice), the custom of offering the *tulasi* leaves to God Siva, and the celebration of a peculiar ceremony, known as the 'Banavrata' in the month of Magha. On the basis of these peculiar customs an antiquity of at least seven or eight centuries is claimed for this place, which is further corroborated by the existence of a number of images and inscribed pillars. *Paikore.*

"The most important antiquities at Paikore are the two inscribed pillars at Narayanachatvara lying on a masonry platform by the side of a tank, along with an image of Narasimha and several others. Both the pillars seem to have been crowned by images, and the inscriptions engraved on them must have referred to the dedication of the images. The Vijayasena pillar clearly exhibits the headless figure of the goddess Manasā, while the Karnadeva pillar being broken off just at the commencement of the inscription shows no trace of the image. The pillars must have been sunk into the floor, as we see from the rough-hewn surface of the lowermost portion of the Karnadeva pillar, the square and octagonal sections of the shaft above being highly polished and decorated with beautiful tracery. The design on each side of the square section is that of a vase (*mangala kalasa*) the top and bottom of which are covered with full-blown lotuses and foliage while at the centre appears a *kīrtimukha*, the necklaces of pearls issuing from which are held by bearded attendants. The carving of this pillar has been done so beautifully as to entitle the sculptor to a high rank. It is very probable that the artist belonged to Bengal, rather than to the Chedi country, firstly because the polish and finish of the black basalt stone from the Rajmahal hills used in the sculpture indicates a thorough mastery over the material, which cannot be acquired without the efforts of generations; and, secondly, the inscription engraved on the pillar is not in the Central Indian script, but in the Proto-Bengali characters prevalent in N. E. India.

"The inscription, which consists of six lines, is rather hastily engraved. It begins on the tapering circular portion of the shaft, and is continued over the octagonal section.

Paikore. It is written in shallow, cursive letters of the 11th century north-eastern characters. It was first partially deciphered by Mahāmahopādhyāya Hara Prasād Sāstrī, whose tentative readings were published in the *Birbhum-bibaran*, without facsimiles. It is with some diffidence that I publish below my own readings of the inscription —

1. *Srī Srī Gaṇapati.*
2.
3. *Om deva-dvija-guru [bhajah] ntari.....*
   daya bhaktinānta X
4. *nehayan—X [sraddha] yā-smin karmmaṇi rājasrī-Karṇadeva*
5. *Om svasti samṛiddha rājya-srī-Chedi*
   r (ā jya) śrī-Karṇa-deva [sya]
   jya nantarā kīrti prasāsti (?).

   Śrī viśva karmā charaṇa-prasādāt
   devī-murtti nrimita X ptīya Śrī Kārtti.....

"The gist of the record seems to be that at the order of King Karnadeva of Chedi, an image of the goddess was made by a certain sculptor.

"The other inscription reads—*Rajena-Sri-Vijayase.*

"Besides the pillars, several interesting images mostly fragmentary or obliterated, representing Vishnu, Hara-Gauri, Astabhuja, etc., are collected and now lying about the platform at Narayana-chatvara. One of these, the image of Nrisimha, of which the head is separated from the torso, is particularly interesting [Plate XXVIII *d*]. The scene of the appearance of the man-lion incarnation from the midst of a pillar, which the proud and unbelieving Asura Hiranyakasipu had the audacity to kick, has been depicted here to the left of the main figure. The story as narrated in various Puranas is practically unanimous in saying that the occasion for the appearance of the incarnation was the kicking of the pillar by the Asura as a challenge to his son Prahlad, who would argue with his father that his God existed everywhere—in land and water, wood and stone. In the Paikore image, we probably had on the right of the main figure the earlier scene at the throne-room of the Asura King, where the recalcitrant son was summoned to his father's presence, and questioned about his belief. We only see the left half of a figure seated on a throne with a standing figure turned towards the former probably in the attitude of making obeisance. We can easily identify the two figures as Hiranyakasipu* and Prahlad respectively. In the scene to the left of the central figure, we see Hiranya raising his right leg to the very top of the pillar, and the half-length figure of the man-lion emerging out of the pillar with the right hand raised. The concave curve described by the up-turned leg of Hiranya is unnatural, but is frequently met with in Indian sculpture, especially in connection with the Vamana or dwarf incarnation of Vishnu. The main man-lion image is shown as trampling on a prostrate figure with the left foot and with the two lower hands cutting open the abdomen and drawing out the entrails of the Asura, who lies in a recumbent position resting on the knee of the incarnation. The upper two hands of the figure are lost. The mane of the lion is disposed

* *Vide* Matsya-purana.

on either side of the face to resemble an aura. A long garland reaching to the knees and a necklace, torque, bracelets, armlets and the other usual ornaments decorate the body. The two kneeling figures on the pedestal probably denote the donor and his wife. The image cannot be later than the 12th century in date. *Paikora.*

"Another collection of sculptures housed in a small room in the Bura Sibtala quarter of the village, contains some interesting pieces. One of these is a fine Makara head with the characteristic small ears and big twisted horns. Another interesting image is a four-handed one, identified by Mr. Nagendra Nath Vasu as representing the Lokesvara of Mahayanism ; but the identification is open to great doubt. Two of the hands of the figure hold a conch and *akshamala* respectively, the other two being placed over the heads of two figures standing by the sides, one of which is a male and the other a female. The presence of a high crown (*mukuta*) on the head and matted hair (*jata*) on the shoulders, and a long garland reaching to the knees, makes it more probable that the image was Brahmanical, most probably a form of Harihara. A peculiar feature of another image here, representing the Sun-god, is the presence of a lotus on the pedestal in place of the usual seven horses drawing the Sun's chariot. One of the epithets of the Sun-god as found in the sadhanas is *padmasanah* (or lotus-seated), but this only refers to the lotus-seat on which the God may be represented as seated and not to the vehicle. The present image is, however, standing, and has all the other usual charateristics, *viz.*, lotuses in the hands, high *kirita* and boots, and Pingala and Danda holding the ink-pot and the lance respectively on either side.

"A short inscription in twelfth century characters on a *linga*, mentions one Pahidatta, who was most probably the donor of the *linga*.

"The only part of India where the once paramount religion of Buddha is still a living faith today with at least a section of the population, is Chittagong and its neighbourhood. There are, however, no great traditions of long standing among the Buddhist population, nor does the country abound in remains of antiquity such as stupas, viharas or even images connected with the practice of the Buddhist religion. Literary evidence about the antiquity of Chittagong compiled from Tibetan sources by the late Rai Bahadur Sarat Chandra Das, was published in a note in the J. A. S. B. for 1898, pages 20-28. We read there that in the seventh century A. D. when Gopi Chandra the son of Vimala Chandra ruled over East Bengal, with his capital at Chatigrama (the ancient name of Chittagong) there were many Tirthika or Brahmanical temples and viharas of the Buddhists, the latter belonging mostly to the Tantrik Mahayana school. We further note that the city of Chatigrama was the capital of the Ramma (lit ; beautiful) country and was the headquarters of Buddhism after the decline of Nalanda. *Chittagong.*

"There was a large Buddhist monastery at Chatigaon called the Pandita-vihara. The origin of the Lamaistic conical cap, called in Tibetan *pan-shva* or the Pandit's cap, is traced to a successful religious controversy against the Brahmanas held at the Pandita-vihara by the Buddhist Pandits, who were led by a person wearing a pointed cap. In the tenth century the great Tantrik Buddhist sage Tila-yogi is said to have lived in Chatigaon. It is satisfactory to note that at the Buddhist monastery recently established in Chittagong, a number of ancient Buddhist images in bronze, stone and wood found mostly in Chittagong district have been collected, thanks to the energy of the learned Bhikkhu in charge, Rev. U. Dhammavansa, lecturer in Pali at the local College. These images thus offer a substantial corroboration of the evidence obtained from

Chittagong.

Tibetan works as to the existence of Mahayanism in Chittagong at least from the 8-9th century. Through the courtesy of the reverend lecturer, I was able to obtain photographic records of 13 of the images described below. They represent the Buddha, Padmapani Avalokitesvara, Tara and other cult images, and range in date from about the 9th century to the 12th or 13th, being closely allied to the products of the Magadha school. The bronzes are similar in workmanship to the Nalanda bronzes and it is possible to imagine that the worshippers in this remote corner of India requisitioned images from more inland parts of the country, unless they had them manufactured locally in imitation of models obtained from the Magadha country. A detailed description of these Buddhist images in Chittagong follows :—

(1) Bronze image (height 7¼") of Buddha seated in the *Bhumisparsa mudra* originally found in a mosque. The left hand is placed palm upwards a little below the navel. The right hand passing over the knee-joint points to the earth. The end of the upper garment hangs in folds from the left shoulder. A *vajra* is shown in the centre of the pedestal. The original bronze colour with its green patina is still preserved in this image. There is a circular seal on the back, as in the Nalanda images, which must once have contained the Buddhist creed. The inscription on the pedestal in characters of the 10th-11th century reads—

'*1. Om deya-dharmmo-yam pravara-mahayayinah*
x cha (?) *ndra vijaya putrasya* (?) *yadatra......*
2. mata pitri..........................'

(2) Bronze image (height 7¼") of Buddha seated in the *Bhumisparsa mudra*; similar to No. (1) in almost every respect; covered with gold leaf. Inscription on pedestal in one line, consisting of the Buddhist creed and the words—

'*deya-dharmo-yam Dharmikasya*'—the gift of Dharmika.

(3) Bronze image of Padma-pani (?) Avalokitesvara (height 9"), seated on a lotus seat; left hand on seat behind left leg; right hand holding lotus bud supported on right knee; decorated with all the usual ornaments; has a *dhyani*-Buddha in his crest; lotus-stalk to left. Inscription on the petals of the lotus-seat in triangle-headed characters of about the 9th-10th century,—

'*Om deya-dharmo-yam Nagirikasya*'—the gift of Nagirika.

(4) Stone bas-relief (height 7") of Tara; seated in the *lilasana*; holds the stalk of a lotus in the left hand, the right being placed over the knee; fully ornamented; stupa in relief on the back slab; lions couchant on either side; kneeling figures in front on pedestal, probably representing donor and his wife. The inscription in 7 lines in characters of the 9th century on the back reads,—

'1. *Om ye dharma hetupra*

2. *bha (ava) hetum tesanta* 3. *thagatah evam vani jo*

4. *nirodho brihadharma* 5. *mahasramah* 6. *Om ye dharma paramopa*

7. *sakah Kadainda.'* Chittagong.

The first five lines give a corrupt and incomplete creed; the last two give the name of the donor which was Kadainda.

(5) Bronze image (height 6") of Padmapani Avalokitesvara seated in the *lilasana*; circular halo behind; covered with silver leaf; left hand holds stalk of lotus; dhyani-buddha in crest. Inscription on pedestal below lotus seat—

deya-dharmo—yam Sri Haritaka (?)

(6) Bronze image (height 5") of Tara seated in the *lilasana*; circular halo behind; covered with silver leaf; uninscribed.

(7) Hollow bronze cast image (height 4¼") (most probably of foreign origin) of Buddha, seated in the *Bhumisparsa mudra*; on reverse, stupa with 10 umbrellas. The technique is very defective, as shown by the bulging eyes.

(8) Bronze image (height 6") of Buddha standing in the *Abhaya mudra*. Small round seal on reverse.

(9) Bronze image (height 3¾") of Buddha, seated in the *Bhumisparsa mudra*; oval shaped halo with beaded border, behind; square pedestal with double lotus seat; on reverse, small round seal inscribed with Buddhist creed in 11th century characters.

(10) Bronze image (height 4¼") of Jambhala, seated in the *lilasana*, with right foot hanging down and the left folded on the seat. The god is characterized by the distended abdomen and the row of seven auspicious jars on the pedestal; his left hand holds a toy elephant and the right holds some kind of fruit; the figure is fully ornamented.

(11) Small soapstone sculpture (length 3½") shaped like a boat with a lamp receptacle on the left and a bearded sadhu with distinctly Chinese features, leaning on it to the right. This must have been left by some Chinese visitor or pilgrim.

(12) Bronze image (height 3½") of Buddha, seated cross-legged, with the hands in the *Dharmachakra-mudra*; behind, broken halo with decorated borders; on reverse, ring with hole, meant for holding the staff of an umbrella.

(13) Wooden image (height 7") of Buddha, seated on double-lotus seat in the *Bhumisparsa mudra*; *Vajra* in front and branches of the Bodhi tree on the halo behind the head; surface damaged and cracked; right arm broken; originally from Vikrampur, District Dacca.

"*Devikot of Bangarh.*—The ancient city of Kotivarsha, which was the seat of a district (*vishaya*) under the Paundra-vardhana province (*bhukti*) at the time of the Guptas; (*vide* the article on the Domodarpur plates *Epi. Ind.* Vol. XV, pages 133—145) is now represented by the extensive mounds of Bangarh or Ban Rajar Garh on the Punarbhaba, about 16 miles from Dinajpur and 2 miles from Gangarampur Police Station. The older site was in continuous occupation till the invasion of the Muhammadans in the thirteenth century to whom it was known as Devkot or Devikot. It possesses Muhammadan records ranging from the thirteenth to the sixteenth century. The later Sanskrit Lexicons Haima and Trikanda mention Devikota, Kotivarsha, Banapura, Sonitapura, and Bangarh.

Bangarh. Umavana as different names of one and the same place. The last two are not known from any other source to denote the present site, but it is interesting to find that Banapura and Sonitapura are synonymous terms applied to the modern town of Tezpur in Assam. The fact seems to be that the names of kings like Bana and Birata, well known in popular mythology, were foisted at one time or other on different places laying claim to antiquity.

" The extant ruins at Bangarh are almost in the same condition as they were when described by General Cunningham, more than forty years ago (A. S. R., Vol. XV, pages 95—100). The thick jungle that existed in his time is not there, and the level area on the top is now cultivated by Santals. The Rajbari mound at the south-east corner is one of the highest mounds at Bangarh and must contain some important remains. The Dargah of Sultan Pir is a Muhammadan shrine built on the site of an old Hindu temple of which four granite pillars each 15′ in height are still standing in the centre of the enclosure, the door jambs having been used in the construction of the gateway.

" The Dargah of Shah Ata on the north bank of the Dhaldighi tank is another building built on the ruins of an older Hindu or Buddhist structure. The four inscriptions noticed by Cunningham are still preserved in the walls of the Dargah. The walls are in good condition, but overgrown with jungle trees. The tops of the wall have a surkhi plaster coping and it is very doubtful if the inner apartment of the Dargah ever had the domed roof Cunningham supposed. The female figure on the lintel of the doorway now fixed in the east wall of the Dargah appears to be Tara, from which it would seem that the temple destroyed was Buddhist. It is proposed to bring the Dargah within the provisions of the Ancient Monuments Preservation Act, for the sake of the inscriptions.

" A fine terracotta head (height 9″) discovered in the ruins of Bangarh was picked up by me from a modern Siva temple and presented to the Indian Museum, Calcutta (*vide* Plate XXIX *b*). Its thick lower lip, straight nose, and broad forehead are among the most noticeable features ; and it can safely be assigned to a period not later than the early Pala period (8th-9th century). Another stone at the same Siva temple is a fragmentary door-jamb ornamented with beautiful scroll-work containing figures of men and animals.

" The Rajbari or Raja's palace at Dinajpur contains several important pillars, architectural stones and images taken from Bangarh. The best known antiquity here is the inscribed basalt pillar of the Kamboja king, whose date has been the subject of a long controversy. Another sandstone pillar crowned by a black basalt image of Garuda is standing in the courtyard of the temple of Kaliya-kanta. Other important antiquities in the palace are a miniature shrine with a *sikhara* (spire) of the Orissan temple type, a very beautiful carved doorway, with two female Naginis on the lintel and serpents' coils entwined on the door-jambs, and a collection of images in the eastern enclosure, including an interesting image of a female deity, similar in other respects to Chamunda, but whose vehicle is a horse.

Bahulara. " *Siddhesvara temple at Bahulara.*—Bahulara is about 3 miles distant from Onda station. The temple of Siddhesvara here is one of the finest brick temples in the district. It must have been prior in date to the Vaishnava temples at Vishnupur, as can be seen from its style which is more similar to the older North Indian style than to the later Bengali type. The plan of the temple is polygonal with a tall sikhara (54 feet in height) the surface of which is richly decorated with moulded bricks, one of the ornamentations being a repetition of the temple itself. The shrine is approached through a portico in the thickness of the wall, with a tall triangular corbelled arch opening. By the side of the linga which is the main object of worship there is an interesting standing image of the Jaina Tirthankara Parsvanatha (see Plate XXIX *d*). Besides the usual accompaniments of a seven-hooded cobra canopy over the head, the chowrie-bearers by the side, a male and female Naga attendant below the lotus seat, and Gandharvas flying in the air, it is interesting to find on the back slab of the image, seated figures of the 8 planets (Ketu being omitted), four on each side. *Bahulara.*

" *Dharmaghar.* 3½ miles from Harashpur Railway Station on the Tippera border, contained an old temple of Kali, which was destroyed during the last earthquake. The image of Kali originally enshrined here is traditionally reported to have been removed to Kasba (District Tippera) by the Tippera king Kalyanmanikya (*circa* 1650 A. D.) through fear of desecration by Muhammadans, who then threatened to invade this part. The only interesting object now left here is a bronze-image of Buddha (height 8") seated in the *Bhumisparsa mudra* with the branches of the Bodhi tree overhead. A peculiarity noticeable in this image is the existence of some object in Buddha's left hand. The border of the halo is decorated with wavy line and cable designs, and on the reverse is seen the circular ring, which must have had the creed stamped on it. [*Vide* Plate XL, Fig. (*b*).] The style of the image is similar to that of the Chittagong bronzes and it may safely be assigned to the 9th or 10th century. No Buddhist antiquities have previously been discovered so far to the north-east. *Dharmaghar.*

" *Comilla, Satara Ratna Temple.*—About two miles to the east of the modern town of Comilla is the Satara Ratna temple built by one of the Rajas of Tripura in the eighteenth century. It is about 45′ to 50′ in height and when complete with its seventeen towers must have commanded respectful attention. As it is, the main spire and a part of the western side alone is preserved, the rest of the temple having fallen at least 25 years ago. The chief architectural feature is the spire with 17 towers, (*Satara-ratna*) a stage in the development of the five tower (*Pancha-ratna*) and nine tower (*Nava-ratna*) type into the full-fledged twenty-five tower (*Pancha-vimsati-ratna*) Sikhara. The plan of the temple consists of an octagonal central room rising to a height of three stories and crowned by a high conical Sikhara, and double octagonal galleries around the sanctum, the inner one reaching to the second story and surmounted by 8 conical Sikharas, the outer one, restricted to the ground floor, being covered by a curved cornice-type roof. The temple is still owned by the Tripura Raj and no action on the part of Government is necessary. *Comilla.*

" *Unakoti* (*Koilashahar Division*).—One of the most important discoveries in Bengal during the year under report is that of the colossal rock-cut sculptures at Unakoti hill in the Koilashahar Division of the Tripura State. The place is about 14 miles from Shamshernagar Railway Station on the A. B. Railway and about 5—6 miles from Koilashahar. It is known to the people of the neighbourhood as an ancient holy place of the Saivas and an annual fair is held in the month of Pausha (January-February) when the State authorities usually clear a path-way through the thick bamboo jungle which grows here so luxuriantly. This year at the instance of the Archæological Superintendent, who first visited the place in November 1921, the State Divisional officer opened a direct road to the hill, cleared jungle and loose earth from the sides of the hill where the rock carvings are situated, and brought to light several new sculptures and rock-cut figures. *Unakoti.*

Unakoti.

" The existence of this interesting group of antiquities was first brought to the notice of this Department in 1914 by Captain Williams, then political agent to the Tripura State. Besides a Bengali pamphlet recently published by Mr. Debabarman of the Botanical Survey, there are no other publications referring to Unakoti. The Rajmala, a Bengali metrical history of the Tripura Raj family, contains two or three references to the visits of some of the Tripura Rajas to this holy place. The name Unakoti (which is also applied to another well-known holy place in Assam, *viz.*, Bishvanath in Tezpur District) means ' one less than a crore ', and the propriety of denoting a *tirtha* by this name will be apparent when it is remembered that Kashi or Benares, the holiest of all holy places is the only Koti-tirtha, (either because it is supposed to contain one crore of Siva-emblems within its boundaries or because of its outstanding religious merit), all other places, however successful in emulating it, falling just short of the crore.

" The remains at Unakoti consist of a number of stone sculptures, now mostly worn and defaced, on the top of the knoll, and others scattered here and there, together with a series of colossal heads and figures carved partly in the rocky bed of a stream which issues from the hills at this place, and partly on the face of the rocky slopes on either side of the stream. The most central and conspicuous figure is the colossal Siva head [Plate XXX *b*] in the stream bed, at the point where it issues from a succession of pools. The spot is one of great natural beauty and the outcrop of stone must have been a great attraction to the religious sculptor. Indeed, the choice of Unakoti as a Tirtha may be due to this combination of circumstances. The activity of the people who popularized the Tirtha by converting large masses of rock surface into images of their gods, must have extended over a fairly long period, but it is a pity that the heavy rainfall and the frequent earthquakes have not left more of the carvings intact.

" The central head is about 30' high, including the high embroidered head-dress which is itself 10' in height. The face is carved out of a flat square block of stone ; the third eye is shown in the middle of the forehead and the mouth is a long narrow slit with vertical lines representing the teeth. The ears are carved on the side in lower planes than the central plane of the face, their lower extremities being hidden beneath bold flower ornaments. The moustache is turned upwards ending in a loop. The figure is much damaged, as can be seen from the crack running through from ear to ear just below the eyes, the flaked off surface at the left cheek and the gaps in the right ear and the head-dress. At some distance to the left are the Trident of Siva and some stone heads, while in front are three representations of Siva's bull. In the rock above the head, the figure of Durga standing on her lion can be distinguished to the right and another female figure to the left.

" On the left bank of the stream there are several colossal rock-cut figures. One of these probably represented Vishnu, as a lozenge-shaped jewel ornaments the breast of the figure, the face being lost. Another gigantic Siva figure has merely the huge ears with ear-rings left. Among the numerous figures on the right bank, two arches, a lion-faced goddess, a standing Siva figure holding the conch (*sankha*) in the right hand and the rosary (*akshamala*) in the left, may be specially mentioned. The last described form is seldom found in other Siva images, but is common at Unakoti. Other peculiar forms in which Siva was worshipped here are represented by three boulders fairly rounded, each with five, eleven, or twenty-eight balls at the top, representing Siva lingas, and on the sides, rows of crude faces in low relief.

"A little lower down the valley a group of Ganesa figures carved in the perpendicular face of the rock in the stream bed was discovered in course of clearance. [Plate XXX *a*]. This group having been so long covered with jungle and earth is in better preservation than the other figures, but its situation in the bed of the stream makes it particularly liable to the action of water. The group consists of a seated Ganesa (height 22') to the extreme left and to his right two standing elephant-headed figures, with an image of Vishnu at the proper right end. Iconographically, the two central figures are unique. They are undoubtedly connected with the cult of Ganesa, but they differ widely from the usual image of that God. They are standing erect, whereas Ganesa is usually seated with his legs apart; they have attenuated waists, while Ganesa has a distended abdomen; they have three and four tusks and six and eight hands respectively, while Ganesa has only one tusk and two or four hands; the objects held as emblems are the *sankha, chakra, akshamala, damaru*, etc., and they have conchs on their ears, a feature not noticed elsewhere. The image of Vishnu at the right end is a standing four-handed image holding the usual *Ayudhas*, the pose resembling that of the Sun-god more than that of Vishnu. *Unakoti.*

"The style of the rock-cut carvings at Unakoti betrays a rudimentary and crude conception of the sculptor's art and illustrates in a remarkable way the canons of primitive art. The anatomical features of the different parts of the body are treated only in their broadest aspects, without any attempt to harmonise the whole. It is extremely difficult to fix the period of the rock-carvings, as no material for comparison with them exists in north-east India. The Surma valley tract is one of the poorest parts of India so far as historical materials or even literary references are concerned. The only indications of the probable age of the sculptures is afforded by the detached stone images, The older collection at the hill-top which has badly weathered contains images of Vishnu, Hara Gauri, Harihara, Narasimha, Ganesa, and Hanuman, which could scarcely be placed earlier than about the 11-12th century. But the discovery of two *chaturmukha-lingas* and an *ekamukha-linga* (lingas with four and one faces respectively) during the year gives for the first time excellent material, which can bear comparison with products of art from other places in Eastern India. The *chaturmukha-linga* (height 3') lying on the bank of the stream a short distance below the Ganesa group, is a fine specimen of early mediæval art. Two of the four figures are in good preservation, and they testify to the skill of the sculptor in delineating the contemplating form of Siva. The beatific smile of the Yogi has been successfully shown on the face [*vide* Plate XXIX (*c*)] The right hand, holding the rosary (*akshamala*) is, true to the canon, shown in the 'treble-bending' (*tribhanga*) pose, as also are the fingers; the left hand holds a *sankha* The ornaments of the figure are a high head-dress, necklace and torque, bracelets, armlets, ear ornaments and a snake in place of the sacred thread. The other *chaturmukha* linga though similar in detail (except that it has one bearded face), is much inferior in execution.

"The only inscriptions at Unakoti are a couple of records in old Bengali characters of the 11-12th century on the last mentioned linga, which mention one Sri-Jayadeva, probably a pilgrim. The linga with one face, which is similar to these, has weathered a good deal and is now enshrined on the highest point of the Unakoti hill.

"On the whole, judging by the extant remains at Unakoti, it may be concluded with some certainty that the site has been sacred to the worship of Siva at least from the 8-9th centuries, if not some centuries earlier."

Places visited in the Southern Circle.

Southern Circle.
Cochin.

Mr. Longhurst could not take up any excavation work this year as, owing to the transfer of his headquarters from Madras to Kotagiri in the Nilgiri District, he was very busy in arranging his records and fixing up the office. Consequently the amount of Rs. 1,000 sanctioned for exploration, lapsed to Government.

The Officiating Superintendent, Pandit Hirananda Shastri, reports, however, that "During his tours of inspection Mr. Longhurst visited several interesting monuments. Some of these have already been described by him in detail in his annual reports, while others like the Bandar Fort at Masulipatam have just been noticed. Of the rest the most important is the church of *St. Francis at Cochin*, which is probably the oldest existing European church in India [Plate XVI(*a*)]. The exact date when it was built is not known, but presumably it owes its origin to the Franciscan Friars who accompanied the first Portuguese expedition under Pedro Alverez Cabrel, and if so it must have come into existence soon after A. D. 1500, the year of the expedition. It is said to have been of wood originally but was soon afterwards re-built in stone. In 1502 Vasco Da Gama landed at Cochin and concluded a treaty of commerce with the local Raja. In 1524 he paid his second visit to Cochin, but this time he came only to die. He expired on the 24th or 25th December and was interred in the chancel of this church, though fourteen years later his corporeal remains were removed to Portugal by one of his sons. In 1663 the Dutch took Cochin and, remaining in possession of it for some one hundred and thirty-two years, greatly improved the town as well as its fortifications. They expelled the Portuguese and Spanish priests and destroyed most of their convents and all the churches, except the St. Francis Church, which they converted into a chapel for their own use. In consequence of these measures the Roman Catholic community deserted the town in a body and declined to trade with the Dutch. A compromise was finally effected and permission given to the Roman Catholics to erect a church on the Island of Vypeen. In 1795 the old church of St. Francis passed into the hands of the English. In 1806, fearing that Cochin was to be restored to the Dutch, the East India Company blew up the old Roman Catholic cathedral of Santa Cruz, which the Dutch had converted into a storehouse, and destroyed the fort with some of the quays and rest-houses. The church of St. Francis very nearly shared the same fate, for barrels of gunpowder had been already placed inside, and everything was ready for its demolition, when at the eleventh hour, the officer in command relented, and happily, this historical old building escaped destruction. The massive buttresses which are such a striking feature of all the larger buildings in the town are said to have been erected about this time to shore up the cracked walls of the houses shaken by the force of the explosions. The church is of no particular architectural merit but it is a big lofty building of massive construction and mainly built in the Dutch style in brick and plaster with a timber-framed roof covered with modern tiles. It has a lofty gable front facing the west with a semi-circular arched entrance and windows above. The façade is decorated with three rows of brick and plaster super-imposed columns carrying horizontal string courses which divide the front into three compartments. On each side at the angles is a tall buttress terminating in a stepped pinnacle and on the summit of the gable is a bell turret in the same style. The entrance has no porch, but immediately above it, obscuring the three windows in the middle compartment of the façade, an unsightly tiled pent-roof has been erected to serve as a shelter to the entrance below. This being an eyesore should be removed and replaced by a proper porch built in keeping with the style of the old doorway. A row of massive buttresses, six feet square at the base, supports the side walls of the building which are four feet thick. The nave is 142 feet in length, 51 feet in width and about 50 feet in height and is bright, airy, and simple in style. A plain broad-spanned arch with simple mouldings divides the nave from the chancel. *Cochin.*

"This church was restored by the Dutch in 1779 and has been repaired from time to time at Government expense since and is now in a good state of preservation. The floor of the nave until 1867 was paved with carved and inscribed tombstones of former distinguished Portuguese and Dutch officials and merchants, but for the sake of safety they were removed and fixed in an upright position in the side walls of the nave. The earliest Portuguese inscription is dated 1562 and the earliest Dutch record 1664. As shown in the accompanying illustrations some of the heraldic designs and armorial bearings depicted above the quaint old epitaphs are well-executed and very interesting [Plate XVII (*a*) and (*c*)]. Immediately in front of the main entrance is a small stone-built War-memorial erected in 1921 to the memory of those Europeans from Cochin who fell in the Great War.

Dutch Cemetery, Cochin.

"Close to St. Francis Church and facing the sea, is the old Dutch Cemetery which is crowded with curious old tombs of various forms in brick and plaster and much blackened by long exposure. Some are flat, domed or pyramidal, while others are occasionally diversified by broken columns, urns and sarcophagi. They form an interesting group of old Dutch monuments well worth preservation at Government expense.

Rock Fort at Dindigul.

"This Hindu Fort is said to have derived its name from the rock on which it stands which is shaped like a pillow (Tamil *Tandu*—pillow, *Kal*—stone). It dates from about the 17th century A. D. and contains the remains of some interesting structures such as the temple of the goddess Abhirāmi on the summit of the hill, the extensive pillared mandapa and a group of small shrines and tanks. Much clearance is required to keep the interior of this fort tidy. The old drain should be opened and the tops of the ramparts sloped and dressed where necessary to prevent water collecting during the rains. The space within the main gate should be converted into a grass plot without attempting to have a garden, and be provided with proper drainage. The fort has extensive underground barracks located in the basement of the ramparts around the main gate, in the form of a series of underground brick and plaster galleries with bomb-proof roofs supported on rows of low round arches. The entrances are all on the inner side of the rampart wall facing the high sloping surface of the rock above, down which during the rains a considerable volume of water flows towards the gateway and the underground barracks. In order to prevent the latter from getting flooded, a large subterranean drain passes under the floor of the barracks to the outside of the fort. The outer end of this drain is now blocked with silt and should be cleaned and put in working order. The steps to some of the entrances to these barracks should be raised to a height of about 1 foot to prevent surface water getting into the interior. The cracks in some of the roofs require patch-repairs. The tanks within the fort should be cleaned out, repaired and made watertight where necessary with new cement work. The group of small temples and *mandapas* on the top of the hill are in good order. These together with the ruined buildings in the fort, the barracks, the magazines and others do not stand in need of any repair but should be kept tidy and free from rank vegetation.

Dutch Fort at Sadras.

"At Sadras in the Chingleput District there is an old Dutch fort which was blown up when abandoned by the British. Its fortifications and circular bastions standing at

Dutch Fort at Sadras.

each of the four angles are in ruins. At the basement of the south-west bastion two cannons are lying. The ramparts on the east side facing the sea have been destroyed. The main gateway on the west side is not in so decayed a condition as the rest of the fortifications. On the south side of this gateway within the fort is a small Dutch cemetery which is enclosed by a brick and plaster wall. On the north side, outside the fort is another similar cemetery which is also enclosed by a brick wall. On inspection it was found that the fort and the ruined buildings within were overgrown with rank vegetation and full of rubbish requiring thorough clearance. The floors of the ruined buildings needed levelling and sloping to ensure proper drainage. The buildings are mostly in an advanced stage of decay and beyond repairs, but both the cemeteries should be maintained in good order."

Burma Circle.

Sameikshe.

For some years past lack of funds has prevented the Superintendent in Burma from doing any excavation work. The excavations at Sameikshe were undertaken because, from the very first, the villagers themselves offered their services free from remuneration for a number of days. M. Duroiselle says: "Men from three villages turned out for the work in a fine enthusiastic spirit and the monks themselves were not slow in contributing their spiritual influence and their help in that gentlemanly and broad-minded way so widely prevalent among the Burmese bhikkhus. In 1920 unauthorized excavations had been made at Sameikshe by a villager, the principal find being a bronze image of Dipankara Buddha, a good find, considering how very scarce are the images of this Buddha in Burma. The spot where this was found had been thoroughly dug up, and in the process, the foundations of an old building had been somewhat damaged. It was to avoid further damage to this or any other monument which might be excavated that the Superintendent was asked to come and supervise the work himself. The site already dug by the villagers yielded nothing more ; but further traces of walls were discovered. The monument must have measured 25 feet in plan, and was no doubt of the type so numerous in Pagan, that is, a square central pile of bricks with a vaulted corridor all round it. From the nature of the objects found in it, mention of which has been made in a previous report, this temple was probably built in the 11th or 12th century. Nothing whatsoever is known about it, nor about the numerous remains scattered all about over a large area ; there appears to be no local tradition, and this seems to point to comparatively recent immigration. My attention was next directed to another mound of ruins close by about which many strange tales were told by some of the villagers. Very large bricks were strewn about, pointing to the fact that the site was probably an old one. From a low depression in the centre of the mound, it was clear that it had already been dug into, but no one present could remember any digging having taken place here. A trench was dug from north to south across the mound and about one foot below the surface on the north side, a course of bricks was brought to light ending abruptly on the east and south, but continuing on the north and west. A little lower down was discovered the corner of an exterior wall, traces of plaster still adhering to it. Further digging only disclosed other courses of bricks forming the foundation of an old monument. Nothing of moment was found excepting, at the lowermost layer of the foundations, a few terracotta votive tablets. The most interesting of these was one measuring $6'' \times 4\frac{3}{4}''$; it is of a kind common enough in Burma, representing the Buddha in the *bhumi-sparsa mudra* with beneath, the representation of the temple at Bodh-Gaya. The throne is flanked on either side by a Bodhisattva seated with one leg pendant. Below is a short inscription in Nāgari characters in which appears the name of King Anorata (1044-1077). This fixes the date of the tablet, as well as that of the ruined building, which must have been contemporary. The other tablets were of a common type and call for no remarks. It will be seen that these excavations were not very successful. What the other mounds, scattered, as has been said above, over a large area, may yield, remains for the future to disclose, when sufficient funds will be available."

To the south of Sameikshe, M. Duroiselle visited two old buildings; a pagoda called the Patodawgyi and a Sima. Both are evidently old from their style, the pagoda dating probably from the 13th century. At the Sima was found a very beautiful bronze image of a Bodhisattva going back probably to the 11th century. These two buildings were in a bad state of repairs, but the Superintendent induced the residing monk, U Vasavinda, to repair them, which he promised to do as soon as he had collected the necessary funds.

At Nyaungbingan, somewhat to the west of Sameikshe, was found, in a field, a votive tablet with a legend in old Talaing of the 10th or 11th century on the reverse face; but the letters have very much weathered and are so faint that nothing satisfactory has yet been made out.

Another votive tablet was found of a kind rather scarce in Burma; it represents in bold relief, the figure of Buddha seated European fashion, with his hands in the *dharmacakra mudra*; two bodhisattvas flank him; above the latter there appear to be some writing in north-Indian characters, but so very faint that nothing much can be deciphered. The most interesting feature consists of a Burmese legend on the reverse face in very archaic language which presents some difficulties for translation.

Notes on places visited by Mr. Duroiselle.

"Pagan being, as has often been stated, the principal centre of conservation work in Burma, owing to its numerous monuments, among which are found some which may rank among the finest in India, might be thought to be also a centre for fruitful excavation work. Such, however, is not the case; excavations executed in the past did not justify this expectation, and nothing really valuable from an antiquarian point of view has been found there. But the place is very rich in votive tablets. These tablets are of importance as a help in elucidating the history of Burma and its relations with India, above all north-eastern India. Many are inscribed with legends in Pali or Sanskrit, sometimes with both, the one being on the obverse, the other on the reverse face; some are inscribed in mixed Pali and Sanskrit; and the characters belong mostly to North-Indian alphabets of the 10th and 11th centuries and in some cases probably earlier. At that period, and somewhat earlier, many monks from India, it is well known, crossed over to Burma and Cambodia, among whom was the famous Sangama Srīnāya, and in Bengal and Bihar were many monks from Indo-China. Moreover, there is evidence of intercourse other than religious between these countries. This no doubt explains the large number of votive tablets evidently manufactured in India which are now found at Pagan. *Pagan.*

"Another find of very interesting tablets was made by me while examining an old ruined pagoda near the Mingala-zedi. I found that a moulding on one of the terraces was actually built up with votive tablets. But it was impossible to detach many of them without endangering the stability of the building which, on that side, tilts very dangerously. A certain number were recovered from the moulding itself and from among the *débris*. Most of them bear an inscription, but the striking feature

Pagan. is that legends in different languages were found collected in the same monument. Some of the legends are in Sanskrit, some in Pali, some tablets bear a Burmese legend and others a Talaing one. Again others are bi-lingual, that is Sanskrit and Burmese or Sanskrit and Talaing. All these legends belong to the 10th or 11th century.

Old Prome. "Old Prome is the oldest place in Burma so far as archæology is concerned, and contains monuments, such as the Bawbawgyi for instance, which have no counterpart anywhere else. The Bawbawgyi was repaired in 1910-14, but unfortunately the three lower terraces which have been buried under earth and *débris* probably for centuries, were not cleared at that time. Some of the most important and oldest finds ever made in Burma were obtained by digging into a very small portion of this *débris*. The probability is that other important finds will be made if the whole be dug. There seems to have been a vague idea that, if the three lower terraces were uncovered, the whole building would topple down, as the earth and *débris* strengthen the building. There appears to be no adequate reason for thinking so. Mr. Chan Toon, Public Works Department Officer in charge, accompanied me and after very careful examination of the building and the nature of the rubbish, came to the opinion that the lower terraces could be brought to light without the least danger to the monument, those terraces, judging from the two above, being very broad, and having nothing to do with the building's foundations. The removal of this rubbish and earth, besides the probable yield of finds, would restore the monument to its original state and add to its beauty. This work will be undertaken as early as possible."

Kashmir.
Harwan.

On his exploratory work during 1921-22 Mr. Ramchandra Kak, the State Superintendent of Archæology in Kashmir writes : "The excavation of the stupa at Harwan which last year's trial diggings had brought to light was completed. A number of other structures, the most important among which are a set of chapels and an apsidal temple were also excavated. The site is an extensive one and judging from the different styles of masonry employed in the various buildings and their stratigraphical relation to one another, it seems certain that the buildings belong to different periods. The styles of masonry are three ; *viz.*, (*a*) the pebble style, consisting of small pebbles built in mud and originally covered with plaster ; this seems to be the oldest style ; (*b*) the diaper pebble style, consisting of pebbles with large stones interspersed at short distances, and (*c*) the diaper-rubble style, consisting of large and small rubble stones so arranged as to form something like a diaper pattern.

"Perhaps the most interesting finds at Harwan are the carved tiles which were used not only in the pavements of the courtyard but also as the face decoration of the buildings. All of them are marked with Kharosthi numerals. This script was in vogue in North-Western India during the three centuries preceding and the three or four centuries succeeding the Christian Era. This circumstance, coupled with the fact that the style of art revealed by the figure decoration on the tiles has a distinct resemblance to the later Gandhara Art, and also bears some traces of Sassanian influence, determines their date as about 300-400 A. D. These tiles have been found *in situ* in or about the buildings of the diaper-pebble style only, which consequently may also be assigned to about the fourth century A. D.

"Stratigraphical evidence also indicates that the diaper-pebble stands, in point of time, between the pure pebble style and the diaper-rubble style. It is difficult to define precisely the date of these two styles, but we shall not be far wrong in fixing their upper and lower limits as the 2nd century and the 7th century A. D. respectively."

In addition to this excavation work, Mr. Kak also explored the little-known valleys of Wadwan, Marev, and Dachhan, which in modern times form part of the Kashtwar Tahsil. "As a matter of fact," Mr. Kak says, "the very same valley bears each of these three names at different places. The valley, exclusive of the numerous side Nallas, which in themselves are extensive tracts, is over 80 miles long and stretches from the mountains which form the water-shed between Ladakh and Kashtwar almost to the very town of Kashtwar itself. The principal objects of interest discovered were as follows :— *Kashtwar.*

"1. An unique Hindu temple built of piles of pine-wood and stones, constructed exactly on the same structural principles as the wooden mosques of Kashmir. This is situated at Dilguth in the Nanth Nallah.

"2. A natural grotto known as Bathastal near Dachhan. A number of early Gupta characters, mostly of the cursive type, are painted on its ceiling in dark red, white and yellowish colours.

"3. Two Sanskrit inscriptions, (*a*) one engraved on the stone known as the Kalpa-Kan, 'the stone of doomsday' in the Little Zaji-Nai. It records the construction of a stable for horses, presumably those which were then as now sent in summer to graze in the alpine regions of the Little and Great Zaji-Nai. This inscription is said to belong to the time of Zain-ul-abidin (1422-1472) A. D. (*b*) Another carved on a granite boulder near the bridge at Dachhan. It mentions the name of Anantadeva (A. D. 1081-1089) and may record the construction of a bridge across the Marev-send, on the bank of which the boulder is situated.

"4. A number of Mughal and Afghan *farmans* and miscellaneous documents, in possession of Rasul Malik of Marev."

SECTION III.

OFFICERS ON SPECIAL DUTY.

Sir Aurel Stein gives me the following note on the work done by him, as Officer on Special Duty :— **Sir Aurel Stein's work during 1921-22.**

"My work during the official year 1921-22 was devoted almost exclusively to tasks connected with the results of my second and third Central-Asian expeditions. By using in 1920 all available leisure during a period of leave in Europe, as well as by unremitting efforts during six months of deputation in England granted to me in continuation of it by His Majesty's Secretary of State, I had succeeded in passing through the Oxford University Press the text, close on 1500 pages quarto, of *Serindia*, the detailed report on the explorations of my second Central-Asian expedition, 1906—08, (1)

(1) *Serindia.*—Detailed Report of Explorations in Central Asia and Westernmost China, carried out and described under the orders of His Majesty's Indian Government by Aurel Stein, K.C.I.E. With Descriptive Lists of Antiques by F. H. Andrews, F. M. G. Lorimer, C. L. Wolley, and others ; and Appendices by J. Allan, L. D. Barnett, L. Binyon, E. Chavannes, A. H. Church, A. H. Francke, A. F. R. Hoernle, T. A. Joyce, R. Petrucci, K Schlesinger and F. W. Thomas.

Five volumes, royal 4to (13¾ × 10), pages XXIX+1580, with 175 plates in collotype in colour, 345 illustrations in half-tone, 9 figures in the text, 59 plans, and 96 maps. Oxford : At the Clarendon Press, MCMXXI.

Sir Aurel Stein's work.

together with the hundreds of plates, photographic reproductions and plans comprised in that publication. There remained, however, the revision and printing of the necessarily elaborate Index which alone could render reference to the many ruined sites, the varied historical and geographical subjects discussed, and the thousands of individual antiques described and figured conveniently practicable for purposes of research. Though the materials for this Index had been previously collected at Oxford by Mr. New of the Clarendon Press, a professional Indexer working under my direction, the final arrangement and revision of these voluminous materials, filling 240 columns quarto in close print, kept me as well as my second assistant Miss F. Lorimer fully occupied during the month of April and the first half of May.

"Here it may be conveniently recorded that *Serindia*, filling with its plates and atlas of 96 map sheets, five stout volumes of Royal Quarto, was published early in December 1921. Gratifying evidence of the widespread interest with which this publication met from its first appearance was afforded by the rapidity of its sale. Though after the first few months the price was raised from 12 guineas to 18 guineas, the whole of the edition was exhausted within less than twelve months and the greater portion of Government's heavy outlay on the publication thus recovered.

"Ever since systematic examination and treatment at the British Museum had revealed the great importance and exceptional artistic interest of the hundreds of ancient Buddhist paintings which in course of my second Central-Asian journey I had recovered from a walled-up chapel of the 'Caves of the Thousand Buddhas' near Tun-huang, on the westernmost border of China, I had wished for a publication which would allow of select specimens from among them to be made accessible to students interested in Eastern art by reproductions representative in character and more adequate in size and execution than it had been possible to provide within the scope of *Serindia.*

"It was largely due to the generous interest shown by the Right Honourable Mr. Austen Chamberlain, then His Majesty's Secretary of State for India, that it became possible on my return from my third Central-Asian journey to arrange, with the ready assistance of the India Office and the co-operation of the Trustees of the British Museum, for the publication of the portfolio of *The Thousand Buddhas*, containing in 48 plates reproductions, half of them by photography in colour, of selections from the mass of those pictorial treasures. Mr. Laurence Binyon, Deputy Keeper of the Department of Prints and Drawings in the British Museum and a leading authority on Far-Eastern Art, contributed to the publication a lucid *Introductory Essay*. In it he discussed on the one hand the importance of these paintings dating from the T'ang period (7th-10th century A. D.) for the history of Chinese Art, and on the other the great interest they present as illustrating how the designs and methods of treatment first developed in Græco-Buddhist art penetrated through Buddhist Central-Asia and made their influence felt on the arts of the Far East.

"There remained, however, the task of furnishing a sufficiently detailed descriptive account of these pictures with special regard to the iconography of the subjects they represent, almost all derived from the Mahāyāna system of Indian Buddhism. The preparation of this account, in which I was much helped by the very useful Descriptive List previously prepared by Miss F. Lorimer for *Serindia*, as well as by the interpretations of my lamented collaborator M. Raphael Petrucci, Mr. F. H. Andrews and other scholars, kept me fully occupied during the months of May and June. Accompanied by this text filling over 60 pages royal folio in print, the portfolio of *The Thousand Buddhas* was published in March 1922 for the India Office by Messrs. B. Quaritch ([2]). This publication has proved equally successful with *Serindia*, as at the time of writing the edition is reported to be nearly exhausted, thus fully covering the original cost of production and leaving hope of some profit to Government. *Sir Aurel Stein's work.*

"The summer and early autumn months following had to be devoted mainly to the preparation of a detailed *Memoir* on my maps of Chinese Turkistan and Kansu, embodying the results of the surveys made during my three Central-Asian expeditions. Though these journeys had archæological exploration for their primary object, I had been equally anxious also to use all opportunities offered by them for geographical work. Through the generous help of the Survey of India which deputed with me experienced Indian Surveyors and provided needful instruments, funds, etc., it had been possible to realize this aim by means of systematic surveys carried out under my direction and with my assistance over the whole of the ground which those protracted travels, with aggregate marching distances of over 20,000 miles, had covered.

"On my return in 1916 from my third expedition it was decided with the ready approval of Colonel Sir Sidney Burrard, R.E., K.C.S.I., then Surveyor General, whose unfailing interest and guidance had from the beginning facilitated those labours, to publish the topographical results of that journey in a series of maps embodying also the surveys of my previous expeditions, though these had already before received cartographical record in connection with my Detailed Reports, *Ancient Khotan* and *Serindia*.

"These new maps, numbering 47 sheets, executed on the scale of 1 : 500,000, have thus come to comprise a vast area of innermost Asia extending in its extreme limits from the Pāmīrs in the west to the Pacific watershed on the Nan-shan in the east, and from the high Tibetan plateaus in the south to beyond the T'ien-shan range in the north. The compilation of the results of these surveys which included, besides continuous plane-table work by my assistants and myself, also triangulation and astronomical observations, was effected by the Trigonometrical Survey Office during the years 1916 and 1917, and occupied a large staff of draftsmen under the direction of several officers from the Provincial and Upper Subordinate Services. The subsequent labours connected with the drawing and reproduction of these maps continued without interruption for five years longer, the revision and correction of the map sheets in all the successive stages of drawings and proofs claiming a great deal of my time to the close of 1922.

"It had been my constant endeavour to make our surveys as careful and detailed a record of the prevailing physical features as conditions would permit. Improved methods of drawing and reproduction, including the use of seven different colours, have allowed in the new maps a clearer and fuller representation of that record than was possible in previous publications. These new maps will thus for some time to come serve as a main source of cartographical reference for a great portion of Central Asia which, by the physical conditions of the present and by its great rôle in the past, as the meeting place of the ancient civilizations of India, China and the West, is attracting more and more interest from the historical student and the geographer.

([2]) *The Thousand Buddhas.*—Ancient Buddhist Paintings from the Cave-temples of Tun-huang on the Western Frontier of China, recovered and described by Sir Aurel Stein, K.C.I.E., with an Introductory Essay by Laurence Binyon. Published under the orders of His Majesty's Secretary of State for India and with the co-operation of the Trustees of the British Museum. 48 Plates (mostly 24 by 20 inches), half of them reproduced by photography in colour. Text, royal folio pages xii and 66. 1922. Price £7-10-0.

Sir Aurel Stein's work.

"It, therefore, appeared appropriate to accompany the issue of these maps (intended for the Report on my third journey but also to be separately published) by a *Memoir* recording all needful information as to the history of these surveys ; the nature of the materials furnished by them ; the chief features determining the geographical character of the regions explored, etc. This *Memoir* to which Major K. Mason, R.E., M.C., Deputy Superintendent of the Survey of India, has added an important Appendix on the triangulation executed during our surveys, was completed by me in manuscript by October 1921. It has been printed since as a volume of the *Survey of India Records*, filling (with a complete Index of local names) over 200 pages foolscap, and will shortly be published. (3).

"While the above tasks kept me occupied during the first half of the official year, the work of cataloguing and systematic description of the antiquities brought back from the explorations of my third journey and temporarily deposited at Srinagar under the care of Mr. F. H. Andrews, in the Annexe to his official residence as Principal of the A. S. Technical Institute, was steadily continued by that old and most helpful collaborator and Miss F. Lorimer, my second assistant. This task to which Mr. Andrews had devoted since 1917 whatever leisure he could spare from his exacting duties under the Kashmir Darbar, and for which Miss F. Lorimer, since her transfer from my collection at the British Museum in 1919, had been able to render experienced assistance, could, owing to the great extent of the collection and the extremely varied character of the thousands of objects comprised in it, not be completed until the succeeding official year.

"The methods followed in this work, an essential corollary to my own Detailed Report, were the same as had proved so effective in the treatment of the collections of antiques resulting from my first two expeditions and described in *Ancient Khotan* and *Serindia*. The thoroughness of the descriptions recorded of all objects, together with the inventory photographs which in May and June 1921, were prepared of all the more important among them, enables me to continue the preparation of my Detailed Report also at a distance from the Collection.

"By the end of October I was able to resume this essential task at Srinagar, after having been kept from it for fully two years by the labours referred to above. Its progress again suffered some unavoidable interruption during the winter months. Before the Christmas holidays I felt induced to devote a short stay at Peshawar to the record of interesting linguistic specimens of *Tirāhī*, a Dardic language surviving in a few isolated settlements of refugees from Tirāh, found to the south-west of Dakka in Afghān territory. The survival of this tongue, hitherto practically unknown, among a population now speaking Pashtu, is of distinct antiquarian and historical interest ; for it affords important fresh proof of the former prevalence along the North-West Frontier of a Dardic-speaking race preceding the Pathān invasion and extending until a comparatively recent period as far south as the territory of the Afrīdīs, the Aparytai of Herodotus, on the borders of Gandhāra. The language specimens taken from the mouths of these Tirāhī-speakers, the tracing of whom I owed to the kind help previously rendered

---

(3) *Memoir on maps of Chinese Turkestan and Kansu*, from the Surveys made during Sir Aurel Stein's Explorations, 1900-1, 1906-8, 1913-15. By Sir Aurel Stein, K.C.I.E., Indian Archæological Survey. With Appendices by Major K. Mason, M.C., R.E., and J. de Graaff Hunter, Sc.D., Trigonometrical Survey Office, Debra Dun, 1923. Foolscap, pages XII and 208, with 2 maps, 9 charts and 30 plates of photographic illustrations.

by the late Sir George Roos-Keppel, have been analyzed by Sir George Grierson, the Director of the Linguistic Survey of India, and will form the subject of an early publication by that great authority. *Sir Aurel Stein's work.*

" The Christmas holidays were used by me for a brief but interesting archæological tour within and outside the borders of the Hazāra District. It was intended in the first place to give me personal acquaintance with the *Agrōr* tract, a portion of the North-West Frontier which I had not been able to visit before. It had acquired special antiquarian interest for me since I had been able to identify it with the *Atyugrapura* of Kalhana's Chronicle of the Kings of Kashmir and the *Ariora* of Marco Polo's account of a Mongol inroad into Kashmir ([4]). At the beginning of my tour, which the kind help of Colonel E. H. S. James, C.I.E., Deputy Commissioner of Hazara, greatly facilitated, I was able rapidly to examine some important remains of the Bhōgarmang Valley where it opens into the fertile plain of Pakhlī proper. As, however, these remains have been described by Mr. Hargreaves, Superintendent in the Frontier Circle, on pages 63 to 65 of this Report, my own notes on Bedadi and its surroundings are omitted here.

" My subsequent necessarily rapid marches up to the head of the Batkhās Nullah through Agrōr and down to Darband, in the Nawāb of Amb's territory on the Indus, acquainted me with ground offering varied antiquarian and geographical interest, but left no time to search for local remains. They sufficed, however, to show the peculiar character, and to explain the historial importance, of the open fertile valley of Agrōr, interposed between the barren ' Black Mountains ' and the narrow gorges of the Indus on the one side and the basin of Pakhli on the other. I also was able to collect a good deal of archæologically interesting information about ruins in the valleys of independent territory draining towards Thākōt on the Indus. A fortunate encounter with Abdul Jabbār Pādshāh, the very capable descendant of the old kings of Swāt and pretender to their throne, enabled me to gather useful data, too, about the hill tracts of Ghōrband, Chakēsar, etc. These tracts, lying between the Upper Swāt Valley and the Indus, may yet prove of importance for the ancient geography of this region.

" From Darband, undoubtedly a place of considerable antiquity, I concluded my short tour on the Hazāra border by a visit to the large village of *Kalinjar*, the chief place of a fertile plateau above the left bank of the Indus. Its name had suggested possible identity with *Kālinjara*, a frontier territory mentioned in Kalhana's *Rājataranginī* ([5]). But though I succeeded in tracing the remains of at least one small fortified site on a hill spur above the village, with walls of ' Gandhāra ' masonry and manifestly pre-Muhammadan, no direct evidence in support of the location could be found.

" Of the remaining months of the year, some time had to be spent by me at Dehra Dun for the sake of miscellaneous urgent work connected with the completion of my maps and the printing of my *Memoir*. Of the rest, most was claimed at New Delhi by arrangements for the setting up of the Buddhist wall-paintings recovered on my third Central Asian journey in the building specially erected for their accommodation. The actual execution of this difficult task was in the expert hands of Mr. F. H. Andrews who utilized for it his winter vacation from Kashmir and who has described the progress achieved in the following note." *Mr. Andrews' work.*

([4]) See *Marco Polo's Account of a Mongol inroad into Kashmir*, by Sir Aurel Stein, in *Geographical Journal*, August, 1919, pages 100 sqq.

([5]) See *Kalhana's Rājatarangiṇī*, translated, etc., by M. A. Stein, *I*, page 366 (note on *vii*. 1256); *II*, page 433.

Mr. Andrews' work on the Stein Collection at New Delhi.

"The work of unpacking, mounting and hanging the ancient Buddhist wall paintings brought from ruined shrines in the Turfān District of Chinese Turkistan by Sir Aurel Stein, K.C.I.E., in the course of his third Central-Asian expedition (1913—16) was commenced in January 1921 at the Depository built to receive them in the Imperial Capital, New Delhi.

"The paintings, which are executed on mudplaster, were removed from the walls of the shrines in slabs of about 1" to 1½" in thickness and of varying sizes averaging about 2' by 20", but not necessarily rectangular in shape. Irregular shapes resulted from the endeavour to avoid cutting across a face or some other interesting detail which it was desired to preserve intact. The removal was directed by Sir Aurel Stein who also supervised all the packing for the long and difficult journey to India. The ingenious system of packing he devised was as follows.

"Each slab, as it was taken from the wall, was backed with strong canvas steeped in glue and numbered in accordance with a key sketch made before any part was removed from its original position. Two slabs of approximately equal size were then placed face to face with an even buffer of cotton wool and smooth paper between. A bed was prepared consisting of two wooden battens laid parallel and a suitable distance apart and on these a second pair at right angles with the first. Above these was placed a level layer of stiff reeds at right angles to the second pair of battens; then another layer of reeds at right angles to the first. On this the pair of slabs was laid and a similar arrangement of reeds and battens in reverse order, placed on top. Strong cords were next passed round the whole and lying along the battens; more reeds were closely packed against all four edges of the bundle and then the cords were drawn tight and firmly tied. (Plate XXXIV, Fig. *a*). This compact bundle was next lowered into a box made to fit, a bedding of reeds having been put inside and ropes placed to permit its being easily lifted out at the end of the journey (Fig. *b*). More reeds were packed round the edges and on top, the lid was screwed on and hoop-iron nailed round the angles. Thanks to this careful packing, the very fragile slabs stood the long journey with a minimum of damage.

"The mud forming the rough ground for the paintings was applied to the wall in successive layers of various thickness from about ½" to ¾" or more. It is very coarse mixed with chopped straw as a bonding, and casual rubbish such as pebbles, chips of stone and wood, nut shells, fruit stones, twigs, etc. Upon this was spread a thin layer of carefully washed mud mixed with scutched hemp fibre and sometimes a small proportion of goat's hair, smoothed to form the *intonaco*. Over the smooth surface was brushed a thin wash of white pigment, probably gypsum, to form a kind of priming on to which the design of the subject to be painted was transferred from the cartoon, probably by means of a pounce.

"The pounced lines were then traced over with a thin grey brush line to fix them. The local colours were next put in, sometimes flat or with a darker tone added to suggest light and shade. Finally, the whole was outlined and contoured with very free sweeping brush lines in one, two or more colours. Generally two outline colours are used, black for everything but flesh, which is outlined with red or crimson. The practice varies, however, with different schools of painting.

"All the work is in tempera, the proportion of medium used varying in different pictures, and it is probable that the medium itself is not always the same. With one or two exceptions the colours are so soft that they can be removed with a dry soft brush.

Mr. Andrews' work.

The exceptions, in the case of certain colours, can be cleaned with damp cotton wool very carefully and tenderly applied. This method is, however, too risky to be recommended.

"In several pictures are inscriptions in Uigur, probably contemporary. In another is a much damaged Chinese inscription written in the usual vertical label provided for the purpose. In others the label is provided but has no inscription. A third type of writing is in a Brāhmī script and Kuchean language written in dense black ink with a reed pen on a heavily sized surface prepared for the pen. The three types of writing coincide with three distinct styles of painting. Space in this Report does not permit of a detailed examination of the styles and the many interesting problems presented.

"The method of treatment employed for preserving and effectively exhibiting the paintings was first used by me in connection with the wall paintings from Mīrān and other Central-Asian sites, brought by Sir Aurel Stein to London from his second expedition (1906-08). Examination showed that the backing of mud and straw was frequently impregnated with salt, inherent in the soil of the greater part of the plains of Turkistan. The action of damp on the mud caused the salt to manifest itself in the form of a fine glistening furry growth on the surface of the picture, and distinct from this a brownish green mildew also developed and caused serious discolouration in patches.

"My first care was to remove as much of the offending mud as possible without damaging the painting. This was done by placing each section of the picture face downwards on glass and by cutting and scraping the mud away from the back until the thinnest possible skin of the *intonaco* remained, with the picture on its lower surface in contact with the glass. A mirror placed below the sheet of glass, by reflecting the face of the picture, permitted the operator to watch for any disturbance of the painted surface during the scraping.*

"A thin layer of plaster of Paris in which a small quantity of formaline was mixed was then spread over the skin of mud as a first backing (Plate XXXIV, Fig. *c*). Next a frame was made, the size of the picture section, and on this was stretched a very open, thin canvas (painter's scrim). The frame with canvas side down, was placed on the plaster surface and more plaster spread over the scrim. The second layer of plaster united with the first through the meshes of the scrim which became embedded between the two. When dry, the whole was lifted from the glass, clean, light and comparatively strong.

"Certain modifications of the process were necessary in the present work. The paintings dealt with in London were small, whereas those brought to Delhi are, when built up, in some cases twelve feet by eight high, ten or even eighteen feet wide (Plate XXXV, Fig. *c*).† They had been cut from the walls of the shrines in slabs, as already described, and the task before me was to reassemble all these sections in their original positions, reconstructing complete pictures, or as complete as when they were found. It seemed inadvisable to use material such as wood and scrim in a climate subject to so many changes as that of Delhi, and where the white ant is ever seeking what it may devour. Iron and steel, copper and brass were all disqualified on account of the inevitable stain they give when in contact with plaster of Paris. Aluminium seemed to be the only practicable material remaining, and this I adopted.

* The mirror is seen in use in Plate XXXIV, Fig. *c*.

† The picture representing two Buddhas with attendants, donors, etc., measures 18′ 2″ × 12′ 1″. It is composed of 37 slabs mounted on 16 aluminium frames.

Mr. Andrews' work.

"I decided to make the frames of angle iron and to use expanded aluminium as the web in place of canvas. Expanded aluminium, I found, was not a regular article of commerce; in fact the makers had found it unsatisfactory and demurred at my request for further trials. However, they eventually worked to my specification and the result has been an unqualified success.

"The process of clearing away the mud and of coating with plaster remains as described. The next step is to assemble two or three adjoining slabs on a glass table and after connecting them with plaster, to fit an aluminium frame to hold them together. The frame with the expanded aluminium as web is placed on the assembled slabs, and plaster applied all over (Plate XXXV). The plaster unites with the backing, gripping the web of aluminium between the two, and when set, the whole is lifted from the glass table as a single section (Plate XXXV, Fig. *b*).

"Having thus made up the original small sections into larger ones, as large as can be safely handled, the next procedure is to hang them on the wall and to adjust them exactly to one another (Plate XXXV, Fig. *c*). To effect this, the walls of the Depository had been fitted with channel irons placed horizontally at a vertical distance apart of about 3 feet. The large sections are hung to these channels, and adjustment is made by a system of lifting-screws fitted to the aluminium frames.

"The method described may be regarded as satisfactory. The first experiment with aluminium was made in January 1921 and the sections then mounted show no change—no shrinkage, cracking or any chemical activity. The aluminium is light and tough, and as the plaster strengthened by the expanded metal reinforcement, need not be thick, the sections have a minimum of weight and may be conveniently moved about as needed.

"By the courtesy of the Kashmir Durbar I was permitted to devote the period of the annual winter vacation of the Amar Singh Technical Institute, Srinagar, to this work and was also able to secure the assistance of certain of my students for the same period. An intelligent local smith and his assistant were engaged to make the frames, and under my instruction and direction, the process for the treatment of the paintings was quickly learned by all and the work progressed smoothly and quickly. The assembling and joining of the small slabs to form larger sections, as already explained, was a part of the work which I could not entrust to other hands and eyes than my own, as errors were easily made but most difficult to correct.

"The number of original slabs treated was 102. These were joined to form 38 larger sections, each contained on one aluminium back frame. The larger sections joined together formed 22 compositions or more or less complete wall paintings, of which the largest measures 18 feet 2 inches by 12 feet 1 inch. The aggregate superficial area of the painted surface mounted totals 514 square feet.

"Two pieces of wall painting are here reproduced of which the following are brief descriptions. Plate XXXV, Fig. *b* from the north wall of the ambulatory of Bezeklik shrine iii, is a fragment of a large subject similar to that of Fig. *c*, and represents a celestial attendant standing in an attitude of reverence to the left of the vesica surrounding a figure of Buddha. The pattern of the outer border of the vesica is a Chinese cloud scroll repeated in various colours. The drapery of the figure is a good example of the skill of the Turkistan designers in expressing freedom, while strongly schematizing the drawing. Size 6½ feet by 2 feet, or about life size.

"Fig. *c* is from the S. E. wall of shrine xii at Bezeklik, a site of cave temples in the Turfān District, and represents to L. a standing Buddha figure over life size within a halo bordered by a repeated wing-like ornament and surrounded by attendants and probably donors. In the upper corner is a small Chinese pavilion in a paved courtyard surrounded by a wall provided with a pair of doors slightly open. In the centre is a second Buddha standing on a Chinese raft of wood resting on water. His feet which, like the first, have sandals, are supported by lotuses. Worshipping figures at the lower part present gifts of food and treasure (?) with which a sitting camel to L. is fully laden. The dresses and faces of these donors are interesting. To R. is a Nirvāna scene with two followers of Buddha and a lamenting figure half kneeling and supporting his aching head on his L. hand. Below are three musicians playing drum, cymbals, *biwa* and a fourth of whom his instrument, the flute, is partly preserved. A finely designed seated figure entirely in white, the Chinese mourning colour, in meditation below is very Byzantine in style. Part of the upper border of seated Buddhas is preserved; size 18 by 12 feet. *Mr. Andrews work.*

"The necessity for providing protection against dust and flies for the delicate surface of the paintings is obvious, and wall cases of teak fitted with plate glass have been designed and are under construction. Blinds will be arranged inside the cases to protect the colours as far as possible from the action of light."

SECTION IV.

MUSEUMS.

Indian Museum, Calcutta.

Ever since Sir John Marshall accepted his Trusteeship for the Indian Museum, Calcutta, and assumed responsibility for the Archæological Section of that institution, it had been his constant ambition to secure the services of a whole-time Curator, but the ambition was perennially thwarted by lack of funds. The result was that for several years the heavy responsibilities for this Section were unavoidably placed as an additional burden upon one already overworked official after another, to the inevitable dissatisfaction of all concerned and most of all the officers themselves. The collection, which is the most extensive and important in India, called urgently for re-arrangement and development, and offered almost unlimited scope for study. But with multiple other duties pressing upon them, including the obligation to be away from Calcutta for a large part of the year on tour, the part-time Officers-in-charge found it out of the question to undertake the development of the section seriously, and what was practically stagnation resulted. It is therefore with peculiar satisfaction that we record the termination of these make-shift arrangements by the appointment on the 23rd May 1921 of a whole-time Superintendent for the Archæological Section in the person of the well-known Bengali scholar, Mr. Ramāprasād Chanda, who since that date has been in exclusive charge of the Calcutta collections of antiquities. During the winter of 1920-21 M. Foucher had kindly consented to fill a temporary gap at the Museum, and his charge extended by six days into the year under review. Charge was then taken for a brief space by Mr. K. N. Dikshit, Archæological Superintendent for Bengal, in addition to his other duties; but this was a purely provisional arrangement, extending only to the 23rd May as mentioned above. What substantial improvements the appointment of a whole-time Curator has rendered possible will be apparent from Mr. Chanda's first Report, which follows.

Indian Museum, Calcutta.

"The beginning of the year was marked by the opening to the public of the spacious hall of the groundfloor of the new wing of the Museum buildings (called the New Hall) wherein miscellaneous antiquities are exhibited. Labels have been put on the show cases of this Hall in course of the year. A scheme for arranging the sculptures in the galleries in, as far as possible, a chronological order was adopted. The Trustees of the Indian Museum by placing the Eastern Verandah and the entire Entrance Hall of the main Museum Building at the disposal of the Archæological Section, rendered the execution of the scheme possible. The later mediæval sculptures and architectural pieces hitherto exhibited in the Entrance Hall were transferred to the Southern and the Eastern Verandahs respectively, and the Hall itself was reserved for Mauryan and other archaic or Early Sunga sculptures. Two rows of pillars divide this Entrance Hall into twelve equal squares. In the middle square just in front of the entrance door are fixed on individual pedestals the cast of the lion capital of the Sarnath pillar of Asoka, the original lion capital of the Rampurwa pillar of Asoka, the bull capital of another monolithic pillar at Rampurwa ascribed to the same emperor, and the Kalpadruma or Wishing Tree from Besnagar in Gwalior State, Central India, which evidently served as the capital of a column. In the space between the third and the fourth pillars on the right side of the visitor entering the hall are exhibited the two big Patna statues, while the big female statue from Besnagar and the cast of the colossal statue from Parkham in the Mathura Museum of Archæology are installed on the left side. The two Patna statues and the Kalpadruma and the Besnagar female statue have been transferred to the Entrance Hall from the adjoining Bharhut Gallery where they were originally exhibited. On the shelf in the right wall of the Hall has been placed the arch stone from Patna (see below), and on the shelf in the left wall the stone receptacle of the relics, evidently of Gautama Buddha, of the so-called Jagat Singh stūpa of Sarnath. A group of later mediæval Buddhist and Brahmanic sculptures from Bihar, Bengal and Orissa have been arranged on the bench along the wall of the Southern Verandah, and the spaces between the columns in front of this Verandah have been cleared of antiquities.

"The five cellars of the New Wing of the Museum Building that serve as the godown of the Archæological Section were almost inaccessible on account of old rejected show-cases deposited therein. These cellars were cleared and the show-cases placed with the Trustees for sale. After defraying all expenses in connection with the removal and sale of these show-cases, the Trustees handed over to the Superintendent Rs. 309 out of the sale proceeds with which a wooden dark room has been erected in a corner of the office room of the Section originally marked off for the purpose. The antiquities in the cellars have been arranged and listed. In this connection the Superintendent desires to thank Dr. S. W. Kemp, the Offg. Honorary Secretary to the Trustees for the greater part of the year, whose sympathetic co-operation greatly facilitated the work.

"Antiquities other than coins acquired by purchase and received as presents or on loan number 175 pieces, including pictures [*vide* Plate XXXVI]. This collection consists of specimens representing all stages of the artistic history of India. The earliest in age is a granite arched torana stone (Figs. *a* and *b*) received on loan from Mr. K. P. Jayaswal, M.A., Bar-at-Law, the well-known Archæologist of Patna. The upper and lower curved faces of this piece bear Mauryan polish, and on three corners of the lower face are three mason's marks, *ko, kau, chu* (?) in archaic Brāhmī characters (*vide* Plate XL, Fig. *c*). The stone was discovered some years ago when the roots of an old tree were being dug out of the compound of the Muhammadan Shrine (*Dargāh*) near the site of Pataliputra. Mr. Jayaswal acquired the stone from the Manager (Sajjadānashīn) of the Dargāh. The polish on both the upper and lower faces may lead one to suppose that this stone originally belonged to the circular plinth round the mouth of a well. But indentations on all the four rough sides indicate that the stone was originally placed in a suspended position and evidently belonged to a free arch that crowned a torana. The stone measures 2′ 9″ in length, 2′ 1½″ in breadth at the upper end and 11″ at the lower end, and 13″ in thickness.

Indian Museum, Calcutta.

" *Samkhapāla-jātaka* (?) Perhaps next in order of time is a sculpture of Gandhāra slate in high relief measuring 13″ by 10″. This sculpture was found near Mathura (Muttra) in the bed of the Jumna and has been acquired through Rai Bahadur Radha Krishna, Honorary Curator of the Mathura Museum of Archæology. Unfortunately the effacement of almost all the characteristic features of the figures in this remarkable composition renders identification very difficult. On the background is a serpent with a hood of six or seven heads and at the foot of the back slab is a conch shell (*samkha*). To the left a layman of rank is seated on a stool. On his left hand resting on his left knee is probably a small serpent. One person is bowing low at his feet and another person, evidently a male attendant, is standing behind the stool. In the left upper corner of the back slab is seen hanging the foot of a human figure. Opposite the seated figure is standing a man with a staff slung on his right side. There is a water vessel behind him. The presence of the conch shell and the seven headed Nāga tempt me to identify the scene with an episode in the Samkhapālajātaka, No. 524 of the Pali collection. The Bodhisattva was born as the Nāga king Samkhapāla. Once every fortnight he used to leave the Nāga world, come to the earth, and coil himself round an ant-hill on a high road in order to practise virtues. One day sixteen wicked men caught hold of him and began to pull him cruelly in order to eat his flesh. The Nāga king was rescued by a householder named Alāra. Out of gratitude Samkhapāla took Alara to his palace in the Nāga world and entertained him for a year. Some of the *gāthās* (stanzas) in the Pali story give an account of the manner in which Alara was entertained in the Nāga palace (*The Jātaka*, Vol. V, translated by H. F. Francis, p. 88). Though this sculpture does not quite agree with the stanzas, it looks more like a scene in the Nāga world than anything else. (Plate XXXVI, Figs. *c* and *d*).

"The very small collection of Amarāvatī sculptures (only two in number) in the Indian Museum has been replenished by the addition of eighteen pieces presented by the authorities of the Madras Government Museum from their duplicate set. Forty-two pieces of fragmentary sculptures, besides the Gandhāra piece noticed above, have been purchased at Mathura through Rai Bahadur Pandit Radha Krishna. Most of these are of red sandstone and belong to the Kshatrapa-Kushan period (first and second centuries A. D.). There are a few pieces of grey sandstone belonging to the mediæval period. One of these pieces (Plate XXXVI, Fig. *e*) represents the child Krishna lifting up Mount Govardhana on his left hand. This piece was found at Jatipārā, near the village called Govardhana in the Muttra District, and measures 5⅔″ by 4½″. Once in the beginning of autumn, Nanda, the foster-father of Krishna, and other cowherds engaged themselves in making preparations for a sacrifice to Indra. Krishna told them that Indra was the god of cultivators and not of nomadic shepherds. Cattle and mountains were proper objects

Indian Museum, Calcutta.

of worship for shepherds, he said, so that they ought to offer sacrifice to Mount Govardhana instead of to Indra. Nanda and the other shepherds did as they were bidden by Krishna. This greatly annoyed Indra who ordered his attendant clouds to afflict the cattle of the shepherds with rain and wind. 'The clouds roared aloud, as if in terror of the lightning's scourge and poured down uninterrupted torrents. The cattle pelted by the storm, shrunk, cowering, into the smallest size, or gave up their breath. The calves trembling in the wind, looked piteously at their mothers' (Wilson's *Vishnu Purana*, V, II). The child Krishna then uprooted the spacious mountain Govardhana and held it up over the camping-ground of Nanda and his followers for seven days and nights. The sculpture shows Krishna holding up the mountain. The cow under the mountain is the very picture of peacefulness and security, and the eagerness with which the calf has just rushed to drink its mother's milk is portrayed with skill (Plate XXXVI, Fig. *e*).

" *Pāla Sculpture.*—There are two Tibetan works relating to the history of Buddhism, one of which is known after its author as Tārānāth, while the other is Pag Sam Jon Zang. [1] These works contain short sketches of the legendary history of sculpture in India that agree in substance and are evidently derived from a common source. According to both versions, miraculously gifted human and Deva artists made images before the time of Asoka. Yaksha artists were employed in Asoka's time and Nāgas were employed during the time of Nāgārjuna. Somewhat later, in King Buddhadisa's reign an artist named Bimbasara flourished in Magadha ; and during Sila's reign lived a clever image-maker named Srigadhari who was born in the Maru country. Then in the reign of King Dharmapāla and Devapāla there lived in the Varendra Country (Nalendra according to the Pag Sam Jon Zang) two clever artists, Dhiman and his son Bitpalo, who founded new schools of sculpture and painting. Whether these legends have any historical basis or not, they roughly correspond to the successive schools of sculpture that flourished in Eastern India and Hindustan. We have not yet come across any authentic specimen of the work of the miraculously gifted artists of the pre-Mauryan period. The sculptures produced in the reign of Asoka, the capitals of his edict-bearing monolithic columns, form a group by themselves, attributed to Yaksha artists by the Tibetan writers and to Bactrian sculptors by modern archæologists. The works of the Nāga artists of the time of Nāgārjuna correspond to the ancient Indian National School represented by the sculptures of Bharhut, Sânchī and Amarâvatī. This ancient school was succeeded by the early Gupta school of Hindustan proper. Whether the artists Bimbisara and Srigadhari and their royal patrons are historical personages or not, the sculptures of the Gupta period (fifth and sixth centuries A. D.) discovered at Sarnath near Benares, at Deogarh in the Jhansi district of the United Provinces, and at certain other places in Hindustan proper, make up the most valued contribution of India to the artistic heritage of mankind. The sculpture from Mathura showing the child Krishna with Mount Govardhana should probably be assigned to the post Gupta period.

" With Kings Dharmapāla and Devapāla we reach the firm ground of history in the narrative of the Tibetan writers. These two kings of the Pāla dynasty of Bengal and Bihar probably reigned in the ninth century A. D. Though the names of the artists Dhiman and Bitpalo are not met with elsewhere, we find in great abundance in Bihar

(1) For Taranath, see Indian Antiquary, Vol. IV., p. 102. I am indebted to Mr. J. Van Manen for an English translation of the passage in the Pag Sam Jon Zang and for a revised translation of the passage in Taranath.

and Bengal a new type of sculpture dating from the eighth or ninth century A. D. The material used is black shale called *kashti-pāthar* or touchstone in the vernacular, which is more tractable than sandstone. The inscribed image of Buddha calling the earth to witness (Plate XXXVI, Fig. *f*) is an early specimen of the sculpture of this type. It has been presented to the Indian Museum with eight other pieces by Mr. D. Sunder, F.L.C., F.R.G.S. of Bhagalpur, who found it at Rajgir in the District of Patna in Bihar. The Buddhist creed and the name of the donor, the Reverend (Bhanta-Bhudhuta) Silagupta are engraved on the pedestal in nail-headed characters that mark the transition between the Gupta and the old Nāgari scripts and were commonly used in Eastern India in the eighth and ninth centuries A. D. As distinguished from Gupta sculpture we may designate sculptures of this new school as Pāla sculptures. The Pāla sculpture is marked off by a peculiar development, a tendency to decorate the back slab more and more elaborately, which may be considered as a sign of decadence. But the technical skill of the artists of this period shows little sign of abating, and in the best images the expression discloses little or no loss of idealism.

"*Crowned Buddha.*—Another remarkable sculpture of black shale from Bihar presented by Mr. Sunder is a seated image of the crowned Buddha (Plate XXXVII, Fig. *a*). The main figure in the composition (10″ × 7⅝″) wears a crown and a necklace and holds in both hands a bowl which reminds us of the bowl-full of honey which a monkey offered to Buddha at Vaisālī. The seven figures on the back slab illustrating well-known events in the life of Buddha which with the main image make up the number eight, clearly indicate that the crowned figure actually does represent the Sākya monk. In the scenes from Buddha's life on the back slab Buddha is figured as a monk without ornament. The scenes to the proper right from the bottom upward are; Buddha calling the earth to witness just before attaining supreme knowledge; the descent from the heaven of the thirty-three gods; Buddha preaching at Sarnath. The topmost scene which is broken off undoubtedly represented the Death or Parinirvāna of Buddha. The scenes represented on the proper left of the figure from the bottom are:—Buddha in meditation evidently after attaining supreme knowledge; the taming of the elephant Nālagiri at Rājagriha; Buddha preaching after the performance of the miracles at Srāvastī. In the relief reproduced in Figure *f* of Plate XXXVI we have the same scenes with the exception of the first, for which the birth scene in the Lumbini garden is substituted. Six other figures of the crowned Buddha are exhibited in the Gupta Gallery. Figure *b* of Plate XXXVII shows a Buddha of this type in the attitude of calling the earth to witness, with seven other events of the Buddha's life figured on the back slab, where the Buddha is represented as a monk. The main image in Figure *c* represents Buddha preaching at Sarnath. Three of the seven scenes on the back slab of this sculpture are lost. In three others Buddha wears the crown. Two of these images (Figs. *b* and *c*) are from Bihar. Figure *d* is an image of sandstone from Sarnath. The head is unfortunately lost, but the necklace indicates that it is also an image of the crowned Buddha preaching at Sarnath. Figure *e* is another sandstone image of the crowned Buddha from the same site. The few remaining letters of the Buddhist creed originally engraved on its pedestal indicate that the image should probably be assigned to the ninth century A. D. In Figure *f* is reproduced a sandstone image of the same type from Bodh Gaya in the attitude of offering protection. The inscription on the pedestal gives the name of the donor as Pidumākā and dates from the tenth or eleventh century A. D. This group of crowned figures evidently represent a new type of Buddha that originated in Eastern India in the Pāla period. We recognize an

Indian Museum, Calcutta.

intermediate stage in the evolution of this type in Figure *g*, an image of black stone evidently from Magadha. It is a seated Buddha offering protection. The head wears curled hair and shows the usual protuberance called the *ushnīsha*. But there is a necklace round the neck. The next step after the necklace was of course the crown on the head. The Buddhist creed is engraved on the pedestal of this image in the nail-headed characters commonly used in the eighth and ninth centuries A. D.

"The Buddhist image makers could not stop with necklace and crown but went on adding other ornaments as well. A fine figure evidently of Buddha which wears not only the crown and the necklace, but also bangles and armlets, was excavated from site No. III at Nalanda in 1919-20. It measures 2 ft. by 11½ inches. The monkish dress of this image offers a strange contrast to these ornaments, and precludes us from identifying it with a Bodhisattva like Maitreya or Avalokitesvara. The lower garment (*antaravāsaka*) of a monk, as distinguished from the *dhoti* or loin cloth of a layman, is shown over the lower portion of the legs, and the *samghāti* or upper garment is quite prominent. I am therefore inclined to identify it as a standing crowned Buddha offering a boon, with the open right palm marked with the symbol of the Wheel and with the left hand holding the hem of the upper garment (Plate XXXVII, Fig. *h*). In Plate XXXVII, Fig. *i*, is reproduced the photograph of a headless image of evidently a crowned Vajrāsana Buddha in earth-touching attitude also wearing armlets and bangles. It was found in the Rajshahi District in Northern Bengal and is now exhibited in the Museum of the Varendra Research Society at Rajshahi.

"The Director-General of Archæology in India presented to the Indian Museum six bronze images unearthed at a village called Rayanallur in the Tiruturaipundi Taluk of the Tanjore District in the Madras Presidency and acquired by the Government of Madras as Treasure Trove. Two of these images, Vishnu and Lakshmī, are reproduced in Plate XXXVIII, Figs. *a* and *b*, respectively. Fourteen other bronze images were received in exchange from the Madras Museum through the good offices of Mr. Percy Brown, Officer-in-Charge of the Art Section of the Indian Museum.

"After mentioning the sculptures of the Pāla period Taranath writes, 'In Nepal also the early style was like the old western one (*i.e.*, Gupta). The paintings and bell metal (castings) of the middle period, which were mostly very closely like the eastern ones were regarded as of distinctly Nepalese style. Later they were no longer strictly so regarded' (Van Manen). The Director-General of Archæology in India presented 16 bronze images from Nepal purchased from a vendor at Delhi. Two of these, an image of Buddha calling the earth to witness and an image of Tārā, are reproduced in Figures *c* and *d* respectively. The drapery of the Buddha with border discloses Chinese influence.

"Among miscellaneous antiquities acquired during the year are two wooden shrines one from Gujarat presented by the Director-General of Archæology (7′ 8″ by 4′ 10″ by 4′ 10″) which has been installed near the entrance door of the New Hall, and another purchased at Mathura (3′ 5″ by 1′ 8″ by 1′ 1½″). The legs attached to the Kīrtimukha and the winged Makaras engraved on the top piece of the latter shrine indicate Nepalese origin. Mr. D. Sunder of Bhagalpur has also presented a stone cannon ball, 5 inches in diameter, which he found among the ruins of the palace of Mahārāja Pratāpāditya in the Sunderbans in the Khulna District in Bengal. Pratāpāditya, a semi-independent zemindar of Bengal, refused allegiance to the Mughal Emperor and was subdued by the famous Raja Mansing in the beginning of the reign of the Emperor Jahangir (A. D. 1605-27). According to tradition such balls were used by the imperial army in bombarding the palace of Pratāpāditya. Dr. Annandale, Director of the Zoological Survey of India, has transferred from the Anthropological Section of the Indian Museum two pieces of cannon of historical interest, a big inscribed brass kettle-drum (4′ 8″ in diameter and 3′ 6″ in height) made under the orders of Sivasimha the Ahom King of Assam in the Saka year 1652 (A. D. 1734), and a brass Astrolabe made in Herat. The Director-General of Archæology has presented a curious Persian vase which was found by British soldiers digging trenches near Baghdad at a depth of nearly 18′. Three sides of this vase are reproduced in Plate XXXIX. Figure 20 shows a Chinese dragon and a Persian horseman; Figure 21 shows a Chinese bowman shooting a bird; and Figure 22 shows an Indian elephant with a rider seated in a chair. *Indian Museum, Calcutta.*

"Other donors of sculptures and miscellaneous antiquities are, the Superintendent of Archæology, Eastern Circle, the Sub-Divisional Officer of Diamond Harbour, and Mr. H. Hodgart of the Zoological Survey of India.

"The Director-General of Archæology also presented a copy of a fresco painting at Polonnaruwa in Ceylon, and the Hon'ble Mr. Justice Beaufort of South Africa has presented through the Marquis Curzon 39 old pictures of some of the most notable Muhammadan Monuments of Eastern India as they existed towards the close of the eighteenth century.

"A whole-time modeller was added to the staff of the Archæological Section in the beginning of the year to fill up the gaps in the collection of sculptures with plaster casts of typical pieces in other Museums. A cast of the colossal Parkham image in the Mathura Museum of Archæology, and a cast of the inscribed statue of Kanishka exhibited in the same Museum have been installed in the galleries. Mr. Puran Chand Nahar, M.A., B.L., a scholar and a zemindar, has raised funds from the Svetāmbara Jains of Calcutta with which casts of ancient Jain sculptures from Mathura deposited in the Museums of Mathura and Lucknow are in course of preparation. From Mr. Fritz Holm of New York was procured a cast of his replica of the famous Chinese Nestorian Monument at Sian-Fu. This monument was set up in A. D. 781, and the Chinese and Syrian inscriptions engraved on it give a short history of the Nestorian Christian mission in China. The replica from which the cast is taken is now deposited in the Lateran Palace, Rome.

"(*a*) *Coins of non-Muhammadan dynasties.*—The Director of Industries, Central Provinces, presented 3 gold coins, two of which are of Prithvideva, and one of Ratnadeva of the Kalachuri-Haihaya dynasty of Ratnapura, and date from the twelfth century A. D. Five silver Gadhiya coins of the Rajputana and Gujarat currency of the eighth to the eleventh centuries A. D. have been presented by the Sardar Museum and Summair Public Library of Jodhpur.

"(*b*) *Coins of Muhammadan dynasties.*—Out of the Taylor collection (630 coins) purchased last year, 160 coins were added to the cabinet of the Section, 194 were presented to the Delhi Museum, and the rest were offered for sale to Provincial Museums. Three gold coins of the Barakzai dynasty of Afghanistan have been acquired

Indian Museum, Calcutta. by purchase. Besides the coins purchased, 37 have been received as presents from the following donors :—Bikanir Darbar, the Government of the United Provinces, Raja of Kharsama, the Government of Bengal and the Director of Industries, Central Provinces.

" A short pamphlet Guide was issued during the year in connection with the Second Session of the Oriental Conference held in Calcutta in January 1922.

" When the Archæological Section was separated from the Natural History Section of the Indian Museum in 1911, about 1900 volumes were transferred from the Zoological Library and formed the nucleus of the library of the Archæological Section. About 800 volumes have been added since then, 70 having been added during the year 1921-1922 excluding Journals.

" Since the creation of the Archæological Department all the circles of the Archæological Survey and the office of the Director-General of Archæology in India have been regularly supplying prints of photographs taken by them during each official year. This Section has received photographs from the office of the Director-General of Archæology in India up to the year 1919-20 ; from the Northern Circle, Agra Office, and from the Burma Circle, up to the year 1920-21 ; from the Southern Circle, Madras, up to 1917-1918. Other circles have not yet sent photographs taken after 1916-17. There is also a considerable collection of old photographs."

The Delhi Museum. Mr. Blakiston, as Honorary Curator of the Delhi Museum of Archæology, reports that " During the year 31 new exhibits and 438 coins were received at the Delhi Museum as detailed in Appendix C (*vide* page 254 pp.). Of the former some are of exceptional interest, the inscribed stone filter of the Emperor Aurangzeb and the Farman (Royal patent) of Ahmad Shah Durrani being worthy of particular notice [*vide* Plate XL. Fig. (*d*)]. The filter bears the inscription " Distilled water of the filter stone of Aurangzeb Alamgir, the king champion of the faith. The year 1080 " (1669-70 A. D.). Its characteristic is that when immersed in water it allows only pure water to percolate through, all impurities remaining without. Ahmad Shah Durrani attained renown through his defeat of the Mahratas on the plains of Panipat in 1761. The Museum is now in possession of a very fair collection of Farmans and other Moghal documents. Of the coins, 36 were purchased from dealers, 352 were received from various Provincial Governments and the remainder (50) were placed on loan in the Museum. It may not be out of place to mention that eight new wall cases and two standard cases which have been made for the display of the collection of pictures are now finished and will shortly be erected. They are a very great improvement on the old ramshackle frames that previously did service. It is hoped that it may be possible to report next year that the new cases for exhibits, which are being made to take the place of the heterogeneous collection now in use, have also been completed. This year new sun curtains also have been provided, as the old ones were entirely worn out."

Peshawar Museum. The Peshawar Museum is, strictly speaking, a Provincial institution, but the Archæological Superintendent for the Frontier Circle acts *ex-officio* as Honorary Curator, and the annual statement of progress is therefore included here. Mr. Hargreaves reports as follows :

" The total number of visitors to the Peshawar Museum was 54,386 as compared with 52,583 in the preceding year, an increase of 1,803.

Peshawar Museum.

" Two hundred and twenty-four antiquities including coins were acquired during the year. A hoard of 194 copper coins, principally of the early Pathan kings of Delhi and their contemporaries, which were discovered by some labourers when road-making near Charsada, was purchased for Rs. 12-2-0. Two stone mortars and a roughly-shaped stone with scroll ornamentation in very low relief which were obtained at the ancient site of Bedadi in the Hazara District were presented by Mr. T. B. Copeland, I.C.S. One silver coin of Shah Ālam II was contributed by the Government of the United Provinces and one smaller silver Gadhiya coin by the Superintendent, Sardar Museum, Jodhpur. Six copper Kushan coins, one iron implement, one arrow-head, two thin pieces of sheet copper, one copper bangle, four iron finger-rings, one copper signet and two other copper rings were sent on loan by the Superintendent, Archæological Survey, Frontier Circle, being part of the antiquities recovered during the operations at Jamālgarhī in 1920-21. The Director of Industries, Central Provinces, also presented to the Museum one silver and six gold coins.

" Thirty-six books have been added to the Museum Library, twenty-eight being presentations from official sources and eight being purchases. The Museum already possesses the nucleus of an excellent library dealing with the ancient history of the province and the antiquities in the Museum, and purchases are limited to works dealing with these and allied subjects. A special effort will be made to strengthen it in works dealing with numismatics. It is hoped that in time the library will be able to meet all the needs of students and others requiring works of reference dealing with the history and antiquities of the Frontier Province.

" The Museum was closed to the Public for 16 days, for various public purposes, examinations, committees and meetings and also for two days for the Hunt Ball. For committee meetings and examinations the body of the Hall alone is required and no inconvenience is experienced, but the Hunt Ball is always a source of danger, as it necessitates the removal of table cases, heavy images and inscriptions. On the last occasion the head of a heavy image was broken off during removal, and even with the greatest care safety cannot be ensured when antiquities have to be removed and replaced. Until the antiquities can be housed in some building where their removal is unnecessary they must be exposed to the risk of damage and it is, therefore, to be regretted that the proposed extension of the Victoria Memorial Hall, which was referred to in last year's report, could not, in view of the financial stringency, be built, and that the projected extension is now indefinitely postponed.

" The repairs to the exterior of the building which were so greatly needed have been executed during the year under report and the Victorial Memorial Hall is now in sound condition. No funds, however, have been available for the improvement of the Museum grounds and they continue in their previous unsatisfactory condition. In the past the brick piers and iron railings of the Museum grounds, where they are bounded by the Grand Trunk Road, have been constantly overthrown and damaged by the projecting loads of heavily laden carts and buffaloes. The attention of the Public Works Department was directed to this and the boundary wall and railings have now been adequately protected by the provision of a raised footpath three feet wide on the outer side of the boundary wall.

Peshawar Museum.

"All objects acquired during the year have been listed first in the Accession Register and then in the special registers and many of the antiquities exhibited in the table cases have been provided with explanatory labels.

"As the proposed Museum extension is now indefinitely postponed and the Museum cases are unlikely to undergo any re-arrangement in the near future, an endeavour will be made during the ensuing year to revise and republish the *Handbook to the Sculptures in the Peshawar Museum*, as Dr. Spooner's original edition has been long out of print, and many applications for copies are received from visitors and others.

"The question whether the Museum coin collection should not be more restricted in scope and limited to the coins of dynasties which have ruled on the North-West is under consideration. In the meantime Major H. M. Whittell, an active member of the Numismatic Society of India, has most generously offered to survey the collection and to make a selection of the coins worth retention in the coin cabinets, and at the same time prepare a list of duplicates which might better be transferred to other Museums or exchanged for those now lacking in the Museum. Should Major Whittell remain in Peshawar he has promised to draw up a manuscript catalogue of the coins.

"Numerous antiquities of stucco and stone, which have been recovered in excavations carried out in the Frontier Province since 1907, lie in the godowns of the Superintendent, as the Peshawar Museum affords no accommodation for their exhibition. Under instructions from the Director General of Archæology a representative selection of these stucco heads and images was made for loan to the Indian Museum, Calcutta, and supplemented by seven duplicate antiquities formerly exhibited in the Peshawar Museum. Of this selection 66 were carefully packed and despatched on March 31st to the Superintendent, Archæological Section, Indian Museum, Calcutta, and arrived in good condition. Five large and heavy statues, already packed, still await dispatch on receipt of further instructions from Calcutta. As the extension of the Museum is indefinitely postponed, it becomes a matter for consideration whether similar selections of the antiquities still in the godowns should not be offered to other Museums in India, which it is believed would welcome an opportunity of supplementing their collections with representative specimens of the Græco-Buddhist School of Gandhāra."

Prince of Wales' Museum, Bombay.

"The Prince of Wales' Museum of Western India," Mr. Banerji reports, "was opened to the public by Her Excellency Lady Lloyd on 10th January 1922. The Archæological Section of this Museum was classified, arranged and labelled by the Superintendent of the Western Circle, who acted as its Honorary Curator throughout the year. The Madras Central Museum presented a number of Amaravati sculptures, prehistoric pottery and iron implements, together with a large collection of neolithic stone implements from among its duplicates. Some heads and crossbars of railings were also received from the duplicates in the Lucknow Provincial Museum. Images and sculptures found in the excavation of the later Chalukyan temple in the fort at Sholapur were also transferred to this Museum at Bombay. The following sections were opened to the public:—I. Brahmanical, II. Buddhist, III. Epigraphical, IV. Jain, foreign and Prehistoric, V. Pottery and VI. Hero-stones and Miscellaneous.

Bijapur Museum.

"Only one meeting of the committee of management of the Bijapur Museum was held during the year, and a few articles of interest were purchased. The Museum was created by the Government of Bombay and its management entrusted to a committee of five, of whom three were officials (*vide* Bombay Government Resolution No. 4679, General Department, dated 19th July 1912), according to the suggestions made in a note dated the 30th January 1911, by Dr. J. Ph. Vogel, then Officiating Director-General of Archæology in India. According to this resolution the scope of the Museum was confined to antiquities of the Adilshahi period only. During the earlier years of its existence all portable antiquities found in the Bijapur District were stored in this Museum. In 1921 when a proposal for the transfer of non-Adilshahi antiquities was raised informally before the committee of management, they decided to keep all specimens already in the Museum and moreover applied to the Government for permission to increase the scope of the Museum. The Government of Bombay sanctioned this proposal in their letter No. 203-G., dated the 14th September 1921, stating that the Government had approved the resolution passed by the Committee of the Bijapur Museum at their meeting held on 1st July 1921 that the scope of the Museum should extend to all antiquities of the Adilshahi period and any other antiquities of local interest." Both of these Museums at Bombay and Bijapur are provincial and therefore the statements of acquisitions are not printed here in accordance with recent orders of the Government of India to the effect that the Archæological Department need not in future report in detail on the growth and progress of Provincial collections of antiquities. **Bijapur Museum.**

As has been stated elsewhere excavation as such was not in progress at Nalanda during 1921-22, although a few antiquities were incidentally recovered in the course of such clearance as became necessary in connexion with the conservation work. A brief account of the chief discoveries has been given already in the section on Conservation (page 19ff. *ante*), and Mr. Page has accordingly sent no formal report on the so-called "Museum" at Nalanda beyond the tabular statement of fresh acquisitions given in Appendix D page 259. I say "so-called" Museum because in reality the accommodation so far provided at Nalanda for the housing of antiquities recovered from the site amounts only to one room of the small bungalow built as a rest-house for the Archæological Officer in charge, and being without any staff of regular attendants cannot be called a Museum in any usual acceptance of this term. It is in some ways unfortunate that this purely provisional deposit has been popularly glorified by the name Museum, because a natural consequence of this designation is that the public are thereby led to suppose that they have a right to admittance. Admittance is, of course, conceded to the public whenever possible during those periods when the Archæological Officer is in residence. At other times, since there is no regular Custodian, and by no means enough glazed cases to render the antiquities safe, it is manifestly out of the question that the collection should be open to the public. Nalanda is not altogether easy of access, despite the existence of the toy railway running past it to Rajgir Kund, and it is not surprising therefore that when visitors take the trouble to come here from a distance and find the supposed Museum closed to them, disappointment is not only felt but expressed. With our present funds, however, it is impossible for the Department to do other than it does, although it is obviously to the advantage of the Department and of the work that public interest in the excavations and the resultant finds should be stimulated. As soon as the financial position permits of the provision of funds it is hoped that increased accommodation, preferably in a detached building, can be arranged for, and that a sufficient staff of permanent attendants can be secured to make it possible to open the Museum to visitors at all times of the year. But the safety of the antiquities **Nalanda Museum.**

Nalanda Museum. will have to be secured first of all by the provision of more show-cases. During 1921-22 six table cases were received from the Archæological Section of the Indian Museum from stock being given up by them, and a strong safe was purchased at a cost of Rs. 491. But the great majority of the finds, mostly small and very portable statuettes in stone and bronze, are merely laid out on open shelves which it is not possible to glaze. I should add that a sum of Rs. 3,014 was spent during the year towards the erection of a much needed godown, together with chowkidars' quarters, in the Museum enclosure.

Eastern Circle.

Apart from the Archæological Section of the Indian Museum, none of the museums of Eastern India are administered by the Archæological Department, but the following brief notes on three of these institutions have been included in the present Report at the special request of Mr. Dikshit, who as Superintendent in the Eastern Circle, co-operating with the local Museums, desires that the more important of their new acquisitions should be recorded here for future reference, as none of the institutions in question issue a formal report.

Dacca Museum.

"No important sculpture was added to the collection of the Dacca Museum during the year, but the Coin Cabinet received notable additions through the purchase of a collection of about 300 ancient Indian coins, mostly copper, from Mr. Russel of the Railway Department. The collection includes numerous interesting specimens of Tribal, Indo-Greek, Indo-Scythian and Pre-Moghul coins. It also contains two coins of Siladitya, with a clear legend. Another important addition to the Coin Cabinet is a gold coin of the later Gupta type found at Sabhar, and purchased for Rs. 16. The representative series of 32 coins of Shah Jahan presented by the Bengal Government from the find at Parsundi in the Birbhum District, also deserves mention."

Rajshahi Museum.

"The Secretary to the Varendra Research Society reports that 15 antiquities were added to their collection during the year. The number includes two gold coins of the Gupta Emperors Chandragupta II and Skandagupta acquired by purchase, and some stone and metal images from the Dinajpur District. Among stone sculptures the following deserve special notice: (1) an image of Sadāsiva (a ten-armed form of Siva, figured on the seals of the Sena kings of Bengal), of which the main figure with two hands in the *Vyākhyāna-mudrā* is in excellent preservation; (2) a square stone tablet (4" sq.) in good preservation, representing Vishnu on one side and his ten incarnations on the other; (3) a stone image (ht. 1' 10") representing the snake-goddess Manasā, in *alto relievo*. The delineation of the figures is graceful and artistic. Its chief iconographical feature of interest is the existence of a Siva-linga placed overhead at the top of the halo. Two miniature metal images, one of Avalokitesvara and the other of Ganesa, riding astride of his *vāhana* the rat (a rare form of the deity) are also worthy of mention."

Gauhati Museum.

"The Gauhati Museum is the only public collection in Assam worthy to form the basis of a future Museum for the province. The additions during the year are a fragmentary stone inscription from Jorapukur, District Nowgong, presented by Mrs. Tunstall at the instance of the Archæological Superintendent, and a number of ornamental pieces of pottery found at a great depth below ground level, in digging the foundations of a house at Ujan Bazar in Gauhati. The pottery exhibits a variety of shapes and designs indicative of a skill not inherited in any degree by the modern Assamese potter.

Mr. Garde, the Archæological Superintendent in Gwalior State, reports as follows :— Gwalior Museum.

"The formation of the Archæological Museum was the chief achievement of the Department in the year of report. The work of adapting the building known as Gujari-mahal for accommodating the Archæological Museum and of collecting exhibits on the spot had been already started last year. The building and initial collection having been completed early this year the work of classifying, arranging and labelling the exhibits was taken in hand immediately and was finished before the end of January so that the museum was ready by the time His Royal Highness the Prince of Wales visited Gwalior. Since then the museum has been open to visitors.

"The exhibits have been classified into the following groups :—(1) Inscriptions, (2) Capitals of monolithic pillars, (3) Jaina Tirthamkaras, (4) Vishnu and Lakshmi, (5) Avataras of Vishnu, (6) Siva and Parvati, (7) Saiva deities, (8) Minor gods, (9) Minor goddesses, (10) Yakshas and demi-gods, (11) Miscellaneous figures, (12) Figurines and limbs, (13) Figures of animals, (14) Architectural pieces and (15) Pictures and small antiquities. Each group is arranged in a separate room. There are, however, a few large and important sculptures which, though they may fall into one or other of the aforesaid groups, have been exhibited in separate cells by themselves as by being so placed their individual importance is emphasised and they are able to attract the particular attention of visitors. In each room prominent places are reserved as far as possible for well preserved sculptures of artistic merit, thus sacrificing to a certain extent the chronological order. The arrangement is such that commencing at one end of the quadrangle the visitor can see the whole museum in one single round.

"The museum contains nearly 250 sculptures and 21 stone inscriptions picked up from various places in the State and ranging in date from the 2nd century B. C. to the 13th century A. D. There are a few Buddhist carvings and a fair collection of Jaina sculptures but by far the largest number of images are Brahmanical. Besides these the minor antiquities such as coins, heads, inscribed seals, pieces of pottery and iron implements exhumed in the excavations at Besnagar (Vidisa) and a number of large sized photographs of the more important ancient monuments in the State have been exhibited separately in a spacious hall. The most valuable exhibits, however, are the excellent copies of the very interesting fresco-paintings in the Buddhist caves at Bagh.

"For the guidance of visitors sign boards have been provided for all important rooms, indicating the general nature of their contents, and all important exhibits are furnished with labels showing their name, find spot and approximate age, also specifying exact dates where available. When time permits it is proposed to publish a catalogue giving full descriptive and historical notes on the antiquities for the use of those who wish to study them more closely.

"The specimens now exhibited are all local, *i.e.*, collected from the territories of Gwalior State alone. The present museum is, however, only a nucleus to be developed hereafter. There is still a wealth of antiquities lying scattered in the districts which will be brought to the museum in due course. Although the museum is thus intended to be primarily a store house of local antiquities exclusiveness will not be pushed to an extreme and small antiquities also from other parts of India such as coins, pictures and photographs of representative monuments of all periods of Indian History will be added to the museum as far as practicable. It is also proposed to exchange duplicates with other museums. In short every effort is being made to make the Institution useful and interesting."

SECTION V.

EPIGRAPHY.

Sanskrit Epigraphy.

M. R. Ry. Rao Bahadur H. Krishna Shastri having been on leave when the materials for this Report were being prepared, Mr. K. V. Subrahmanya Aiyer sends me the following general statement of the progress made in this branch of the Department.

"During the year 1921-22 the *Epigraphia Indica* was under the joint editorship of Dr. F. W. Thomas and Rao Bahadur H. Krishna Sastri. Five parts of the journal, *viz.*, part VII of Volume XV and parts I to IV of Volume XVI were passed for printing and issue. The Ghosundi stone inscription edited by Mr. K. P. Jayaswal, M.A., is the earliest Sanskrit inscription yet discovered in India. It refers to the deified Vaishnava statues of Sankarshana and Vāsudēva who also appear as Gods belonging to the Lunar family in the Nanaghat inscription. The record accordingly is an additional valuable evidence for the early history of Vaishnavism. Two copper-plate grants from Indore, edited by Dr. R. C. Mozumdar, are dated in years 67 and 107, probably of the Gupta Era, corresponding to 386-7 and 426-7 A. D., the former being the earliest dated inscription of the Guptas, and the earliest copper-plate grant ever discovered in Northern India. They belong to the reigns of the feudatory chiefs Svāmidāsa and Bhulunda and mention the *dūtakas* Nannabhatti and Skanda. The Shorkot inscription of the Gupta year 83 (= A. D. 402), edited by Dr. Vogel, is of importance as it gives us to understand that its ancient name was Sibipura, the capital of the Sibis, one of the races of North India overcome by Alexander the Great, according to the Greek geographers. The indistinct Kharoshthi inscription on the Bimaran Vase in the British Museum was successfully deciphered by Dr. Pargiter, and the much worn Prākrit epigraphs from Cutch were made out by Mr. R. D. Banerji. These latter belong to the reign of the Western Kshatrapa king Rudradāman, son of Jayadāman, grandson of Chashtana and great grandson of Ysāmotika. They are dated in the Saka year 52 (= A. D. 130), dark half of Phalguna, 2, and refer to the erection of funeral monuments *lashtis*. The Tipperah grant of the feudatory chief Lōkanātha published by Mr. R. G. Basak, is dated in the year 44, taken to be of the Harsha Era (= A. D. 650) and is a record of importance. According to it, the chief Lōkanātha was a *Karana* by caste ; his maternal grandfather was one Kēsava, the leader of an army and a *Pārasava* ; the latter's father and grandfather were prominent Brahmins. The members on the paternal side of Lōkanātha may have been Kshatriyas ; among them was an *adhimahārāja*, a *sāmanta* and another, who, renouncing the world, led the life of a *rishi*. The inscription thus brings strongly into evidence the prevalence in East Bengal in A. D. 650, *i.e.*, just before the rule of the Buddhist Pāla Kings, of the Hindu creed and of *anulōma* marriages. It shows also that persons of mixed caste were not held in disrepute in those days but were honoured with high social position. Lōkanātha's contemporary was a certain Jayatungavarsha, whose name reminds us of a much later Jayatungasimha of the Kamā country. Of the fourteen records published by Dr. Barnett out of those bequeathed to the British Museum by the late Dr. Fleet, there are two which refer to the grammarian Narēndrasēna, the author of *Pramāna-pramēya-kalika*, a work on logic. These records state that the author was a disciple of Kanakasēna, who was himself a disciple of Ajitasēna ; that he had mastered the *Chāndra*, *Kātantra*, *Jainēndra*, *Sab-dānusāsana*, *Aindra* and *Pānini* and flourished about Saka 975 (= A. D. 1053). The Bhamodra Mahota Plates edited by the same author belong to the time of Dronasimha the second son of Bhatārka, the founder of the Maitraka dynasty of Vallabhi and are dated in the

Gupta Vallabhi samvat 183 (=A.D. 501) being thus the earliest Vallabhi grant extant. The Damoh Hindi inscription published by Mr. Hira Lal refers to the reign of Mahmud Shah II, the last king of the Khiljis of Malwa; it is dated in Vikrama Samvat 1570 and contains a proclamation recording remission of taxes on seed-lenders, midwives and tailors. Mr. Sewell has contributed a valuable paper on the Ārya Siddhānta. Sanskrit Epigraphy.

"In the Central Circle, Babu Manmatha Nath Sen presented to the Patna Museum a copper-plate grant of the time of the Vākātaka king Pravarasena II; and an old inscribed wooden pillar of the 4th or 5th century A. D., found in the middle of a dried up tank at Kirāri in the Chandrapur-Padampur Taluk of the Bilaspur District, Central Provinces, was brought to the notice of the Archæological Department by Pandit Lochan Prasad Pandeya and was removed to the Nagpur Museum. The Epigraphist to the Patna Museum took estampages of the Asokan edict at Lauriya-Nandangarh and the Assistant Archæological Superintendent of the Circle copied 13 inscriptions in connection with the listing of ancient monuments.

"The Provincial Museum at Lucknow acquired a set of two inscribed copper-plates with ring and seal, of the time of the Gāhadavāla king Gōvindachandra, of Kanauj, dated in Vik. Samvat 1177 (=A. D. 1121); and a fragmentary sun-dried brick containing a cuneiform inscription, obtained from the ruins of a sun temple at Ur, the ancient city of the Chaldees in Mesopotamia, was presented by Lieutenant-Colonel C. A. Sprawson.

"No Epigraphical acquisition was made during the year to the Indian Museum at Calcutta.

"In the Eastern Circle, a number of bronze Buddhist images were discovered in different parts of the Chittagong District, with dedicatory inscriptions, ranging in date from the 9th to the 12th century A. D. engraved on their backs and pedestals. They are now preserved in the Chittagong monastery. The missing leaf of the Nidhanpur plates of Bhāskaravarman was traced at Silchar and found to embody the interesting information that this grant was originally made by Bhūtivarman, the great-great-grandfather of Bhāskaravarman, but was renewed by his descendant owing to the destruction by fire of the original document. The name of the village granted is given as Mayūrasalmalī, which is most probably in the Assam Valley. Mr. K. N. Dikshit says 'It now seems possible that the discovery of the plate in Sylhet has no bearing on the question whether Sylhet formed part of ancient Kāmarūpa.' Of greater interest is the Chēdi inscription of the 11th century A. D., of the time of king Karna, discovered on a small decorative pillar at Paikore in Birbhum District. It records that the image of a goddess was made by an order of the king himself. Its main interest lies in the fact that it confirms the conjectural invasion of Bengal by this powerful ruler of Central India, gathered from references in Chēdi inscriptions and in the Tibetan life of the Buddhist Achārya Atīsa or Dīpankara. Another pillar found along with the above record mentions Vijayasēna, apparently the well-known king of the Sēna dynasty, who lived a century later than the Chēdi king. A huge semi-circular stone found at Maharani in the Udaypur Division of the Tripura State contains 4 inscriptions in elegant Sanskrit verse, relating to the building of a Vishnu temple by King Vijayamanikya in 1548 A. D. These are the earliest inscriptions of the Tripura dynasty discovered so far. Copies of the famous Bangarh pillar inscription of the Kamboja king (now at the Rajbari, Dinajpur) and the Gaganēsvara fragmentary inscription of Kapilesvaradeva of Orissa (A. D. 1434-70) were also made.

Sanskrit Epigraphy.

"In the Southern Circle, ten new copper-plates were examined, 808 stone inscriptions copied, and 3,327 manuscript pages of texts of South-Indian Inscriptions sent to the Superintendent, Government Press, Madras, partly to complete Volumes V and VI and partly to form Volume VII of the new series of the *South-Indian Inscriptions :—Texts*. Of this collection, 61 are copies of records previously secured and 82 have not been examined. The rest are noticed in the Annual Report on Epigraphy, Southern Circle, Madras.

"Indra Bhattāraka of the Eastern Chalukya family whose succession to the throne remained till now in doubt owing to the fact that earlier charters mentioned him even without the title of Mahārāja and omitted to give the extent of his reign as they did for others, but who according to the later charters reigned for seven days, is represented by a copper-plate grant which calls him Indravarma-Mahārāja, the son of Vishnuvardhana (I) and grandson of Kīrttāvarman. The seal of the grant bears the legend '*Tyāgadhēnu*' which must have been one of his titles.* The inscription registers the gift of the village of Kondanagūru to a brahman named Chandisarman and it is to be published in the *Epigraphia Indica* by Professor Hultzsch. A copper-plate belonging to the time of the Chalukya-Chōla King Rājarāja II, son of Kulōttunga I, issued in the second year of his viceroyalty of Vēngi, states that he was crowned in Kulira *ba*, *Dasamī* Wednesday, Tulā-laghna (roughly 27th July 1076 A. D.). It registers a grant of 12 villages to a favourite chief named Mummadi-Bhīma who was brought up in the royal household of the Chalukyas. It is reported that the chief rendered valuable service in the wars waged against the kings of Ganga, Kalinga, and Kuntala and that in recognition of this, he was given the governorship of 1,000 villages in Vēngīpura-vishaya.

"A hitherto unknown king Bhavadatta of the Nala race is found to figure in a fragmentary lithic record of the 5th century A. D. discovered near the Podagadh hill in the Jeypore Agency.

"The largest number of the year's collection belongs to the Chōlas and almost all the kings of the line are represented. A record of Rājakēsarivarman found at Takkōlam, where the Chōla prince Rājāditya was killed by Būtuga, is referable to Aditya I as it mentions Aparājita-chaturvēdimangalam, a name derived from the last member of the Pallavas whom he vanquished. One of the inscriptions of Parāntaka dated in the 7th year of his reign (A. D. 914) registers a gift of gold made by a lady for plying a boat in the big tank of the village, and the village assembly of Parundur undertook to supply 150 *kādi* of the *Panchavāra* paddy for its maintenance. The boat was evidently meant to remove silt from the tank when there was water in it. The Uttaramallūr inscription published in the Archæological Survey Report for 1904-05, page 131 ff. gives us to understand that the *Panchavāra* committee was one of the committees forming the village assembly. What its duties were, it was not possible to know. The inscriptions of the year seem to indicate that the collection of assessment in paddy was left with the members of this committee. One of the records brings to light a hitherto unknown daughter of Parāntaka I, Vīramādēvī by name, who was the queen of Gōvinda Pallavarayar. It is interesting to notice that a stone inscription found at Pullamangai in the Tanjore district, is dated in the sixth year of Parakēsarivarman (*i.e.*, Parāntaka I)

---

* *Cf.* the title *Kamadhenu* which his father Vishnuvardhana I is given in his Chipurapalle grant (*Ind. Ant.*, vol. XX, page 16, text-line 5). [K.S.]

and introduces Sembiyan Māvali Vānarāyan as the king's vassal. From the Tamil portion affixed to the Udayēndiram grant of the Ganga king Prithivīpathi II. which states that Parāntaka I defeated two Bāna princes and conferred their territory on the Ganga, with the title of 'Banāditya', we know that the the name Sembiyan Māvali Vānarāyan was borne by Prithivīpathi II. In another record of Parāntaka, found at Tiruvadi, figures the Kongavānar which testifies to the king's conquest of Kongu. Sanskrit Epigraphy.

"Rājarāja I may be said to be the foremost among the kings of Southern India who took a keen interest in the administration of endowments made for charitable purposes. From previous collections we know that he appointed Madurāntakan Gandarādittan at the head of a committee to overhaul the accounts of temples, to conduct inquiries in cases of misappropriations and to set right matters by punishing the offenders. Rājēndra-Chōla I appears to have followed his father closely in this respect. One of his Tiruvallam inscriptions copied during the year, states that Pūvattabhatta-Sōmāyajiyār of Kottayūr scrutinised the accounts of the temple of Tiruvallam from his camp at Mēlpādi and fixed the scale of expenditure in conformity with an order issued by Madhurāntakan Gandaradittanar in the seventh year of Rājarāja's reign. The epigraphs of Tenneri, record that the village Assembly of Uttamachōla-chaturvēdimangalam laid down that only those who were capable of reciting the *Mantra-Brāhmana* were eligible for membership in the *Ūr-vāriyam* (*i.e.*, the village supervision committee), it being stipulated also that those among them who were guilty of misappropriating the property of Brāhmanas or of other heinous crimes should not be given the privilege. Some of the inscriptions of Parakēsarivarman Rājēndradēva refer to the image of the Sōla-Kēralavitankar set up in the temple of Tiruvallam. This is evidently named after the Chōla prince of that name who figures as one of the sons of the king.

"Two inscriptions from the Cuddalore District, of the time of Jatāvarman Sundara-Pāndya, refer to extensive salt works that existed at several places and state that one *ulakku* of salt was the tax on 1 *urai*. It is interesting to point out that a record of Kulōttunga III discovered during the year at Tiruvadi introduces a lady with the title of *talaikkōli*. One of the Tiruvorriyūr inscriptions states that on the 8th night of the Avani festival, the Chōla king Rājarāja III attended the dancing of *agamārga* performed by a lady who bore the title Uravakkinān-*talaikkōli*. Ancient Tamil literature informs us that expert lady dancers, who had acquired distinction in the art of dancing were publicly favoured by kings with a special mark of honour and were invested with the title of *talaikkōli*. The investiture of this title was preceded by a grand ceremony and followed by the presentation of a staff embellished with the nine gems and covered with gold plates. The two records afford epigraphical confirmation of the ancient practice.

"In the 13th century A. D. the power of the Chōlas waned considerably. The decline was greatly aggravated by the advance of the Pandya on the one hand and by the prevalence of discord among the several Chōla subordinates on the other. Compacts were entered into with the latter and this saved the situation for a time. But many of the subordinates soon asserted their independence. And in the reign of Rājarāja III, a chieftain named Perunjinga, of Pallava extraction, rebelled against the central authority, took the king captive after defeating him in several engagements and proclaimed himself ruler. In the current year's collection, there are a few records which introduce certain Sambuvarāyans, who might be regarded as the lineal descendants of

Sanskrit Epigraphy.

those with whom compacts were entered into; others which were issued by certain chieftains who might be the successors of those that threw off the Chōla yoke; and the rest belong to the reign of the later Pallava ruler Perunjinga. The inscriptions of the last show that he was a great admirer of the arts. It is said that he made large additions to the temple at Chidambaram by building for it the finely sculptured seven-storied tower on the southern side, delineating the various poses of dancers as described in the *Bharata-Nātya-Sāstra*. One of the inscriptions of this year states that the village of Āttūr in the Chingleput District was granted for meeting the cost of building this *gopura*. Another record, also secured this year, gives him the significant *birudas Kshīrāpagādakshina-nayaka, Pennai-nadīnātha, Kāvērikāmuka, Sabhāpatisabhā-sarvakārya-sarvakāla-nirvāhaka, Khaddgamalla Bharatamalla Sāhityaratnākara.*

"The services rendered to the Chidambaram temple by a chief who is variously named Kūttan Tondaiyarkōn, Naralōkavīran and the lion of the Kalingar, forms the subject of a bi-lingual metrical composition in Sanskrit and Tamil (No. 120 of 1888), wherein it is stated that in addition to the *gōpura* at the south entrance, he built also several *mandapas* supported by numerous pillars, constructed with stone the temple tank, covered with gold the dancing hall and presented valuable jewels, vessels and live-stock and provided richly for all the requirements of the temple. In the current year's collection, there is a similar metrical record in Tamil, which registers the contribution made by the same chief to the temple at Tiruvadi. As this chief is stated to have conquered the Pāndyas, the Chēras and the kings of the north, he must be different from Parākrama-Pāndya, who also bore the surname Naralōkavīra (Annual Report for 1909, Part II, paragraph 29). To judge from the Palæography of the inscription the chief appears to belong to the 13th century A. D. Another later Pallava chief Bhasavasankara, with a string of high sounding *birudas*, figures in an inscription of the 17th year of the reign of Rājanārāyana Sambuvarāya. He seems to be a later member of the family to which Bhasavasankara Allādi Pammayadēva-Māharāja of Tripurāntakam belonged.

"Three other epigraphs in the year's collection show the patronage given by Hindu sovereigns to literary men. Varakavi Rāmalingayya of the time of Sāluva Narasimha received 60 *panam*; the poet Uddandavēlāyuda-Bhārati received a *sarvamanya* gift of land for composing a *kalambagam* on Tiruvadi; and Varadaya of Kuratti who composed the *Tiruvallai-andādi* obtained a similar gift. Though the encouragement given to these men is thus known, the compositions themselves remain yet to be discovered.

"Among the numerous Vijayanagara records secured during the year, there are two belonging to the reign of Vīra-Bhūpati son of Bukka II. One of them mentions his officer Mahapradhāni Annādata-Udaiyar. An inscription of Dēvarāya II, dated in Saka 1352 registers an order issued by the king's younger brother Srīgiri whom we know from the Satyamangalam and Madras Museum plates to have been governing the Maratakanagara country. The records of this year's collection belonging to the time of Sāluva Narasimha show that he had for his commander (*dalavāy*) Isvara-Nāyaka, who is probably the ancestor of Krishnarāya-Mahārāya. Rāhutta-Perumāl and Annamarasayya are reported to be the agents of this Isvara-Nāyaka.

"In the Western Circle, two new inscriptions were discovered. One of them is a copper-plate grant of three leaves found at Kalyan in the Nasik District. It belongs to the time of Yasōvarman, a subordinate of the Paramāra king Bhōja of Malwa. Referring to Bhōja, the record says that he conquered the kings of Karnāta, Lāta, Gūrjjarat

Chēdī and Komkana ; and meditated on the feet of Sindhurājadēva who meditated on the feet of Vākpatirājadēva and who again meditated on the feet of Sīyakadēva. The date of the inscription which is not furnished by the plates, may be said to fall before A. D. 1056, when Bhoja I was defeated by the Kalachuri-Chedi King Karnadeva. The inscription registers the grant of certain pieces of land, oil-mills, shops for merchants and 14 *drammas* to the Tirthankara Muni-Suvratadeva of the Jain temple at Mahīshavuddhika in the holy *tīrtha* of Kalkalēsvara, situated in the Svetapada country. Mr. R. D. Banerji states that Svetapada is probably the ancient name of the country of Dandesh, surnamed Khandesh after its conquest by the Mughal Emperor Akbar I. The other record is a stone inscription discovered at Jura in the state of Maihar and sent by Mr. Banerji to the Government Epigraphist for being deciphered. It is a *prasasti* of the Rāshtrakūta king Krishna III engraved in the Kanarese language by a certain Chimmayya at the instance of Tuyyala Chandayya the younger brother of Kāmesetti and contains some well-known *birudas* of the king, besides three verses which describe him as a son to women folk other than his wife. Most of these *birudas* have been collected from a number of inscriptions by the late Dr. Fleet, and their significance noticed in the *Epigraphia Indica*, Volume VI, pages 178 ff. ; but it has to be pointed out here that the *biruda* ' *Kabbega* ' ' a poet ' which actually occurs as such in line 3 of the Atakur inscription (*ibid* page 54) has been misread as ' *Kachchēga* ' and interpreted to mean ' he who wears the girdle (of prowess).' Both these interesting inscriptions are to be published in the *Epigraphia Indica* under the editorship of Messrs. Banerji and T. T. Sharma.

Sanskrit Epigraphy.

" Twenty-two inscriptions were copied during the year for the Rajputana Museum, Ajmere. Out of these, 3 come from Sirohi, 3 from Chitor (Mewar State) and the rest are from Partabgarh State. Two of the records of Chitor are dated in H. 705 and 709 and belong to the reign of Allauddin Khilji, the king being called Sultan Shah-i-jahan Muhammad Shah and Sultan Muhammad Shah Bul Muzaffar Sikandar. The other inscription registers the construction of a building by Tughlaq Shah and Assauddin Arsalan. Mr. G. S. Ojha points out that this Assauddin Arsalan was the nephew of Ghiyas-ud-din Tughlaq and was appointed by him as Naib Barbak in the year of his accession, and as such the record must belong to the period A. D. 1320--25. All the other inscriptions, which range in date from Samvat 1135 to 1524, are engraved on the backs of brass images found in Jain temples said to be of the Tīrthankaras Rishabhadeva, Sāntinātha, Pārsvanātha, Dharmanātha, Vimalanatha, Padmaprabha, Ādinātha and Neminātha. They mention the names of donees, the year of gift and the names of the Jain teachers who performed the consecration ceremonies. Various castes including the Balāhī are also mentioned. As Mr. Ojha says that the Balāhīs are at present an untouchable caste among the Hindus, the mention of the name as a class in the Ukesa caste is a proof of the story of the wholesale conversion of the town of Osian (Ukesa) to Jainism.

" In the Northern Circle Rai Bahadur Daya Ram Sahni discovered and deciphered eighteen new inscriptions. As many as eleven of these which were unearthed at Sarnath, are short dedicatory epigraphs which record the installation of images by Buddhist monks or laymen, though one of them is much defaced and appears to contain the name of Budha-gupta. Mr. Sahni thinks that this last may be the same as the Gupta King of that name, inscriptions of whose reign were unearthed by Mr. Hargreaves in 1914-15 close to the spot where the inscription in question was found last year. One short inscription

Sanskrit Epigraphy.

was copied at Amīn in the Kurukshetra area, which is believed to mark the spot where Abhimanyu, the son of the great Pāndava hero, Arjuna, was slain by the Kaurava forces. It is engraved in Brāhmī characters of the Kushān period, on the top of a short stone pillar, 3'-9½" in height, and embellished with carvings on all the four faces. The inscription merely states that the post, on which it is cut, was the gift of a certain Isimitra (Sanskrit *Rishimitra*).

"The remaining six inscriptions were recovered by Mr. Sahni in the course of a search made in the villages in and around Kosam in the Allahabad District, one of them being found on the hitherto concealed portion of the shaft of the Kosam pillar itself. This last mentioned inscription, which General Cunningham correctly assigns to the 6th or 7th century A. D. has already been published by Mr. Pargiter in the *Epig. Ind.*, Vol. XI. It was composed by a certain Sankhadeva and consists of a single stanza in the Upendravajrā metre, which states that 'the man who fixes his look on this tall pillar will preserve fortitude during the adversity of the planets, and being delivered from sin he purifies his kindred and proceeds without doubt to Indra's world'. Other earlier writings on the visible portion of the shaft, including the surface of the lower portion laid bare this year, consist of two short epigraphs of a few characters each, which are assignable to the 4th or 5th century A. D. As the southern half of the lower portion of the shaft is still hidden from view it is impossible to say whether it contains any inscription which would throw light on the early history of the monument.

"The longest and best preserved inscription discovered in the neighbourhood of Kosam is a document of thirteen lines neatly cut in Brāhmī characters of the 2nd or 3rd century B. C. on a railing post, 2'-10" in height, which is built into the parapet of a well in the village of Masharfa situated about a mile and a half to the north-west of the pillar at Kosam. The inscription begins with a salutation to a certain Bhagavat and records that a certain householder named Gotiputa, who was the son of Seliya-puta Kusāpala, who again was the son of a certain Vāri, a votary of Manibhadra, caused a stone rail to be made. Unfortunately the name of the deity which was engraved at the end of the inscription is broken away. Mr. Sahni is of opinion that as the grandfather of the donor is specifically described as a Mānibhadra, *i.e.*, an adherent of the Yaksha Manibhadra, the deity in whose honour this railing was set up must have been Manibhadra himself. The deity is known to us from the Pawaya Manibhadra image inscription and two others. Mr. Ramāprasād Chanda has discussed the prevalence of the cult of this deity in his article entitled *Four ancient Yaksha Statues* in the Journal of the Department of Letters, University of Calcutta, Volume IV. The inscription discovered near Kosam provides further epigraphical evidence on the subject.

"Two other inscriptions discovered by Mr. Sahni near Kosam are much mutilated. They contain, however, the names of two rulers which he reads as Mahārāja Bhadramegha, and Mahārāja Sivamegha. One of these inscriptions is dated in the year 80 presumably of the Kushan era. These rulers are not yet known from contemporary coins or any other source.

"The latest, though perhaps the most valuable inscription brought to light in the neighbourhood of Kosam is a short Nāgarī inscription engraved on a door jamb, 4'-10" in height, which was lying in front of a ruined temple in the village of Meohar, distant 7 miles from Kosam. The purport of the inscription is that in the year Samvat 1245 (1189 A. D.) in the reign of King Jayachchandra of Kanauj a certain Sirvāstavya

Thakkura whose name is missing, caused a temple of Siddhesvara to be built at the village of Mehavada in the district of Kausāmbī. As the village of Maohar where this inscription has been found is identical with the Mehavada village mentioned in the epigraph, and as it is situated within 7 miles of Kosam, Mr. Sahni regards this inscription as affording incontestable evidence of the identity of Kosam and Kāusambī.

Sanskrit Epigraphy.

"One other inscription deciphered by Mr. Sahni this year deserves special mention here. It was originally engraved on an image pedestal, and the extant portion of the epigraph has come down to us on fourteen pieces of different sizes which were fitted together by Dr. Vogel. The inscription consists of six lines in Sanskrit and Brāhmī characters of the Kushan period. Imperfect as it is, the document is of interest in connection with the history of the Kushan dynasty. It appears to record that a certain temple was built by or for the grandfather (*pitāmaha*) of Huvishka, whose name is lost in the inscription. This temple fell to ruin and was restored out of regard for the then reigning King Huvishka by one of his officers, who held the rank of Mahadandanayaka. Something else is also stated to have been done for the benefit of the daily guests and Brahmanas at the same temple. None of the numerous Kushan inscriptions known to us from Mathurā or other places have anything to tell us about the mutual relationship of the Kushan Kings. The gap after the word *pitāmahasya* is unfortunate though it is possible to conjecture that it might refer to Kanishka. Further researches alone can definitely settle this point.

"No epigraphical discoveries were made on the Frontier during the year but Mr. Hargreaves writes: 'Mr. T. B. Copeland, I.C.S., forwarded for examination a small copper oil-measure, *karandi*, which he obtained from the ancient site of Bedadi in the Hazara District. This *karandi* is 9" in length and weighs 2·7 ounces. The diameter of the bowl is 1·9" and its height 1·4". The long thin handle is at right angles to the diameter of the bowl and terminates in an oval ring formed by bending backwards the top 2½" of the wire-like handle. Just below the rim of the bowl on the outer side are twenty-eight stippled Kharoshthī *aksharas*. The oil-measure was sent to Rai Bahadur Daya Ram Sahni for decipherment, but he reports that he has been unable in the time at his disposal to decipher the whole of it, and that it does not appear to be an inscription of special importance. He believes he can read two names in the genitive case. Although the oil-measure is excellently preserved it appears to have had some use, as the bottom is slightly indented and some of the characters are partly defaced. It was in all probability a gift to one of the religious establishments of Bedadi by some zealous laymen about the 2nd century A. D. Its exact find-spot has not been recorded. The antique is not at present in India, but it is hoped to obtain it later—at least on loan—for the Peshawar Museum, when more prolonged and closer examination of the inscription will then become possible'."

"In Burma" M. Duroiselle says, "this year saw the issue from the press of Volume II, Parts I and II of the *Epigraphia Birmanica*. Volume III, Part I, of the same publication is practically ready, and is awaiting copies of the plates for issue. This Part contains three inscriptions, No. IX—XI, which are the last of the 'Early Môn Inscriptions.' No. IX is remarkable both for its contents and its length. It records very circumstantially the erection of a palace at Pagan; and considering the probable date of the inscription, about the last two decades of the 11th century, it must have been the palace erected for King Kyanzittha (1084—1112). The palace of course, has, completely disappeared after so many centuries, the structure being of wood. The site on which it

Burmese Epigraphy.

Burmese Epigraphy.

stood is still well known in Pagan, and a commemorative pillar has been erected in the centre of it. It is situated not far from the Ananda temple between the Shwegugyi and the Gawdawpalin temples. From the inscription we know that already at that time Brahmins played an important part in ceremonies and festivals; most of them appear to have come from Lower Burma and to have been Vaishnava; they are represented as constantly bringing lustral water in vases of gold, silver, brass and clay. The Buddhist monks held a service of blessing and recited *paritta* for the protection of the new building. The inscription contains many technical terms relating to portions of the palace and its decorative architecture. Unfortunately, the meaning of a good number of these terms is still very doubtful, their equivalent not having been found in modern literary Talaing.*

"Inscription No. X consists of only four lines. It records a royal gift, probably the dedication of land to a pagoda. It contains mention of a king whose style is Sri Tribhuwanaditya-pawaradhammarāja. This title belonged to at least four kings of Pagan; *viz*: Alaungsithu (A. D. 1112—60), Narapatisithu (1169—1204), Nandaungmya (1204—27) and Uzana (1243-44). Mr. Blagden, on palæographical grounds, is of opinion that the writing is nearer 1112 than 1248, the two dates between which it would fall.

"M. R. Ry. Diwan Bahadur L. D. Swamikannu Pillai Avergal, I. S. O., Secretary to the Madras Legislative Council, the well-known author of *Indian Chronology* and *Indian Ephemeris* has kindly volunteered to check the dates found in the several volumes of Burmese Inscriptions. After a careful study of about 200 dates given in the *Inscriptions of Pagan, Pinya and Ava* and those found in the Kalyani inscriptions of King Dhammacheti, he comes to the following conclusions :—

(*i*) the most reliable guide in the verification of Burmese dates is the Surya Siddhanta;

(*ii*) that many of these dates can easily be verified from his *Ephemeris, A. D. 700 to A. D. 2000*, which has now been published by the Government of Madras;

(*iii*) that the proportion of unverifiable Burmese dates (less than 20 per cent.) is much smaller than the proportion of similar dates in Indian inscriptions of the same period;

(*iv*) that a reckoning of 'Expired' or *gata* years side by side with 'current' or *vartamāna* years is found in ancient Burmese inscriptions to the same extent (about 20 per cent.) as in Indian inscriptions dated in the Saka era;

(*v*) that the week-day has to be relied on as the chief test in determining whether a particular year is an expired year or a current year;

(*vi*) that a Burmese Sakkaraj year rendered into English by the addition of 638, may be regarded as a current year; while one rendered into English by the addition of 639 is an expired year.

"He adds that it is noteworthy that the following calendrical details ordinarily met with in Indian inscriptions, more especially in those of South India, are entirely or almost entirely absent from these Burmese inscriptions :—

(1) full moons are occasionally referred to, but rarely new moon or Amāvāsya;

---

*One of the terms *tircul* (tirukula) which Mr. Duroiselle explains as being "applied in a limited sense to the Cholas" occurs in a few Vaishnava inscriptions of the twelfth century A. D. in South India and is there applied to division of the outcast classes of Holeyas (Tamil Parayas) who however are given special privileges in the Vaishnava Temple at Melukote in Mysore. (Mr. Rice's Mysore Gazetteer, Vol. II, p. 273). [K. S.]

(2) citation of days by Nakshatras is not found ; Burmese Epigraphy.

(3) citations of Saura or Solar months like Mesha, Rishabha, etc., or of Sankrantis, Uttarāyana or Dakshināyana, are not found ;

(4) citation of days of Solar months is not found ;

(5) citations of positions of planets properly so called, *viz.*, Mars, Mercury, Jupiter, Venus and Saturn are not found ;

(6) citation of eclipses is not found. An auspicious moment is occasionally referred to, and certain *tithis* seem to have been favourites for making donations and Mr. Taw Sein Ko notes that the Burmese, though professing Buddhism, were firm believers in astrology ; but Lagna, Yoga and other astrological combinations are never alluded to in these inscriptions and Adhika months do not seem to be avoided although in India it is not usual to make donations during Adhika months.

(7) The Sakkaraj year is regularly cited, but Kaliyuga and Saka years are not referred to ; Buddha's era (543 B. C.) is sometimes cited ;

(8) a cyclic year corresponding to Prabhava, Vibhava, etc., seems to be occasionally cited.

" Estampages were procured of fifteen new inscriptions during the year. They consist mostly of short dedication records on votive tablets in Talaing, Burmese and Pali, in Burmese and Nagari characters, the earliest of which may be placed on palæographic grounds in the XIth century A. D. Two new inscriptions in Burmese with dates 671 and 684 in the common Burmese era (A. D. 1309 and 1322, respectively) were found in the Kyaukse District, and Mr. J. A. Stewart, M.A., I.C.S., Settlement Officer, Kyaukse, very kindly supplied this office with estampages. They record the dedication of lands, and slaves to monasteries, but apart from this, have no historical interest."

Mr. Yazdani, Epigraphist to the Government of India for Moslemic Inscriptions, who is now abroad writes :— Moslemic Epigraphy.

" In last year's Report, a reference was made to the systematic survey of the inscriptions of ' Ala-ud-din Husain Shah of Bengal, during whose reign the artistic genius of Islam reached its zenith in this part of the world. The exquisite *Tughrá* writings of the period appeal to the imagination not only by their beauty and grace, but by a sense of mystery which their intricate arrangement imparts, and which is the keynote of Islamic art in all its aspects. Through the kind co-operation of Mr. K. N. Dikshit, Archæological Superintendent, Eastern Circle, the survey is nearing completion and by the time I return to India (June, 1924) material will be available to publish a detailed monograph on the subject." In the meantime Mr. Dikshit himself records his progress in the following terms :

"36 Moslem inscriptions were also copied, of which 32 were from Malda, 2 from Sylhet District and 2 from Devikot in Dinajpur District. The inscriptions at and near Malda were copied at the instance of Mr. Yazdani for his projected article in the *Epigraphia Indo-Moslemica* on the inscriptions of Ala-ud-din Husain Shah of Bengal, in whose reign the *Tughra* script reached its high water mark. The inscription copied at Hatkhola in Sylhet District is an unpublished record of the reign of Barbak Shah, Sultan of Bengal, dated 877 A. H. Of the 4 inscriptions in Ata Shah's Dargah on the banks of the Dhaldighi at Debikot, District Dinajpur, the inscription of Sikandar bin Ilias dated 765 A. H. was photographed, and those of Rukn-ud-din Kaikaus Shah dated 697 A. H. and Shams-ud-din Muzaffar Shah dated 896 A. H. were copied."

Moslemic Epigraphy.

Mr. Yazdani notes further that, "During the year under review thirty-four new inscriptions have been copied; sixteen of which come from the historic fort of Udgir and the rest from various places in the district of Bidar. The majority of them belong to the reign of Aurangzeb and when studied collectively they may throw interesting light on the military administrations of the Deccan after its conquest by him.

"For the article on the inscriptions of Bid, to be published in the ensuing number of the *Epigraphia Indo-Moslemica* (1921-22), Dr. L. D. Barnett, Keeper, of Oriental Mss., British Museum, has been kind enough to decipher and translate for me the texts of certain Mahratti inscriptions the Persian versions of which have been dealt with by me. I take this opportunity to acknowledge his courteous help."

SECTION VI.

ARCHAEOLOGICAL CHEMIST.

Mr. Sana Ullah's work.

The deputation of the Archæological Chemist to Ajanta, where he had been deputed to assist Professor Cecconi in the restoration of the frescoes came to an end in the middle of April 1921. He had then to go to Calcutta to dismantle his laboratory in the Indian Museum, where he had completed the special work for which he was temporarily stationed there, and to make arrangements for the safe transport of the equipment to his new headquarters at Dehra Dun. At this time the Government of India had under consideration a scheme for building laboratories at Dehra Dun for the proposed Imperial Chemical Institute, so that a temporary laboratory was fitted up for Mr. Sana Ullah's work until the larger scheme should be realised.

A number of interesting investigations have been carried out by him this year. The composition of the white pigment employed by the painters of the Ajanta frescoes was not clear. Griffiths* has stated that "It is free from carbonates. Its principal constituents appear to be calcium sulphate and white silicious matter insoluble in acids." Mr. Sana Ullah has now made careful analyses of several specimens of this white pigment and has come to the conclusion that it consisted principally of white silicate minerals such as the zeolites, albite-anorthite feldspars, epidote, or kaolin, to which lime or burnt gypsum were added to impart setting properties. These minerals which abound in the Deccan trap, were probably ground fine in water and mixed with some medium before use. Gums of *nim*, *kikar* and wood-apple trees are mentioned in Sanskrit literature for the medium. Three typical compositions of these white pigments may be quoted here :—

——	Cave VI.	Cave XVII.	Cave XIX.
Silicate mineral	*Nil*	75	70
Kaolin	50	*Nil*	*Nil.*
Calcium carbonate	36·5	*Nil*	30
Gypsum	11·6	22·5	*Nil.*
Impurities	1·9	2·5	*Nil.*
Total	100·0	100·0	100·0

* *Cave Temples of Ajanta*, page 18, report of the Analyst to the Bombay Government.

The rough cast of mud which covers the rock was given a preliminary coating of lime plaster followed by a wash of kaolin incorporated with lime or burnt gypsum, to form the ground for receiving the brush work, but the compositions mentioned above were substituted if a brilliant white surface was required. The yellow and black pigments are ochre and lampblack, respectively.

The cause of decay of marble in the Dilwara temples at Mt. Abu was investigated and attributed by the Archæological Chemist to the action of soluble chlorides which were present in the affected parts. The chlorides have probably been deposited by the monsoons which pick up minute quantities of sea-salts when sweeping over the ocean.*

The problem of the decay and preservation of the stone temples at Halebid and Belur in Mysore State, was also referred to him. The stone employed in these temples is known as potstone which is a variety of altered pyroxenites. By comparing the analyses of sound and of decaying fragments it was found that the rock had suffered a net loss of about a quarter of its constituents in the course of decay; the changes undergone being due to the oxidation of the ferrous oxide and the solution of other constituents by the action of rain water charged with carbonic acid, it was suggested that the decaying parts should be hardened by means of magnesium fluate and the whole surface rendered waterproof, as far as possible, by the application of beeswax in turpentine spirit or hard paraffin wax in petrol.

A metal plate recovered at Taxila, was found, on analysis, to be of the following composition :—Cu 77·45 %, Ni 21·35 %, Co 0·52 %, Fe 0·68 %, Sb 0·03 %; total 100·03. This nickel-copper alloy is, therefore, identical with that employed by the Indo-Bactrian kings for their coinage.

Two curious porcelain-like fragments, also from Taxila, were analysed. One of these proved to be a variety of quartz and the other a kind of white glass. A red opaque glass, similar to the Roman Haematinum, has also been discovered at Taxila. Mr. Sana Ullah's analyses of these two forms of glass are given below :—

——	White opaque glass.	Red opaque glass.
SiO_2	61·32 %	37·09 %
Sb_2O_3	5·08	*Nil.*
PbO	*Nil*	34·85
$Al_2O_3 + Fe_2O_3$	1·70	3·16
MnO	0·26	0·11
CaO	9·74	6·46
MgO	1·64	0·70
Cu_2O	*Nil*	7·20
Na_2O	20·26†	10·33
K_2O		0·87
Total	100·00	100·77

In fact several specimens of coloured glass have been found at Taxila and in other parts of India, and are the subject of further investigation by the Archæological Chemist. For the present it may be stated that they confirm Pliny's statement that the ancient

* *Cf.* Holland and Christie : *The Origin of the Salt Deposits of Rajputana.* Read G. S. I., XXXVIII, 154—186

† Contains $K_2O > 1$ %.

Indians knew the art of making glass and colouring it by the addition of metallic salts, as practiced in modern times.

In February 1922, Mr. Sana Ullah visited Gwalior State to advise on the preservation of the frescoes at Bagh and the Udaygiri caves.

The total number of antiquities treated by him for cleaning and preservation consist of Terracotta 111, Copper and Bronze 11, Iron 53, Silver 3, Bone and Ivory 2, Wood 21 and miscellaneous 2 ; total 203. The bronzes were mostly from Nalanda, including the massive inscribed plate referred to on page 19. He also trained for 2 months the Assistant Curator, Patna, in the cleaning of antiquities by chemical means.

SECTION VII.

ANCIENT MONUMENTS ACT AND LISTING OF MONUMENTS.

In Sir John Marshall's Report for 1920-21 it was explained (p. 40) that one of the immediate effects of the Reforms had been entirely to change the position in regard to monuments protected under the Ancient Monuments Preservation Act. So long as the responsibilities of the Archæological Department were not defined, and we were entrusted with the inspection and repair of all ancient monuments irrespective of their status, the application of the Ancient Monuments Preservation Act was apt to be more or less haphazard, as there was a natural tendency not to invoke this Act except in special cases where its application was necessary. Under the Reforms, however, the scope of the Archæological Department is limited to those monuments only which have been declared protected under the Act, and this has of course necessitated a complete stock-taking of all the ancient monuments throughout the country. The beginnings of this stock-taking were described by Sir John Marshall in the report under reference, but the task has involved much more work and much more correspondence than was at first anticipated, and is still in progress. Many of the Provincial lists call for further scrutiny, as very few of them have attained to final form during 1921-22.

LISTING OF MONUMENTS.

Delhi.

The third and fourth volumes of the list of Muhammadan and Hindu Monuments in the Delhi Province are still in the Press. The second proof of the former has been received back for correction and the latter has been sent for final printing.

Central Circle.

Owing to various causes, and the pressure of other work, comparatively little progress could be made with the revised list of ancient monuments in Bihar and Orissa until Mr. Muhammad Hamid Kuraishi, the present Officiating Assistant Superintendent, was appointed to take up this task on May 1st, 1921. To enable him to concentrate on this work, with a view to its early completion, he was relieved of all other duties. Mr. Hamid began his work on the Tirhut Division (as the one on which most materials had previously been collected) in close consultation with the Archæological Superintendent, and the finished lists for this area were finally submitted in typescript to the Local Government, together with a number of photographic illustrations of the more important monuments described therein, early in March 1922. The Assistant Superintendent then proceeded to Orissa to take up the listing of that division ; and it is hoped that the lists for the whole Province will be completed by the end of 1923.

The preparation of Antiquarian maps of Bihar and Orissa was first suggested by Sir Edward Gait, the late Lieutenant-Governor of the Province, early in 1916; but owing to pressure of other duties no substantial progress in this direction was possible before May 1917 when work was started on the Champaran District. A specimen map of this district was submitted to the Local Government in the following June; and, their approval of it having been secured, the map of the whole Tirhut Division was completed a year later. This was followed by maps of the Patna and Bhagalpur Divisions, which were submitted to Government in December 1918 and April 1919, respectively. Owing to difficulties encountered by the Assistant Superintendent, who had this work in hand, in the completion of the remaining Divisions of the Province (Chota Nagpur and Orissa), the preparation of these maps was entrusted to the Officer-in-charge, Bihar and Orissa Drawing Office, Gulzarbagh, Patna. These last Divisions have now been completed, and it is hoped that maps for the whole Province will be printed off shortly. Alphabetical lists of the ancient sites and monuments marked in the five Divisional maps, as well as a comprehensive bibliography, are under preparation in the Archæological Superintendent's office, and will be published along with the maps.

Eastern Circle.

The Indian States of Tripura and Cooch Behar sent a list of 8 and 4 monuments respectively in their States which they desire to conserve. The Sikkim Darbar inform us that there are no monuments which they propose to conserve, but there are 34 monasteries which are being maintained by the Darbar and by public donations.

Southern Circle.

A new list of protected monuments in the Madras Presidency is under preparation. The list that existed already has been revised according to the orders of Government with regard to the addition or deletion of monuments, and a corrected copy of it was sent to Government showing the number of Protected Monuments in the Southern Circle to be three hundred and thirty-three on the 31st March 1922.

Burma Circle.

No additions were made to the List of Ancient Monuments in Burma. From this list a selection of 102 monuments was made and submitted to Government for preservation by the Imperial Government. These monuments are scattered all over Burma, and in age range from the 6th to the 19th century. The oldest are those at Prome, some of which date from the 6th or 7th century; the latest are found in Mandalây and consist of the Palace and of the *Pyatthats* (bastions) on the City walls. They were built in 1857—59; but though not old, they are invested with an historical and architectural interest now unique, and would soon disappear but for the help and care of the Archæological Department. Under orders from the Government of India a special list of European burial grounds in Burma was compiled, including all tombs with inscriptions anterior to the 1st of January 1858, those later than this date being considered too recent for inclusion. The list comprises 27 European cemeteries containing a total of 266 tombs with epitaphs. The oldest tomb so far found is that of a Mrs. Samuel White, who died in 1682 at Mergui.

SECTION VIII.

TREASURE TROVE.

Northern Circle.

There is nothing to report in the Northern Circle, although it is remarkable that, despite the amount of excavation both around ancient monuments and in the new Capital at Delhi, finds of coins or other antiquities are hardly ever reported.

Frontier Circle. No finds of Treasure Trove were reported during the year in the Frontier Circle, but it cannot be assumed that antiquities coming under the operations of the Act were not recovered. As finds are very rarely reported in the Frontier Province it was suggested by the Superintendent to the Local Government that to make the Treasure Trove Act and its recent modification by the Government of India more widely known, it might be well to enlist the assistance of the Education Department of the Province. The Director of Public Instruction has expressed his readiness to help and has been furnished by the Superintendent with a note explaining what Treasure Trove is, the rules governing it, and how Inspecting Officers and teachers can assist in dispelling the wide-spread idea that Government takes finds of Treasure Trove without payment, and can aid very materially in this and other ways in recovering for permanent preservation in Museums valuable relics of India's past.

Western Circle. Fifty-one pigs of lead, weighing approximately 5 tons and valued at about Rs. 3,000 were found during the excavations at the back of the old gate to the palace inside the Ahmadnagar fort, in the Nagar Taluka of the Ahmednagar District. Orders about their final disposal were not issued up to the end of the year under review. Treasure Trove coins found in the Western Presidency are examined by the Bombay Branch of the Royal Asiatic Society. The Honorary Secretary of that Society reports that "There were 3,854 coins under examination at the close of 1920, and 1,017 were received during the year. Of the latter, 804 silver were received from the Collector of Kolaba, 83 gold from the Collector of Bijapur, 7 gold from the District Magistrate, Kanara. Fifty silver from the Mamlatdar of Sinnar, 46 silver from the Mamlatdar of Chorasi, 17 gold from the Mamlatdar of Sirur and 10 silver from the Mamlatdar of Kopergaon. Out of these 804 silver from the Collector of Kolaba were returned as they possessed no numismatic value. 3495 have been reported to Government and are awaiting distribution. There are 572 coins still under examination."

Central Circle. (*i*) *Treasure consisting of coins.*—No new finds were reported in Bihar during the year; but as a slight error appeared in the report of the find of 96 gold coins in the Monghyr District, published in the Annual Progress Report of the Eastern (now Central) Circle for the year 1918-19, a corrected account of the same is republished here: *vide* the tabular statement below :—

District.	Locality.	No. of coins.	Metal.	Examined by.	Circumstances of find.	Classification and description.
Monghyr ..	Village Sindhi P. S. Barbigha.	96	A. N.	Mr. R. D. Banerjee	Found by Birhaspat Kahar in a *Debia* of copper in a *garh* while digging for earth.	3 Allauddin Md. Shah. 1 Ghiyasuddin Tughlak. 61 Muhammad Tughlak. 31 Firoz Shah.

Central Provinces. (*ii*) *Treasure of other than coins.*—One new find of 3 gold rings was reported this year from the Central Provinces. The rings were found by gold-washers in the bed of the Mahanadi river, and were forwarded for examination to the Archæological Superintendent by Pandit Lochan Prasad Pandeya of Balapur in the Bilaspur District, who remarks that such rings were in early times used as hair ornaments. As the present rings are quite modern and possess no artistic or archæological interest they have been returned to the Pandit.

Eastern Circle

Treasure consisting of coins.—Three new cases of treasure trove consisting of coins have been reported in the Eastern Circle during the year 1921-22 and the expert's report on the highly interesting find of 346 coins found in 1917 at Keteen, thana Rupganj, Dt. Dacca (noticed on page 6 of the Annual Report of the Eastern Circle for 1919-20) has been forwarded to the Superintendent for publication. Of the new finds one consisting of 57 coins of the late Mughal period from Dt. Bakarganj is of little interest. About the find of 25 coins from Atturanayarbad, Dt. Dacca, Colonel A. R. Nevill, the Government expert who examined them, reported :—

> "With the exception of two coins, struck at Surat* and Bombay, all belong or appear to belong to the Arkat mint. Some were struck by the French at Pondicherry, the name of Arkat being retained as the place of mintage ; but in these cases the date is missing. During recent years the Museums have received a plethora of these common Arkat coins of Muhammad Shah, and apart from the two others mentioned above, I recommend the acquisition at one rupee apiece of only five coins, which show both mint and date, for the Dacca Museum. The rest may be returned to the sender."

Some interest is attached to the find of four gold Mohurs of the time of Shah Jahan in a small silver casket, reported from Mahimapur, Dt. Murshidabad. The finder of the treasure trove, Dal Chand Singhi of Azimgunj, has under an indenture of lease and agreement from the owner taken possession of the land and premises known as the old residential site of the well-known family of Jagat Seths, the Bankers of the Nawabs of Bengal. The lessee, it is understood, is conducting operations to search for hidden treasure on the premises, in course of which the silver casket containing the gold coins was found. The finder forthwith sent the treasure to the Collector of Murshidabad, who forwarded the same to Government for disposal. It is a very rare instance of a treasure trove case, systematically conducted and promptly reported.

The following extracts from Colonel Nevill's report to the Government of Bengal on the 346 Bengal Sultan coins found at Keteen, Dt. Dacca, in 1917, will show the exceptionally great historical and numismatic interest attached to this find, which has gone to enrich the Bengal Sultan series in the various Museums, especially the Indian Museum, Calcutta and the Dacca Museum. These coins were correctly classified by the Curator, Dacca Museum, as issues of the Muhammadan Sultans of Bengal, with the exception of four struck by the Hindu Rajas Danuja-Mardana and Mahendradeva at the beginning of the fifteenth century in a style closely resembling that adopted by the Sultans, during the confusion that ensued on the death of Hamza Shah. The earliest coin of the find is a solitary piece of Ghias-ud-din Bahadur Shah dated about 720 A. H. Then follows one of Fakhr-ud-din Mubarak, and then a large number† of coins struck by Ilias Shah and his successors. These are mainly of interest for the reason that they enable us to determine the chronology of that period with much greater certainty than has yet been found possible ; and on this account alone, the find can claim historical importance. The main interest however attaches to the later period included in the range covered by this *trouvaille*. We have, in the first place, a remarkable assortment of the very rare coins of Shahab-ud-din Bayazid, which are of numismatic importance, but these are eclipsed by the discovery of coins struck in the name of Ala-ud-din Firoz ibn Bayazid,

*Issued in the reign of Farrukhsiyar.

†There are 33 coins of Shams-ud-din Ilias Shah, 60 of Sikandar bin Ilias, and 72 of Ghias-ud-din Azam Shah.

Eastern Circle. who occupied the throne of Bengal in the year 817 A. H. No reference to this king has yet come to light in any history. The find proves that Bayazid ruled from 814 to 817 and not from 812 as was previously held, and that his son occupied the throne in 817 and possibly for a portion of the succeeding year, the earliest known coin of the following Sultan, Jalal-ud-din Muhammad, being dated in 818. That Firoz may definitely be numbered among the Sultans of Bengal is established by the fact that he controlled the three mints of Firozabad, Satgaon and Muazzamabad.

" In the case of the previous reigns we find that while the accepted dates of Iliyas and Sikandar may stand, the reign of Ghias-ud-din Azam must be extended to 813, leaving only the inside of two years to his successor, Saif-ud-din Hamza Shah, instead of the ten assigned to this monarch by Sir John Woodburn and other authorities. The find unfortunately affords us no further information as to the reputed son of Hamza traditionally know as Shams-ud-din.

" The dates recorded on these coins run on to 823* A. H. the series ending with a number of pieces struck in that year by Jalal-ud-din Muhammad Shah at the mint of Chatgaon or Chittagong. Incidentally it is proved that the coins of this king hitherto attributed to the Satgaon mint are in reality from Chatgaon, as those now discovered from the former mint are of an entirely different type.

" A remarkable curiosity is a coin of this king bearing on one side the usual legend and on the other the lion of Tippera. I greatly regret that though this unexampled piece is in fine condition, I am unable to decipher the mint or to find any trace of a date.

" According to your instructions I have allotted only to the Indian Museum, Calcutta, such coins as are required to improve that unexampled collection of Bengal rupees, provided that they are in sufficiently good condition to warrant a place in that cabinet. As is often the case with Muhammadan coins of this series, the great majority of the pieces under examination are extensively defaced in consequence of repeated shroffing ; and this has unfortunately happened to a number of unique coins, whose numismatic value has in consequence been seriously impaired. In such cases I have allotted the coins to the Dacca Museum. This institution gains by this find the nucleus of a valuable collection of the Bengal series, owing to its position as second on the list I have been unable, as in previous reports, to make any allotment to the Madras Museum because it is at present impossible to ascertain the possessions and needs of that unlisted collection.

" In all, on this distribution, the Dacca Museum receives 101 coins, Calcutta 54, Bombay and Lucknow 23 each, Delhi 16, Lahore 15, Nagpur 13, Shillong 12, Peshawar 10, Quetta 9, Ajmere and Patna 8 each and Rangoon 6, while 2 coins go to the British Museum. The remainder I have recommended to be kept for sale at Dacca. I fear they are not worth much from a numismatic point of view, but they are too uncommon to deserve the melting-pot.

" In this connection I would beg to observe that this find was reported to the Collector in March 1920†. I greatly regret that press of official work has prevented me from dealing with it in a more expeditious manner, but none the less I would respect-

*Colonel Nevill's distribution list shows one coin dated 828 A. H.

†It must have been reported before April 1918, as the coins were then sent to the Curator, Dacca Museum, who after close study communicated the classification to the Collector in February 1920.

fully protest against the previous delay of more than eighteen months. Experience has shown abundantly that in order to encourage the finders of treasure trove to report their discoveries promptly and honestly, it is essential that the price due to the finder under the law should be paid with the utmost possible despatch. I am not aware that these coins have yet been acquired by Government. I am much indebted to the Curator of the Dacca Museum for the careful attention he has given to this interesting find, but properly such an examination should have been undertaken after it had been decided to acquire them. I lay the greater stress on this point, because of late there has been evident a tendency to conceal such treasure trove, judging from the very meagre receipts in other provinces where the annual number of reports had previously been more or less constant; a tendency that is influenced no doubt by the general political atmosphere*.

"If acquisition has not yet been effected, I would recommend that all the coins be acquired at a cost of 15 annas apiece."

Gwalior. Two thousand and sixty coins were recovered as Treasure Trove in the State territories were examined in the year. Out of these 40 were of silver, 7 of bullion and the rest of copper. From the dynastic point of view 93 belonged to the Emperors of Delhi, 10 to the Sultans of Jaunpur, 1,193 to the Sultans of Malwa and 858 to the Sultans of Gujarat, while six were miscellaneous.

SECTION IX.

PUBLICATIONS.

Director General. The following publications were issued by the Director General of Archæology during the year :—

(1) Annual Report of the Director General of Archæology in India for the year 1919-20.

(2) Catalogue of the Museum of Sanchi, Bhopal State.

(3) A Guide to Taxila—2nd edition.

Northern Circle. *Agra Office.* In the Northern Circle, Agra, Maulvi Zafar Hasan contributed two papers, *viz.* "The Mosque of Shaikh Abdu-n Nabi" and "A guide to Nizam-ud-din" (both at Delhi) which were published as Memoirs of the Archæological Survey of India. The Annual Progress Reports of the Superintendent, Muhammadan and British Monuments, for the three years ending 31st March 1919 and 1919-20 were finally distributed, while the Report for the year 1920-21 and the third and fourth volumes of the *List of Muhammadan and Hindu Monuments in the Province of Delhi* were in the Press. Two little guides to the Agra Fort and Fatehpur Sikri containing short notes on the principal buildings of interest were prepared by the Superintendent for the visit of H. R. H. the Prince of Wales to Agra. The publication of a number of drawings executed under the supervision of the late Mr. E. W. Smith nearly thirty years ago were in hand, and short historical and descriptive accounts of the places they illustrate were under preparation. The

---

* The view expressed here by Colonel Nevill deserves serious consideration. The present find was made as far back as July 1917 and if the payment of the claims due has taken as much as four or five years, it is but natural that the claimants must have lost considerable interest in the discovery, which is of much historical value. It is gratifying to note in this connection that the Government of India have recently issued a resolution offering special rewards for finds of objects of historical or archæological interest, in addition to the price admissible under section 16 of the Treasure Trove Act, *viz.*, 120 per cent. of the intrinsic value of a treasure. It is proposed to invoke this sanction in the present case, and to give the finder of these interesting coins a special reward over and above the amount due to him under the Treasure Trove Act.

Northern Circle. Memoir on the Qutb at Delhi by Mr. J. A. Page, on which he was engaged while he was Superintendent of the Northern Circle, was practically completed and ready to go to Press. The work, when published, should prove of considerable interest. Finally the catalogue of exhibits in the Fort Museum, Delhi, was under revision, the previous catalogue published some 9 years ago having been sold out.

Lahore Office. In the Lahore office Mr. Sahni prepared the Annual Progress Report of the Superintendent, Archæological Survey, Hindu and Buddhist Monuments, Northern Circle, for the year ending 31st March 1921, and in addition read two short articles at the Second Oriental Conference, which was held in Calcutta from 28th January to 1st February 1922. These are a note on three Kushan Inscriptions found at Muttra, one of which will be found briefly noticed under the Epigraphical work of this year in this report; and another note dealing with the ancient names of Bhatinda in the Punjab.

Frontier Circle. The Superintendent in the Frontier Circle, in addition to his Annual Report for the year 1920-21, translated from the French, and prepared for the press, an hitherto unpublished monograph by M. Foucher, *Les représentations figurés de la Nativité du Buddha*, which is to be published as a Memoir of the Archæological Survey.

Central Circle. The only publication issued during the year in the Central Circle was the Annual Progress Report of the Superintendent for the year ending 31st March 1921.

Western Circle. The Superintendent of the Western Circle finished his memoir on *The Basreliefs of Badami* in which he describes in detail for the first time the Saiva and Vaishnava basreliefs in the caves at Badami, in the Bijapur District. The larger basreliefs and a general description of the caves were published by Fergusson and Burgess, but the series of Saiva basreliefs in Cave No. I and the unique Vaishnava basreliefs in Caves Nos. II and III had never been correctly described or illustrated so far as is known. These basreliefs represent—(1) The early life of Krishna from his birth to the death of his uncle Kamsa, (2) The churning of the Ocean by the Gods and Asuras (in both Caves; Nos. II and III). In addition to these subjects the basreliefs in Cave No. III, which is the largest and most elaborate of the group, illustrate—(1) the removal of the Parijata tree from the heaven of Indra to Dvaraka by Krishna, (2) the fight of Garuda with the Gods for the jar of nectar found during the churning of the ocean, (3) the removal of Subhadra, the sister of Krishna, by Arjuna the third Pandava, and (4) the death of Hiranyakasipu in the hands of the Man-lion (*Narasimha*). The memoir on the punch-marked coins discovered in the village of Patraha of the Purnea District of Bihar and Orissa was also completed and typed. The memoir on the monuments of the Chedi country approached completion but could not be completed during the year under review as some of the monuments which lie in the Jubbulpore District had not been visited by the Superintendent, who had inspected all important monuments of ancient Chedi or Dahala, now lying in the states of Nagod, Maihar, Ajaygarh and Rewa. This memoir deals with—(1) The Chronology of the Haihaya dynasty of Tripuri, a subject not adequately discussed before, (2) The monuments of the Chedi country, (3) Images and Sculptures found within this area and (4) Saiva influence. The Annual Progress Report for the year 1920-21 was sent to the press for printing, but was not completed up to the end of the year.

Eastern Circle.

Besides the Annual Report for 1920-21, Mr. Dikshit's contribution on *Six Sculptures from Mahoba* was published during the year as a Memoir of the Archæological Survey. Another paper written by him for the Epigraphia Indica on the Garra plates of the Chandella King Trailokyavarman (A. D. 1205) was in the press. He also read two papers at the Second Oriental Conference held in Calcutta in January-February 1922. One of these relates to the chronology of the Maukhari kings, a dynasty that ruled in the 6th-7th centuries A. D. Mr. Dikshit proposes to read the dates on the coins of the Maukharis in a different way and interpret them as dates in the Gupta era, thus fixing the approximate reign-periods of the king Isanavarman, Sarvavarman and Avantivarman, but it is doubtful if this view will be accepted without further discussion. The other paper *On the localities mentioned in the Bhandek plate of Krishnaraja* (772 A. D.) was read before the Ancient Geography Section of the Conference and is being published by the Conference. In this paper Mr. Dikshit identifies the place of encampment, the village granted, and the boundary villages mentioned in the plates, with certain places in the Yeotmal District of Berar, against Rai Bahadur Hira Lal who had placed them elsewhere (*vide Epig. Ind.*, Vol. XIV, page 129).

Southern Circle.

Mr. Longhurst contributed Part I of a Monograph on Pallava Architecture, which will be published as an Archæological Memoir.

Burma Circle.

In Burma, the following publications were issued during the year :—

1. Epigraphia Birmanica, Vol. II, Parts I and II.
2. List of inscriptions found in Burma, Part I.
3. Amended list of Ancient Monuments in Burma.

In the First Part of Volume II of the Epigraphia Birmanica, Mons. Duroiselle has deciphered, translated and explained the short Talaing inscriptions found on 389 plaques which adorn the upper terraces of the Ananda Temple at Pagan. These plaques illustrate the last ten long stories of the Jātakas, from Temi Jātaka to Vessantara Jātaka. The meaning of old words long fallen into disuse is traced to, and their form deduced from modern Talaing literature. The scenes in the plaques are explained. At the end of the volume are found three vocabularies : (*a*) old forgotten words found in the plaques ; (*b*) words in literary Talaing not found in any existing vocabulary and (*c*) a list of words under which grammatical information is given not found elsewhere.

The Ananda Temple at Pagan, built by King Kyanzittha, was completed in 1090. It is the most graceful temple in Pagan and probably in Burma. But its interest does not rest alone in the beauty of its architectural design. It is also the most important in this Province, from the artistic and philological point of view. The interior contains, besides very numerous statues of the Buddha in every possible attitude, a series of eighty stone sculptures representing the career of the Buddha, from the Tusita Heaven to his Parinirvāna. The exterior is practically covered with glazed plaques. On the basement they represent his contest with Māra's host, and his apotheosis ; all these contain short legends in Talaing. The anterior lives of the Buddha, or Jātakas, adorn the first and second roof and the three terraces above them ; these bear inscriptions in Pali. The 389 plaques explained in the volume above mentioned are found on the upper terraces, and constitute a unique collection for, so far as has been ascertained, the last ten great Jātakas are illustrated with such a profusion of scenes on no other monument of the Buddhist world. Part II of the same volume contains the plates with short explanations of the scenes.

Burma Circle. In the *List of inscriptions found in Burma*, all the epigraphs so far published and which are contained in six large volumes covering altogether 2,802 pages, are arranged according to their dates, with references to volume and page ; information is also given as to (*a*) the place of origin, (*b*) the founder's name and (*c*) brief indication of the contents. In his Preface, M. Duroiselle gives information on a variety of points which will prove useful to the historian and philologist, on the languages used in these inscriptions ; their age ; their value, etc.

Kashmir. In Kashmir, Mr. Kak has completed his "Guide to the Kashmir Monuments" but no arrangements have yet been made for the publication either of this work or of his "Handbook to the Archæological and Numismatic Sections of the Srinagar Museum."

SECTION X.

LIBRARY.

Northern Circle. In the Northern Circle 34 new volumes were added to the reference library attached to the Agra Office and 33 to the office in Lahore.

Frontier Circle. In the Frontier Circle the books purchased during the year dealt exclusively with numismatics, Buddhism and the early history of India and adjacent countries. The library is deficient in works of reference such as the earlier issues of the J. R. A. S., J. A. S. B., and Indian Antiquary, and also lacks copies of several of the expensive publications dealing with the ancient monuments of India, but requirements in these directions were met by loans from the libraries of the Director General of Archæology and the Peshawar Museum.

Central Circle. The library maintained in the office of the Archæological Superintendent, Central Circle, comprised 1,185 volumes of a generally reprasentative character, dealing principally with the history, archæology, ethnography, epigraphy and religion of the two provinces constituting the Circle, as well as of India generally. The great bulk of the books are in English ; though the vernaculars are fairly well represented. The collection, however, contains no volume of special rarity that calls for mention in this very brief résumé. Gazetteers, Imperial and Provincial, figure largely in it, as well as the Journals of the Royal Asiatic Society and the Asiatic Society of Bengal ; while a nearly complete series of Cunningham's Archæological Reports is also included, in addition to the later Archæological Annuals issued by Sir John Marshall, and the several volumes of the *Epigraphia Indica*. Forty-one new volumes were acquired during the year.

Western Circle. In the Western Circle 39 books were added to the library during the year, the most important among which is Martin's *Miniature Paintings of Persia, India and Turkey*, Vols. I & II, purchased with the sanction of the Government of Bombay. The library contains complete sets of the *Epigraphia Indica*, *Epigraphia Indo-Moslemica*, *Indian Antiquary*, *Journal of the Bombay Branch of the Royal Asiatic Society*, *Journal and Proceedings of the Asiatic Society of Bengal* (new series), *Journal of the Bihar and Orissa Research Society* and Cunningham's *Archæological Survey Reports*. Recent numbers of the *Journal of the Royal Asiatic Society* (from 1888, new series, Vol. XX, up to date) and the *Journal of the Asiatic Society of Bengal*, old series, Part I (from 1875, Vol. XLIV to 1903, Vol. LXXII) are also included in this collection. Complete sets of the Annual Reports of the Director General of Archæology, of the Superintendents of the Northern Circle, both Hindu and Buddhist Monuments and Muhammadan and British Monuments, as well as of the Superintendents of the Central, Eastern, Burma, Southern, Western and Frontier Circles are kept. Annual Reports are also received from the Patna and Rajputana Museums and the Mysore Archæological Survey. Complete sets of the Reports on Epigraphy of the Madras Presidency and all publications of the Hyderabad Archæological Survey are also included in this collection. The library also contains a good working set of coin catalogues, such as those of the Indian Museum, Calcutta, the Punjab Museum, Lahore, and British Museum Catalogues such as Rapson's *Coins of the Andhras and Western Kshatrapas* Percy Gardner's *Coins of the Greek and Scythic kings of Bactria and India*, and Allan's *Gupta Dynasties*. It also contains the recent publications of the American Bureau of Ethnology and some Pali books, such as Fausböll's *Jatakamala* (Vol. I wanting), Oldenberg's *Vinaya pitaka*, etc.

Eastern Circle.

The library attached to the office of the Superintendent in the Eastern Circle in 1920 consisted of 564 volumes, of which 147 were added during the year under report. Besides the available publications of the Archæological Department, *viz.*, Provincial Annual Reports, D. G. A.'s Annual, Parts I and II, and volumes of the *Epigraphia Indica*, etc., and the series of Gazetteers for the two provinces, the library now contains a number of local Gazetteers in the Bengali language, all other volumes of the new series and such of the numbers of the old series of the Journal of the Asiatic Society of Bengal as contain references to antiquities in the Eastern Circle, and the usual reference books on Indian numismatics, architecture, etc.

Southern Circle.

Eighty-six volumes were added to the reference library maintained in the office of the Superintendent at Kotagiri. Out of these, seventeen are official reports. This brings the number of books in the office to 1,442. A separate catalogue of books is in course of preparation by the Superintendent.

Director General's Library.

During the year 280 books in all were added to the Central Archæological Library of the Director General of Archæology. Of these, 117 were purchased, 47 were received in exchange, while 116 were received as gifts. Of the acquisitions worthy of note may be mentioned a complete set of Vasari's Lives of the Painters, Sculptors, etc., published by the Medici Society of London, an edition now grown rare, Svorono's Das Athener National Museum in 4 volumes of Text and Plates, 50 volumes of the Loeb Classical Library, besides some rare books on the Antiquities of Babylon, Nineveh, Egypt and India, these last having been presented by the India Office, London. About 300 volumes were bound or rebound for the Library.

Journals and periodical publications received in the library amounted to 50. With the resumption of exchange of publications with the Learned Societies and Academies of the late enemy countries, the library is now regularly receiving the Journals and Proceedings of these Institutions.

The library was extensively used by the officers of the Department at Headquarters and in the Circles, and its importance and value as a reference library for subjects dealing with Archæology, Indology and allied branches are daily increasing.

SECTION XI.

PHOTOGRAPHS.

D.G.A.'s Office.

3,858 photo prints in all were received in the office of the Director General of Archæology in India during the year. Of these, 1,258 were supplied by the Archæological Superintendents of the various Circles in India and 2,600 were purchased from Captain K. A. C. Creswell of Cairo. This set of 2,600 prints, representing as it does a perfectly clear and intelligible development of Saracenic architecture through its various stages with reference to the historic monuments of Egypt, Syria, Palestine and Constantinople, is a most valuable addition to what is by far the largest collection of Archæological photos in India. All the prints received were mounted in Albums and arranged according to the localities to which the monuments belong. In addition to these, 110 fresh negatives were prepared. They represent in the main sites excavated at Taxila and antiquities unearthed in the course of Sir John Marshall's exploration. 363 prints were supplied to the public on payment.

Southern Circle.

In the Southern Circle, 104 negatives were prepared and properly listed under their respective heads, the total number of negatives at the close of the year amounting to 2,905. The photo-albums require overhauling which is being done. Several photos have weathered, and these will be replaced in the near future. 67 photographic prints were sold to the public.

Northern Circle.
Agra.

The photographic collection of the Agra office dates back to the year 1892 and consists at present of 29 volumes of photographs of Monuments in the United Provinces, Punjab, Ajmer and Delhi. Many gaps existed in the volumes but these except in the case of a few volumes have now been filled and are complete. Amongst the photographs taken during the year may be mentioned 17 at Tughlaq's Fort at Delhi showing various gateways and walls, etc., after conservation, and 10 at Kotla Firoz Shah also after repairs. Two photographs of Qadam Sharif were taken while repairs were in progress and seven views of Hauz Khas. A number of plates were exposed at Itimad-ud-Daulah's Tomb at Agra and photographs of the newly restored dalans at the Taj and the platform at Akbar's Tomb were made, 24 photographs of pointing experiments were taken showing walls before and after raking out and after being re-pointed. Four photographs of Iftikhar Khan's Tomb at Chunar were obtained after repairs had been executed.

Lahore.

In the Northern Circle (Hindu and Buddhist Monuments) 279 new photographs were taken during the year under review. They include 24 photographs of the principal sculptures, etc., in the Sarnath Museum including some unearthed by Mr. Oertel in 1904-05 and some by Sir John Marshall during the winters of 1906-07 and 1907-08 of which no photographs existed in the Lahore office. Among the rest, there were 38 photographs of the antiquities brought to light by Mr. Sahni at Raja Karn ka Kila at Thanesar (Skt. Sthānvīsvara), 29 of objects discovered by him at Kosam and 57 photographs of Gandhara and other sculptures in the Mathura Museum or in the possession of the Hony. Curator of that institution. The photographic albums in the Lahore office are quite up to date. They contain all the photographs taken since 1902-03 except 293 prints which will be prepared and put into the albums as soon as practicable.

Frontier Circle. The photographic negatives preserved in the Frontier Circle number 1,936 and these are generally in excellent condition. The photographic albums are complete, all missing prints having been replaced. Sixty-nine new negatives were made during 1921-22. Most of these are of general interest, but seventeen were taken in connection with conservation at Jaulian, while three are field inventories of the sculptures recovered at Jamalgarhi. The more important of these finds have also been re-photographed at headquarters separately and on a larger scale and three of them are published in this report [Plate XXIV, Figs. (*c*), (*d*), Plate XXV, Fig. (*b*)]. Besides photographic prints forwarded to officers of the department for official purposes, photographs to the value of Rs. 41-4-0 were supplied to various persons in India and Europe. A list of negatives of exhibits in the Peshawar Museum is being drawn up and will be placed in the museum to enable visitors to purchase photographs of antiquities in which they are interested.

Western Circle. In the Western Circle 282 negatives were taken this year, out of which 231 were taken in the Bombay Presidency, 32 in Central India, and 29 in Rajputana. All negatives of Central India and Rajputana were made over to the Director General of Archæology in March 1922 in accordance with orders received from the Government of India, as that officer has been placed in charge of archæological work in that region. A set of prints from negatives taken by Dr. Burgess which are now in Simla are mounted in albums. Sets of photographs taken up to the end of 1916 are mounted on cardboards but those taken during the last five years are slipped in on cartridge paper. Numerous gaps exist in the collection but steps are being taken to complete the sets as early as possible. Mr. Banerji reports that all negatives and prints taken in his circle during the last ten years are excellent, the improved quality being due in his opinion to the exceptional ability and perseverance of the Head Photographer, Mr. J. P. Joglekar, whose work has been appreciated by all Superintendents of the Poona Office.

Central Circle. The number of photo-negatives stored in the Archæological Superintendent's office, Central Circle, totals 2,959 of which 2,317 are of monuments in the Bihar and Orissa Province and the remainder in the Central Provinces. The more interesting records are those of the several excavated sites, and the antiquities recovered from them, around Patna, *viz.*, Kumrahar (Pataliputra), Bara Pahar, and Bulandibagh, which date from the Mauryan period. Sites of similar antiquity are represented in the photographs taken of Basarh in the Muzaffarpur District, and again in those of the Asoka columns in Champaran District. The ancient caves in the Khandagiri and Udaygiri Hills in Orissa have also been fairly completely photographed ; while a representative series of photos of the Gupta site at Nalanda and the antiquities it has yielded is also included in the collection. The early mediæval temples at Bhuvaneshwar and Konarak in the Puri District are other monuments so recorded, as well as the two early Hindu bridges of characteristic corbel-construction in the same neighbourhood. At the other end of the chronological scale are many monuments of the Muhammadan period, among which may be mentioned the tomb at Manair, Patna District, and the Sher Shahi monuments at Sassaram and Rohtas. In the Central Provinces the Muhammadan monuments are the more prominent in the photo-negative list, and include the Bahmani forts of Narnalla and Gawilgarh in the Akola and Amraoti Districts, respectively, as well as the Tombs of Ellichpur and the remarkably fine gates of its Nawabi city walls. The monuments of Burhanpur, and the neighbouring fortress Asirgarh in Berar—relics of the Faruqi dynasty of Khandesh— are also numbered among these negatives ; while remote antiquity is represented by the famous Rock Edict of Asoka at Rupnath, Jubbulpur District, of which inscription a photograph exists ; and of the intervening Gupta period the monuments at Eran in Saugor District have been photographed. The principal photographs taken during 1921-22 were of the excavations carried out at Nalanda, and of the monuments in the Orissa Division ; these latter are in connexion with the listing of monuments in Bihar and Orissa. In the Central Provinces, photos were taken of conservation works in progress or in prospect at Asirgarh, Burhanpur, and the other forts abovementioned, as well as of the Hemadpanth Temple under repair at Lasur in the Amraoti District. The photo-albums maintained in the office are now practically complete, steps having been taken to make good previous deficiencies.

Eastern Circle. The total number of photo-negatives stored in the Eastern Circle office is 808, of which 551 represent the collection made before 1920, when the present Eastern Circle was constituted. The new series commenced in 1920-21 now totals 257 negatives, of which 109 were added during the year under report. The most important additions are a set of 31 photographic records of the antiquities at Unakoti in Tripura State. The album of photo-prints from negatives preserved in this office is not complete, but it is hoped to fill up the existing gaps shortly. Rs. 34 were realized from the sale of photoprints, which amount was duly credited to Government.

Burma Circle. A detailed list of the 77 photographs prepared in The Burma Circle during the year is given in Appendix E at pages 40—42 of the Annual Report of that office for the year ending 31st March 1922, which has been published separately. Among the principal additions may be mentioned the fresco-paintings found on the walls of certain temples at Mandalay, Amarapura and Minnanthu at Pagan, and Pagan. The frescoes at Pagan and Minnanthu are fast disappearing, and drawings, paintings and photographs are being prepared of them wherever possible. Although there is no doubt that, except in a few isolated instances, the art of painting never attained a very high degree of perfection in Burma, still these pictures hold an honourable place in the history of painting in the East. In many cases, their importance is mainly historical, but they date from the early part of the 12th century down to a very late period, and thus furnish the student with a continuous series of examples of remarkable interest.

SECTION XII.

DRAWINGS.

Agra Office. Work in the drawing office at Agra mainly consisted in the preparation of working drawings for designs by the Superintendent. Amongst them may be mentioned a design for new gates for the Entrance Gateway of the Shalamar Garden at Lahore, and designs for new doors and windows for Wazir Khan's Baradari now used as the Public Library of that city. Designs for new picture-cases and show-cases for the Delhi Fort Museum were prepared, as also were designs for a new door in the Tah Khana under the Rang Mahal in the Fort. Drawings for a suggested lay-out of the enclosure of the tomb of Shah Burhan at Chiniot in the Jhang District of the Punjab were also made. Tracing of all drawings received from the Public Works Department in connection with estimates were made, and a number of drawings for Dr. Hankin's Memoir on Saracenic Patterns were commenced. The Head Draughtsman for the greater part of the year was engaged on the survey of the Delhi Monuments with the four special Draughtsmen, temporarily employed for making measured drawings of the principal monuments in the Delhi Province. During the past year they have been employed at Kotla Firoz Shah, Hauz Khas and Humayun's Tomb. At the former, some thirteen drawings have been commenced, complete measurements of all existing material having been taken, and in the case of eleven drawings a conjectural restoration has been worked out and added. The drawings have been inked in and are almost completed. At Hauz Khas work has been in progress on the sheets of drawings which have been completed except for the finishing touches such as tinting and printing headings, etc. These buildings have also been conjecturally restored on paper by Mr. Page and a very good idea of what they were like in Firoz Shah's time can now be obtained. It is expected that the set of drawings with an explanatory text will be published before long as a Memoir. Measuring work was begun at Humayun's Tomb towards the end of December, and nine drawings have been plotted, but the work is as yet not very far advanced. A list of the drawings prepared this year is given in Appendix E to this Report page 261.

In the Lahore office twelve new drawings were prepared. Out of these, ten pertain to the excavations carried out at Sarnath. **Lahore Office.**

Three plans of ancient sites were prepared by the Draftsman in the Frontier Circle, and he also made numerous sketches and small plans required for working purposes, estimates and the demarcation of sites to be acquired under the Land Acquisition Act. The plan of the Northern Kafirkot monument published as an appendix to this report was also re-drawn by him for reproduction. **Peshawar Office.**

In the Poona office thirteen drawings in all were taken in hand during the year, out of which three only were completed. The drawings of monuments situated in Central India and Rajputana were transferred to the office of the Director General of Archæology in India in March 1922 according to the orders of the Government of India along with the negatives taken in these two provinces. Out of 657 drawings in this office, 4 are still incomplete and 315 require labels to be written on them. **Poona Office.**

The principal drawings stored in the Archæological Superintendent's office, Central Circle, are those of the Puri Temples in Orissa, certain of the Faruqi monuments at Burhanpur in Berar, as well as a plan of the Nalanda excavations and those at Basarh, in the Patna and Muzaffarpur Districts, respectively. Most of the other drawings are plans prepared merely to illustrate specific conservation proposals rather than exhaustive architectural records of the old remains. The only drawings prepared during 1921-22 were also in connection with the conservation work in progress at Nalanda on the excavated site ; and include a record of the stratigraphic evidence apparent in the earth left undisturbed in a corner of one of the monastery courtyards, revealing layers of brick débris, potsherds, ashes, and earth, indisputably recording the vicissitudes through which the old remains have passed since their probable foundation in the 5th century A. D. **Patna Office.**

The number of drawings now stored in the Eastern Circle office at Calcutta totals 36, of which the additions during the year under report were 9. The collection includes a set of plans of the monuments at Vishnupur taken in 1920-21 together with a survey **Calcutta Office.**

map of the same village. The new additions during the year consist of a survey plan of the environs of Mahasthangarh and the plans of seven monuments at Gaur and Pandua in the Malda District. In addition to these, several other tracings and working plans were made.

Kotagiri Office. Ten old pencil drawings were inked and three hundred and sixty-five old drawings were scaled this year in the Southern Circle. The total number of drawings preserved in Mr. Longhurst's office on the 31st March 1922 was 1,280, and like the photo-negatives, they have also been classified under several headings, namely, Primitive Stone Monuments and Antiquities; Buddhist Art and Architecture; Jain Art and Architecture; Hindu Art and Architecture; Muhammadan Art and Architecture; Indo-Saracenic Art and Architecture, and Historical Forts and European Monuments.

Mandalay Office. Seven new drawings were prepared by the Superintendent, Burma Circle, a list of which will be found in his Annual Report which has appeared separately.

Simla Office. Eight drawings were prepared in pencil in the office of the Director General of Archæology, all of which relate to the excavations at Taxila. A few others were also prepared to accompany the Conservation Manual which was under preparation.

SECTION XIII.

PERSONNEL.

The reorganization of the Archæological Department sanctioned by the Government of India in June 1921 added to the cadre of the Department 6 new appointments, *viz*:— 1 Superintendent for the Archæological Section of the Indian Museum, 1 Superintendent for Epigraphy, 2 Assistants for Epigraphy and 2 officers as Leave Reserve. Three out of these six were appointed during the year. Mr. Ramaprasad Chanda, B.A., was appointed Superintendent of the Archæological Section, Indian Museum, on 23rd May 1921; Mr. Hirananda Sastri, M.A., Superintendent for Epigraphy, on 26th November 1921, and Mr. K. V. Subrahmanya Aiyar, B.A., Assistant Superintendent for Epigraphy on 21st February 1922. The appointment of the Deputy Director General of Archæology in India was made permanent. The States of Rajputana and Central India, which had been hitherto grouped in the Western Circle, were separated from that Circle and placed directly under the Director General.

Agra Office. Mr. J. A. Page held the appointment of Superintendent, Muhammadan and British Monuments, Archæological Survey of India, Northern Circle, up to the forenoon of the 24th November 1921, when he was relieved by Mr. J. F. Blakiston, the permanent incumbent, who held the appointment to the close of the year 1921-22. Before resuming charge of this office. Mr. Blakiston had been granted leave for 13 months and 3 days as follows:—

(*a*) On privilege leave from the 21st October 1920 to 21st March 1921.

(*b*) On commuted furlough from the 22nd March 1921 to 21st July 1921.

(*c*) On furlough from the 22nd July 1921 to 23rd November 1921.

Maulvi Zafar Hasan, Assistant Superintendent, Archæological Survey, on special duty at Delhi in connection with the listing of ancient monuments in that Province, completed his work there on the 31st July 1921 and proceeded to Simla to be attached to the office of the Director General as Assistant Superintendent.

Patna Office. Mr. V. Natesa Aiyar, Officiating Superintendent, Archæological Survey, Central Circle, proceeded on combined leave for 7 months and 21 days, with effect from the forenoon of the 5th March 1921 and, I very much regret to report, died on the 13th October 1921, when his place was taken by Mr. Hirananda Sastri who had till then held the post of Assistant Superintendent of this Circle. Mr. Natesa Aiyar was a young scholar of great promise and his death is a sad loss to the Department. In the forenoon of the 26th November 1921 on transfer from the Northern Circle, Agra, Mr. J. A. Page took over charge of the duties of Superintendent from Mr. Hirananda Sastri, who was subsequently appointed as Officiating Superintendent for Epigraphy under the Government Epigraphist at Ootacamund. Maulvi Muhammad Hamid Kuraishi, formerly Excavation Assistant to the Director General, was appointed to officiate as Assistant Superintendent in the Central Circle from the forenoon of the 1st May 1921, in the vacancy caused by Mr. Sastri's appointment as Officiating Superintendent.

SECTION XIV.

SCHOLARSHIPS.

The Sanskrit scholarship for training in Archæology was held by Mr. Madho Sarup Vats, M.A., the scholarship for training in Archæological Chemistry by Mr. Ram Singh Ahuja, and the Architectural scholarship by Mr. Maung Hla Thwin. In Burma the local scholarship was offered to Mr. M. W. Kyin Pu, B.A., who joined the department on 1st August.

SECTION XV.

MISCELLANEOUS NOTES.

In the Provincial Reports hitherto issued from year to year by the several Circles, Part II afforded Archæological officers a convenient medium for recording brief notes and queries on miscellaneous questions of antiquarian interest, either too limited in extent or too tentative in character to come within the scope of our more formal Memoirs. As this channel is now closed by the discontinuance of these Provincial Reports, it has been decided to include in the consolidated report a special section for material of this kind, which is frequently possessed of particular interest for the student of Archæology. Thus in the present report Mr. Hargreaves has contributed a note on certain puzzling figures, shown in Gandhara compositions depicting the Buddha's approach to the Bodhi Tree, Mr. Ramaprasad Chanda a brief note on the Visvantara Jataka at Bharhut and M. Duroiselle a study of the picturesque image of the

Earth-Goddess in Burma, etc. These notes are grouped together in the present section, and are as follows :—

MARA AND HIS DAUGHTER IN GANDHARA RELIEFS.

By Mr. H. Hargreaves.

Mara and his Daughter in Gandhara Reliefs. *(By Mr. H. Hargreaves.)*

"In certain Gandhara reliefs depicting the Approach to the Bodhi Tree appear a couple of striking figures in an unusual attitude.* The male, dressed in the robes of ceremony of a personage of high caste, leans his left elbow familiarly on the right shoulder of his female companion, or amorously throws his left arm around her neck, the left hand resting on her left shoulder. For this amorous couple various identifications have been advanced. M. Foucher had long ago suggested that they were either a divine couple not mentioned in the texts, or else the Nāga Kālika and his wife.† The discovery by Dr. Spooner in 1907-08 of a relief which contained both the Nāga Kālika and his wife and also this couple, rendered the second identification untenable,‡ and Dr. Spooner proposed another interpretation, that these were *devas* of the Suddhavāsa heaven. Against this identification M. Foucher has pointed out that it must be remembered that among the divine beings of the Suddhavāsa heaven, sex is abolished, and that these *devas* are saints among the gods. Moreover he draws attention to the interesting fact that on certain of the reliefs, including that recovered by Dr. Spooner, an attendant holds aloft behind this couple a standard surmounted by a *makara*, and this seems to settle the question, for he whose ensign is a *makara* can hardly be other than Māra.* The amorous couple are, therefore, Māra and his daughter.

"Two reliefs on which this striking couple appear have been recovered in the recent operations at Jamalgarhi, and are reproduced here [Plate XXIV (*c*), Plate XXV (*b*).] It will be noted that in the latter the *makara* standard again appears.

"Now the routine character of the school of Gandhara, its conventionalities and its fondness for *clichés* are marked features, and accepting this identification of Māra and his daughter in reliefs of the Approach to the Bodhi Tree, I would propose to extend the identification to this amorous couple in whatever reliefs they appear, even when the *makara* standard is absent. In support of this a hitherto unpublished relief (No. 353 of the Peshawar Museum collection) brings unexpected confirmation to M. Foucher's identification. This depicts the Buddha seated in *abhayamudra* under a conventional tree with this amorous couple to his left and two other females to his right. It requires but a slight acquaintance with the works of the school to recognize at once that these figures, so lacking in respect, are not those of the usual visitors to the Buddha. And who but Māra and his cortége fail to admit his pre-eminence ? We have, therefore, in this relief what is probably a unique representation of the Temptation of the Buddha by Māra and his three daughters. The school, as usual, here observes its usual restraint and there are none of the lascivious details on which the texts expatiate. [Plate XXIV (*b*).]

"It is in no way surprising that in the reliefs under consideration Mara appears as a princely personage and not as a warrior, for in all scenes he assumes the form most

---

* A. S. I., 1907-08, Plate XLIV (*b*) uppermost scene.

† *L'art greco-bouddhique*, T. I, p. 396.

‡ A. S. I., 1907-08, p. 141, Plate XLII (*b*).

appropriate to his dual character, now as a warrior in the *Attack* and now as the prince of worldly pleasures in the *Temptation of Lust*."

In conclusion M. Hargreaves notes that the same couple appear on the extreme right of the well-known Mahāparinirvāna relief from Loriyan Tangai (now in the Indian Museum, Calcutta) and it is probable that a survey of the sculptures in other museums and albums will reveal their presence in other reliefs also.

The Visvantara Jataka at Bharhut.

By Mr. Ramaprasad Chanda.

"The Visvantara Jātaka which embodies the story of the Buddha's penultimate terrestrial incarnation was a favourite theme with artists in India. An entire architrave of a gateway at Sānchī—the lowest architrave of the North Gateway, both front and back—is devoted to the delineation of the various episodes of this romantic story.† At Ajanta it appropriates the whole central part of the wall to the left in Cave XVII.‡ But though sculptured representations of 29 jātakas have hitherto been traced among the bas-reliefs of Bharhut (19 of which bear ancient Brāhmī labels), no trace of the Visvantara Jātaka has been found among them. Cunningham believed that he had found an episode of the Visvantara Jātaka on a fragment of a corner pillar discovered after the bulk of the relics had been despatched to Calcutta. He writes in the Preface to his *Stupa of Bharhut* (p. vi) :—

Visvantara Jataka at Bhar hut. (By Mr. Ramaprasad Chanda.)

"'In the summer of 1876 I completed the present account of Bharhut, but as I had reason to believe that some further discoveries might well be made, Mr. Beglar and myself visited the place a third time, and once more thoroughly explored the whole neighbourhood. The remains of the corner pillar of one of the missing gateways were then discovered together with several fragments. These are not included in the plates; but I may mention that the story represented on the pillar was almost certainly the celebrated Wessantara Jataka. About two-thirds of each face have been cut away, but in the remaining portion of one of the scenes there is a four-horse chariot with a boy and girl being led by the hand, which leave no doubt in my mind that these are intended for the two children of Prince Wessantara'."

"From this meagre description of the sculpture it is very difficult to say how far Cunningham is right in his identification. But recently, while overhauling the sculptures of Bharhut in the Bharhut Gallery of the Indian Museum, I found fixed up by hooks on the western wall of the gallery a fragment of a coping stone. On taking down the fragment I found in one of the compartments a bas-relief that shows a richly dressed layman with a turban on his head giving away an elephant to a beggar while pouring water from a pitcher (Plate XL, Fig. *e*). As the fragment was evidently accidentally fixed on high, it escaped the notice of Cunningham and Anderson. The bas-relief on it illustrates an episode of the Visvantara Jātaka, the giving away by Prince Visvantara of the white elephant, the incident that proved the first great turning point in his life and led to his banishment to Mount Vanka. The story of Visvantara is told in Jātaka No. 547 of the Pali Collection and in No. 9 of Arya Sūra's *Jātakamālā*.

---

* *L'art greco-bouddhique*, T. II, pp. 194—202.
† Sir John Marshall, *A Guide to Sanchi*, Calcutta, 1918, page 53.
‡ A Foucher in *the Journal of the Hyderabad Archæological Society*, 1919-20, pages 61-62.

" Visvantara (Pali, Vessantara) was the heir-apparent of King Sānjaya of the Sibis. He had a passion for alms-giving. Hearing of it a neighbouring King (the king of Kalinga according to the Pali commentary) sent Brahman emissaries to rob him of his excellent white elephant. One day when Visvantara was inspecting his alms-halls, these Brahmans approached him and requested him to present them with the elephant. Visvantara 'alighted from the back of that excellent elephant and stood before them with uplifted golden pitcher ; then he pronounced the solemn formula) ' Accept.' '"* In the Pali commentary it is said that the King of Kalinga sent eight Brahmans.† In our bas-relief only one Brahman with ' hairy head ' is receiving the gift of the elephant. But this need not stand in the way of the identification. The recipients are represented by one person on account of exigencies of space. Both in the Pali version and by Ārya Sūra the elephant is described as richly decorated, and so the animal is in our relief. This great act of charity on the part of Visvantara led to a revolt of all classes of the Sibi people against him, who compelled his father Sanjaya to banish him to Mount Vanka. The succeeding episodes in the story of Visvantara were probably engraved in the succeeding compartments of the coping stone of which we have only a small fragment."

WATHUNDAYE, THE EARTH-GODDESS OF BURMA.

By M. Charles Duroiselle.

Wathundaye, the Earth-goddess. *(By Mr. Duroiselle.)*

" The story of Wathundaye is one of those quaint legends which seem peculiar to the Buddhists of Indo-China, for, though founded sometimes on some episode in the career of the Buddha, they are not to be traced—at least most of them have not yet been traced, to any Buddhist work in Pali or Sanskrit written in India. A good example is the *Zimmê-pannāsa*, a collection of fifty jātaka stories which have not yet been found elsewhere, but which are well known in Siam and Burma. The story of the Earth-goddess, is not unknown in Indian Buddhist works, but not in the form current among the Indo-Chinese. Some of its representations in stone in Cambodia and Burma are very old, and the question of the place of its origin is an interesting one. The figure of Wathundaye is very common in Burma ; it may be seen in practically every pagoda, and the episode to which it refers is also found painted on the walls of many temples, though by no means so commonly as the goddess herself. She is represented in two postures, either seated or standing ; in both cases a thick braid of hair is brought over the left shoulder before her breast, and she is in the act of squeezing water out of it, by so doing bearing witness in favour of the Buddha. Wathundaye is the Burmanized form of a name : Vasundharī, which appears to be extant neither in Sanskrit nor Pali. The usual and proper form is : Vasundharā, that is, the Earth. She is a Buddhist divinity of inferior rank. M. G. Coedes started the question of the origin of the Indo-Chinese Vasundharā in an interesting paper published in the *Memoires concernant l' Asie Orientale* (Tome II, pages 117-22). He found the legend in a Pali work called the " Pathamasambodhi ", well known in Cambodia and Siam, but which appears to be unknown in Burma. The legend as recorded in the " Pathamasambodhi " runs as follows :—Māra, the Buddhist Satan, has come with his monstrous hosts to oust the future Buddha from under the Bo tree and take his place, for he says that he (Māra)

* J. S. Speyer, *Jātakamālā*, Sacred Books of the Buddhists, Volume I, page 74.
† Cowell and Rouse, *The Jataka*, Volume VI, page 252.

is entitled to it. Then Māra said (showing his army) : Here is my witness, Siddhattha; but where is thine ?' The Buddha replied : 'I have no animate witness, but I will call on the inanimate Earth to bear me testimony' and pointing with his hand to *his witness, recited this stanza : 'This throne is mine, what need of another witness ? Let this Earth, which has quaked when I gave Maddi,† be now my witness.' Then he added— 'O, Wicked One ! By me, who aspire to the possession of this throne, there is no gift which has not been made in my innumerable existences, and no precept which has not been observed. Without mentioning my other liberalities, I have, in my existence as Vessantara alone, reached perfection in giving away Queen Maddi and the Earth quaked seven times. And now that I am seated on this throne which has never been conquered, having for aim victory over the entire world and fighting (for it) with Māra, how is it that the Earth keeps silent ? Māra has taken his army as false witness ; let this Earth hear my voice and be my witness, inanimate yet visible !' Like a golden lightning darting from a red cloud, the right hand of the Bodhisatta issued from his robe, illuminated with the lustre of its nails of the colour of coral, like unto the trunk of an elephant and ornamented with the sign of the Wheel. Pointing this right hand towards the Earth,† he said 'O Earth ! I have realized the thirty perfections and, in my existence as Vessantara, I have made the sacrifice of my wife and of my children, and I have distributed gifts by seven hundred (of each) at a time ; but I have no monk nor brahman to bear testimony (to what I say), O, Earth, why dost thou not come to bear witness ? ' Then the Earth, unable to resist the power of the Bodhisatta's perfection, emerged from the ground under the appearance of a woman and placed herself before the Bodhisatta and, as if to say 'O Great Man, I know that thou hast fulfilled the necessary conditions for the attainment of Supreme Wisdom, my hair is soaked with water poured upon the earth to ratify thy gifts, and now I will squeeze it out ', the Earth squeezed her hair and disappeared. The water flowed from her hair like the waves of the Ganges. Māra's hosts could not withstand the flood, and fled. The feet of Girimekhala (Māra's elephant) slipped and sank to the bottom of the ocean. The umbrellas, standards and fly-flaps were broken and fell. Seeing this wonder, Māra astonished said : 'The power of the Bodhisatta's perfections has conquered Māra's army, and the torrents of water flowing from the hair of his witness have scattered it completely to the four points of the compass.'

Wathundaye, the Earth-goddess. *(By Mr. Duroiselle.)*

" The legend as known to the Buddhists of Burma is exactly the same, but is not recorded in any work written in that Province, in either Pali, Burmese or Talaing ; and this accounts for the fact that it is not found even in that splendid work of Bishop Bigandet *The Life of the Burmese Buddha*, where M. Coedes sought for it in vain, for Bigandet was translating from a Burmese work. That, judging from the representations of it, this legend of Vasundharā is very old, is borne out by the fact that it is found on two carved stones in Cambodia, one at the famous Angkor Vat and the other at Vat-Nokor ; on both stones she is represented exactly as in Burma, that is, in the act of wringing her hair. Again, I found a figure of this goddess in Vesāli in Arakan, which may safely be assigned to the 9th or 10th century. This legend, then, must have been known there very much earlier, and may perhaps, without too much straining be pushed back to the 6th or 7th century. The point, however, is this, that although, the

* This explains the attitude of the seated Buddha, with his left hand palm upwards in his lap, and his right hand falling in front of his knee, in the movement of touching the earth.

† A reference to the story of Vessantara, in which he gives his wife Maddi in alms.

Wathundaye, the Earth-goddess. (*By Mr. Duroiselle.*)

image of Vasundharā has been found in India (see, for instance, *Catalogue of the Museum of Archæology at Sarnath*, pp. 91 and 94), it is not in the same attitude as the one in Indo-China; for in India, she is always represented as emerging from the earth at the call of the Bodhisattva and holding a vase in her hand. And the question arises, which is still unanswered—Where did this charming legend originate? Mons. Coedes is of opinion that it is not a mere modern fancy of Cambodian or Siamese monks, that it has a very old origin which will perhaps have to be looked for outside of Indo-China itself. As may be gathered from what precedes, Burma brings no light whatever on this point; not only is the story not recorded in any writing, but the Burmese themselves point to Zimme (Xieng-mai) in Siam, as to the place they received it from. It must be added, however, that nothing much should be based on this statement, for the Burmese, under the impression that the Siamese monks are not very strictly orthodox in certain of their beliefs, always ascribe any story not found in the canonical books or their commentaries, to Zimme as its place of origin. The only close approach to the Indo-Chinese form of this legend in a Burmese work is found in the Tathāgata-Udāna-dīpanī, Vol. I, p. 199; here we have practically only half the legend. It is said there, that on being called to witness, Vasundharā emerged from the earth, her hair, which she holds before her breast, soaking wet with the water poured on the earth in dedication of gifts by the Bodhisattva in numberless previous existences; then, bearing witness, she wrings it, and the noise of her doing so puts Māra and his hosts to flight; nothing is said of their drowning. The author no doubt knew well the whole story, but stopped short at the drowning of Māra from a sense of orthodoxy; for practically all sources, both Pali and Sanskrit, ascribe Māra's flight to the terrible noise made by the Earth in bearing witness. But the legend does occur in one Burmese work, the "Samantacakkhudīpanī" Vol. I, pp. 205-07. After reviewing the passages in Pali works where the Earth is mentioned as bearing witness, the author comes to the conclusion that this legend as known among the people is not orthodox, for it is found nowhere in Pali; neither is it found in any previous Burmese work; he concludes therefore that the legend is merely a popular fancy, to which no weight should be attached. In this connection, he tells us how the well-known Bishop Tripitakalankara (17th century) caused the representation of this legend to be rubbed out from the wall of a cave on which it had been painted. Such a representation however may be seen now on the walls of the Arakan Pagoda at Mandalay. At the Archæological Museum at Pagan, there is a beautiful wooden figure of Vasundharā in a sitting posture which was found in a ruined temple near Pagan, but it is not older than the 14th or 15th century. The special interest of this figure is that in dress and features it is distinctly Chinese. Unfortunately, nothing whatever is known of this temple, nor consequently of this particular image. It may have been brought to Pagan from Southern China by sea, or perhaps by land from or through Yunnan. At any rate it shows that the legend was known out of Indo-China; but whether it came to Indo-China or was received from it, is a problem which has yet to be solved."

Mongol Frescoes at Pagan.

By M. Charles Duroiselle.

Mongol Frescoes at Pagan. (*By Mr. Duroiselle.*)

"The close of the 13th century witnessed one of the greatest catastrophes which ever overtook Burma. This was, in 1287, the destruction of the Burmese army, the fall of the capital, Pagan, the ultimate dissolution of a great dynasty and the disruption, for a long time, of Burmese political unity, through the invasion of the Mongol warriors of Kublai Kahn aided by border tribes such as the Lo-lo, the Pa-y, the Mossos, etc. The victory was crushing and the Burmese nation received a shock from which it never really recovered. Yet, strange to say, up to the present, no tangible vestige of the passage of the Mongol warriors had yet been discovered. In Europe, the memory of the passage of these hordes under their Khans has not yet passed away ; it is true, as is well known, that there they made their appearance and excursions felt in the most dreadful manner ; leaving behind them smoking cities and villages ; heaping in their trails mounds of aged men, women and children cruelly butchered through mere lust of blood ; collecting from the fallen foes tens of thousands of ears as hideous witness of their prowess. In Asia also their passage traced a path of desolation—raping, killing, burning, piling up pyramids of heads. Their very name had become a terror. As far as one is able to judge, these horrors were not inflicted on Burma, for, had such been really the case, it is impossible that the national memory should have so completely forgotten them as it seems to have done. Nothing in the inscriptions, the chronicles and the traditions gives the least hint of such atrocities having been perpetrated. Only the memory of their victory remained with its aftermath of political dissolution. And no trace, no vestige, nothing, seemed to have been left of their passage. It is true there is, in the Museum at Pagan, a certain inscription, Chinese on one face and Pyu on the other, of which it has been supposed that the Chinese face at least was engraved about 1287 (the year the Mongols took Pagan under Nasr-ed din, the General commanding the expedition) ; but this is merely a plausible surmise, because the inscription has never been read and, owing to its bad state, is now past deciphering at all.

Mongol Frescoes at Pagan. *(By Mr. Duroiselle.)*

" There have now been found, however, a small series of frescoes representing several Mongol types, both religious and laic. They were discovered painted on the walls of the Kyanzittha Cave. Careful copies were made of them. The Kyanzittha Cave is properly a monastery, situated close to the great Shwezigon pagoda at Nyaung-U, some four miles from Pagan. It is a low brick building half under ground and half above. As its name indicates, it was built, or at least tradition has it that it was built, by King Kyanzittha (1084-1112). This is not, however, mentioned in any inscription found at Pagan, nor in any old documents, and we have only the popular tradition. The interior of the building consists of long and dark corridors, some of the walls of which are ornamented with frescoes which are on the whole well preserved. All of these frescoes do not represent Mongolian personages, but those which do were most probably painted during the Mongol occupation of the city in 1287. One represents a Buddha seated European fashion on a high-backed chair ; his feet rest on a lotus ; the back of the chair is tri-foliated, the upper part forming an oval halo round the Buddha's head ; his begging-bowl rests on his lap and is held with both hands. Another fresco shows a Buddhist monk. This, considering his dress, is a Chinese ; but he may also possibly be a Central-Asian. He is holding a rosary in front of his breast, and is seated in the posture of meditation ; his eyes are closed. There are several others, in subjects religious and laic, the technique of which shows strong Central Asian influence. The most interesting, however, are the two which represent, one a Mongol military officer, and the other an archer. The upper part of the officer's body is clad in a close-fitting jerkin adorned with rosaces ; his legs are encased in similarly close-fitting trousers ; his feet are shod with leather boots. On his head is a helmet, from the summit of which hangs backwards the tail of an animal ; a bandana surrounds his waist. He is seated on a low wooden stool. The features are clearly reminiscent of the Tartar type : high cheek bones, almond eyes, faint moustaches and

Mongol Frescoes at Pagan. *(By Mr. Duroiselle.)*

spare beard. A hawk or falcon is perched on his left fist, he having been evidently a devotee of the chase like other Tartars. This method of hunting must have been interesting to the Burmese for, as far as is known, hawking has never been practised in Burma, at least, there is no mention of it in the whole range of Burmese literature known to me. The archer is represented in the act of shooting with bow and arrow. He is dressed apparently very much like the officer, but he is barefooted. These tangible proofs of the passage of Kublai Kahn's warriors in Pagan are unfortunately few, but they are decisive, and of great historical interest."

D. B. SPOONER,

Offg. Director General of Archæology in India.

Simla, 6th June, 1923.

APPENDIX A.

Showing expenditure incurred for the office establishments of the Superintendents, etc., during the year 1921-22.

(a) Superintendent, Muhammadan and British Monuments, Northern Circle.

Heads.	Allotments.	Expenditure.		
1. (*a*) Salaries of Gazetted Officers.	Rs.	Rs.	A.	P.
Superintendent's pay.				
Mr. J. A. Page, salary from 1st March 1921 to 31st October 1921	7,670	9,888	11	4
Mr. J. F. Blakiston, salary from 24th November 1921 to 28th February 1922.		7,888	8	8
Mr. J. F. Blakiston, leave allowance from 1st March 1921 to 5th November 1921.		4,214	13	5
Assistant Superintendent's pay.				
Maulvi Zafar Hasan, from 1st March 1921 to 31st July 1921 .	3,900	6,246	10	8
Total Salaries Gazetted Officers .	11,570	28,238	12	1

Note.—Excess over the allotments is due to the payment of Rs. 3,788-11-4 to Mr. J. A. Page, Rs. 4,493-8-8 to Mr. J. F. Blakiston, and Rs. 4,305-8-7 to Maulvi Zafar Hasan as arrears of salaries at enhanced rate owing to the revised scale of pay, and leave allowance paid to Mr. J. F. Blakiston while on leave in England.

Heads.	Allotments.	Expenditure.		
1. (*b*) Office Establishment.				
One Conservation Assistant	3,600	1,650	0	0
One Munshi	1,680	1,155	14	0
Three Clerks	3,180	2,273	11	4
Three Draftsmen and Photographers	2,400	3,006	11	10
Five Peons, 1 Farrash, 1 Mali, 1 Khalasi and 1 Daftri . .	1,328	1,173	12	4
Temporary Establishment	290	252	0	0
Total Office Establishment .	12,478	9,512	1	6
Establishment Grand Total [total of 1 (*a*) and 1 (*b*)]	24,048	37,750	13	7
Carried over ..	24,048	37,750	13	7

Heads.	Allotments.	Expenditure.
	Rs.	Rs. A. P.
Brought forward	24,048	37,750 13 7
2. CONSERVATION, *see* page 166.		
3. EXPLORATION	*Nil*	*Nil.*
4. MUSEUMS AND DAK BUNGALOWS IN THE UNITED PROVINCES AND THE PROVINCE OF DELHI.		
(*a*) *Delhi Museum of Archæology*—		
Pay of Establishment	580	1,517 0 10
War allowance	260	237 0 0
Allowance for dearness of provision	160	191 15 4
Contingencies	2,870	1,718 7 3
Total Delhi Museum	3,870	3,664 7 5

NOTE.—Allotment for the Delhi Museum Clerk is not included in the figure Rs. 580. Provision for him was made by the Chief Commissioner, Delhi, but figures were not intimated to this office. Funds for the Delhi Museum were provided by the Provincial Government.

Heads.	Allotments.	Expenditure.
(*b*) *Taj Museum at Agra*	250	170 12 3
Total Museums	4,120	3,835 3 8
(*c*) *Dak Bungalow at Sikandara, Agra* —		
Pay of a Chaukidar, etc.	250	157 4 6
Total Bungalow	250	157 4 6
5. PHOTOGRAPHY.		
Photographs and purchase of Photo. materials	800	966 15 0
Total Photography	800	966 15 0
6. LIBRARY.		
Purchase of Books and Newspapers	200	125 15 0
Total Library	200	125 15 0
Carried over	29,418	42,836 3 9

APPENDIX A—*contd.*

Heads.	Allotments.	Expenditure.		
	Rs.	Rs.	A.	P.
Brought forward	29,418	42,836	3	9
7. OFFICE CONTINGENCIES.				
Purchase and repair of tents	50	64	8	0
Belts, badges and liveries for peons	30	68	8	0
Rents, rates and taxes	660	500	0	0
Postage and Telegram charges	220	920	0	0
Conveyance of tents, stores and records	200	639	8	0
Purchase of Stationery	} 2,070	12	1	0
Hot and cold weather charges		132	6	8
Miscellaneous		613	8	3
Total Contingencies	3,230	2,950	7	11
8. TRAVELLING ALLOWANCES.				
Travelling allowance of gazetted officers	} 7,050	2,778	10	0
Travelling allowance for Office Establishment		2,969	4	11
Compensation for dearness of provisions		27	9	3
War allowance	30	36	2	1
Total allowances	7,080	5,811	10	3
9. TEMPORARY DRAFTSMEN EMPLOYED ON THE SURVEY OF ANCIENT MONUMENTS IN THE PROVINCE OF DELHI.				
4 Temporary Draftmen's pay	1,920	1,920	0	0
War allowance	528	528	0	0
Travelling allowance	880	879	12	0
Contingent charges	250	166	12	0
Total Survey Party	3,578	3,494	8	6
10. PURCHASE OF SUPERINTENDENT'S OFFICE BUILDINGS	15,000	15,000	0	0
TOTAL	58,306	70,092	14	5

APPENDIX A—*contd.*

(b) Superintendent, Hindu and Buddhist Monuments, Northern Circle.

Heads.	Allotments.			Expenditure.		
	Rs.	A.	P.	Rs.	A.	P.
Salary of the Superintendent	7,075	0	0	6,240	0	0
Salary of the Establishment	9,884	0	0	9,515	7	7
Travelling allowance of the Superintendent	3,000	0	0	3,414	10	0
Travelling allowance of the Establishment	3,050	0	0	3,328	15	6
Contingencies	5,930	0	0	3,738	4	9
Excavations	6,000	0	0	5,268	4	6
Conservation, *see* page 181.						
TOTAL	34,939	0	0	31,505	10	4

(c) Superintendent, Archæological Survey, Frontier Circle.

Heads.		Allotments.			Expenditure.		
Establishment.—		Rs.	A.	P.	Rs.	A.	P.
Salaries	Superintendent	8,400	0	0	12,600	0	0*
	Indian Assistant	3,120	0	0	3,120	0	0
	Clerks	552	0	0	1,134	3	2
	Photographer	1,220	0	0	1,644	0	0
	Draftsmen	770	0	0	902	11	4
	Servants	624	0	0	547	4	8
	Temporary establishment	84	0	0	144	0	0
Travelling allowance of officers		3,000	0	0	1,797	11	0
Travelling allowance of Establishment		3,000	0	0	2,868	7	0
Grain compensation allowance		80	0	0	125	4	1
	Total	20,850	0	0	24,883	9	3
	Carried over	20,850	0	0	24,883	9	3

*Excess due to revision of pay.

APPENDIX A—*contd.*

Heads.		Allotments.			Expenditure.		
		Rs.	A.	P.	Rs.	A.	P.
	Brought forward .	20,850	0	0	24,883	9	3
Contingencies .	Stationery	1,850	0	0	256	0	0
	Postal and Telegraph charges . .				250	0	0
	Tour charges				78	13	0
	Hot and cold weather charges . .				215	0	10
	Tents				69	10	9
	Pay of menials				65	0	0
	Purchase and repair of furniture . .				26	8	0
	Miscellaneous charges				213	14	10
	Total .	1,850	0	0	1,574	15	5
Conservation, see page 183.							
Publications . . .	Publication of Annual Report . .	200	0	0	79	12	0
	Total .	200	0	0	79	12	0
Photography . . .	Photographic materials .	300	0	0	576	12	0
	Total .	300	0	0	576	12	0
Library	Purchase of publications and books .	150	0	0	205	6	6
	Total .	150	0	0	205	6	6
Excavation	Excavations	5,000	0	0	1,067	1	1*
	TOTAL .	28,350	0	0	28,387	8	3

*Of this sum Rs. 1,003-13-6 was expended on Maintenance until sanction for Rs. 18,900 was received and is included in the Rs. 13,011-0-6 under Head—"Conservation and Maintenance," while Rs. 63-3-7 was expended on the pay of a temporary modeller.

APPENDIX A—*contd.*

(*d*) *Superintendent, Western Circle.*

Heads.	Allotments.			Expenditure.		
1. ESTABLISHMENT.—	Rs.	A.	P.	Rs.	A.	P.
(*a*) *Salary.*—						
(*i*) Superintendent	6,900	0	0	10,879	0	6*
(*ii*) Assistant Superintendent	7,200	0	0	5,205	10	8
(*iii*) Establishment	5,856	0	0	7,936	8	4
(*b*) *Allowances.*—						
(*i*) Travelling allowance, Supdt., Asstt. Supdt.	5,600	0	0	7,736	15	0
				366	8	0
(*ii*) Establishment	2,400	0	0	4,211	13	0
(*iii*) Temporary and Prov : allowance	100	0	0	483	10	6
(*c*) *Contingencies.*—						
(*i*) Photographs and Photo materials	1,000	0	0	1,509	9	0
(*ii*) Other petty supplies (tents, instruments, etc.)	250	0	0	682	13	6
(*iii*) Purchase of books, newspapers, etc.	300	0	0	683	4	0
(*iv*) Liveries to peons	50	0	0	109	14	6
(*v*) Rents, Rates and Taxes	..			28	2	0
(*vi*) Postage and Telegram charges	500	0	0	1,175	10	0
(*vii*) Conveyance of tents, stores and records	1,200	0	0	5,075	12	0
(*viii*) Purchase of furniture	1,900	0	0	..		
(*ix*) Purchase of stationery	..			14	1	6
(*x*) Office expenses and Miscellaneous	550	0	0	1,253	15	11
(*xi*) Telephone charges	..			205	0	0
(*xii*) Charges for excavation	5,000	0	0	11	4	0
2. CONSERVATION, *see* page 203.						
3. MUSEUMS	*Nil*			*Nil.*		
4. PUBLICATIONS	*Nil*			*Nil.*		
TOTAL	38,806	0	0	47,569	8	5

*Excess due to revision of pay.

Appendix A—*contd.*

(e) *Superintendent, Central Circle.*

Heads.	Allotments.	Exependiture.
	Rs. A. P.	Rs. A. P.
1. Establishment—		
(i) *Salary of gazetted officers*—		
Superintendent's pay	15,600 0 0	9,939 6 8
Assistant Superintendent's pay		3,564 8 3
	..	13,503 14 11
(ii) *Salary of non-gazetted establishment*—		
1 Excavation Assistant	7,906 0 0	2,644 0 0
1 Photographer		1,248 3 7
1 Accountant		1,392 0 0
2 Draftsmen (1,293-10-8 + 404-8-3)		1,698 2 11
3 Clerks (1,949-0-6 +545-0-6)		2,494 1 0
1 Jamadar		177 6 2
5 Peons (447-10-6+314-12-10)		762 7 4
1 Chowkidar		99 11 7
Temporary Establishment (8-0-0+9-6-8)		17 6 8
Grain compensation allowance (48-4-9+21-0-6)		69 5 3
	..	10,602 12 6
(iii) *Allowances*—		
Travelling allowances, gazetted officers	6,850 0 0	3,773 5 5
Travelling allowances, Establishment		3,359 1 9
	..	7,132 7 2
Carried over	30,356 0 0	31,239 2 7

Appendix A—*contd.*

Heads.	Allotments.			Expenditure.		
	Rs.	A.	P.	Rs.	A.	P.
Brought forward .	30,356	0	0	31,239	2	7
(*iv*) *Contingencies*—						
Office Rent, Rates and Taxes	600	0	0	248	4	0
Postage and Telegram charges	450	0	0	400	0	6
Conveyance of Tents, Stores and Records . .	500	0	0	1,031	0	0
Purchase of furniture	400	0	0	121	0	0
Office expenses and Miscellaneous	850	0	0	957	8	3
Menial charges	90	0	0	88	11	0
Telephone charges	150	0	0	155	0	0
Petty supplies (tents and instruments) . . .	250	0	0	6	4	0
Liveries for Peons	80	0	0	57	0	0
Total .	3,370	0	0	3,064	11	9
1. (*a*) Temporary Establishment (non-gazetted)—						
(*v*) *Salary*—						
1 Photographer						
2 Peons	1,706	0	0	1,789	0	0
Grain compensation allowance . . .						
(*vi*) *Allowances*—						
Travelling allowances	1,000	0	0	782	0	0
(*vii*) *Contingencies*—						
Miscellaneous	1,200	0	0	647	0	0
Total .	3,906	0	0	3,218	0	0
2. Conservation, *see* page 185.						
3. Exploration—						
Excavation charges at Nalanda*	5,000	0	0	2,313	0	0
Carried over .	42,632	0	0	39,834	14	4

*(Note.—Carried out in the hot weather of 1921, and included in the account published in the Annual Progress Report of the Central Circle for the year ending March 31st, 1921.)

APPENDIX A—*contd.*

Heads.	Allotments.			Expenditure.		
	Rs.	A.	P.	Rs.	A.	P.
Brought forward .	42,632	0	0	39,834	14	4
4. MUSEUMS—						
Nalanda—						
(*i*) Museum furniture	400	0	0	381	0	0
(*ii*) Show cases and safe	3,000	0	0	761	0	0
(*iii*) Construction of godown and chowkidar's quarters : re-appropriated from unspent residue of Nalanda excavation and conservation grants.	..			3,014	0	0
(*iv*) Upkeep of Museum bungalow . . .	600	0	0	389	0	0
	4,000	0	0	4,545	0	0
5. PUBLICATIONS	*Nil*			*Nil.*		
6. PHOTOGRAPHY	800	0	0	1,518	0	0
7. LIBRARY	400	0	0	354	0	0
TOTAL .	47,832	0	0	46,251	14	4

(*f*) *Superintendent, Eastern Circle.*

Heads.	Allotments.			Expenditure.		
	Rs.	A.	P.	Rs.	A.	P.
1. Establishment :—						
1 Superintendent	6,225	0	0	6,289	10	8
2 Clerks . . . . 1 Photographer . . . . 1 Draftsman . . . . 1 Duftri . . . . 4 Peons	4,006	0	0	4,311	3	1
Grain compensation allowance	..			20	14	9
Travelling allowance	3,000	0	0	2,978	10	9
Carried over .	13,231	0	0	13,600	7	3

APPENDIX A—*contd.*

Heads.	Allotments.			Expenditure.		
	Rs.	A.	P.	Rs.	A.	P.
Brought forward	13,231	0	0	13,600	7	3
2. CONSERVATION, *see* page 196.						
3. Exploration	2,000	0	0	2,802	9	8
4. Museums				..		
5. Publications				..		
6. Photography				820	5	6
7. Library				1,090	2	0
8. Other petty supplies				105	3	0
9. Miscellaneous	5,830	0	0	756	0	9
10. Rents, Rates and Taxes				284	6	0
11. Postage and Telegram charges				275	0	0
12. Furniture				1,063	0	0
13. Belts, badges and liveries to Peons				60	13	0
14. Carriage of office records				326	6	9
	..			7,583	14	8
TOTAL	21,061	0	0	21,184	5	11

(*g*) *Superintendent, Southern Circle.*

Heads.	Allotments.			Expenditure.		
	Rs.	A.	P.	Rs.	A.	P.
1. ESTABLISHMENT —						
Salary of the Superintendent	14,400	0	0	14,673	5	4
Pay of the Establishment	6,342	0	0	4,477	11	5
Travelling allowance	4,500	0	0	3,663	7	6
2. CONSERVATION, *see* page 224.						
Carried over	25,242	0	0	22,814	8	3

APPENDIX A—*contd.*

Heads.	Allotments.			Expenditure.		
	Rs.	A.	P.	Rs.	A.	P.
Brought forward	25,242	0	0	22,814	8	3
3. Exploration	1,000	0	0	*Nil.*		
4. Museums	*Nil*			*Nil.*		
5. Publications	*Nil*			*Nil.*		
6. Photography	2,200	0	0	1,220	11	6
7. Library, etc.	150	0	0	50	0	0
TOTAL	28,592	0	0	24,085	3	9

(*h*) *Superintendent, Burma Circle.*

Heads.	Allotments.	Expenditure.			Remarks.
	Rs.	Rs.	A.	P.	
Establishment.					
Superintendent, Archæological Survey	8,100	11,600	0	0	Excess due to the revision of the scale.
Archæological Assistant Architectural Surveyor Clerks (four) Draftsman Assistant Photographer Burmese Artist Burmese Copyist Servants (three)	10,240	10,245	10	0	Excess due to increments to the pay of the Assistant Photographer and Burmese Copyist.
Carried over	18,340	21,845	10	0	

APPENDIX A—*contd.*

Heads.	Allotments.	Expenditure.			REMARKS.
	Rs.	Rs.	A.	P.	
Brought forward .	18,340	21,845	10	0	
Temporary allowances and Burma allowance to Superintendent.	1,300	1,574	4	0	
Travelling allowance	4,000	*3,990	11	0	*Includes also the travelling allowances of Honorary Archæological Officer for Arakan.
Conservating, see Annual Report of the Superintendent, Archæological Survey, Burma Circle, for the year 1921-22.					
Supplies and Services.					
Preservation of Archæological Remains	500	100	0	0	
Purchase of photographs and photographic materials.	650†	597	6	6	†Deducting Rs. 166-9-0 recovered from the sale of photographs.
Mandalay and Pagan Museums and Archæological scholarships.	1,250	1,050	0	0	
Purchase and translation of ancient manuscripts.	2,700‡	1,580	4	0	‡ Rs. 1,700 paid by the Local Government out of Provincial Revenues.
Contingencies.					
Contract contingencies	2,500	2,453	6	0	
Rents, Rates and Taxes	960	960	0	0	
TOTAL .	32,200	34,151	9	6	

APPENDIX A—*contd.*

(i) Government Epigraphist for India.

Heads.	Allotments.	Expenditure.			REMARKS.
	Rs.	Rs.	A.	P.	
Salaries—					
Government Epigraphist for India .	7,400	14,863	5	4	Due to arrears of pay on account of time-scale.
Establishment—					
Clerk	1,284	1,298	11	3	Due to promotion to H. C.'s post on Rs. 150.
Servants	396	194	3	1	
Temporary establishment (Khalasis) .	240	..			
Lump provision for addition of establishment.	4,540	..			
Allowances—					
Travelling allowance—					
Government Epigraphist . .	2,500	765	4	0	
Establishment		872	8	6	
Compensation for dearness of provision	90	..			
Contingencies—					
Liveries and clothing	68	..			
Rents, Rates and Taxes	1,800	1,005	0	0	
Purchase of books and newspapers .	50	2,275	13	9	Excess was met by re-appropriation.
Postage and Telegram charges . .	200	146	15	0	
Conveyance of tents, etc. . .	1,000	314	1	0	
Purchase of furniture	500	677	9	0	Ditto.
Office expenses and miscellaneous .	270	801	10	9	Ditto.
Menial charges	120	74	5	0	
Carried over .	20,558	23,289	6	8	

APPENDIX A—*contd.*

Heads.	Allotments.	Expenditure.	Remarks.
	Rs.	Rs. A. P.	
Brought forward .	20,558	23,289 6 8	
Unallotted special charges—			
Director-General's Library and other publications—			
Reproduction of plates . .	3,000	921 10 0	Excess of Rs. 34-0-11 was met by reappropriation from D. G.'s grant.
Honorariums to contributors .		1,112 6 11	
Honorarium to Dr. Thomas for editing Epigraphia Indica.		1,000 0 0	
Rounding	2	..	
TOTAL .	23,560	26,323 7 7	

(*j*) *Archæological Chemist in India.*

Heads.	Allotments.	Expenditure.
	Rs. A. P.	Rs. A. P.
Salaries—		
Archæological Chemist in India—		
Budget allotment	4,700 0 0	8,002 4 10
Supplementary allotment on account of revision of pay.	3,302 4 10	
Total .	8,002 4 10	8,002 4 10
Carried over .	8,002 4 10	8,002 4 10

APPENDIX A—*contd.*

Heads.	Allotments.			Expenditure.		
	Rs.	A.	P.	Rs.	A.	P.
Brought forward .	8,002	4	10	8,002	4	10
Establishment—						
Pay of Establishment	670	0	0	591	10	3
Travelling allowance—						
Budget allotment	1,500	0	0	2,242	6	6
Supplementary allotment	950	0	0			
Total	2,450	0	0	2,242	6	6
Contingencies—						
Contingencies . . . . . Total .	1,600	0	0	1,599	12	1
Special charges—						
(Charges in connection with transfer of headquarters from Calcutta to Dehra Dun.)						
(a) *Recurring*—						
Pay of Establishment	1,460	0	0	877	3	1
House rent	1,200	0	0	744	12	4
Total .	2,660	0	0	1,621	15	5
(b) *Non-recurring*—						
Transport of apparatus (packing, railway freight, etc.)	800	0	0	800	0	0
Fittings (benches, gas and water pipes) . . .	1,200	0	0	1,165	2	3
Reservoir of concrete, iron tank and stand, semi-rotary pump and iron pipes.	1,000	0	0	152	8	0
Furniture	1,200	0	0	1,196	8	0
Labour (skilled and unskilled)	500	0	0	183	15	6
Petrol Gas Machine	2,000	0	0	2,000	0	0
Total .	6,700	0	0	5,498	1	9
Total Special Charges .	9,360	0	0	7,120	1	2
TOTAL .	22,082	4	10	19,556	2	10

APPENDIX A—*contd.*

(*k*) *Director General of Archæology including Epigraphist for Moslem Inscriptions.*

Heads.	Allotments.			Expenditure.		
	Rs.	A.	P.	Rs.	A.	P.
Establishment charges—						
Salary, officers	38,950	0	0	56,615	14	8
Salary, establishment	37,384	0	0	38,328	7	11
Archæological scholarships	5,520	0	0	2,296	12	4
Total	81,854	0	0	97,241	2	11
Allowances—						
Grain compensation allowance	310	0	0	363	0	1
Travelling allowance, officers	7,400	0	0	7,050	4	0
Travelling allowance, establishment	13,250	0	0	13,240	10	6
Total	20,960	0	0	20,653	14	7
Contingencies	26,942	0	0	25,739	14	9
Special charges—						
Annual Report	2,000	0	0	1,734	9	6
Other Archæological publications	3,810	0	0	3,806	13	0
Library	3,000	0	0	3,008	10	8
Antiquities	6,000	0	0	5,866	0	0
Bakhshali Mss.	4,524	4	0	4,524	4	0
Total	19,334	4	0	18,940	5	2
TOTAL	1,49 090	4	0	1,62,575	5	5

NOTE.—Excess over the allotments is due to revision of pay of officers.

Appendix A—*contd.*

(*l*) *Sir Aurel Stein.*

Heads.	Allotments.			Expenditure.		
	Rs.	A.	P.	Rs.	A.	P.
Establishment—						
Salaries of Officers—						
Sir A. Stein	....			15,687	9	0
Miss F. Lorimer	....			6,000	0	0
Honorarium of Mr. F. H. Andrews	....			3,000	0	0
Temporary Establishment	....			2,440	10	6
Total .	....			27,128	3	6
Travelling allowances—						
Officers' travelling allowance	....			2,092	13	0
Establishment travelling allowance	....			384	2	0
Temporary Craftsmen	....			2,046	6	9
Total .	....			4,523	5	9
Contingencies—						
Contingencies	....			2,440	14	11
Charges on Collection Building, New Delhi	....			2,496	4	9
Aluminium materials for frescoes	....			1,444	15	0
TOTAL .	33,000	0	0	[illegible]8,033	11	11

APPENDIX A—*contd.*

CONSERVATION.

Statement showing the expenditure incurred on the conservation of Muhammadan and British Monuments during the year ending 31st March 1922.

District.	Locality.	Name of work and description.	Amount of sanctioned estimate.	Allotment for the year 1921-1922.	Amount spent during the year 1921-1922.	REMARKS.
1	2	3	4	5	6	7
		UNITED PROVINCES.	Rs.	Rs.	Rs.	
		Special Repairs (non-recurring charges).				
Agra .	Agra . .	Restoring the Colonnades around the Quadrangle of the Taj Mahal.	62,374	28,262	28,261	Completed.
" .	" . .	Restoring inner Delhi Gate, Agra Fort.	39,954	1,000	1,080	Do.
" .	" . .	Special Repair to Marble Chajja of Moti Masjid in Agra Fort.	1,946	1,946	1,739	Do.
" .	" . .	Constructing a bridle path to Itbari Khan, Sadiq Khan and Salabat Khan's Tomb.	1,686	1,686	1,098	In progress.
" .	Sikandrah and Itimad-ud-Daulah, Agra.	Providing sand-stone seats for visitors at Akbar's Tomb and Itimad-ud-Daulah's Tomb.	834	834	409	Do.
" .	Sikandrah .	Completing the restoration of the East Causeway and Central Tank in the Mausoleum.	83,265	10,000	10,143	Do.
" .	" .	Restoring well to the south of East Causeway in the Mausoleum.	7,499	1,500	2,545	Do.
" .	" .	Providing a red sand-stone Jali in Mariam's Tomb.	54	54	52	Completed.
" .	" .	Constructing a tube well with engine house and pumping plant in the Kanch Mahal.	37,194	10,000	2,242	In progress.
" .	Agra . .	Conservation of Itbari Khan's Mosque and three other monuments.	748	748	741	Completed.
Lucknow .	Lucknow .	Providing tablets and railings in the Residency Buildings.	697	697	710	Do.
" .	" .	Special repairs to Chhatar Manzil.	966	966	596	In progress.
" .	" .	Spreading surkhi on existing roads in Residency.	996	996	968	Completed.
		Total .	..	..	50,584	
		Add departmental charges @ 19 per cent.*	..	..	9,611	
		Total Special Repairs .	..	..	60,195	

*Departmental charges have not been shown in returns received from Superintending Engineer, United Provinces, and have therefore been added by this office.

APPENDIX A—*contd.*

District.	Locality.	Name of work and description.	Amount of sanctioned estimate.	Allotment for the year 1921-1922.	Amount spent during the year 1921-1922.	REMARKS.
1	2	3	4	5	6	7
			Rs.	Rs.	Rs.	
		UNITED PROVINCES—*contd.*				
		Annual Repairs (recurring charges).				
Agra .	Agra . .	Taj and adjacent buildings . .		5,915	4,545	Completed.
" .	Fatehpur Sikri.	Buildings and Roads at Fatehpur Sikri.		7,500	6,506	Do.
" .	Agra . .	Chini-ka-Rauza	21,120	150	47	Do.
" .	" . .	Fort at Agra		4,350	4,117	Do.
" .	" . .	Roman Catholic Cemetery . .		264	214	Do.
" .	" . .	Sir John Russel's Tomb . .		30	30	Do.
" .	" . .	Ram Bagh		750	708	Do.
" .	" . .	Itimad-ud-Daulah . . .		750	508	Do.
" .	" . .	Queen Victoria's Memorial . .		60	42	Do.
" .	" . .	Firoz Khan's Tomb . . .		250	206	Do.
" .	" . .	Akbar's Tomb		2,841	2,829	Do.
" .	" . .	Kanch Mahal		75	43	Do.
" .	" . .	Mariam's Tomb . . .		750	60	Do.
" .	" . .	Dak Bungalow and outhouses .		354	68	Do.
" .	" . .	Electric Installation at Taj .	1,430	1,594	1,869	Do.
Allahabad	Allahabad .	Tomb of Sultan Khusru at Khusru Bagh.	450	450	384	Do.
" .	" .	Tomb of Sultan Khusru's mother at Khusru Bagh.				
" .	" .	Tomb of Sultan Khusru's sister at Khusru Bagh.				
" .	" .	Enclosure wall and gateway of Khusru Bagh.				
" .	" . .	Zanana Palace in Fort . .	350	350	231	Do.
Mirzapur .	Chunar .	Iftikhar Khan's Tomb . .	750	750	734	Do.
Meerut .	Meerut .	Tomb of Shahpir . . .	180	180	103	Do.
" .	" . .	Tomb of Abu Muhammad Khan .	150	150	66	Do.
		Carried over .	..	..	23,310	

APPENDIX A—*contd.*

District.	Locality.	Name of work and description.	Amount of sanctioned estimate.	Allotment for the year 1921-1922.	Amount spent during the year 1921-1922.	REMARKS.
1	2	3	4	5	6	7
			Rs.	Rs.	Rs.	
		Brought forward .	..	..	23,310	
		UNITED PROVINCES—*contd.*				
		Annual Repairs (recurring charges) —contd.				
Aligarh .	Tappal .	Old gateway at Tappal . .	16	16	10	Completed.
Lucknow .	Mile 4 of Lucknow-Cawnpore road.	Alambagh House	750	750	666	Do.
" .	Lucknow .	Lal Baradari	550	550	546	Do.
"	" .	Chhatar Manzil Palace . .	3,750	3,750	3,667	Do.
" .	" .	Platform in front of Chhatar Manzil	105	105	105	Do.
" .	" .	Farhat Bux Station Library .	1,200	1,200	1,201	Do.
" .	" .	Neil's Gate	15	15	15	Do.
" .	" .	Sikandar Bagh buildings . .	450	450	447	Do.
" .	" .	Qaisar Bagh gates	1,200	1,200	1,095	Do.
" .	" .	Nadan Mahal and Ibrahim Chishti's Tomb.	630	630	625	Do.
" .	" .	Nasir-ud-din Haidar's Karbala at Daliganj.	450	450	435	Do.
" .	" .	Residency buildings	1,500	1,500	1,478	Do.
" .	" .	Bibiapur House	300	300	287	Do.
" .	" .	Dilkusha Palace	750	750	746	Do.
Hardoi .	Tahsil Bilgram Mallawan village.	Fine well	22	22	21	Do.
" .	Shahabad .	Nawab Didar Khan's Tomb. .	495	495	486	Do.
Muzaffarnagar.	Majhera .	Tombs of Syed Hussain, Syed Muhammad Khan, Syed Saif Khan and his mother, Syed Umar Nur Khan and octagonal well.	150	150	140	Do.
Bijnor .	Najibabad .	Nawab Najib-ud-Daulah's Tomb .	127	127	118	Do.
Azamgarh	Mehnagar .	Daulat's Tomb	75	75	35	Do
		Carried over .	..	..	35,433	

Appendix A—*contd.*

District.	Locality	Name of work and description.	Amount of sanctioned estimate.	Allotment for the year 1921-1922.	Amount spent during the year 1921-1922.	Remarks.
1	2	3	4	5	6	7
			Rs.	Rs.	Rs.	
		Brought forward	..	..	35,433	
		UNITED PROVINCES—*concld.*				
		Annual Repairs (recurring charges)—concld.				
Jaunpore	Jaunpore	Jami Masjid	900	900	898	Completed.
"	"	Atala Masjid				
"	"	Lal Darwaza Masjid				
"	"	Jaunpore Fort				
"	"	Gomti Bridge				
"	"	Jhinjhri Masjid				
"	"	Firoz Khan-ka-Rauza				
"	"	Sher Zaman Khan-ka-Rauza				
"	"	Kings' Tomb	75	75	75	Do.
Jalaun	Kalpi	Chaurasi Gumbaz	450	450	362	Do.
"	"	Tomb of Lodi Shah Badshah and Fort wall.				
Farrukhabad.	Mau Rashidabad.	Tomb of Nawab Rashid Khan	10	15	6	Do.
"	Karhar	Tomb of Major Robertson and a well.	20	39	33	Do.
"	Chaudhariapur.	An unknown tomb	10	15	8	Do.
Cawnpore	Cawnpore	Sawada Kothi monuments including flight of steps with the surrounding plateau.	30	45	19	Do.
"	"	The garden known as the Memorial well garden.	186	279	..	Do.
Benares	Dhorara	Aurangzeb's Mosque	112	112	62	Do.
		Total	..	..	36,896	
		Add departmental charges @ 19 per cent.*	..	..	7,010	
		Total Annual Repairs	..	..	43,906	
		Total Special Repairs	..	..	60,195	
		Grand Total for United Provinces	..	..	1,04,101	

*Departmental charges have not been shown in returns received from Superintending Engineers, United Provinces, and have therefore been added by this office.

APPENDIX A—*contd.*

Statement showing the expenditure incurred on the conservation of Muhammadan and British Monuments during the year ending 31st March 1922.

District.	Locality.	Name of work and description.	Amount of sanctioned estimate.	Allotment for the year 1921-1922.	Amount spent during the year 1921-1922.	REMARKS.
1	2	3	4	5	6	7
			Rs.	Rs.	Rs.	
		PUNJAB.				
		Special Repairs (non-recurring charges).				
Gujrat .	Chillianwala	Memorial obelisk	741	815	188	Completed.
Attock .	Attock .	Begam-ki-Sarai . .	7,795	..	11	In progress.
" .	Hasanabdal .	Repairs to Sarcophagus of Lala Rukh's Tomb.	1,020	850	850	*In progress. Work undertaken by the Archæological Department.
Jhelum .	Rohtas .	Certain gates and buildings in Fort.	4,765	785	407	In progress.
Jullundur .	Nakodar and Phillaur Tahsils.	Kos Minars or Mughal mile stones	350	350	350	Completed.
Hissar .	Hissar .	Certain improvements to old fort buildings and town wall.	2,924	2,850	1,920	In progress.
Karnal .	Thanesar .	Sheikh Chilli's Tomb . .	1,367	750	165	Do.
" .	" .	Stone Mosque and Hujra . .	1,365	1,050	1,078	Completed.
Lahore .	Shalamar .	Distempering Baradari . .	1,703	1,703	1,642	Do.
" .	" .	Buildings in Shalamar Garden .	14,643	14,407	14,537	Do.
" .	" .	Shalamar Garden buildings .	630	630	638	Do.
" .	" .	Cleaning silt from covered portion of irrigation channel in front of entrance gate to Shalamar Garden.	210	210	210	Do.
" .	" .	Improvements to Fountains .	209	176	168	Do.
" .	" .	Providing counter for pumping engine.	179	180	89	In progress.
" .	Lahore .	Making foot paths from Gulabi Bagh Gate to Dai Anga's Mosque.	520	520	864	Completed.
" .	" .	Improvements to Chauburja . .	429	360	218	Do.
" .	" .	Samadh of Maharaja Ranjit Singh	1,480	1,300	1,172	Do.
		Carried over .	..	..	24,507	

*Not included for departmental charges.

APPENDIX A—*contd.*

District.	Locality.	Name of work and description.	Amount of sanctioned estimate.	Allotment for the year 1921-1922.	Amount spent during the year 1921-1922.	REMARKS.
1	2	3	4	5	6	7
			Rs.	Rs.	Rs.	
		Brought forward .	..	..	24,507	
		PUNJAB—*contd.*				
		Special Repairs (non-recurring charges)—concld.				
Lahore .	Nawakot .	Nawakot Buildings . . .	3,048	..	2,107*	*In progress. Funds allotted by S. E. by mistake from Provincial funds.
Sheikhupura.	Shahdara .	Improvements to Asaf Khan's Tomb.	38,549	10,660	9,521	In progress.
" .	" .	Providing Historical Notice Board at Nur Jahan's Tomb.	40	34	29	Completed.
" .	" .	Certain Conservation work in Akbari Sarai.	7,650	2,230	1,747	In progress.
" .	" .	Remetalling roads in Akbari Sarai	1,841	1,200	911	Completed.
		Total .	..	..	38,822	
		Add departmental charges @ 18 per cent. on Rs. 35,865†	..	..	6,456	
		Total for Special Repairs .	..	..	45,278	

* Not included for departmental charges.

† Departmental charges have not been shown in returns received from Superintending Engineers or Accountant General, Punjab, and have therefore been added by this office.

APPENDIX A—*contd.*

District.	Locality.	Name of work and description.	Amount of sanctioned estimate.	Allotment for the year 1921-1922.	Amount spent during the year 1921-1922.	REMARKS.
1	2	3	4	5	6	7
			Rs.	Rs.	Rs.	
		PUNJAB—*contd.*				
		Annual Repairs (recurring charges).				
Attock .	Hasanabdal .	Lala Rukh's Tomb . . .	446	445	143	In progress.
„ .	Mile 198 on G. T. Road.	Baolis at Losar and Saidon .	217	105	65	Do.
Rawalpindi	Margalla .	General Nicholson's Monument .	139	50	29	Do.
Gujrat .	Kharian .	Baoli Aurangzeb . . .	105	300	80	Do.
„ .	Chillianwala .	Memorial Obelisk . . .	987			
„ .	Gujrat .	Akbari Baoli in Fort . . .	179			
„ .	„ .	Battlefield cemetry . . .	30			
„ .	Sadullapur .	Monuments	31			
Jullundhar	Dakhni .	Gateway of Sarai . . .	258	110	117	Do.
„ .	Nur Mahal .	Gateway of Sarai . . .				
„ .	Nakodar .	Gateway and tombs . . .				
Firozpur .	Surbraon .	Monuments and antiquities .	775	59	185	Do.
„ .	Misri Wala .					
„ .	Firozpore and Mudki.					
„ .	Firozepore .	Sara Garhi Memorial . . .	1,385	59	109	Do.
Ludhiana .	Aliwal . .	Monuments	178	15	15	Do.
Hissar .	Hissar .	Historical buildings in the district	717	695	451	Do.
Gurgaon .	Gurgaon .	Kos Minars	276	250	107	Do.
„ .	Jharsa .	Tomb of Mr. Jean Ettienn Jharsa	23	20	12	Do.
„ .	„ .	Tomb of Major Franswa Ferey .	15	15	9	Do.
Rohtak .	Sonipat .	Khwaja Khizar's Tomb . .	167	150	130	Completed.
„ .	„ .	Kos Minars	176	170	48	In progress.
Ambala .	Ambala City.	Kos Minars	5	5	5	Completed.
		Carried over .	..	..	1,505	

APPENDIX A—*contd.*

District.	Locality.	Name of work and description.	Amount of sanctioned estimate.	Allotment for the year 1921-1922.	Amount spent during the year 1921-1922.	REMARKS.
1	2	3	4	5	6	
			Rs.	Rs.	Rs.	
		Brought forward .	..	..	1,505	
		PUNJAB—*contd.*				
		Annual Repairs (recurring charges)—contd.				
Karnal .	Thaneswar .	Sheikh Chilli's Tomb . . .	135	104	148	In progress.
" .	" .	Stone Mosque including Hujra .	23	17	54	Do.
" .	Panipat .	Ibrahim Lodi's Tomb . .	30	27	23	Do.
" .	" .	Kabuli Bagh Mosque . . .	212	158	104	Do.
" .	" .	3rd Battle Monument . .	7	5	5	Do.
" .	Gharaunda .	Old Mughal Fort with north and south gateways.	234	175	209	Do.
" .	Grand Trunk Road.	Kos Minars	72	54	58	Do.
" .	Grand Trunk Road, Mile 69.	Old Badshahi bridge . . .	45	34	34	Do.
Lahore .	Lahore .	Historical buildings . . .	6,147	6,116	6,766	Do.
" .	" .	Ditto . . .	4,351	3,804	3,451	Do.
Sheikhupura.	Sheikhupura.	Haran Minara	1,827	827	649	Do.
" .	Shahdara .	Historical buildings . . .	19,545	15,000	16,472	Do.
" .	Ramnagar .	Grave in Barahdari garden . .	26	25	16	Do.
Gurdaspur	Kalanor .	Historical buildings Takht Akbari	211	211	131	Do.
Amritsar .	Amritsar .	Saragarhi Memorial . . .	212	212	196	Completed.
Kangra .	Upper Dharam Sala.	Lord Elgin's Tomb . . .	20	20	13	Do.
Multan .	Multan .	Historical buildings—				
		No. 1 Baba Safra . 103 4 0				
		No 2 Sher Khan's well 77 9 0	232	232	211	In progress.
		No. 3 Daya Ram's well 30 8 0				
		No. 4 Baqar-i-Arabi . ..				
		211 5 0				
		Carried over .	..	..	30,045	

Appendix A—*contd.*

District.	Locality.	Name of work and description.		Amount of sanctioned estimate.	Allotment for the year 1921-1922.	Amount spent during the year 1921-1922.	Remarks.
1	2	3		4	5	6	7
				Rs.	Rs.	Rs.	
		Brought forward .		..	..	30,045	
		PUNJAB—*concld.*					
		Annual Repairs (recurring charges) —concld.					
Dera Ghazi Khan.	Dera Ghazi Khan.	Ghazi Khan's Tomb cemetery at Asni.		206	200	84	In progress.
Muzaffernagar.	Shitpur .	No. 1 Mosque	142				
		No. 2 Tomb of Tahar Khan Nahar.	148	208	208	290	Do.
			290				
		Total .		..	..	30,419	
		Add departmental charges @ 18 per cent.*		..	..	3,475	
		Total for Annual Repairs . .		..	..	33,894	
		Total for Special Repairs . .		..	..	45,278	
		Grand Total for Punjab .		..	..	79,172	

*Departmental charges have not been shown in returns received from Superintending Engineers or Accountant General, Punjab, and have therefore been added by this office.

APPENDIX A—*contd.*

Statement showing the expenditure incurred on the conservation of Muhammadan and British Monuments during the year 1921-22.

Locality.	Name of work and description.	Amount of sanctioned estimate.	Allotment for the year 1921-22.	Amount spent during the year 1921-22.	REMARKS.
1	2	3	4	5	6
		Rs.	Rs.	Rs.	
	DELHI PROVINCE.				
	Special Repairs (non-recurring charges).				
Firozabad .	Conservation work at Firoz Shah Kotla.	9,910	9,900	9,351	In progress.
" . .	Conservation work at Firoz Shah Kotla, river front.	12,475	10,170	9,143	Completed. (?)
Tughlaqabad .	Conservation of Road Front to Tughlaqabad (supplementary).	16,128	7,000	6,961	Do.
Delhi . .	Conservation work in the enclosure wall of Qadam Sharif.	7,390	7,390	6,559	In progress.
" . .	Removal of earth and débris from Sher Shah's Gateway.	2,705	700	700	Do.
" . .	Installing an electric pump with necessary feeder and pipe line at Safdarjang Garden for the irrigation of the western approach.	8,709 3,469	3,400	3,421	Completed.
Delhi Fort . .	Constructing a stable and Godown in the Delhi Fort.	730	730	734	Do.
" " . .	Providing a door to Tab Khana beneath the Rang Mahal, Delhi Fort.	240	240	230	Do.
" " . .	Carrying out certain repair works to the rear portion of the Diwan-i-Am, Delhi Fort.	350	300	352	Do.
" " . .	Special Repairs to Mumtaz Mahal used as Museum.	55	55	48	Do.
" " . .	Repairing an inlaid black marble panel in Diwan-i-Am, Delhi Fort.	156	156	156*	*Completed. Work undertaken by the Archæological Department.
Mehrauli . .	Conservation of Zafar Mahal at Mehrauli.	2,760	2,700	2,373	Completed.
Indarpat . .	Improving the Devi's temple at Purana Qila.	730	730	730	Do.
Khirkee . .	Levelling the ground round Mosque at Khirkee.	3,136	3,100	2,809	In progress.
Humayunpur .	Certain conservation work at Humayun's Tomb.	14,222	450	345	Do.
Near Purana Qila Indarpat.	Conservation work at Khair-ul-Manazil.	16,270	5,900	6,420	Do.
Begumpur . .	Special repair to north and west wall of Begampur Mosque.	472	470	466	Completed.
Ridge and Wazirabad.	Special repairs to Chauburji and Wazirabad Mosques.	437	430	351	Do.
Hauz Khass .	Constructing an approach road from Qutb Road mile 9 to Hauz Khass.	3,500??	..	700	In progress.
	Total	..	..	51,849	
	Add departmental charges at 13½ per cent on Rs. 51,693.†	..	..	6,979	
	Total Special Repairs .	..	..	58,828	

* Not included for departmental charges.

† Departmental charges have not been shown in returns received from Superintending Engineer, Delhi, and have therefore been added by this office.

APPENDIX A—*contd.*

Locality.	Name of work and description.	Amount of sanctioned estimate.	Allotment for the year 1921-22.	Amount spent during the year 1921-22.	REMARKS.
1	2	3	4	5	6
	DELHI PROVINCE.	Rs.	Rs.	Rs.	
	Annual Repairs (recurring charges).				
Delhi . .	Firoz Shah Kotla with all main buildings.				
" . .	Lal Darwaza				
" . .	Purana Qila with Sher Shah's Mosque and Sher Mandal.				
" . .	Khairul-Manazil				
" . .	Buildings between Humayun's Tomb and Purana Qila.				
" . .	Humayun's tomb with tomb of Babar.				
" . .	Nila Burj . . .				
" . .	Arab Sarai Gateways . . .				
" . .	Isa Khan's Tomb				
" . .	Walls and gateways of Bu-Halima Garden.				
" . .	Sabz Burj				
" . .	Chaunsath Khamba . . .				
" . .	Tomb of Taga Khan . . .				
" . .	Junah Shah's Mosque . . .				
" . .	Dargah of Khwaja Amir Khusru and Baoli at Nizam-ud-Din and Khan Khanan's Tomb.				
" . .	Barah and Pulla				
" . .	Kos Minars on Delhi-Muttra Road .				
" . .	Khairpur Lodhi's Tomb . .				
" . .	Tomb of Safdar Jang and Mosque .				
" . .	Darya Khan's Tomb . . .				
" . .	Kotla Mubarakpur group . .				
" . .	Moth-ki-Masjid . . .				
" . .	Muhammadi Masjid . . .				
" . .	Bastion at Siri				
" . .	Hauz Khas group of buildings .				

Appendix A—*contd.*

Locality.	Name of work and description.	Amount of sanctioned estimate.	Allotment for the year 1921-22.	Amount spent during the year 1921-22.	Remarks.
1	2	3	4	5	6
		Rs.	Rs.	Rs.	
	DELHI PROVINCE—*contd.*				
	Annual Repairs (recurring charges)—contd.				
Delhi	Dome between Qutb Road and Hauz Khas.				
"	Humayunpur monuments				
"	Muhammadpur monuments				
"	Mumirka monuments				
"	Zamarudpur monuments				
"	Kalu Sarai Mosque				
"	Bijai Mandal				
"	Begumpur Mosque				
"	Lal Gumbad				
"	Khirkee Masjid				
"	Tomb of Yusuf Qattal				
"	Satpulla				
Tughlaqabad	Tomb of Ghyas-ud-din Tughlaq				
"	Road front of Tughlaqabad Fort				
Mehrauli	Qutb Minar with all buildings in that area.				
"	Muhammad Quli Khan's Tomb				
"	Adham Khan's Tomb				
"	Bahadur Shah II's Palace				
"	Jahaz Mahal				
"	Rajon-ki-Bain				
"	Masjid to south-west of Bagh-i-Nazir				
"	Wall Mosque				
"	Jamali Kamali Tomb and Mosque				
"	Basti Baori group of buildings				
Mehpalpur	Sultan Ghari's Tomb				
"	Shikargah	3,060	4,430	3,033	
	Carried over	..	..	3,033	

APPENDIX A—*contd.*

Locality.	Name of work and description.	Amount of sanctioned estimate.	Allotment for the year 1921-22.	Amount spent during the year 1921-22.	REMARKS
1	2	3	4	5	6
		Rs.	Rs.	Rs.	
	Brought forward .	..	..	3,033	
	DELHI PROVINCE—*concld.*				
	Annual Repairs (recurring charges)—concld.				
Delhi . .	Baradari Roshanara Garden . .	1,010	800	677	Completed.
" . .	Old Magazine Gateway . . .	110	100	111	Do.
" . .	Meterological Observatory . .	12	10	8	Do.
" . .	Historical Buildings in charge of Provincial Division.	1,693	1,680	1,811	Do.
	Total .	..	..	5,640	
	Add departmental charges at 13½ per cent.*	..	..	761	
	Total Annual Repairs .	..	..	6,401	
	Total Special Repairs .	..	..	58,828	
	GRAND TOTAL FOR DELHI PROVINCE	..	..	65,229	

* Departmental charges have not been shown in returns received from Superintending Engineer, Delhi, and have therefore been added by this office.

Appendix A—*contd.*

Statement showing expenditure on Archæological Gardens in the Northern Circle (Muhammadan and British Monuments) during the year 1921-22.

Name of Garden.	District.	Locality.	Expenditure during the year 1921-22.	Remarks.
			Rs. A. P.	
United Provinces.				
Khusru Bagh	Allahabad	Allahabad	22,893 0 0	Funds provided by the Local Government.
Taj	Agra	Agra	41,052 0 0	Ditto.
Agra Fort	"	"		
Itimad-ud-Daulah	"	"		
Chini-ka-Rauza	"	"		
Akbar's Tomb	"	Sikandara		
Ram Bagh	"	Agra		
Khan-i-Alam	"	"		
Roman Catholic Cemetery	"	"		
Residency Garden	Lucknow	Lucknow	5,136 0 0	Ditto.
Sikandar Bagh	"	"	*Nil.*	
Dilkusha Palace Garden	"	"	500 0 0	Funds provided by the Nazul Department of Lucknow.
Total	..	..	69,581 0 0	
Punjab.				
Shalamar	Lahore	Baghbanpura	7,891 8 3	Funds provided by the Punjab Government.
Shahdara Jahangir's Tomb	"	Shahdara	11,800 2 9	Ditto.
Hazuri Bagh	"	Lahore	1,032 3 0	Ditto.
Total	..	..	20,723 14 0	
Delhi Province.				
Humayun's Tomb	Delhi	Humayunpur	20,712 0 0	Funds provided by the Government of India.
Isa Khan's Tomb	"	"		
Buhalima	"	"		
Kotla Firoz Shah	"	Kotla Firoz Shah.	2,893 0 0	Ditto.
Carried over	..	..	23,605 0 0	

Appendix A—*contd.*

Name of Garden.	District.	Locality.	Expenditure during the year 1921-22.	Remarks.
			Rs. A. P.	
Brought forward .	..	..	23,605 0 0	
Delhi Province—*concld.*				
Purana Qila	Delhi . .	Purana Qila .	5,172 0 0	Funds provided by the Government of India.
Hauz Khas	" . .	Hauz Khas .	1,305 0 0	Ditto.
Qutb	" . .	Mehrauli. .	8,066 0 0	Ditto.
Delhi Fort Palace Garden.				
Salary of the Superintendent of Historical Buildings and Establishment. 6,839 1 10*				*Funds provided by the Provincial Government.
Pay of Malis 3,618 15 10†		Delhi Fort .	21,525 0 0	†Funds provided by the Government of India.
Expenditure on motor pump for watering the garden. 8,927 12 8†				
Contingencies and other charges. 2,139 1 10†				
Total 21,525 0 2				
Total .	..	..	59,673 0 0	
Add departmental charges @ 13½ per cent. on 52,834.	..	..	7,133 0 0	
Total .	..	..	66,806 0 0	

Note.—No departmental charges have been added where funds have been provided by Provincial Governments.

SUMMARY.

Province.	Total amount spent on Special Repairs during the year 1921-22.	Total amount spent on Annual Repairs during the year 1921-22.	Total amount spent on the maintenance of gardens during the year 1921-22.	Total.
	Rs.	Rs.	Rs. A. P.	Rs. A. P.
United Provinces	60,195	43,906	69,581 0 0	1,73,682 0 0
Province of Punjab . . .	45,278	33,894	20,723 14 0	99,895 14 0
Delhi Province	58,828	6,401	66,806 0 0	1,32,035 0 0
Total .	1,64,301	84,201	1,57,110 14 0	4,05,612 14 0
Grand Total for conservation of Monuments and maintenance of Gardens.	..	..	..	4,05,612 14 0

Appendix A—*contd.*

Statement showing the expenditure incurred on the conservation and excavation of ancient Hindu and Buddhist Monuments in the Punjab and United Provinces during the year ending 31st March 1922.

District.	Locality.	Name of work and description.	Amount of sanctioned estimate	Allotment for the year 1921 1922.	Amount spent during the year 1921-1922.	Remarks.
1	2	3	4	5	6	7
			Rs.	Rs.	Rs. A. P.	
		PUNJAB.				
Rawalpindi	Rawalpindi .	Annual Repairs to Hindu and Buddhist Monuments in the Rawalpindi District.	20	20	15 0 0	
Jhelum .	Rohtas .	Annual Repairs to Satghara temple.	50	50	10 0 0	
Shahpur .	Amb . .	Annual Repairs to temples inside fort.	279	150	44 0 0	
" .	Bhera . .	Annual Repairs to ancient city of Bhera.	36	35	34 0 0	
" .	Miani . .	Annual Repairs to old site of Vijhi.	52	50	49 0 0	
" .	Amb . .	Special Repairs to temples inside fort.	3,001	2,254	2,120 0 0	
Karnal .	Thanesar .	Acquisition of Mound known as Raja Karn ka Kila.	1,800	1,800	1,531 0 0	
Ambala .	Jagadhari .	Annual Repairs to Kapal Mochan temple.	20	20	13 0 0	
Kangra .	Bajaura .	Annual Repairs to temple of Basheshwar Mahadev.	20	23	19 0 0	
" .	Nagar .	Special Repairs to temple of Gauri Shankar at Dasal and Nagar.	79	50	50 0 0	
" .	Kangra .	Special Repairs to fort at Kangra	399	200	336 0 0	
" .	Kotla . .	Special Repairs to fort at Kotla .	481	200	356 0 0	
" .	Baijnath .	Special Repairs to temple at Baijnath.	1,161	800	994 0 0	
" .	Nurpur .	Special Repairs to fort at Nurpur	1,280	900	1,281 0 0	
" .	Kangra .	Conservation work at Kangra fort	347	323	388 0 0	
		Carried over .	..	..	7,220 0 0	

APPENDIX A—*contd.*

District.	Locality.	Name of work and description.	Amount of sanctioned estimate.	Allotment for the year 1921-1922.	Amount spent during the year 1921-1922.	Remarks.
1	2	3	4	5	6	7
			Rs.	Rs.	Rs. A. P.	
		PUNJAB—*concld.*				
		Brought forward .	..	..	7,220 0 0	
Kangra .	Nurpur .	Annual Repairs to temple at Nurpur.	..	19	18 0 0	
			..	..	7,238 0 0	
		Excavations at ancient Mound known as Raja Karn ka Kila.	..	3,000	2,268 4 6	
			..	..	9,506 4 6	
	Taxila .	Excavation and conservation works including the Museum at Taxila.	..	33,200	33,200 0 0	
		Total Punjab .	..	..	42,706 4 6	
		UNITED PROVINCES.				
Dehra Dun	Kalsi .	Annual Repairs to Asoka stone .	37	37	37 0 0	
Agra .	Agra .	Annual Repairs to Jaswant Singh ki Chhatri.	150	150	63 0 0	
Muttra .	Brindaban .	Annual Repairs to temple of Govindji, Jugal Kishore and Radhaballabh.	600	600	523 0 0	
Hardoi .	Sandi .	Annual Repairs to temple of Phoolmati.	7	7	4 0 0	
Hamirpur	Mahoba .	Conservation of monuments at and near Mahoba.	5,663	1,316	497 0 0	
Benares .	Sarnath .	Asoka Column	..	..	1,189 0 0	
,, .	,, .	Old and New Museum and Archæological remains.	..	..	809 0 0	
Gorakhpur	Kasia .	Annual Repairs to Buddhist ruins at Kasia.	..	..	141 0 0	
			..	..	3,263 0 0	
Benares .	Sarnath .	Excavation and conservation works.	9,000	9,000	8,114 13 4	
Allahabad	Kosam .	Ditto ditto .	..	..	861 8 0	
		Total United Provinces .	..	..	12,239 5 4	
		GRAND TOTAL FOR PUNJAB AND UNITED PROVINCES.	..	..	54,945 9 10	

APPENDIX A—*contd.*

Statement showing the expenditure on the conservation of ancient monuments in the Frontier Circle during the year 1921-22.

District.	Locality.	Name of work and description.	Amount of sanctioned estimate.	Allotment for 1921-1922.	Amount spent during the year 1921-22.			REMARKS.
		FRONTIER CIRCLE.						
		(a) Special Repairs (non-recurring charges).	Rs.	Rs.	Rs.	A.	P.	
Peshawar .	Tahsil Mardan	Conservation at Jamalgarhi . .	..	5,000	3,249	6	0	
„ .	„ „	Conservation at Takht-i-Bahi .	..	2,000	1,987	0	0	
„ .	„ „	Protection of Larger Inscribed Rock at Shahbazgarhi.	..	600	..			
„ .	„ „	Path to Tareli Site	..	1,000	..			
„ .	„ „	Improvement to the path to Kashmir Smas.	..	400	..			
Hazara .	Near Taxila .	Conservation at Jaulian . .	..	6,000	5,827	13	6	
„ .	„ „ .	Works at Archæological Bungalow .	..	..	1,316	2	0	
„ .	„ „ .	Compensation paid for the excavated land at Tofkian.	..	..	297	3	0	
„ .	„ „ .	Cost of boundary pillars, etc., for the acquisition of the following sites :—			..			
		Jandial		400	..			
		Tofkian			..			
		Badalpur			..			
		Lal Chak			..			
		Jaulian	..	..	132	9	0	
Dera Ismail Khan.	..	Path to Fort Northern Kafir Kot .	..	1,000	..			
		Total (*a*) .	..	16,400	12,810	1	6	
		(b) Annual Repairs and Maintenance (recurring charges).						
Peshawar .	Tahsil Mardan	Maintenance charges at Jamalgarhi	..	500	159	0	0	
„ .	„ „	Annual repairs and maintenance charges at Takht-i-Bahi Monuments.	..	700	..			
Hazara .	Near Taxila .	Maintenance charges at Jandial Monuments.	..	280	180	0	0	
„ .	„ „ .	Maintenance charges at Jaulian Monuments.	..	1,020	1,169	7	0	
		Carried over .	..	..	1,508	7	0	

APPENDIX A—*contd.*

District.	Locality.	Name of work and description.	Amount of sanctioned estimate.	Allotment for 1921-1922.	Amount spent during the year 1921-22.	REMARKS.
1	2	3	4	5	6	7
			Rs.	Rs.	Rs. A. P.	
		Brought forward ..	..	..	1,508 7 0	
		FRONTIER CIRCLE—*concld.*				
		(*b*) *Annual Repairs and Maintenance (recurring charges)*—concld.				
Hazara .	Near Taxila .	Maintenance charges at Nikra Archæological Bungalow.	..	700	679 8 0	
,, .	Mansehra .	Annual repairs to Asoka Rock Inscriptions at Mansehra.	..	200	..	
		Total (*b*) .	..	3,400	2,187 15 0	
		GRAND TOTAL (*a*) AND (*b*) .	..	19,800	14,998 0 6*	
		Works executed from funds of Public Works Department.				
Dera Ismail Khan.	..	Repairs to pathway to Kafir Kot (Bilot).	..	..	1,001 14 0	
,,	..	Repairs Kafir Kot (Umar Khel) .	..	..	500 0 0	

* The total expenditure of Rs. 14,998-0-6 includes the following expenditure which was met from this office contingencies under head " Excavation (Rs. 5,000) ":—

	Rs. A. P.
1. Maintenance charges of various sites	1,003 13 6
2. Pay of a temporary modeller	63 3 7
Total .	1,067 1 1

This was necessitated by the fact that no funds were available for these charges until the grant-in-aid Rs. 13,900 and Rs. 5,900 was sanctioned late in the year.

APPENDIX A—*contd.*

Statement showing the expenditure incurred on the conservation of ancient monuments in the Central Circle during the year 1921-22.

District.	Locality.	Name of work and description.	Amount of sanctioned estimate.	Allotment for the year 1921-22.	Amount spent during the year 1921-22.	REMARKS.
1	2	3	4	5	6	7
			Rs.	Rs.	Rs. A. P.	
		I.—BIHAR AND ORISSA.				
		(a) Special Repairs (non-recurring charges).				
		ORISSA CIRCLE.				
Puri .	Konarak .	Black Pagoda at—	1,043	1,043	966 0 0	Completed.
„ .	Dhauli Hill .	Monument at—	39	39	39 0 0	Do.
Cuttack .	Jajpur .	Marhatta Bridge at—Providing stone wheel-guard to.	279	279	288 0 0	Do.
„ .	„ .	Marhatta Bridge at— . .	685	685	687 0 0	Do.
		EASTERN CIRCLE.				
Patna .	Patna City .	Begu Hajjam's Mosque at— .	570	170	172 0 0	In progress
„ .	Rajgir and Nalanda.	Providing Notice Boards to the monuments at—.	102	52	48 0 0	Do.
„ .	Nalanda .	Conservation of excavated remains at—by Archæological Superintendent.	..	5,000	2,859 0 0	Do.
„ .	„ .	Museum at—	..	..	4,156 0 0	
		Total (*a*) .	..	..	9,215 0 0	
		(b) Annual Repairs (recurring charges).				
		SON CIRCLE.				
Shahabad .	Arrah . .	Soldier's tomb at— . . .	5	5	4 12 0	Completed.
„ .	Deo Bonarak	Sculpture Shed at— . . .	15	15	7 12 0	In progress
„ .	Arrah . .	Arrah House at —	100	100	82 8 0	Completed.
„ .	Rohtas .	Rohtas Palace and Inspection Bungalow at—.	500	620	641 0 0 24(*a*)*	Do.
„ .	Sasaram .	Hassan Sur Shah's tomb at— .	160	195	192 0 0 24(*a*)*	Do.
		Carried over .	..	..	976 0 0	

*(*a*) The expenditure was incurred from April to June 1921 against the estimate for 1920-21.

APPENDIX A—*contd.*

District.	Locality.	Name of work and description.	Amount of sanctioned estimate.	Allotment for the year 1921-22.	Amount spent during the year 1921-22.	REMARKS.
1	2	3	4	5	6	7
			Rs.	Rs.	Rs. A. P.	
		Brought forward	..	..	976 0 0	
		I.—BIHAR AND ORISSA—*contd.*				
		SON CIRCLE—*concld.*				
		(*b*) *Annual Repairs (recurring charges)*—contd.				
Shahabad	Sassaram	Alwal Khan's tomb at—	20	25	24 0 0	Completed.
"	"	Sher Shah's tomb at—	60	74	73 0 0	Do
"	"	Do. lightning conductor—removing defects of.	88	109	95 0 0	Do.
"	"	Salim Shah's tomb at—	20	25	25 0 0	Do.
Gaya	Bodh Gaya	Bodh Gaya temple at—	124	124	116 0 0	Do.
"	Guneri	Buddhist statue shed at—	18	18	17 0 0	Do.
"	Ghenjan	Ditto	18	18	16 0 0	Do.
Patna	Manair	Mukhdum Shah's tomb at—	481	481	286 0 0	In progress.
Gaya	Shamshernagar.	Shamsher Khan's tomb at—	62	62	46 0 0	Completed.
Shahabad	Buxar	Fort and Bastion at—	184	184	164 0 0	Do.
"	"	Tomb at—	15	15	12 0 0	Do.
"	Shergarh	Fortress at—	184	150	104 0 0	Do.
"	Buxar	Katkauli tomb at—	5	5	5 0 0	Do.
"	Ramgarh	Mundeswari temple at—	25	25	25 0 0	Do.
"	Chainpur	Bukhtiyar Khan's tomb at—	130	130	127 0 0	Do.
"	Buxar	Monuments in the battlefield at—	50	50	44 0 0	Do.
					2,155 0 0	
		ORISSA CIRCLE.				
Cuttack	Cuttack	Mosque and moat wall in Barabati Fort.	80	80	39 0 0	In progress.
"	"	Barabati Fort gate Q.-R. to—	47	5	5 0 0	Do.
Puri	Bhubaneswar	Khandagiri and Udayagiri caves and temple at—Q.-R.	100 (1920-21)	65	65 0 0	Do.
			199 (1921-22)	60	72 0 0	
"	Khurda and Ganjan.	Monuments—Q.-R. to—	11	11	11 0 0	Completed.
"	Konarak	Sculpture shed at—	15	15	..	
		Carried over	..	..	192 0 0	

APPENDIX A—*contd.*

District.	Locality.	Name of work and description.	Amount of sanctioned estimate.	Allotment for the year 1921-22.	Amount spent during the year 1921-22.	REMARKS.
1	2	3	4	5	6	7
			Rs.	Rs.	Rs. A. P.	
		Brought forward .	..	..	192 0 0	
		I.—BIHAR AND ORISSA—*contd.*				
		ORISSA CIRCLE—*concld.*				
		(b) Annual Repairs (recurring charges)—contd.				
Puri .	Konarak .	Temple at—Q.-R. to . . .	541	341	343 0 0	In progress.
Cuttack .	Jajpur .	Ancient monuments at—Q.-R. to—	68	68	65 0 0	Completed.
Balasore .	Balasore Town	Two Dutch tombs at—Q.-R. to —	44	44	44 0 0	Do.
					644 0 0	
		EASTERN CIRCLE.				
Bhagalpur	Patharghatta Colgong.	Ancient monuments at— . .	131	..	..	
" .	Madhipura .	Tomb of Charles Haye . .	5	5	4 0 0	Do.
" .	Bhagalpur .	3rd Buffs cemetery . . .	9	9	9 0 0	Do.
Purnea .	Gunamati .	Tomb of John Macquire . .	5	5	4 0 0	Do.
Monghyr .	Pirpahar .	Tomb of Mary Annie Becket .	25	25	24 0 0	Do.
" .	Monghyr Fort	Tomb of Pir Shah Naffa . .	100	89	75 0 0	Do.
Santal Parganas.	Rajmahal .	Juma Masjid and Bridge at Hadaf	150	150	51 0 0	In progress.
" .	" .	Endowed tomb of James Scott .	2	2	2 0 0	Completed.
" .	Gudda .	Tomb of John Scott at— .	5	5	3 0 0	Do.
Patna .	Rajgir .	Maniyar Math (temple) at— .	20	20	7 0 0	In progress.
" .	" .	Mahadeo temple at— . .	25	25	9 0 0	Do.
" .	" .	Jain temple at—	10	10	9 0 0	Completed.
" .	Patna City .	Agam Kuan (well) at— . .	10	10	6 0 0	In progress.
" .	" " .	Tall stone shaft at—	10	10	8 0 0	Completed.
" .	Bankipur .	Gola (granary) at—. Spent Rs. 10 (*a*)*.	90	90	96 0 3	Do.
" .	" .	Major Knox's tomb ; cenotaph on—	10	10	10 0 0	Do.
" .	Bihar . .	Syed Ibrahim's tomb . . .	40	40	22 0 0	In progress.
" .	Nalanda .	Upkeep of monuments . .	..	2,500	560 0 0	
					899 0 0	
		WESTERN CIRCLE.				
Hazaribagh	Chatra .	Monument to commemorate some soldiers who fell in combat with mutineers in 1857.	13	13	10 0 0	Completed.
		Carried over .	..	..	10 0 0	

*(*a*) Spent between April and June 1921 against the estimate for the previous year.

APPENDIX A—*contd.*

District.	Locality.	Name of work and description.	Amount of sanctioned estimate.	Allotment for the year 1921-22.	Amount spent during the year 1921-22.	REMARKS.
1	2	3	4	5	6	7
			Rs.	Rs.	Rs. A. P.	
		Brought forward	..	..	10 0 0	
		I.—BIHAR AND ORISSA—*concld.*				
		WESTERN CIRCLE—*concld.*				
		(*b*) *Annual Repairs (recurring charges)*—contd.				
Hazaribagh	Hazaribagh	Major Roughsedge monument (No. 60).	12	12	15 0 0	Completed.
Sambalpur	Sonepur	Tomb of Amelia, wife of Captain Russell, M. S. C.	15	15	15 0 0	Do.
					40 0 0	
		GANDAK CIRCLE.				
Saran	Chapra	Soldiers' tomb at—	40	40	29 0 0	Do.
"	Bargaon	Ditto	20	20	21 0 0	Do.
"	Revelganj	Ditto	15	15	10 0 0	Do.
Muzaffarpur.	Majorganj	Ditto	20	20	19 0 0	Do.
Champaran	Lauriya	Asoka Pillar at—	20	20	16 0 0	Do.
"	Gobindganj	Ditto	15	15	15 0 0	Do.
"	Rampurwa	Ditto	25	25	23 0 0	Do.
					133 0 0	
		Total	..	..	3,871 0 0	
Patna	Nalanda	Upkeep of Museum at—	..	..	389 0 0	
		Total (*b*)	..	..	4,260 0 0	
		GRAND TOTAL (*a*) AND (*b*)	..	..	13,475 0 0	

Appendix A—*contd.*

District.	Locality.	Name of work and description.	Amount of sanctioned estimate.	Allotment for the year 1921-22.	Amount spent during the year 1921-22.	Remarks.
1	2	3	4	5	6	7
			Rs.	Rs.	Rs.	
		II.—Central Provinces & Berar.				
		(a) *Special Repairs (non-recurring charges).*				
Bilaspur ..	Pali ..	Mahadeo temple at—	121	92	92	In progress.
" ..	Arbhar ..	Temple at—	365	283	283	Do.
" ..	Ratanpur ..	Kanthi Deval temple at— ..	349	219	219	Do.
Damoh ..	Rajnagar ..	Jungle clearance from the Fort and uprooting big trees inside the Fort.	107	107	102	Completed.
Saugor ..	Rahatgarh ..	Old Fort—certain repairs to the—	1,656	1,656	1,258	Do.
" ..	Khimlassa ..	Ancient monuments; Old mosque and Idgah, etc., etc.	2,436	1,000	1,000	In progress.
Nimar ..	Asirgarh ..	Compound wall of the tomb of Shah Gohar.	148	148	118	Completed.
" ..	" ..	Jumma Masjid—replacing broken brackets of chhajja stones by new ones at—	6,431	1,150	839	In progress.
" ..	" ..	Fort; removing jungle from— ..	1,551	1,350	864	Do.
" ..	Burhanpur ..	Nadir Shah's tomb at— ..	6,208	1,255	858	Do.
" ..	" ..	Fort—repairing damaged walls and roof, etc.	1,680	700	507	Do.
Chhindwara ..	Deogarh ..	Fort—repairs to the buildings in the—	1,841	1,841	978	Do.
Amraoti ..	Chikaldah ..	Gawilgarh Fort—certain repairs to buildings in the—	1,441	332	332	Do.
" ..	Lasur ..	Anandeswar temple at— ..	2,132	875	875	Do.
Akola ..	Shahnoor ..	Narnalla Fort at—	3,111	1,777	1,777	Do.
Buldana ..	Lonar ..	Old mosque adjoining the Dhar temple. Providing barbed wire fencing to the—	542	51	51	Completed.
Nagpur ..	Ghogra and Khapa.	Mahadeo temple at—	911	388	388	Do.
Raipur ..	Sirpur ..	Construction of a shelter for sculptures near Laxman temple.	4,249	2,539	2,539	Do.
		Total (*a*) ..	..	..	13,080	

APPENDIX A—*contd.*

District.	Locality.	Name of work and description.	Amount of sanctioned estimate.	Allotment for the year 1921-22.	Amount spent during the year 1921-22.	REMARKS.
1	2	3	4	5	6	7
			Rs.	Rs.	Rs.	
		II.—CENTRAL PROVINCES—*contd.*				
		(*b*) *Annual Repairs (recurring charges).*				
Nagpur ..	Junapani .. Ubali. Takalghat. Nildho. Ghogra and Khapa. Wathoda.	Masonry, etc.	90	90	110	Completed.
" ..	Ramtek Hill Dongartal. Nagardhan.	Do.	370	370	440	Do.
Balaghat ..	Langi ..	Fort and temple	50	50	48	Do.
" ..	Garhi ..	Fort at—	10	10	9	Do.
" ..	Baihar ..	Temple	25	25	19	Do.
Raipur ..	Arang ..	Jain temple at—	15	15	32	Do.
Drug ..	Deo Baloda	Temple at—	20	20	18	Do.
" ..	Gandai ..	Do.	20	20	46	Do.
Bilaspur ..	Pali ..	Mahadeo temple at—	40	40	16	Do.
" ..	Janjgir ..	Large Vaishnab temple at— ..	40	40	3	Do.
" ..	Kharod ..	Brick temple of Savari south of the village.	8	8	6	Do.
" ..	" ..	Small brick temple north of the village.	3	3	2	Do.
" ..	Ratanpur ..	Doorway built into the ruined wall beside the north gateway of the fort; and the carved stones and images lying about within the boundaries of the village.	20	20	20	Do.
" ..	" ..	Whole area round the Ratanpur Town.	20	20	25	Do.
" ..	Janjgir ..	Small temple at—	40	40	46	Do.
" ..	Arbhar ..	Temple at—	50	50	22	Do.
" ..	Sheorinarayan	Do.	35	35	38	Do.
" ..	Bamhu ..	Do.	10	10	12	Do.
		Carried over ..	..	..	912	

APPENDIX A—*contd.*

District.	Locality.	Name of work and description.	Amount of sanctioned estimate.	Allotment for the year 1921.	Amount spent during the year 1921-22.	REMARKS.
1	2	3	4	5	6	7
			Rs.	Rs.	Rs.	
		Brought forward ..	..	..	912	
		II.—CENTRAL PROVINCES—*contd.*				
		(*b*) *Annual Repairs (recurring charges)*—contd.				
Bilaspur ..	Gatora ..	Temple at—	10	10	12	Completed.
" ..	Bhatgaon ..	Do.	8	8	10	Do.
" ..	Belpan ..	Do.	8	8	10	Do.
" ..	Malhar ..	Image of Parvati	5	5	4	Do.
" ..	Kampti ..	Temple of Sankarji	10	10	12	Do.
" ..	Khaira Waigan.	Temple of Ram Chandra Swami ..	10	10	12	Do.
" ..	Semarsol ..	Stone with Pali inscription ..	5	5	4	Do.
" ..	Sheorinarayan	Ruined brick temple (Keshonarayan).	35	35	23	Do.
" ..	Kharod ..	Very old Suraj temple	15	15	21	Do.
" ..	" ..	Two inscriptions inside the Luxmaneswar temple.	2	..	..	Not repaired.
" ..	Chandrapur	Temple of Mahadeo	15	15	19	Completed.
" ..	Kanki (Korbad).	Do. do.	15	15	26	Do.
" ..	Kudarmal (Korbad).	A walled enclosure containing 3 tombs of Kabirpanthi Satgurus.	29	29	36	Do.
" ..	Panditole Chhuri.	Kosgaigarh	15	15	23	Do.
" ..	Dhanpur ..	Rock	5	5	6	Do.
" ..	Bagdera ..	Lafa Fort	35	35	5	Do.
" ..	Ramgarh ..	Fort	20	20	8	Do.
" ..	Kotmi ..	Do.	35	35	44	Do.
" ..	Malhar ..	Do.	20	20	30	Do.
" ..	Bawan Badi	Kashigarh Fort	25	25	11	Do.
" ..	Konar ..	Konargarh Fort	25	25	40	Do.
" ..	Amnalla ..	Ajmirgarh Fort	5	5	6	Do.
" ..	Ratanpur ..	Musa Khan's Dargah . ..	5	5	6	Do.
		Carried over ..	..	..	1,280	

APPENDIX A—*contd.*

District.	Locality.	Name of work and description.	Amount of sanctioned estimate.	Allotment for the year 1921-22.	Amount spent during the year 1921-22.	REMARKS.
1	2	3	4	5	6	7
			Rs.	Rs.	Rs.	
		Brought forward ..	..	..	1,280	
		II.—CENTRAL PROVINCES—*contd.*				
		(*b*) *Annual Repairs (recurring charges)*—contd.				
Bilaspur ..	Balanpur ..	Gateways in the Fort	10	10	19	Completed.
„ ..	„ ..	Pandrinath temple, Qila ..	10	10	16	Do.
„ ..	„ ..	Madarbada	5	5	6	Do.
Narsinghpur	Chamragarh	Temple in the Fort	47	47	30	Do.
Hoshangabad	Pachmarhi ..	Caves at—	15	15	15	Do.
Nimar ..	Burhanpur ..	Tomb of Shah Nawaz Khan ..	116	120		
		„ Adil Shah ..	201	281		
		„ Nadir Shah ..	..	..		
		Churi walon ki Masjid ..	..	..	1,215	Do.
		Rajas' chhatri	113	147		
		Tomb of Shah Shuja	90	165		
		Bibi ki Masjid	120	236		
		Palace in the Fort	208	266		
		Juma Masjid	..	..		
„ ..	Asirgarh ..	Tomb of Shah Numa	88	52		
		Fort	648	158		
		Sat Darwaza	43	81		
		Mosque	145	84		
		Temple inside the Fort ..	195	157		
		Mahadeo temple	90	..	638	Do.
		Tomb of Shah Gohar	135	60		
		Idgah	104	46		
„ ..	Mandhata ..	Chaubis Avatar temple ..	..	..		
		Sidhnath temple	..	..		
		Chand Suraj gateway	..	..		
„ ..	Nimbola ..	Tomb of Colonel Fraser ..	55	..		
		Carried over ..	..	..	3,219	

APPENDIX A—*contd.*

District.	Locality.	Name of work and description.	Amount of sanctioned estimate.	Allotment for the year 1921-22.	Amount spent during the year 1921-22.	REMARKS.
1	2	3	4	5	6	7
			Rs.	Rs.	Rs.	
		Brought forward ..	..	..	3,219	
		II.—CENTRAL PROVINCES—*contd.*				
		(*b*) *Annual Repairs (recurring charges)*—*contd.*				
Jubbulpur ..	Karanpur kari talai.	Temple and Tumuli, and linga of Siva.	26	26		
	Tegowa ..	Kankali Devi temple	12	12		
	Nanhwara ..	Temple of Siva	12	12		
	Bilheri ..	Vishnu Varaha temple	12	12		
	Bheraghat ..	Chausath Jogini temple Panch Matha and temple of Gouri Shankar.	218	218	193	Completed.
	Burgaon ..	Temple of Somnath	36	36		
	Karitalai ..	Kacha and Macha	4	4		
	Do. ..	Varaha temple	27	27		
	Padaria ..	Rupnath ; Asoka inscription ..	5	5		
	Panagarh ..	Large effigy of Vishnu Varaha ..	5	5		
Damoh ..	Damoh ..	Sculptures at Phutera Tank ..				
		Slabs in Deputy Commissioner's garden.				
" ..	Kundalpur ..	Jain temples on the hills (1—43)				
		Jain temples below the hills (1—16)				
		One flat roofed temple below the hill.				
" ..	Nohta ..	Temple at -				
" ..	Rajnagar ..	Fort	199	199	159	Do.
" ..	Hatta ..	Rang Mahal Palace				
" ..	Kanorabari ..	Temple				
" ..	Jatashanker	Fort				
" ..	Hatta ..	Sakhar temple				
" ..	" ..	Matha at Raneh				
" ..	Kadol ..	Old temple				
" ..	Narsinghgarh	Mosque				
		Carried over ..	..	..	3,571	

APPENDIX A—*contd.*

District.	Locality.	Name of work and description.	Amount of sanctioned estimate.	Allotment for the year 1921-22.	Amount spent during the year 1921-22.	REMARKS.
1	2	3	4	5	6	7
			Rs.	Rs.	Rs.	
		Brought forward ..	..	..	3,571	
		II.—CENTRAL PROVINCES—*contd.*				
		(b) *Annual Repairs (recurring charges)*—contd.				
Saugor ..	Garhpahra ..	Fort Mahal	903	903	468	Completed.
	Dhamoni ..	Fort Mahal				
	" ..	Tomb of Baljati Shah				
	Eran ..	Ruined temple				
	Bamora ..	Temple				
	Khimlassa ..	Tomb of Panj Pirs				
	"	Old mosque, etc.				
	Rahatgarh ..	Fort				
Betul ..	Bhainsdehi ..	Mahadeo temple	20	20	20	Do.
Chhindwara..	Nilkanthi ..	Temple	10	10	9	Do.
" ..	Deogarh ..	Fort	30	30	25	Do.
Amraoti ..	Amner ..	Tomb of Lal Khan	185	185	147	Do.
" ..	Chikalda ..	Gawilgarh Fort and Tomb of Lieutenant G. Young.	510	510	354	Do.
Yeotmal ..	Lohara ..	Lohara monuments	25	25	16	Do.
Akola ..	Balapur ..	Fort	100	100	123	Do.
" ..	Barsi Takli	Black stone temple of Bhawani ..	50	50	95	Do.
" ..	Shahnoor ..	Narnalla Fort..	500	500	113	Do.
" ..	Patur ..	Two caves	50	50	54	Do.
Buldana ..	Sindkhed Raja	Well near Chandni Talao ..	25	25	49	Do.
" ..	Sakegaon ..	Old temple of Mahadeo ..	30	50	47	Do.
" ..	" ..	Old temple of Vishnu	50	90	127	Do.
" ..	" ..	Images in the vicinity of the old temple of Vishnu.	40			
" ..	Dhotra ..	Three old temples	100	100	117	Do.
" ..	Kothali ..	Old temple inside village, and others outside village.	50	50	60	Do.
" ..	Rohinkhed ..	Mosque	40	40	45	Do.
		Carried over ..	..	..	5,440	

APPENDIX A—*contd.*

District.	Locality.	Name of work and description.	Amount of sanctioned estimate.	Allotment for the year 1921-22.	Amount spent during the year 1921-22.	REMARKS.
1	2	3	4	5	6	7
			Rs.	Rs.	Rs.	
		Brought forward ..	..	..	5,440	
		II.—CENTRAL PROVINCES—*concld.*				
		(*b*) *Annual Repairs (recurring charges)*—contd.				
Buldana ..	Lonar ..	Temple of Daityasudana ..	75	75	38	Completed.
" ..	Mehkar ..	Madha monuments	50	50	76	Do.
Chanda ..	Chanda ..	Gond Raja's tomb	150	150	199	Do.
" ..	" ..	Monuments of officers who fell in the siege of Chanda City (No. 6).	20	20	7	Do.
" ..	" ..	Fort wall	430	430	558	Do.
" ..	" ..	British monuments at Lalpeth ..	20	20	12	Do.
" ..	" ..	Temple of Mahadeo close to Municipal Office.	..	..	..	Not repaired.
" ..	" ..	Pasely monument	4	4	11	Completed.
" ..	" ..	Lalpeth monoliths consisting of 16 colossal stone images.	50	50	72	Do.
" ..	Ballarpur ..	Fort wall, with the ruins of a palace and gateway.	50	50	49	Do.
" ..	Dewalwada..	Old fort and ruined temple	10	10	15	Do.
" ..	Bhandak ..	Old temple near Taka Talao ..	20	20	4	Do.
" ..	" ..	Bijasaw cave	4	4	2	Do.
" ..	" ..	Old temple of Chandika Devi ..	15	15	6	Do.
" ..	Bhatala ..	Mahadeo temple	12	12	13	Do.
" ..	Neri ..	Mahadeo temple	18	18	10	Do.
" ..	Markhandi ..	Group of temples	16	16	15	Do.
		Total (*b*) ..	..	..	6,527	
		GRAND TOTAL (*a*) AND (*b*) ..	..	..	19,607	

APPENDIX A—*contd.*

***Statement** showing the expenditure incurred on the Conservation of Ancient Monuments in Bengal and Assam during 1921-22.*

District.	Locality.	Name of work and description.	Amount of sanctioned estimate.	Allotment for the year 1921-22 (excluding P. W. D. charges).	Amount spent during the year 1921-22 (excluding P. W. D. charges).	REMARKS.
1	2	3	4	5	6	7
			Rs.	Rs.	Rs. A. P.	
		I.—BENGAL.				
		(a) *Special Repairs (non-recurring charges).*				
Malda . .	Gaur . .	Providing wire fencing to the compound of the Gumti gateway.	840	2,000	146 0 0	In progress.
" . .	" . .	Special repairs to the Gumti gate .	1,594		1,361 0 0	⅞ths done.
" . .	" . .	Special repairs to the Darasbari mosque.	1,950	1,100	855 0 0	⅓rd done.
" . .	" . .	Special repairs to the Chamkatti mosque.	1,235		267 0 0	⅛ths done.
Dacca . .	Rajabari .	Repairs to Moth	300	270	147 6 0	
Bakarganj .	Masjidbari .	Certain additional works to the mosque.	860	860	427 0 0	
Murshidabad .	Katra . .	Repairs to the tomb and mosque of Murshid Kulikhan.	1,729	1,000	572 0 0	In progress.
Bankura .	Vishnupur .	Repairs to Radhabenode, Rashmancha, Murali Mohan temple, etc.	11,120	4,000	3,998 11 0	Executed by the Archæological Department. (In progress).
		Total (a) .	..	..	7,774 1 0	
		(b) *Annual Repairs (recurring charges).*				
Calcutta .	Calcutta .	Repairs to the 2 and 12 tombs at North and South Park Street cemeteries respectively.	188	188	181 0 0	Completed.
" .	" .	Repairs to 6 tombs at Lower Circular Road cemetery.	138	138	138 0 0	Do.
24-Parganas .	Sundarbans .	Jatardeul temple	274	274	298 0 0	Do.
Malda . . .	Gaur and Pandua.	Repairs to the Archæological buildings at Gaur and Pandua.	1,812	1,450	1,251 0 0	Almost completed.
		Carried over . .	..	..	1,868 0 0	

APPENDIX A—*contd.*

District.	Locality.	Name of work and description.	Amount of sanctioned estimate.	Allotment for the year 1921-22 (excluding P. W. D. charges).	Amount spent during the year 1921-22 (excluding P. W. D. charges).	REMARKS.
1	2	3	4	5	6	7
			Rs.	Rs.	Rs. A. P.	
		Brought forward .	..	..	1,868 0 0	
		I.—BENGAL—*contd.*				
		(b) *Annual Repairs (recurring charges)*—contd.				
Rajshahi .	Bagha .	Repairs to Bagha mosque . .	200	150	200 0 0	Completed.
,, .	Kusumba .	Repairs to Kusumba mosque .	134	150	134 0 0	Do.
Darjeeling .	Darjeeling .	Repairs to monument over the grave of Cosma-dekoros.	5	..	5 0 0	(Included in list 'B' for being maintained from the Provincial funds.)
,, .	,, .	Repairs to the tomb of General Lloyd.	4	..	4 0 0	Ditto.
Dacca . .	Satmasjid .	Repairs to Satgumbaz mosque .	92	150	78 3 0	
,, . .	Munshiganj .	Repairs to remains at Idrakpu Fort.	30	82	30 7 0	
,, . .	Lalbagh .	Repairs to old mosque . .	38	82	37 4 0	
,, . .	,, .	Repairs to tomb of Bibi Peri .	40	165	38 10 0	
,, . .	,, .	Repairs to remains of old Fort	400	495	373 15 0	
,, . .	Dacca . .	Repairs to Husaini Dalan . .	500	500	488 8 0	
,, . .	,, . .	Repairs to Dewan Bazar mosque in the Dacca college compound.	349	120	358 1 0	
Mymensingh .	Masjidpara .	Repairs to Aurangzeb mosque .	10	10	6 8 0	
,, .	Agarsindur .	Repairs to Shah Mahmud mosque.	21	20	13 3 0	
,, .	,, .	Repairs to Sadi mosque . .	24	24	11 0 0	
,, .	Astagram .	Repairs to Kutub mosque . .	15	15	13 3 0	
Khulna .	Bagerhat .	Repairs to Satgumbaz and Khan Jehan Ali's tomb near Bagerhat.	431	360	138 0 0	
,, .	Masjidkur .	Repairs to Khan Jehan Ali's mosque.	40	35	21 0 0	
Jessore . .	Sagardhari .	Repairs to Memorial tablet of Michael Madhusudhan Dutta.	4	..	4 0 0	
		Carried over . .	..	..	3,822 14 0	

APPENDIX A—*contd.*

District.	Locality.	Name of work and description.	Amount of sanctioned estimate.	Allotment for the year 1921-22 (excluding P. W. D. charges).	Amount spent during the year 1921-22, (excluding P. W. D. charges).	REMARKS.
1	2	3	4	5	6	7
			Rs.	Rs.	Rs. A. P.	
		Brought forward ..	..	..	3,822 14 0	
		I.—BENGAL—*contd.*				
		(*b*) *Annual Repairs (recurring charges)*—contd.				
Chittagong .	Fatehpur .	Repairs to Alwal mosque . .	95	45	33 0 0	Government have decided to have the mosque maintained from the Provincial funds. Only the inscription is on the books of this Department.
Tippera .	Barkamta .	Surveying the land for preparing the site plan of the mound.	..	..	2 0 0	
Hooghly .	Chinsurah .	Repairs to the cemetery (English portion).	47	41	20 1 0	Completed.
" .	" .	Repairs to the cemetery (Dutch portion).	88		73 4 0	Do.
" .	Serampur .	Repairs to Danish cemetery including tomb of Mr. J. H. Munjir.	77	64	62 0 0	Do.
" .	Bullavpur	Repairs to Henry Martin's Pagoda	149	150	140 13 0	Do.
" .	Saptagram .	Repairs to mosque and tomb .	59	50	40 0 0	Do.
" .	Tribeni .	Repairs to mosque and tomb of Jafar Khan Gazi.	194	164	139 5 0	Do.
Burdwan .	Near Sabibganj	Repairs to Clerk's temple . .	30	30	36 0 0	Do.
" .	Kalna . .	Repairs to mosque . .	47	82	47 0 0	Do.
" .	" . .	Repairs to mosque and tomb of Majlis Saheb.	45		35 0 0	Do.
" .	Buddipur .	Repairs to two ancient temples .	41	41	36 7 0	Do.
" .	Burdwan .	Repairs to Behram Sakka . .				
" .	" .	Repairs to tomb of Sher Afghan .	90	82	76 9 0	Do.
" .	" .	Repairs to tomb of Kutubuddin .				
" .	Arrah, (Asansol Sub-Division).	Repairs to Rarheswar Siva temple	96	83	96 6 0	Do.
" .	Gaurangapur	Repairs to Ichai Ghosh's temple .	240	200	230 13 0	Do.
Birbhum .	Sanatore near Suri.	Repairs to temple of Damodar .	52	42	28 0 0	Do.
		Carried over .	..	..	4,928 10 0	

APPENDIX A—*contd.*

District.	Locality.	Name of work and description.	Amount of sanctioned estimate.	Allotment for the year 1921-22 (excluding P. W. D. charges).	Amount spent during the year 1921-22 (excluding P. W. D. charges).	REMARKS.
1	2	3	4	5	6	7
			Rs.	Rs.	Rs. A. P.	
		Brought forward .	..	..	4,928 10 0	
		I.—BENGAL—*contd.*				
		(*b*) *Annual Repairs* (*recurring charges*)—contd.				
Birbhum .	Kenduli .	Repairs to temple of Joydeb or Radha Binode.	38	40	38 0 0	Completed.
Nadia . .	Plassey .	Repairs to new Plassey monument	48	40	30 13 0	Do.
" . .	" .	Repairs to the pillars demarcating the battle field.	60	50	49 14 0	Do.
" . .	Chakdah .	Repairs to the Palpara temple .	76	63	62 13 0	Do.
Murshidabad .	Near Dadpur	Repairs to the tomb of Mirmadan	15	13	11 14 0	Do.
" .	Katra .	Repairs to the tomb of Azimunnessa Begum.	35	27	21 9 0	Do.
" .	Nazimbagh .	Repairs to tomb of Nawab Sarfaraz Khan.	10	8	7 14 0	Do.
" .	Khoshbagh .	Repairs to Mausoleum of Alivardi Khan.	10	8	7 14 0	Do.
" .	" .	Repairs to tomb of Sirajuddoula .	5	4	4 0 0	Do.
" .	Roshnibagh .	Repairs to tomb of Sujauddin .	10	8	6 5 0	Do.
" .	Jaffarganj .	Repairs to tablet of Mirjafar .	2	2	1 8 0	Do.
" .	Kunjaghata .	Repairs to tablet of Maharaja Nanda Kumar.	2	2	1 8 0	Do.
" .	Katra .	Repairs to tomb and mosque of Murshid Kuli Khan.	209	165	165 0 0	Do.
" .	Kharaul .	Repairs to mosque . . .	150	124	126 0 0	Do.
" .	Babulbona .	Repairs to residency cemetery .	220	183	167 2 0	Do.
" .	Panchanontola.	Repairs to the tomb of Burmese prince and princess.	70	65	55 1 0	Do.
" .	Jaffarganj .	Repairs to Dewankhana of Mirjafar.	200	200	151 5 0	Do.
" .	Cassimbazar	Repairs to old residency burial ground.	45	40	36 1 0	Do.
" .	" .	Repairs to tombs of Mary Hastings and her daughter.	12	10	9 12 0	Do.
" .	Kalikapur .	Repairs to Dutch cemetery . .	46	38	32 10 0	Do.
		Carried over .	..	..	5,915 9 0	

APPENDIX A—*contd.*

District.	Locality.	Name of work and description.	Amount of sanctioned estimate.	Allotment for the year 1921-22 (excluding P. W. D. charges).	Amount spent during the year 1921-22 (excluding P. W. D. charges).	REMARKS.
1	2	3	4	5	6	7
			Rs.	Rs.	Rs. A. P.	
		Brought forward .	..	..	5,915 9 0	
		I.—BENGAL—*concld.*				
		(*b*) *Annual Repairs* (*recurring charges*)—concld.				
Murshidabad .	Kalikapur .	Repairs to seventeen other tombs bearing no inscriptions.	99	83	82 9 0	Completed.
" .	Berhampur .	Repairs to the monuments of Henry Sherwood.	7	6	5 0 0	Do.
" .	" .	Repairs to the monument of Henry Creighton.	7	6	5 0 0	Do.
Hooghly .	Chinsurah .	Repairs to five tombs in (Dutch portion).	47	100	25 13 0	Do.
Murshidabad .	Kalikapur .	Repairs to minor tombs in Dutch cemetery.	30	25	23 3 0	Do.
" .	Khoshbagh .	Repairs to Khoshbagh tomb and Mousoleum with compound wall and gate.	362	290	310 9 0	Do.
" .	Roshnibagh .	Repairs to Roshnibagh tombs with compound wall and gate.				
Bankura .	Vishnupur .	Repairs to nineteen temples .	752	620	456 0 0	Do.
" .	Shushunia Hill	Repairs to Rock inscription of Raja Chandravarman.	24	20	16 0 0	Do.
Midnapur .	Midnapur .	Repairs to John Pierce tomb .	30	25	25 0 0	Do.
		Total (*b*) .	..	..	6,834 13 0	
		Total (*a*) and (*b*) .	..	..	14,608 14 0	
		P. W. D. charges @ 21 % .	..	..	2,238 15 6	
		GRAND TOTAL BENGAL .	..	..	16,847 13 6	
		II.—ASSAM.				
		(*a*) *Special Repairs* (*non-recurring charges*).				
Darrang .	Tezpur .	Clearing jungles, arranging and staking stones in the Bamuni Hills.	5,982	300	300 0 0	In progress.
" .	" .	Collection of ancient sculptures and curved stones in the Tezpur Municipal Park.	3,086	797	814 0 0	Do.
" .	Bishnath .	Special repairs to Bordole temple	1,912	1,346	994 0 0	Do.
		Carried over .	..	..	2,108 0 0	

APPENDIX A—*contd.*

District.	Locality.	Name of work and description.	Amount of sanctioned estimate.	Allotment for the year 1921-22 (excluding P. W. D. charges).	Amount spent during the year 1921-22 (excluding P. W. D. charges).	REMARKS.
1	2	3	4	5	6	7
			Rs.	Rs.	Rs. A. P.	
		Brought forward .	..	..	2,108 0 0	
		II.—ASSAM—*contd.*				
		(a) *Special Repairs (non-recurring charges)*—concld.				
Cachar .	Khaspur .	Improvement to the Cachari ruins at Khaspur.	1,547	1,547	1,323 0 0	In progress.
Sibsagar .	Sibsagar ..	Providing platform and a concrete bed for the erection of the old cannon in the Kutchery compound.	342	342	344 0 0	Do.
" .	" .	Special repairs to Garhgaon palace at Nazira.	1,437	350	348 0 0	Do.
" .	" .	Reconstruction of the Namghar attached to the Bishnudole temple.	1,654	115	115 0 0	Completed.
" .	" .	Providing a wicket gate to the Sibdole temple.	25	Lump grant Rs. 350 for petty items below Rs. 50.	25 0 0	Do.
" .	" .	Special repairs to Sibdole temple .	498	1,000+250 for employment of 3 chowkidars at Sibsagar for 8½ months.	302 0 0	Do.
Kamrup .	Gauhati .	Conservation of the Rock-cut sculptures of Vishnu-Janardan.	101	101	90 0 0	In progress.
		Total (a) .	..	..	4,655 0 0	
		(b) *Annual Repairs (recurring charges).*				
Cachar .	Maibong .	Annual repairs to two inscriptions and a temple made of one stone.	5	5	5 0 0	Completed.
" .	Badarpur .	Annual repairs to old Fort at Badarpur.	20	20	20 0 0	Do.
Naga Hills .	Dimapur .	Annual repairs to ruins at Dimapur.	Part of estimate for Rs. 5,365 for 1920-21, and Rs. 400 for 1921-22.	400	393 0 0	Do.
		Carried over .	..	..	418 0 0	

APPENDIX A—*contd.*

District.	Locality.	Name of work and description.	Amount of sanctioned estimate.	Allotment for the year 1921-22 (excluding P. W. D. charges).	Amount spent during the year 1921-22 (excluding P. W. D. charges).	REMARKS.
1	2	3	4	5	6	7
			Rs.	Rs.	Rs. A. P.	
		Brought forward	..	..	418 0 0	
		II.—ASSAM—*concld.*				
		(b) Annual Repairs (recurring charges)—contd.				
Sylhet	..	Surveying the site of enclosure wall of Jaintiapur Nizpat.	4	..	3 0 0	Completed.
Sibsagar	Sibsagar	Repairs to Joysagar temple	413	1,284	449 0 0	In progress.
Do.	Do.	Repairs to Karanghar Ruins	202		123 0 0	Do.
Do.	Do.	Repairs to Runghar Ruins	100		126 0 0	Do.
Do.	Do.	Repairs to Gaurisagar temple	198		181 0 0	Do.
Do.	Do.	Repairs to Ahom Raja's palace at Garhgaon.	210		120 0 0	Do.
Do.	Do.	Repairs to temples at Sibsagar	271		249 0 0	Do.
Kamrup	Kamakhya	Repairs to Duarganga rock inscription at the foot of the hill.	10	10	13 0 0	Do.
Do.	Gauhati	Repairs to carving inscription and pillar on the Urbasi Island.	50	50	59 0 0	Do.
Do.	Jogighopa	Repairs to ancient tombs	120	120	124 0 0	Do.
Khasi and Jaintia Hills.	..	Repairs to ancient monuments and buildings of historical interest.	50	50	50 0 0	Do.
Darrang	Tezpur	Clearing jungles round the Bamuni Hills.	60	75	62 0 0	Do.
		Total (*b*)	..	..	1,977 0 0	
		Total (*a*) and (*b*)	..	..	6,632 0 0	
		P. W. D. charges calculated by pro-rata distribution.	..	..	2,551 8 0	
		GRAND TOTAL ASSAM	..	..	9,183 8 0*	

* Rs. 9,458-0-3 according to the calculations of the Comptroller, Assam.

APPENDIX A—*contd.*

Statement showing the expenditure incurred on the Conservation of Ancient Monuments in the Bombay Presidency including Sind during the year ending 31st March 1922.

District. (P. W. D.)	Locality.	Name of work and description.	Amount of sanction-ed esti-mate.	Allot-ment for the year 1921-22.	Amount spent during the year 1921-22.	REMARKS.
1	2	3	4	5	6	7
			Rs.	Rs.	Rs.	
		BOMBAY PRESIDENCY.				
		Northern Division.				
		(*a*) *Special Repairs* (*non-recurring charges*).				
Ahmedabad	Ahmedabad .	Rani Sipri's mosque and tomb :—Resetting old coping on the top of the compound wall; providing new coping for compound wall; providing collapsible gate; making new water connection in the new tank and urinals; providing new steps to the urinals; removing pillars of the gate and resetting them with additional masonry and levelling the compound by filling the hollows with hard Kankar.	840	840	671	Completed.
Do. .	Dholka .	Khan Masjid :—Erecting scaffolding for the repairs of the chhattri on the south pylon, making reinforced concrete for the platform of the chhattri and superstructure of the missing pillars of the same. (Total expenditure up to date Rs. 7,289).	5,373 8,568	2,802	2,797	In progress.
Do. .	Ahmedabad .	Providing leather belts and brass badges for caretakers.	100	100	100	Completed.
Kaira and Panch Mahals.	Thasra .	Galtesvara Mahadeva's temple :—Construction of retaining walls. (Total expenditure up to date is Rs. 7,948).	12,084	800	748	In progress.
Do. .	Champaner .	Certain monuments at Champaner (15 in number, revised) :—The dome over the porch of Lila Gumbaz and the tops of the minars of Bohra-ki-Masjid were repared. Repairs to the bulged walls of Sat Manzil were partly carried out. (Total expenditure up to date is Rs. 59,844).	1,05,223	6,200	3,486	Do.
		Carried over .	..	..	7,802	

Appendix A—*contd.*

District. (P. W. D.)	Locality.	Name of work and description.	Amount of sanctioned estimate.	Allotment for the year 1921-22.	Amount spent during the year 1921-22.	Remarks.
1	2	3	4	5	6	7
			Rs.	Rs.	Rs.	
		Brought forward ..	..	..	7,802	
		Bombay Presidency—*contd.*				
		(*a*) *Special Repairs (non-recurring charges)*—contd.				
Kaira and Panch Mahals.	Champaner .	Clearing the *débris* and opening the plinths of certain monuments at Champaner :—The work of clearing the *débris* and opening buried plinths by excavating all round Kevda, Lila Gumbaz, Khajuri, Nagina, Kamani, and Baba Man's Masjids have been done.	3,006	..	2,399	Completed.
Do. .	Do. .	Providing leather belts and brass badges for caretakers.	70	70	70	Do.
Thana .	Bassein .	Providing leather belt and brass badge.	10	10	10	Do.
Do. .	Do. .	Portuguese monuments :—Trees, jungles, and weeds. etc., were removed from the top of the rampart wall. Various, 241 big and small pipal, baniyan, pimpar trees of average diameter of roots varying from 5" to 9" were cut down and roots removed completely by chiselling from the inner face of the fort wall. The dangerous overhanging portion of the barrel vault of the Dominican Church was removed, stones and *débris* were separated and stacked at different places. Cut timber has been stacked at different places.	24,621	3,000 1,000	4,000	In progress.
Presidency	Gharapuri .	Providing leather belts and brass badges for caretakers.	70	70	70	Completed.
Do. .	Do .	Elephanta Caves :—Cutting jungles from all round the seven caves on two hills, removing huge accumulation of *débris* and big boulders from the fronts of all the caves except No. 1 ; opening out two blocked up drains to Cave No. 1, providing a pathway to go up to Cave Nos. 5 and 6 ; clearing tops of all caves for building water channels as at Bedsa and Nasik ; new steps built by P. W. D. in Cave No. 1 were removed ; tools and plant were purchased for the Department.	7 estimates. 33,831	14,000	14,000	In progress.
		Carried over .	..	..	28,351	

APPENDIX A—*contd.*

District. (P. W. D.)	Locality.	Name of work and description.	Amount of sanction-ed estimate.	Allotment for the year 1921-22.	Amount spent during the year 1921-22.	REMARKS.
1	2	3	4	5	6	7
			Rs.	Rs.	Rs.	
		Brought forward	..	..	28,351	
		BOMBAY PRESIDENCY—*contd.*				
		(*a*) *Special Repairs* (*non-recurring charges*)—contd.				
Presidency	Gharapuri	Elephanta Cave No. 1	11,128	.	130	In progress.
Kolaba	Revdanda	Portuguese remains. (Total expenditure up to date is Rs. 1,125). *The allotment could not be utilised by P. W. D.	1,546	1,000*	25	Do.
		Total (*a*) Northern Division	..	..	28,506	
		(*b*) *Current Repairs and Maintenance* (*recurring charges*).				
Ahmedabad	Ahmedabad and Suburbs.	Pay of a Karkun for Archæological buildings for 12 months.	420	420	420	Completed.
Do.	Do.	Sidi Sayyad's mosque	204	204	163	Do.
Do.	Do.	Azam Khan's palace	60	60	19	Do.
Do.	Do.	Ahmedshah's mosque	232	232	160	Do.
Do.	Do.	Three gates	50	50	9	Do.
Do.	Do.	Bhadar tower	80	80	20	Do.
Do.	Do.	Rani Sipri's mosque and tomb	212	212	134	Do.
Do.	Do.	Muhafiz Khan's masjid	20	20	17	Do.
Do.	Do.	Queen's mosque at Sarangpur	30	30	23	Do.
Do.	Do.	Baba Loli's mosque	232	232	148	Do.
Do.	Do.	Dutch tombs on Kankaria tank	60	60	19	Do.
Do.	Do.	Dada Harir's well	222	222	159	Do.
Do.	Do.	Dada Harir's mosque	60	60	19	Do.
Do.	Do.	Mian Khan Jahan's masjid	50	50	34	Do.
Do.	Do.	Tomb of Mir Abu Turab	60	60	33	Do.
Do.	Do.	Sidi Basir's minars and tombs	70	70	30	Do.
Do.	Do.	Achyut Bibi's mosque and tomb	222	222	114	Do.
		Carried over	..	..	1,531	

APPENDIX A—*contd.*

District. (P. W. D.)	Locality.	Name of work and description.	Amount of sanctioned estimate.	Allotment for the year 1921-22.	Amount spent during the year 1921-22.	REMARKS.
1	2	3	4	5	6	7
			Rs.	Rs.	Rs.	
		Brought forward .	..	..	1,531	
		BOMBAY PRESIDENCY—*contd.*				
		(*b*) *Current Repairs (recurring charges)*—contd.				
Ahmedabad.	Ahmedabad and Suburbs.	Maintaining a garden in Ahmedshah's mosque.	145	145	136	Completed.
Do. .	Do. .	Maintaining a garden in Sidi Sayyad's mosque.	145	145	48	Do.
Do. .	Vasna .	Tomb of Azamkhan and Muazzamkhan.	50	50	30	Do.
Do. .	Kochrab-Paldi.	Small stone masjid	20	20	13	Do.
Do. .	Adalaj .	Stepped well	242	242	49	Do.
Do. .	Dholka .	Bahlol Khan Qazi's mosque .	232	232	135	Do.
Do. .	Do. .	Khan masjid	232	232	45	Do.
Do. .	Do. .	Khan tank	100	100	23	Do.
Do. .	Isanpur .	Small stone mosque to the south of Malik Isan-ul-Mulk's mosque.	60	60	34	Do.
Do. .	Vatwa .	Tombs	336	336	200	Do.
Do. .	Viramgam .	Mansar tank	60	60	23	Do.
Kaira and Panch Mahals.	Sojali .	Tombs of Saif-ud-din and Nizam-ud-din	172	172	172	Do.
Do. .	Mehmedabad	Bhamaria well	150	150	150	Do.
Do. .	Champaner .	Archæological buildings . .	1,810	1,810	1,810	Do.
Do. .	Halol .	Sikandar Shah's Rauza . .	30	30	30	Do.
Surat and Broach.	Dhao .	Vaux's tomb at the mouth of the River Tapti near Hajira:—Repairs to masonry and plastering done where found necessary and all other required repairs were carried out.	31	31	30	Do.
Do.	Rajgiri (Suvali).	Tomb:—Removing rank vegetation and other required petty repairs were carried out.	6	6	5	Do.
Do. .	Broach City .	Dutch tombs:—Removing rank vegetation and filling in cracks where found necessary were carried out.	35	35	35	Do
		Carried over .	..	..	4,499	

Appendix A—*contd.*

District. (P. W. D.)	Locality.	Name of work and description.	Amount of sanctioned estimate.	Allotment for the year 1921-22.	Amount spent during the year 1921-22.	Remarks.
1	2	3	4	5	6	7
			Rs.	Rs.	Rs.	
		Brought forward .	..	..	4,499	
		Bombay Presidency—*contd.* (*b*) *Current Repairs* (*recurring charges*)—contd.				
Surat and Broach.	Broach City.	Jami Masjid :—Removing rank vegetation from the masonry, recessed pointing to masonry inside the building, filling in cracks to the terraced roof, etc., were carried out.	160	160	160	Completed.
Thana .	Ambernath .	Temple at Ambernath :—Clearing and removing grass and repairing foot-path in the compound.	35	35	35	Do.
Do.	Kalyan	Motabar Khan's tomb and Kali masjid.	24	24	24	Do.
Do. .	Thana .	Graves of two English factors .	10	10	10	Do.
Do. .	Wasbeli .	Caves :—Clearing the precincts of vegetation, rubbish and also of big trees obstructing the approach road is done, and also the water tank is cleared of rubbish.	15	15	16	Do.
Do. .	Nanaghat .	Brahmanical Caves :—No work was done during the year as no subordinate was available for carrying out the work, who could be despatched to such an out of the way place as Nanaghat to do petty works costing Rs. 15. Next year a S. O. or S. D. O. or Executive Engineer will visit it.	15	..	..	
Do. .	Mahuli .	Fort :—The precincts of the mosque and one temple have been cleared of rank vegetation and big trees growing into masonry of the remains, also the difficult portions of the approach road to the fort have been made easy by providing a 4′ wide level pathway by excavation from the hill side.	80	80	53	Completed.
Do. .	Andheri .	Caves at Jogesvari :—Catch water gutters were excavated, gutters cleared and caves cleaned where necessary.	68	68	68	Do.
Do. .	Do. .	Caves at Kondivata :— Do. .	54	54	54	Do.
		Carried over .	..	..	4,919	

APPENDIX A—*contd.*

District. (P. W. D.)	Locality.	Name of work and description.	Amount of sanctioned estimate.	Allotment for the year 1921-22.	Amount spent during the year 1921-22.	REMARKS.
1	2	3	4	5	6	7
			Rs.	Rs.	Rs.	
		Brought forward .	..	..	4,919	
		BOMBAY PRESIDENCY—*contd.*				
		(*b*) *Current Repairs* (*recurring charges*)—contd.				
Thana .	Mandapesvara	Caves :—Catch water gutters were excavated, gutters cleared and caves cleaned where necessary.	95	95	95	Completed.
Do. .	Kanheri .	Caves :—General clearing was started and some work was done but as the *khot* in whose limits the caves are situated objected to the further work being done, work had to be stopped.	190	190	35	Stopped.
Do. .	Bandra .	Fort :—The area was cleared .	40	40	40	Completed.
Do. .	Bassein .	Fort :—Clearing jungle and removing rubbish and pay of caretaker.	342	342	257	Do.
Do. .	Arnala .	Fort :—Clearing jungle . .	60	60	60	Do.
Do. .	Barat .	Caves :—Clearing jungle, removing grass, whitewashing, repairing footpath, etc.	75	75	75	Do.
Presidency	Gharapuri .	Elephanta caves . . .	3,194	3,194	3,219	Do.
Do. .	Do. .	Custodian's quarters . . .	112	112	106	Do
Do. .	Do. .	Assistant Custodian's quarters .	18	18	15	Do.
Do. .	Do. .	Police Chowki and watchmen's quarters.	18	18	15	Do.
Kolaba .	Agarkot .	Portuguese remains :—Weeds and shrubs were removed from the masonry of (1) Chowkoni buruj, (2) Fort walls, (3) Kothi, (4) Two gates, (5) Fort wall of the old factory at Revadanda, (6) Mosque, (7) Hammam Khana, (8) Arch, and (9) Barber's mahal.	595	595	109	Do.
Do. .	Revadanda	Portuguese remains . .	350	350	86	Do.
Do. .	Korlai .	Fort :—Overgrown shrubs on the fort walls were removed and other ordinary repairs to the road executed.	50	50	53	Do.
		Carried over .	..	..	9,084	

APPENDIX A—*contd.*

District. (P. W. D.)	Locality.	Name of work and description.	Amount of sanctioned estimate.	Allotment for the year 1921-22.	Amount spent during the year 1921-22.	REMARKS.
1	2	3	4	5	6	7
			Rs.	Rs.	Rs.	
		Brought forward .	..	..	9,084	
		BOMBAY PRESIDENCY—*contd.*				
		(*b*) *Current Repairs (recurring charges)*—contd.				
Kolaba .	Alibag .	Fort :—Portion of the footpath was improved by removing *débris*. Fallen portion of the Fort wall near the storm signal is under repairs. Weeds and shrubs were removed.	175	175	55	Completed.
Do. .	Ambivli .	Caves :—Grass and vegetation were removed, caves and surroundings cleared and sand spread.	60	60	60	Do.
Do. .	Peth .	Kotali Fort : Footpaths leading to the fort and guns were cleared. Shrubs and grass round the tomb, the gun, and on the top of the fort were removed. The fallen boulders obstructing the footpaths were removed.	75	75	75	Do.
Do. .	Pal .	Caves :—3 furlongs of the footpath was broadened so as to enable visitors to approach caves easily, kerbing put in order ; weeds removed. Small tanks and caves were cleaned.	60	60	59	Do.
Do. .	Raigadh .	Shivaji's Samadhi and Mahadeva temple .—Footpaths to Shivaji's Samadhi and Mahadeva's temple were repaired. Weeds and shrubs removed : cement pointing done to the sides of the Samadhi and the terrace.	125	125	107	Do.
Do. .	Kuda .	Caves :—1,600 r.ft. of footpaths repaired with murum, and kerbing stones put in order ; weeds removed and caves were cleared of dirt, etc.	60	60	60	Do.
		Total (*b*) Northern Division .	..	..	9,500	
		CENTRAL DIVISION.				
		(*a*) *Special Repairs (non-recurring charges)*				
West Khandesh.	Balsana .	Providing leather belt and brass badge for caretaker.	10	10	10	Do.
		Carried over .	..	..	10	

APPENDIX A—*contd.*

District. (P. W. D.)	Locality.	Name of work and description.	Amount of sanctioned estimate.	Allotment for the year 1921-22.	Amount spent during the year 1921-22.	REMARKS.
1	2	3	4	5	6	7
			Rs.	Rs.	Rs.	
		Brought forward ..	..	..	10	
		BOMBAY PRESIDENCY—*contd.*				
		(a) *Special Repairs (non-recurring charges)*—contd.				
Nasik .	Anjanneri .	Providing leather belts and brass badges for caretakers.	30	30	30	Completed.
Ahmednagar	Ahmednagar	Providing leather belt and brass badge for caretaker.	10	10	10	Do.
Do.	Pedgaon .	Lakshmi Narayan temple . .	580	..	13	Do.
Do.	Ahmednagar	Historical buildings in the fort :—Excavation of *débris*.	5,328 3,968	2,000	1,353	In progress.
Do.	Do. .	Faria Bagh Palace :—Unsightly additions and alterations were removed ; earth and *débris* also were removed ; stone and *débris* from top of the domes on top were removed ; urgent underpinnings to jambs of door and arch were completed ; all trees were cut down from the platform as well as from the bed of the surrounding tank.	7,748	2,800	2,800	Do.
Poona ..	Poona ..	Providing leather belts and brass badges for caretakers.	90	90	90	Completed.
Do. ..	Poona City ..	Shanwar Wada :—The collapsed portions of masonry on the north, east and west of the citadel walls, both from inside and outside were repaired with brick in lime on the lines of old construction. Numerous additions and alterations to the Naqqarkhana were dismantled and removed. One wooden chajja suitable to the design of the structure was constructed before the visit of His Royal Highness the Prince of Wales. The floors of the hall of the Naqqarkhana and Delhi gate were paved with stones. The entire old wood-work was washed with hot water and soap and finished with waxing ; wooden railings were provided. Numerous other minor items of work were also carried out.	29,748 2,966	10,800	10,800	In progress.
		Carried over ..	..	..	15,106	

APPENDIX A—*contd.*

District. (P. W. D.)	Locality.	Name of work and description.	Amount of sanctioned estimate.	Allotment for the year 1921-22.	Amount spent during the year 1921-22.	REMARKS.
1	2	3	4	5	6	7
			Rs.	Rs.	Rs.	
		Brought forward ..	..	..	15,106	
		BOMBAY PRESIDENCY—*contd.*				
		(*a*) *Special Repairs (non-recurring charges)*—contd.				
Poona ..	Bhaja ..	Caves :—Providing compound wall with self-closing gate and some other minor additions. (The total expenditure up to 31st March 1922 is Rs. 4,164.)	4,535	1,200	843	In progress.
Sholapur..	Sholapur ..	Old fort :—Closing the breach in the fort wall and sorting and stacking carved stones.	289	289	282	Completed.
Do. ..	Do. ..	Providing leather belt and brass badge for caretaker.	10	10	10	Do.
Do. ..	Do. ..	Excavating the old temple in the fort :—Finishing the sides of the excavation with stone pitching, dry stone retaining wall and providing steps to go down to the excavation and underpinning the gaps in the wall. (The total expenditure up to 31st March 1922 is Rs. 7,133.)	9,054	1,000	1,000	In progress.
		Total (*a*) Central Division ..	..	..	17,241	
		(*b*) *Current Repairs and Maintenance (recurring charges).*				
East Khandesh.	Patna ..	Mahesvara Mahadeva temple :—Repairs executed to floors, compound, approach road, and roof. Preserved the temple by removing stumps of trees and weeds.	55	55	55	Completed.
Do. ..	Do. ..	Shringar Chavdi :—Repairs done to the approach road and the compound cleared of *dèbris*, etc.	80	80	80	Do.
Do. ..	Do. ..	Nagarjun Cave :—Cleared the temple and repairs done to the approach road.	80	80	80	Do.
Do. ..	Do. ..	Caves (Sita's Nahani) :—Cleared the caves and the approach road, and paths repaired.	80	80	80	Do.
		Carried over ..	..	..	295	

APPENDIX A—*contd.*

District. (P. W. D.)	Locality.	Name of work and description.	Amount of sanctioned estimate.	Allotment for the year 1921-22.	Amount spent during the year 1921-22.	REMARKS.
1	2	3	4	5	6	7
			Rs.	Rs.	Rs.	
		Brought forward ..	..	..	295	
		BOMBAY PRESIDENCY—*contd.*				
		(b) *Current Repairs (recurring charges)*—contd.				
East Khandesh.	Waghli ..	Mudhai Devi's temple :—Repairs done to the floors, vaulted roof, back yards, steps and the compound.	80	80	79	Completed.
Do. ..	Dighi ..	Temple of Devi and Sambha :—Cleared the floors, repaired the front portion and plinth with earth bank, stray stones and *débris* removed and the compound cleared.	35	35	34	Do.
Do. ..	Sangamesvara	Temple of Mahadeva :—Repaired the cracks in walls with chips and mortar with cement pointing; also repaired the roof and the compound.	70	70	70	Do.
Do. ..	Changdeva ..	Changdeva's temple :—Cleared the jungle and repairs done to the terraced roof and masonry of the parapet walls.	160	160	159	Do.
West Khandesh.	Balsana ..	Temples :—Caretaker's pay ..	36	36	36	Do.
Nasik ..	Sinnar ..	Gondesvara temple	188	188	186	Do.
Do. ..	Do. ..	Aisvara temple	15	15	15	Do.
Do. ..	Pathardi ..	Pandu Lena caves	218	218	218	Do.
Do. ..	Ankai ..	Caves	272	272	271	Do.
Do. ..	Jhodga ..	Mankesvara Siva temple ..	130	130	130	Do.
Do. ..	Anjanneri ..	Old temple	46	46	46	Do.
Ahmednagar.	Tisgaon ..	Five stone gates	50	50	50	Do.
Do. ..	Harischandragadh.	Caves and temples	10	10	10	Do.
Do. ..	Tahakari ..	Tripad Srinivas temple ..	10	10	10	Do.
Do. ..	Ratanwadi ..	Temple of Amritesvara.. ..	10	10	10	Do.
Do.	Bamni ..	Hemadpanti tank	22	22	22	Do.
		Carried over ..	..	..	1,638	

APPENDIX A—*contd.*

District. (P. W. D.)	Locality.	Name of work and description.	Amount of sanctioned estimate.	Allotment for the year 1921-22.	Amount spent during the year 1921-22.	REMARKS.
1	2	3	4	5	6	7
			Rs.	Rs.	Rs.	
		Brought forward ..	..	..	1,638	
		BOMBAY PRESIDENCY—*contd.*				
		(*b*) *Current Repairs (recurring charges)*—contd.				
Ahmednagar. ..	Kokamthan	Old temple	96	96	96	Completed.
Do. ..	Ahmednagar	Damri masjid	20	20	20	Do.
Do. ..	Do. ..	Faria Bagh Palace	228	228	228	Do.
Do. ..	Dhoka ..	Caves at Dhokesvara	22	22	22	Do.
Do. ..	Mandavgaon Katrabad.	Temple of Devi	19	19	19	Do.
Do. ..	Karjat ..	Mallikarjuna's temple	20	20	20	Do.
Do. ..	Pedgaon ..	Bablesvara temple	22	22	22	Do.
Poona ..	Karla ..	Caves	1,159	1,159	799	Do.
Do. ..	Ghatghar ..	Do.	50	50	50	Do.
Do. ..	Bhaja ..	Do.	310	310	141	Do.
Do. ..	Shelarwadi ..	Do.	160	160	153	Do.
Do. ..	Bedsa ..	Do	143	143	138	Do.
Do. ..	Junnar ..	Do.	868	868	472	Do.
Do. ..	Lohagadh ..	Fort	240	240	240	Do.
Do. ..	Rajmachi ..	Do.	200	200	200	Do.
Do. ..	Visapur ..	Do.	160	160	162	Do.
Do. ..	Bhamburda ..	Caves	321	321	249	Do.
Do. ..	Tulapur ..	Sambhaji's Samadhi	110	110	110	Do.
Do. ..	Sinhagadh ..	Fort	125	125	66	Do.
Do. ..	Do. ..	Rajaram's Samadhi	167	167	160	Do.
Do ..	Poona ..	Kotwal's residence	23	23	11	Do.
Do. ..	Poona City ..	Shanwar Wada	1,652	1,652	1,665	Do.
Do ..	Do. ..	Old European tombs	38	38	27	Do.
Do. ..	Koregaon ..	Monument Memorial pillar ..	67	67	56	Do.
		Carried over ..	..	..	6,764	

APPENDIX A—*contd.*

District. (P. W. D.)	Locality.	Name of work and description.	Amount of sanctioned estimate.	Allotment for the year 1921-22.	Amount spent during the year 1921-22.	REMARKS.
1	2	3	4	5	6	7
			Rs.	Rs.	Rs.	
		Brought forward ..	..	..	6,764	
		BOMBAY PRESIDENCY—*contd.*				
		(*b*) *Current Repairs (recurring charges)*—contd.				
Satara ..	Jakhinwadi ..	Buddhist caves	100	100	84	Completed.
Do. ..	Pratapgadh ..	Afzulkhan's tomb	10	10	8	Do.
Do. ..	Karanja ..	Brick column erected by Aurangzeb.	10	10	10	Do.
Sholapur ..	Sholapur ..	Old fort	641	641	479	Do.
Do. ..	Karmala ..	Old fort	100	100	75	Do.
		Total (*b*) Central Division ..	..	..	7,420	
		SOUTHERN DIVISION.				
		(*a*) *Special Repairs (non-recurring charges).*				
Belgaum ..	Gokak falls ..	Group of temples on the right and left sides of Gokak falls — The work was not in progress owing to want of funds. (Total expenditure up to 31st March 1922 is Rs. 1,019-12-7.)	2,598	..	..	In progress.
Kanara ..	Bhatkal ..	Narasimha Devasthan :—Purchase of steel clamps and copper dowels.	1,226	..	917	Do.
Dharwar ..	Rattihalli ..	Kadambeshvara temple :—Removing the whitewash clearing the interior and filling gaps with single stones including scaffolding, and removing whitewash and paint from exterior, clearing compound and levelling, clearing drain and washing tank including repairs to north side of temple, collecting and setting up inscribed stones and providing notice boards. (Total expenditure up to 31st March 1922 is Rs. 198-7-0.)	1,425	..	18	Do.
		Carried over ..	..	..	935	

Appendix A—*contd.*

District. (P. W. D.)	Locality.	Name of work and description.	Amount of sanctioned estimate.	Allotment for the year 1921-22.	Amount spent during the year 1921-22.	Remarks.
1	2	3	4	5	6	7
			Rs.	Rs.	Rs.	
		Brought forward ..	..	..	935	
		Bombay Presidency—*contd.*				
		(a) Special Repairs (non-recurring charges)—contd.				
Dharwar ..	Haralhalli ..	Somesvara temple:—Putting in copper clamps, big and small, including jacking up and fixing together broken chhajja, cement concrete 1½" thick on chunam terrace. Metal has been collected, lime has been conveyed to the site of work; sand is collected. Clearing vegetation and levelling up the ground and scraping off whitewash coating. (Total expenditure up to 31st March 1922 is Rs. 2,189-13-3.)	2,167	..	285	In progress
Bijapur ..	Bijapur ..	Gol Gumbaz:—Erecting a compound wall round the open site of Gol Gumbaz. The compound wall has almost been completed except at four places. Passage is left open to the people and the cart traffic as the question of land compensation has not yet been settled by the Revenue Department. (Total expenditure is Rs. 9,642.)	10,110	6,826	6,353	Do.
Do. ..	Do. ..	Gol Gumbaz:—Payment of land compensation for diversion of the station road (originally passing through Gol Gumbaz area).	759	759	759	Completed.
Do. ..	Do. ..	Jumma masjid:—Providing ½" galvanised water pipe connection.	275	275	250	Do.
Do. ..	Do. ..	Ibrahim Roza:—Paying compensation for extending the compound.	1,433	863	1,433	Do.
Do. ..	Do. ..	Fort wall:—Near Malik-i-Maidan Gun:—Reconstructing the fallen portion of the Fort wall.	249	307	230	Do.
Do. ..	Do. ..	Masabavdi near Gol Gumbaz:—Fixing pumping plant and emptying water of the bavdi. As the water level was about 30' the work could not be taken in hand. The expenditure is on account of making preliminary arrangements.	2,400	151 *plus* 40	194	In progress.
		Carried over ..	..	..	10,439	

APPENDIX A—*contd.*

District. (P. W. D.)	Locality.	Name of work and description.	Amount of sanction-ed esti-mate.	Allot-ment for the year 1921-22.	Amount spent during the year 1921-22.	REMARKS.
1	2	3	4	5	6	7
			Rs.	Rs.	Rs.	
		Brought forward ..	..	..	10,439	
		BOMBAY PRESIDENCY—*contd.*				
		(*a*) *Special Repairs* (*non-recurring charges*)—concld.				
Bijapur ..	Kumatgi ..	Water pavilion No. 1 :—Fallen portion of the back wall was reconstructed.	432	432	425	Completed.
Do.	Bijapur ..	The bridge of old approach road to Bijapur Station :—The bridge was dismantled.	154	154	102	Do.
Do. ..	Do. ..	Masjid attached to the Ibrahim Rouza: —Expanded metal frames were fixed to the windows of the masjid.	197	197	192	Do.
Do. ..	Ainapur ..	Way to the south of the masjid at Ainapur :—The way to the south of the masjid was widened.	328	784 (for both items)	328	Do.
Do. ..	Do. ..	Palace of Jahan Begum :—The work consisted of dismantling the terrace roof of the verandah of the Mahal, etc., and was completed.	370		367	Do.
Do. ..	Bijapur ..	Gagan Mahal :—Underpinning work of fort wall with recessed pointing was completed; work of filling open chases in masonry wall with stone and lime concrete (gauge) including raking; providing reinforced concrete lintels, filling cracks, lime plaster, repairing plinths, providing gate, etc., are in progress.	5,991	5,352	5,100	In progress.
Do. ..	Torvi ..	Sangit Mahal :—Building two support pillars, underpinning and water-tightening the tops of walls and making approach road were in progress.	4,389	4,389	3,176	Do.
Do. ..	Bijapur ..	Providing leather belts and brass badges for the caretakers.	240	240	240	Completed.
		Total (*a*) Southern Division ..	..	..	20,369	

APPENDIX A—*contd.*

District. (P. W. D.)	Locality.	Name of work and description.	Amount of sanctioned estimate.	Allotment for the year 1921-22.	Amount spent during the year 1921-22.	REMARKS.
1	2	3	4	5	6	7
		BOMBAY PRESIDENCY—*contd.*	Rs.	Rs.	Rs.	
		(*b*) *Current Repairs and Maintenance (recurring charges).*				
Belgaum	Deogaon ..	Old Jain temple:—Repairs to stone pitching, roof, and stopping leakages with cement and dry dammer, pointing stone slabs and removing shrubs and bushes, etc.	33	33	32	Completed.
Do. ..	Golihalli ..	Temples of Ramlingdeva, Shidlingdeva and Kalmesvara with inscriptions Removing the growth of vegetation round the building and repairing the doors.	35	35	35	Do.
Do. ..	Konnur ..	Dolmens on the road from Gokak Road Railway Station to Gokak mills:—Removing prickly pears and rubbish round the monuments.	150	150	150	Do.
Ratnagiri..	Vijayadurga	Fort wall:—Cutting trees and roots, etc., from the fort walls and repairs to masonry at places.	300	300	290	Do.
Do. ..	Malwan ..	Sindhudurga (fort):—Cutting trees and roots, etc., from the fort walls and repairs to masonry at places.	225	225	201	Do.
Do. ..	Jaigadh ..	Fort wall:—Removing roots, clearing fort wall, clearing compound and filling in cracks, etc.	150	150	149	Do.
Do. ..	Harnai ..	Suvarnadurga (fort):—The trees and shrubs grown on the fort wall have been cut down from inside and also some from south and north sides of the fort gate.	150	150	150	Do.
Do. ..	Dabhol ..	Mosque:—The trees and shrubs have been removed from the masonry and some patches of chunam plaster have been repaired.	65	65	64	Do.
		Carried over ..	..	..	1,071	

APPENDIX A—*contd.*

District. (P. W. D.)	Locality.	Name of work and description.	Amount of sanctioned estimate.	Allotment for the year 1921-22.	Amount spent during the year 1921-22.	REMARKS.
1	2	3	4	5	6	7
			Rs.	Rs.	Rs.	
		Brought forward	..	..	1,071	
		BOMBAY PRESIDENCY—*contd.*				
		(b) *Current Repairs* (*recurring charges*)—contd.				
Kanara ..	Bhatkal ..	Jettappa Naikan Chandranathesvara Basti :—Murum filling for making the uneven ground level.	3	3	6	Completed.
Do. ..	Nagar Bastikeri, Gersappa.	Chaturmukha Basti :—Fixing notice board, clearing compound and making passage.	29	29	29	Do.
Do. ..	Do. ..	Vardhamanswami's temple :—Fixing notice board, clearing compound and making passage and clearing inscription stones.	20	20	20	Do.
Do. ..	Do. ..	Virbhadra temple :—Clearing compound and making passage.	20	20	20	Do.
Do. ..	Kumta ..	Tombs on the right side of Manki Kumta Road :—Cleaning and painting inscriptions and repairing plaster.	10	10	10	Do.
Do. ..	Mirjan ..	Fort :—Repairing approach road by removing shrubs, etc., and laying murum on the path.	50	50	47	Do.
Do. ..	Bilgi ..	Small deserted temple dedicated to Siva :—Removing rank vegetation and clearing compound.	9	9	9	Do.
Do. ..	Sonda ..	Temple close to the south of the King's seat :—Removing rank vegetation, clearing compound, replacing missing parts of the compound wall and clearing the temple.	14	14	14	Do.
Do. ..	Do. ..	King's seat :—Removing rank vegetation and repairing the floor and roof.	20	20	19	Do.
Do. ..	Somsagar ..	Temple of Siva :—Clearing the compound, removing rank vegetation and clearing the building.	9	9	9	Do.
		Carried over	..	..	1,254	

APPENDIX A—*contd.*

District. (P. W. D.)	Locality.	Name of work and description.	Amount of sanctioned estimate.	Allotment for the year 1921-22.	Amount spent during the year 1921-22.	REMARKS.
1	2	3	4	5	6	7
			Rs.	Rs.	Rs.	
		Brought forward . .	..	..	1,254	
		BOMBAY PRESIDENCY—*contd.*				
		(*b*) *Current Repairs (recurring charges)*—contd.				
Dharwar ..	Bankapur ..	Nagaresvara temple :—Clearing compound, removing small shrubs from Sikhara and sides and cleaning spots on masonry.	32	32	32	Completed.
Do. ..	Unkal ..	Four-porched temple	7	7	7	Do.
Do. ..	Amargol ..	Sankarlinga temple	11	11	11	Do.
Do. ..	Naregal ..	Sarvesvara temple	12	12	12	Do.
Do. ..	Hangal ..	Old ruined temple between fort and tank.	45	45	44	Do.
Do. ..	Do. ..	Tarakesvara temple	50	50	46	Do.
Do. ..	Balambid ..	Kalmesvara temple	40	40	40	Do.
Do. ..	Haveri ..	Sidhesvara temple	15	15	15	Do.
Do. ..	Lakhundi ..	Namesvara temple	15	15	15	Do.
Do. ..	Do. ..	Jain Basti	15	15	15	Do.
Do. ..	Do. ..	Kumbhargiri temple	24	24	21	Do.
Do. ..	Do. ..	Kashivishveshvara temple ..	25	25	24	Do.
Do. ..	Dambal ..	Dodda Basavanna temple ..	15	15	15	Do.
Do. ..	Do. ..	Somesvara temple	15	15	15	Do.
Do. ..	Gadag ..	Somesvara temple	30	30	30	Do.
Do. ..	Do. ..	Sarasvati temple	20	20	20	Do.
Do. ..	Chowdhanpur	Muktesvara temple	25	25	21	Do.
Do. ..	Galagnath ..	Galgesvara temple	45	45	42	Do.
Do. ..	Rattihalli ..	Kadambesvara temple ..	25	25	31	Do.
Bijapur ..	Bijapur, Badami, Aiholi and Pattadkal.	Archæological buildings in the District.	2,055	2,055	2,050	Do.
Do. ..	Do. ..	Pay of the Establishment ..	6,636	6,636	6,154	Do.
Do. ..	Bijapur ..	Bijapur museum :—Contribution for the maintenance of the Bijapur museum.	1,064	1,064	1,064	Do.
		Total (*b*) Southern Division ..	..	..	10,978	

APPENDIX A—*contd.*

District. (P. W. D.)	Locality.	Name of work and description.	Amount of sanctioned estimate.	Allotment for the year 1921-22.	Amount spent during the year 1921-22.	REMARKS.
1	2	3	4	5	6	7
			Rs.	Rs.	Rs.	
		SIND.				
		INDUS RIGHT BANK DIVISION.				
		(a) *Special Repairs (non-recurring charges).*				
Karachi Buildings.	Hyderabad ..	Ghulam Shah Kalhora's tomb (Total expenditure up to date from 1908 is Rs. 3,196.)	1,744	..	..	In temporary abeyance.
Do. ..	Do. ..	Ghulam Nabi Kalhora's tomb (Expenditure up to date from 1908 is Rs. 10,199.)	1,298	..	..	Do.
Do. ..	Do. ..	Sarfaraz Khan Kalhora's tomb (Expenditure up to date is Rs. 869.)	1,203	..	..	Do.
Do. ..	Do. ..	Providing leather belts and brass badges for caretakers.	40	40	30	Completed.
Karachi Canals.	Makli Hills ..	Archæological remains on Makli Hills. (Expenditure incurred up to date by the Executive Engineer amounts to Rs. 4,213.)	14,240	3,800	..	In progress.
Do. ..	Tatta ..	Providing leather belt and brass badge for caretaker.	10	10	10	Completed.
Western Nara.	Khudabad ..	Providing leather belts and brass badges for caretakers.	20	20	20	Do.
Do. ..	Do. ..	Yar Muhammad Khan's tomb. (Expenditure up to date is Rs. 1,350.)	1,356	..	..	In progress.
Do. ..	Do. ..	Jami Masjid :—Expenditure up to date is Rs. 1,652.	2,561	..	..	Do.
Shikarpur Canals.	Rohri ..	Satyan-jo-than :—Expenditure up to date on S. R. amounts to Rs. 3,348.	1,383	1,383	1,349	Completed.
		Total (a) Indus Right Bank Division.	..	..	1,409	

APPENDIX A—*contd.*

District. (P. W. D.)	Locality.	Name of work and description.	Amount of sanctioned estimate.	Allotment for the year 1921-22.	Amount spent during the year 1921-22.	REMARKS.
1	2	3	4	5	6	7
			Rs.	Rs.	Rs.	
		SIND.—*contd.*				
		(*b*) *Current Repairs and Maintenance* (*recurring charges*).				
Karachi Buildings.	Hyderabad	Gulam Shah Kalhora's tomb:—Resetting fallen tiles and lime-plastering wherever necessary both on the walls and floors inside and outside the tomb. Roofs were also repaired with lime plaster in some places, repairs to other tombs in the compound and repairs to notice boards were done.	102	102	88	Completed.
Do. ..	Do. ..	Gulam Nabi Kalhora's tomb:—Resetting fallen tiles and lime-plastering wherever necessary both on the walls and floors inside and outside the tomb. Roofs were also repaired with lime plaster in some places, repairs to other tombs in the compound and repairs to notice boards were done.	130	130	139	Do.
Do. ..	Do. ..	Sarfaraz Khan Kalhora's tomb:—Resetting fallen tiles and lime-plastering wherever necessary both on the walls and floors inside and outside the tomb. Roofs were also repaired with lime plaster in some places, repairs to other tombs in the compound and repairs to notice boards were done.	263	263	259	Do.
Do. ..	Do. ..	Haram of Mirs in the fort:—Sweeper's pay.	24	24	22	Do.
Do. ..	Gidu Bunder	Memorial pillar at the site of the old Residency at Gidu Bunder:—Repairing, fencing round the stone pillars. The stone was given a "Metore" wash and the area inside fencing was cleared.	75	75	41	Do.
		Carried over ..	..	..	549	

Appendix A—*contd.*

District. (P. W. D.)	Locality.	Name of work and description.	Amount of sanctioned estimate.	Allotment for the year 1921-22.	Amount spent during the year 1921-22.	Remarks.
1	2	3	4	5	6	7
			Rs.	Rs.	Rs.	
		Brought forward ..	..	..	549	
		SIND—*contd.*				
		(*b*) *Current Repairs and Maintenance (recurring charges)*—contd.				
Karachi Canals.	Makli Hills ..	Archæological remains on Makli Hills :—Lime or cement plaster or pointing where necessary and renewing rusty wire netting.	352	352	203	The Executive Engineer surrendered the balance.
Western Nara.	Khudabad ..	Yar Muhammad Khan's tomb :—Cement pointing, chunam pointing, B. B. and mud masonry mud plaster, ½" thick, chunam plaster, ½" thick, removing and relaying flat bricks in yard.	237	237	237	Completed.
Do.	Do. ..	Jami masjid :—Chunam plaster ¾", earth filling, ramming and lime pointing.	201	201	201	Do.
Ghar Canals.	Near Ratodaro	Rato-bhando (tomb):—Earth work for platform and painting doors.	105	105	103	Do.
		Total (*b*) Indus Right Bank Division	..	..	1,293	
		Indus Left Bank Division.				
		(*a*) *Special Repairs (non-recurring charges).*				
Eastern Nara.	Mirpurkhas..	Providing leather belt and brass badge for caretaker.	10	10	10	Do.
Northern District, Jamrao Canals.	Brahmanabad	Providing leather belt and brass badge for caretaker.	10	10	10	Do.
		Total (*a*) Indus Left Bank Division	..	..	20	
		(*b*) *Current Repairs and Maintenance (recurring charges).*				
Fuleli Canals.	Near Gaja mouth.	Buddhist stupa	30	30	25	Do.
Nasrat Canals.	Tul-Mir-Rukan.	Buddhist stupa :—Cement pointing.	15	15	15	Do.
		Carried over ..	..	..	40	

APPENDIX A—*contd.*

District. (P. W. D.)	Locality.	Name of work and description.	Amount of sanctioned estimate.	Allotment for the year 1921-22.	Amount spent during the year 1921-22.	REMARKS.
1	2	3	4	5	6	7
			Rs.	Rs.	Rs.	
		Brought forward .	..	..	40	
		SIND—*contd.*				
		(b) Current Repairs and Maintenance (recurring charges)—contd.				
Nasrat Canals.	Kubo Nurmuhamad.	Tomb of Nur Muhammad Kalhora :—Lime plastering.	56	56	56	Completed.
Eastern Nara.	Kahu-jo-daro, about ½ mile to the north of Mirpurkhas.	Buddhist stupa	203	203	192	Do.
Do. ..	Naokot ..	Fort :—Jungle cutting, filling in rain "gbaras", cement pointing to steps.	56	56	90	Do.
Northern District Jamrao Canals.	Dalore ..	Brahmbra-ka-thul :— do. do.	218	218	220	Do.
		Total (*b*) Indus Left Bank Division	..	..	598	

		Special repairs.	Current repairs and maintenance.
		Rs.	Rs.
Bombay Presidency including Sind.	Northern Division	28,506	9,500
	Central Division	17,241	7,420
	Southern Division	20,369	10,978
	Indus Right Bank Division ..	1,409	1,293
	Indus Left Bank Division	20	598
	Total ..	67,545	29,789
	GRAND TOTAL ..	97,334	

Appendix A—*contd.*

Statement of expenditure on Conservation Works executed during the year 1921-22 in the Southern Circle.

District.	Locality.	Name of work and description.	Amount of sanctioned estimate.	Allotment for the year 1921-22 (excluding P. W. D. charges).	Amount spent during the year 1921-22 (excluding P. W. D. charges).	Remarks.
1	2	3	4	5	6	7
		Madras Presidency.	Rs.	Rs.	Rs. a. p.	
		(a) *Special Repairs (non-recurring charges.*				
Kistna . .	Masulipatam	*Bandar Fort including Armoury, Belfry and Powder Magazine.*—Restoration of walls where attacked by saline action; removing and renewing damaged lintels over doors, stopping leaks in terrace, re-building compound wall at certain places, plastering and general clearance.	5,850	5,000	4,552 0 0	The work is in progress.
Guntur . .	Motupalle .	*Virabhadra Chōla temple.*—The north-western wall, the terrace and the floor of the temple have been repaired, the gopuram was grouted and plastered.	940	200	200 0 0	
" . .	Undavalli .	*Cave temple.*—Decayed pillars re-constructed and flight of steps formed with cut stone.	390	390	345 0 0	
Bellary . .	Hampi Ruins	*Vitthala temple.*—Iron clamps fixed to cracked pillars in the south-east Kalyana Mandapa. Flooring in the Goddess temple reset where damaged and buttresses provided where needed.	600	600	299 0 0	
" . .	" .	Laying out a new approach road and acquisition of land.	2,000	2,000	336 0 0	The work is in progress.
Chittoor .	Chandragiri .	*Fort and Palace.*—Clearing surroundings and whitewashing.	730 500	955	838 0 0	Work completed.
Malabar .	Palghat .	*Fort.*—Removal of water hyacinth from the moat.	240	240	239 14 6	Completed.
" . .	" . .	*Fort.*—Removing vegetation, grouting, pointing, plastering, sundry repairs to roadway, etc.	500	500	469 1 6 23 11 0	Work in progress.
Salem . .	Atur . .	*Hill Fort.*—Removing vegetation and repacking revetment.	330	330	290 9 6	
" . .	Sankaridrug	*Hill Fort.*—Forming pathways, removing trees and vegetation and repairs to Fort walls.	770	480	392 2 0	Work in progress.
" . .	" .	*Kabir mosque in the Hill Fort.*—Clearance, plastering, pointing and rebuilding parapet wall where broken.	1,140	1,000	906 12 0	
		Carried over .	..	..	8,892 2 6	

APPENDIX A—*contd.*

District.	Locality.	Name of work and description.	Amount of sanctioned estimate.	Allotment for the year 1921-22 (excluding P. W. D. charges).	Amount spent during the year 1921-22 (excluding P. W. D. charges).	REMARKS.
1	2	3	4	5	6	7
			Rs.	Rs.	Rs. A. P.	
		Brought forward .	..	..	8,892 2 6	
		MADRAS—*contd.*				
		(*a*) *Special Repairs (non-recurring charges)*—contd.				
North Arcot .	Walajapet .	Masjid to the west of the citadel, colour washing, plastering the walls and general clearance.	100	100	99 0 0	Completed.
„ .	Wandiwash .	*Fort.*—Removing vegetation and underpinning brickwork.	..	40	42 0 0	Do.
„ .	Sholavaram .	*Siva temple.*—Renewing the walls around the shrine and levelling ground.	1,600	..	23 0 0	Work in progress. Revised estimate for Rs. 2,780 is submitted for sanction.
„ .	Siyyamangalam.	*Rockcut temple and inscriptions.*—Repairing the roof.	1,030	400	465 0 0	Excess due to actual expenditure found necessary. Work in progress.
Chingleput .	Mahabalipuram.	Planting of avenue trees from temple tank to Shore temple.	190	190	255 0 0	
„ .	„ .	Watering Casurina plants in front of the 5 *rathas.*	110	110	92 0 0	
„ .	„ .	*Thirukandana Jain Temple.*—Special repair to monument at—.	..	35	35 0 0	
„ .	Sadras .	*Dutch cemetery.*—Reconstructing the north-east portion of the compound wall of—.	..	170	144 0 0	
„ .	Pulicat .	*Dutch cemetery.*—Special repairs to —.	270	119	119 0 0	
„ .	Alambarai .	*Fort.*—Special repairs to —. .	930	930	846 0 0	
„ .	Conjeevaram	*Matharigesvara temple.*—Special repairs to —.	30	30	30 0 0	
Tanjore . .	Tanjore .	*Schwartz church.*—Special repairs to —.	720	500	488 0 0	
„ . .	Tranquebar .	*Dansborg castle.*—Special repairs to —.	1,330	730	758 0 0	
South Arcot .	Gingee .	*Gingee Fort buildings.*—Special repairs to —.	21,600	2,600	2,599 0 0	
„ . „ .	Porto-Novo .	*Roman Catholic Portuguese church*—Special repairs to —.	4,000	2,500	497 0 0	
		Carried over . .	..	..	15,284 2 6	

APPENDIX A—*contd.*

District.	Locality.	Name of work and description.	Amount of sanctioned estimate.	Allotment for the year 1921-22 (excluding P. W. D. charges).	Amount spent during the year 1921-22 (excluding P. W. D. charges).	REMARKS.
1	2	3	4	5	6	7
			Rs.	Rs.	Rs. A. P.	
		Brought forward .	..	..	15,284 2 6	
		MADRAS—*contd.*				
		(*a*) *Special Repairs (non-recurring)*—concld.				
Madura .	Dindigul .	*Rock Fort.*—Special repairs to the compound wall of —.	190	144	41 14 0	Completed.
Tinnevelly .	Anjengo .	*Old Fort.*—Special repairs to —	2,300	400	63 10 0	Debits for Rs. 250 on account of land charges by Travancore Government will be adjusted in supplemental accounts for March 1922.
Trichinopoly .	Perambalur-Vallapuram Hamlet of Brahmadesam.	*Voltyar Masjid and Cuddapah Nawab's tomb.*—Pointing, plastering, removing vegetation and underpinning.	510	151	142 0 0	
„ .	Valikondapuram.	*Valisvara temple.*—Pointing with Surkhi mortar, plastering with chunam, clearing prickly pear and petty repairs to Mandapam, etc.	450	226	155 0 0	
„ .	„ .	*Shamaskhan mosque.*—Pointing, plastering the flooring and removing vegetation.	143	143	114 0 0	
„ .	Ranjangudy.	*Fort.*—Underpinning the archwork and minor repairs to walls.	96	94	67 0 0	
South Kanara	Karkal .	*Jain statue of Gummatesvara.*—Pointing the walls and flooring of cut stone with cement, grouting with concrete and clearing the weeds from the walls.	160	150	94 3 3	
		Total (*a*) Special Repairs .	..	..	17,931 13 9	

APPENDIX A—*contd.*

District.	Locality.	Name of work and description.	Amount of sanctioned estimate.	Allotment for the year 1921-22 (excluding P. W. D. charges).	Amount spent during the year 1921-22 (excluding P. W. D. charges).	REMARKS.
1	2	3	4	5	6	7
		MADRAS—*contd.*	Rs.	Rs.	Rs. A. P.	
		(*b*) *Annual Repairs* (*recurring charges*).				
Ganjam .	Jongoda .	*Asoka Rock inscription.*—Annual repairs to—. The leak in the roof over the inscription was caulked with lead wool and the notice board were repainted.	25	25	16 12 4	
Kistna .	Bezwada .	Two rockcut cave temples on Indrakila hill, filling cracks, plastering and clearance of vegetation.	80	42	41 4 0	
" . .	Kondapalle .	Hill Fort and ruined palace .	100	100	97 0 0	
" . .	Gudivada .	*Mound containing Buddhist remains and ancient village site.*—Repairs to the notice board and the Mound such as painting and fixing the demarcation stones round the Mound.	40	50	53 0 0 11 0 0*	Work completed. *The work is in progress and will be completed during the current official year.
" . .	Arugolanu .	*Mound containing Buddhist remains.*—putting up notice board.	25	25	21 10 0	
Guntur . .	Amravati .	*Buddhist stupa and other remains.*—The carved stones stacked and proper drainage provided.	470	..	50 0 0	The incomplete work of an estimate, sanctioned in 1919-20 and executed under provincial funds, was finished in 1921-22.
Anantapur .	Kalayanadrug	*Siva temple.*—Plastering, pointing and clearance.	15	15	13 0 0	
" .	Penukonda .	*Citadel and ruined buildings on the hill.*—Doors and windows and expanded sheets were provided.	250	250	234 0 0	
" . .	" .	*Gagan Mahal.*—Doors and windows and expanded metal sheets were provided.	760	300	304 0 0	
Bellary . .	Hampi Ruins	*Queen's bath.*—Plastering with lime mortar. Gravelling the pathway, etc.	85	85	63 0 0	
" . .	" .	*Sarasvati temple.*—Removing and stacking loose stones, etc., etc.	100	100	70 0 0	
" . .	" .	*Ranga temple.*—Plastering the two mandapams, grouting and pointing big voids on walls. Providing lintel stones at the main entrance with side walls.	190	190	162 0 0	
		Carried over . .	..	..	1,136 10 4	

APPENDIX A—*contd.*

District.	Locality.	Name of work and description.	Amount of sanctioned estimate.	Allotment for the year 1921-22 (excluding P. W. D. charges).	Amount spent during the year 1921-22 (excluding P. W. D. charges).	REMARKS.
1	2	3	4	5	6	7
			Rs.	Rs.	Rs. A. P.	
		Brought forward .	..	..	1,136 10 4	
		MADRAS—*contd.*				
		(*b*) *Annual Repairs (recurring charges)*—contd.				
Bellary .	Hampi Ruins	Removing and carrying carved stones to inspection bungalow at Kamalapur and fixing them in masonry.	25	25	20 0 0	
" .	" .	*Hazara Ramachandra temple.*—Plastering the top of verandah. Reconstructing the fallen compound wall, providing a cut stone pillar for the slipped beamstone in the west verandah, grouting and pointing where necessary, resetting in position the fallen stones, etc.	215	215	164 0 0	
" .	" .	*Chandrasekara temple.*—Removing the loose stones and stacking them.	85	85	78 0 0	
" .	" .	Ruined tank adjoining the Soolai Bazaar removing rank vegetation.	220	220	24 0 0	
" .	" .	Provision of Notice Boards. .	65	65	66 0 0	
" .	Thimmalapur	Siva temple	100	100	5 0 0	The work was completed last year but the amount of Rs. 5 was paid in this year.
Chittoor .	Mangapuram	*Venkatesvara temple.*—Sundry repairs and clearing vegetation.	10	10	10 0 0	Work completed.
" .	Melpadi .	*Somanatha temple.*—Pointing in front verandah of temple and floor of the entrance.	10	15	15 0 0	Do.
" .	Gurramkonda	*Fort.*—Clearing pathway and rebuilding displaced revetment at sides of pathway, etc.	100	200	172 0 0	Do.
Cuddapah .	Sidhout .	*Fort and ancient buildings therein.*—Clearing vegetation, etc.	165	170	147 0 0	
" .	Pushpagiri .	*Temples.*—Repairs to notice board, etc.	30	..	24 0 0	
Coimbatore .	Avanashi .	Siva temple	35	35	19 0 0	
" .	Tirumuruganapundi.	Murugunatha temple . .	48	48	45 0 0	
		Carried over .	..	..	1,925 10 4	

Appendix A—*contd.*

District.	Locality.	Name of work and description.	Amount of sanctioned estimate.	Allotment for the year 1921-22 (excluding P. W. D. charges).	Amount spent during the year 1921-22 (excluding P. W. D. charges).	Remarks.
1	2	3	4	5	6	7
			Rs.	Rs.	Rs. A. P.	
		Brought forward .	..	..	1,925 10 4	
		MADRAS—*contd.*				
		(b) *Annual Repairs (recurring charges)*—contd.				
Malabar .	Wynaad .	*Sultan's Battery.*—Clearing jungle.	..	20	19 14 0	
South Canara	Bekal .	*Fort.*—Removing rank vegetation, earth work and pointing with surki mortar.	225	225	205 1 1	
„ .	Mangalore .	*Sultan's Battery.*—Removing rank vegetation, pointing and plastering with surki mortar and tarring gate.	60	60	57 0 0	
„ .	Mudabidri .	*Seventeen Jain statues.*—Clearing rank vegetation. Painting notice boards, etc.	50	50	39 0 0	
„ .	Nada .	*Jamalabad Rock Fort.*—Clearing vegetation, cutting and removing trees grown on walls and grass on steps.	225	200	105 0 0	
Salem .	Namakkal .	*Hill Fort.*—Removing vegetation on the walls.	140	100	86 1 0	
North Arcot .	Abdullapuram	*Mahal.*—Removing vegetation .	50	50	21 0 0	
„ .	Vellore .	*Old Mosque.*—Whitewashing and patch plastering.	40	65	61 0 0	
„ .	Tirumalai .	*Jain temple.*—Clearing vegetation.	70	70	55 0 0	
The Nilgiris .	Banagudi Shola 3 miles south of Kotagiri.	*Group of large dolmens.*—Maintaining the drain along the road, removing jungle growth in the road and round the dolmens.	70	..	45 0 0	This represents the cost of repairs done relating to the estimate for the year 1920-21. Bill amounting to Rs. 68 being the cost of repairs for 1921-22 was paid in April 1922.
Chingleput .	Mahabalipuram.	Acquisition of land for roadways	102	102	102 0 0	
„ .	Sadras .	*Dutch cemetery.*—Annual repairs, etc.	170	13	13 0 0	
Tanjore .	Negapatam .	*Dutch cemetery*	150	180	180 0 0	
„ .	Tanjore .	*Arsenal Tower in Tanjore Palace* .	880	500	501 0 0	Since deleted from the list.
„ .	„ .	*Statue hall in Tanjore Palace* .	280	260	261 0 0	Since deleted.
Tinnevelly .	Tuticorin .	*Dutch cemetery*	75	..	71 8 0	
		Carried over .	..	..	3,748 2 5	

APPENDIX A—*contd.*

District.	Locality.	Name and description of work.	Amount of sanctioned estimate.	Allotment for the year 1921-22 (excluding P. W. D. charges).	Amount spent during the year 1921-22 (excluding P.W.D. charges).	REMARKS.
1	2	3	4	5	6	7
			Rs.	Rs.	Rs. A. P.	
		Brought forward	..	..	3,748 2 5	
		MADRAS—*contd.*				
		(*b*) *Annual Repairs* (*recurring charges*)—contd.				
Trichinopoly .	Tandoni .	*Rock cut carvings* . . .	40	40	1 0 0	
Ganjam .	Kottakolla .	*Siva temple on Brudhakolla hill* .	100	80	78 4 5	
Vizagapatam .	Sankaram .	Maintenance of watcher to Buddhist remains.	144	144	155 0 0	
" .	" .	Repairs to Buddhist remains .	70	50	50 0 0	
" .	Ramatirtham	Maintenance of watcher to Buddhist remains.	144	144	144 0 0	
Kistna .	Bezwada .	Akkanna Madanna caves.—Clearance of vegetation.	5	5	5 0 0	
" .	Mogalrajpuram.	*Rock cut cave temples on the hill.*—Clearance.	10	10	11 1 0	
" .	Adamalle .	Ancient mounds	85	10	10 14 0	
" .	Pedavegi .	Ditto	55	10	9 14 0	
" .	Guntapalle .	Buddhist monuments . .	85	50	49 15 0	
Guntur .	Amaravati .	Maintenance of a watchman for the Buddhist stupa.	100	110	90 0 0	
Nellore .	Udayagiri .	Hill Fort with ancient buildings .	..	30	27 0 0	
Anantapur .	Tadpatri .	*Ramaswami temple.*—Repairs to the gopuram.	470	470	15 0 0	Monument since deleted from the list.
" .	Gooty .	*Fort and its buildings including the fortifications at the foot of the hill.*—Maintenance of watchmen.	685	685	315 0 0	
" .	Anantapur .	*Sir Thomas Munro's house and two wells.*—Colour washing and white washing the building and repairs to doors and windows.	65	65	48 0 0	
" .	Penukonda .	*Ancient monuments.*—Maintenance of watchmen.	150	200	203 0 0	
" .	Sethutirtham	*Sethutirtham well.*—Clearance of site around the well.	40	40	40 0 0	
		Carried over .	..	..	5,001 2 10	

APPENDIX A—*contd.*

District.	Locality.	Name of work and description.	Amount of sanctioned estimate.	Allotment for the year 1921-22 (excluding P. W. D. charges).	Amount spent during the year 1921-22 (excluding P. W. D. charges).	REMARKS.
1	2	3	4	5	6	7
			Rs.	Rs.	Rs. A. P.	
		Brought forward .	..	..	5,001 2 10	
		MADRAS—*contd.*				
		(b) *Annual Repairs (recurring charges)*—contd.				
Malabar .	Tellicherry .	*Fort.*—Removing jungle growth and vegetation.	150	150	148 11 0	
" .	Kodur .	*Kannesvara temple.*—General clearance and petty repairs.	12	25	11 9 0	Since deleted, no provision to be made in future.
" .	" .	*Krishnamurthi temple.*—General clearance.	15	25	14 3 0	
North Arcot .	Vellore .	*Fort.*—Clearing vegetation from the inner and outer rampart walls of the tank.	530	530	535 0 0	
" .	" .	*Jalakanthesvara temple in the Fort.*—Maintaining two watchmen and pointing, etc.	400	400	399 0 0	
" .	Arcot .	*Delhi Gate.*—Maintenance of a watchman.	180	150	150 0 0	
The Nilgiris .	Hulikaldrug	*Ruined Fort.*—Clearing heavy jungle inside.	25	25	25 0 0	Since deleted, no provision to be made in future.
" .	Batlada Acheni 3 miles S. E. of Kotagiri.	*Group of sculptured dolmens.*—Removing rank vegetation.	5	5	5 0 0	
Madras .	Tondiyarpet	*R. S. Pillar No. 1697.*—Annual repairs to—.	10	10	9 0 0	
" .	" .	*R. S. Pillar No. 1793.*—Annual repairs to—.	10	10	10 0 0	
" .	Washermanpet.	*R. S. Pillar No. 1764.*—Annual repairs to—.	8	10	8 0 0	
" .	" .	*R. S. Pillar No. 1816.*—Annual repairs to—.	15	10	11 0 0	
" .	" .	*Madras old town wall.*—Annual repairs to—.	98	100	91 0 0	
" .	George Town	Joseph Hymner's tomb in Law College compound.	25	25	19 0 0	
Chingleput .	Mahabalipuram.	*Ancient monuments.*—Conservation of—.	420	300	281 0 0	
" .	" .	Repairs to roads at Mahabalipuram.	1,175	1,175	1,129 0 0	
" .	Chingleput .	*Ther Mahal.*—Annual repairs to—	160	151	151 0 0	
		Carried over .	..	..	7,998 9 10	

APPENDIX A—*contd.*

District.	Locality.	Name and description of work.	Amount of sanctioned estimate.	Allotment for the year 1921-22 (excluding P. W. D. charges).	Amount spent during the year 1921-22 (excluding P. W. D. charges).	REMARKS.
1	2	3	4	5	6	7
			Rs.	Rs.	Rs. A. P.	
		Brought forward .	..	..	7,998 9 10	
		MADRAS—*concld.*				
		(*b*) *Annual Repairs* (*recurring charges*)—concld.				
Tanjore .	Tanjore .	*Sivaganga little fort.*—Maintenance of—.	240	240	214 0 0	
South Arcot .	Gingee .	*Gingee Fort.*—Maintenance of watchman.	580	600	576 0 0	
Madura .	Dindigul .	*Rock Fort.*—Employment of watchman from 1st October 1920 to 30th September 1922.	180	144	76 8 0 92 3 10	In progress.
Tinnevelly .	Adichanallur	*Prehistoric remains.*—Maintenance of a watchman.	144	108	99 0 0	
Trichinopoly .	Ranjangudi .	*Fort.*—Maintenance of a watchman.	144	36	10 0 0	
" .	Gangaikonda sholavaram.	Brihadisvara temple . . .	..	..	38 0 0	No work was carried out this year but the amount spent the previous year was paid from grant under urgent contingencies. The monument has now been ordered to be deleted.
Bellary .	Hampi Ruins	Maintenance of watchman and establishment charges for 1921.	970	960	699 0 0	
" .	" .	Maintenance of watchman and establishment charges for 1922.	970	970	234 0 0	
		Total (*b*) Annual Repairs .	..	..	10,037 5 8	
		COORG.				
Coorg .	Mercara .	*Fort and Raja's seat.*—Repairs to roads, elephants, Raja's seat and clearing surroundings and keeping a watchman.	..	240	218 5 0	
" .	Nalkanad .	*Nalkanad Palace.*—Repairs to doors and windows. White-washing and paying a watcher.	..	340	405 6 5	There is no sanctioned estimate for these works in this office.
		Total Coorg .	..	..	623 11 5	
		Total Madras (*a*) and (*b*) .	..	..	27,969 3 5	
		GRAND TOTAL .	..	..	28,592 14 10	

Appendix A—*contd.*

Summary of expenditure on salaries, establishments, excavations, etc.

Circles.	Allotment.	Expenditure.
	Rs.	Rs.
(a) Superintendent, Muhammadan and British Monuments, Northern Circle	58,306	70,093*
(b) " Hindu and Buddhist Monuments, Northern Circle	34,939	31,506
(c) " Frontier Circle	28,350	28,387
(d) " Western Circle	38,806	47,569
(e) " Central Circle	47,832	46,251
(f) " Eastern Circle	21,061	21,184
(g) " Southern Circle (Provincial grant)	28,592	24,085
(h) " Burma Circle do. do.	32,200	34,151
(i) Government Epigraphist for India	23,560	26,323
(j) Archæological Chemist in India	22,082	19,556
(k) Director General of Archæology including Epigraphist for Moslem Inscriptions.	1,49,090	1,62,575
(l) Sir Aurel Stein	38,000	38,033
Total	5,22,818	5,49,712

*Rs. 3,664 provided by Provincial Government for the Delhi Museum.

APPENDIX A—*concld.*

Expenditure incurred on Conservation works by Provinces during the year 1921-1922.

Province.	Allotment.	Expenditure.
United Provinces—	Rs.	Rs.
Muhammadan and British Monuments	2,05,400	1,73,682*
Hindu and Buddhist Monuments		12,239
Punjab—		
Muhammadan and British Monuments	1,19,100	99,895†
Hindu and Buddhist Monuments		42,706
Delhi	1,34,000	1,32,035‡
North-West Frontier Province	38,200	14,998
Bihar and Orissa	26,300	13,475
Central Provinces and Berar	34,000	19,607
Bengal	21,000	16,847
Assam	7,500	9,458
Bombay	1,10,000	97,334
Madras	54,000	28,592
Coorg	600	
Burma	62,700	56,363
Ajmere	7,200	7,200
Chattarpur State (grant-in-aid)	5,000	5,000
Dhar State (grant-in-aid)	15,000	15,000
Reserve	30,000	..
Total	8,70,000	7,44,431

* Includes Rs. 69,581 provided by Provincial Government for Gardens.

† Includes Rs. 20,724 provided by Provincial Government for Gardens.

‡ Includes Rs. 6,839 provided by Provincial Government for salary of caretaker and establishment at the Delhi Fort.

APPENDIX B.

MUSEUMS.

List of exhibits received in the Delhi Museum of Archaeology during the year 1921-22.

PURCHASED. Rs.

1. A specimen of calligraphy written in Naskh characters by Muhammad Afzal who records himself a servant of Dara Shikoh. It was written in Kabul on 15th Shawwal 1062 A. H. (19th September 1652) 25
2. A specimen of calligraphy by the same scribe in Naskh characters. It was also written in Kabul in the month of Ramzan 1062 A. H. (August 1652) but the name of writer, date and place are transcribed in different style . . 25
3. Ditto ditto ditto ditto ditto . 25
4. A specimen of calligraphy in Naskh characters written by Asad Ali . . 15
5. A specimen of calligraphy in Nastaliq characters written by Muhammad Ali, who was a court calligraphist of the late Mughal Emperors. It is dated 1196 A. H. (1781-82 A. D.) 20
6. A specimen of calligraphy in Nastaliq characters written by Safdar Ali . 15
7. A specimen of calligraphy in Nastaliq characters written by Muhammad Subhan 20
8. A specimen of calligraphy written in Nastaliq characters by Muhammad Baqar 15
9. A specimen of calligraphy in Nastaliq characters written by Ahmad Riza . 25
10. A specimen of calligraphy in Nastaliq characters written by Shamsuddin . 30
11. A specimen of calligraphy in Nastaliq characters written by Muhammad Husain Ata Khan. It is dated 1192 A. H. (1778 A. D.) 25
12. A specimen of calligraphy in Nastaliq characters written by Muhammad Muqim, who was one of the calligraphists of Shahjahan's time and lived in the Kali Masjid at Delhi 20
13. A specimen of calligraphy in Naskh characters written by Abdurrahman . 15
14. A specimen of calligraphy in Nastaliq characters written by Arab Shirazi. It is dated 1041 A. H. (1631-32 A. D.) and contains a verse in praise of Abdullah Qutb Shahi, the king of Golkanda 40
15. A specimen of calligraphy in Nastaliq characters written by Sarab Sukh Rai, a pupil of Hafiz Nurullah who flourished during the time of Nawab Asif-ud-Daulah of Oudh (1775—1797 A. D.) 20
16. A specimen of calligraphy in Nastaliq characters written by Tajammul Husain Khan, who was a pupil of Hafiz Ibrahim and served Mr. Montague Turnbull of the Civil Service in 1828 20
17. Seal impressions (more than one hundred) of European and Indian officers of the later Mughal period 100
18. A specimen of calligraphy in Nastaliq characters written by Ustad Haider Ali 15

PRESENTED.

Presented by C. J. Brown, Esq., Professor, Canning College, Lucknow.

1. Sanad issued under the seal of Sayyid Amjad Khan Sadr-i-Jahan, an official of Shah Alam Bahadur Shah I addressed to the authorities of Pargana Jullander, Subah Punjab, granting 65 bighas of uncultivated land of the Pargana to one Niyaz Bano and others as assistance to their livelihood. It is dated 6th Zulhijja (1123 A. H.) of the 5th regnal year (16th January 1712).

ON LOAN.

Lent by the Director General of Archæology in India.

1. Sanad marked with the seal impressions of Majd-ud-Daulah Abdul Majid Khan and Sayyid Umar Khan officials of the Emperor Aurangzeb and dated the 23rd Safar

Appendix B—*contd.*

the year 1068 A. H. (30th November 1657 A. D.). It was issued in favour of a lady named Sharifa Bano and others, permitting them to retain possession of 50 bighas of land in the Pargana of Mihrabad in the Province of the Punjab.

2. Sanad marked with the seal impressions of Sayyid Shahmat Khan and Sayyid Mirak, officials of the Emperor Muhammad Shah, and dated the 14th Muharram the year 1153 A. H. (11th April 1740). It was issued in favour of Sharifa Bano and others, permitting them to retain possession of 50 bighas of land in the Pargana of Mihrabad in the Province of the Punjab.

3. Sanad marked with the seal impression of Hidayatullah, son of Sayyid Ahmad Qadiri, the Sadr-us-Sadur (Chief Judge) of Shahjahan, and dated the 27th of Shawwal, the first year of Aurangzeb corresponding to 1069 A. H. (18th July 1659). It was issued in favour of Nizam-ud-Din, permitting him to retain possession of 85 bighas of land in the village of Baddhi Gharib Rao in the province of Dar-us-Saltanat, Lahore.

4. Sanad marked with the seal impressions of Saadatmand Khan and Sayyid Ashraf Khan, officials of Shah Alam Bahadur Shah I, and dated the 19th Jamadi-ul-Awwal, the year 1121 A. H. (26th August 1709). It was issued in favour of Gul Muhammad, the son of Khan Muhammad, permitting him to retain possession of 60 bighas of land in the village Mihri in the Punjab.

5. Sanad issued under the seal impressions and signatures of Sadr-us-Sadur Sadr-i-Jahan Sayyid Muhammad Afzal Khan and Kutbu Mulk Sayyid Abdullah, the prime minister of the Emperor Farrukhsiyar, granting 40 bighas of land to Shaikh Ismail, the grandson of Makhdum Ilm-ud-Din Suharwardi in the pargana Kulanki in the Province of Multan. It is dated the 14th Rabi-ul-Awwal, the 4th year of the reign of Farrukhsiyar.

6. Sale deed dated the 2nd Rabi-ul-Awwal the year 1177 A. H. (10th September 1764) and marked with the seal impressions of Shaikh Aziz, the Shaikhul Islam, and Faiz Muhammad and Abd-ur-Rahman, the Qaziz, respectively. It refers to the sale of a house at Lahore by Hafiz Muhammad Azam to Muhammad Zarif.

7. Parwana issued under the seal impression of ..... Khan, the Sadr-us-Sadur of Timur Shah, the eldest son of Ahmad Shah Durrani, appointing Mir Masud as a Muazzin of the Jami Mosque of Lahore with an allowance of one rupee a day in supersession of Nazar Muhammad who ran away. It is dated 8th Ziqad the year 1170 A. H. (25th July 1757).

8. Farman of Ahmad Shah Durrani, marked with his seal impression and Tughra. It is dated 1182 A. H. (1768 A. D.) and was issued in favour of Mulla Salih Muhammad, the Shaikhul Islam of Peshawar.

9. Farman of Mahmud Shah, the son of Timur Shah, issued in favour of Mulla Sharfuddin of Peshawar: permitting him to retain possession of 20 Jaribs (chains) of land in the village of Pachki. It is dated 1216 A. H. (1801 A. D.).

10. Farman of Shuja-ul-Mulk, the son of Timur Shah, marked with his seal impression and Tughra and dated the year 1218 A. H. (1803 A. D.). It was issued in favour of Bahram Khan Firoz Kohi, the chief of Afghanistan.

11. Inscribed filter vessel of the Emperor Aurangzeb. It is dated 1080 A. H. (1669-70 A. D.)

12. Specimen of calligraphy by Muhammad Husain. It is written on both sides and contains 12 small pictures of birds. Muhammad Husain was a resident of Kashmir and given the title of Zarrin Qalam (gold pen) by the Emperor Akbar.

APPENDIX B—*contd.*

List of coins received for the Delhi Museum of Archæology during the year 1921-22.

From whom received.	Ruler's name.	Dynasty.	Gold.	Silver.	Copper.	Billon.	Total.
(Presented.)							
Director General of Archæology in India (from Dr. Taylor's collection).	Qutbuddin Mubarak Shah	Khalji	..	..	..	2	2
Do.	Ghiyasuddin Tughlaq	Tughlaq	..	..	..	1	1
Do.	Muhammad bin Tughlaq	Do.	..	..	1	3	4
Do.	Firoz Shah Tughlaq	Do.	..	..	3	17	20
Do.	Firoz Shah with Fath Khan	Do.	..	..	..	1	1
Do.	Muhammad Shah ibn Firoz Shah.	Do.	..	..	1	..	1
Do.	Muhammad Adil Shah	Sur	..	..	3	..	3
Do.	Akbar	Moghal	..	35	..	..	35
Do.	Jahangir	Do.	..	1	..	..	1
Do.	Shah Jahan	Do.	..	1	..	..	1
Do.	Aurangzeb	Do.	..	2	..	..	2
Do.	Shah Alam I	Do.	..	..	4	..	4
Do.	Murtaza I	Nizam Shahi	..	..	8	..	8
Do.	Murtaza II	Do.	..	..	13	..	13
Do.	Ali I	Adil Shahi	..	..	2	..	2
Do.	Ali II	Do.	..	..	4	..	4
Do.	Ibrahim II	Do.	..	..	13	..	13
Do.	Muhammad	Do.	..	..	7	..	7
Do.	Ahmad Shah I	Bahmani	..	..	3	..	3
Do.	Ahmad Shah II	Do.	..	..	3	..	3
Do.	Muhammad Shah bin Humayun Shah.	Do.	..	..	2	..	2
Do.	Kalimullah	Do.	..	..	2	..	2
Do	Ahmad Shah I	King of Gujrat	..	..	8	..	8
Do.	Mahmud Shah I	Do.	..	..	11	..	11
Do.	Ahmad Shah II	Do.	..	..	3	..	3
Do.	Muhammad Shah II	Do.	..	..	2	..	2
	Carried over	..	..	39	93	24	156

APPENDIX B—*contd.*

From whom received.	Ruler's name.	Dynasty.	Gold.	Silver.	Copper.	Billon.	Total.
	Brought forward .	..	..	39	93	24	156
(Presented.) Director General of Archæology in India (from Dr. Taylor's Collection.)	Muzaffar Shah II . .	King of Gujrat.	..	..	1	..	1
Do. .	Bahadur Shah . . .	Do. .	..	..	1	..	1
Do. .	Mahmud Shah II . .	Do. .	..	..	1	..	1
Do. .	Ahmad Shah III . .	Do. .	..	..	5	..	5
Do. .	Muzaffar Shah III . .	Do. .	..	..	6	..	6
Do. .	Tippu Sultan . . .	Rajas of Mahisur.	..	..	16	..	16
Do. .	Krishna Raja . . .	Do. .	..	..	2	..	2
Do. .	Muhammad Akbar Badshah Ghazi II.	Mughal .	..	..	2	..	2
Do. .	Shah Jahan II . .	Do. .	..	..	2	..	2
Do. .	Sahibqiran probably Maharaja Gwalior.	Native State	..	..	1	.	1
Do. .	Bahadur Shah II . .	Mughal .	..	..	1	..	1
Government of the United Provinces.	Shah Alam II . .	Do. .	..	3	..	..	3
Do. .	Muhammad Shah . .	Do. .	..	7	..	..	7
Do. .	Ahmad Shah . . .	Do. .	..	1	..	..	1
Do. .	Muhammad Shah . .	Do. .	..	1	..	..	1
Do. .	Alamgir II . . .	Do. .	..	1	..	..	1
Government of Bengal.	Akbar . . .	Do. .	..	1	..	..	1
Do. .	Jahangir . . .	Do. .	..	1	..	..	1
Do .	Shah Jahan . . .	Do. .	..	116	..	..	116
Do. .	Aurangzeb . . .	Do. .	..	2	..	..	2
Do. .	Farrukhsiyar . . .	Do. .	..	1	..	..	1
Do. .	Muhammad Shah . .	Do. .	..	2	..	..	2
Director of Industries, Central Provinces.	Aurangzeb . .	Do. .	..	2	..	..	2
Do. .	Farruksiyar . . .	Do. .	..	2	..	..	2
Do. .	Muhammad Shah . .	Do. .	..	7	..	..	7
Do. .	Ahmad Shah . . .	Do. .	..	3	..	..	3
Do. .	Shah Alam II . . .	Do. .	..	6	..	.	6
Do. .	Akbar II . . .	Do. .	..	2	..	..	2
	Total presented .	..	..	197	131	24	352

Appendix B—*concld.*

From whom received.	Ruler's name.	Dynasty.	Gold.	Silver.	Copper.	Billon.	Total.	
	Brought forward ..	..	..	197	131	24	352	
(On loan).								
Director General of Archæology in India.	Jahangir . . .	Mughal .	..	1	..	..	1	
Do. .	Aurangzeb . . .	Do. .	8	21	..	..	29	
Do. .	Shah Alam I . . .	Do. .	..	9	..	..	9	
Do. .	Jahandar Shah . .	Do. .	..	2	..	..	2	
Do. .	Farrukhsiyar . . .	Do. .	..	7	..	..	7	
Do. . .	Muhammad Shah . .	Do. .	1	1	..	..	2	
	Total on loan .	..	9	41	..	..	50	
(Purchased) .	Akbar . . .	Mughal .	1	..	..	..	1	Rs. 2[illegible]4-0-0
Do. .	Aurangzeb . . .	Do. .	3	7	..	..	10	
Do. .	Shah Alam I . . .	Do. .	..	3	..	..	3	
Do. ..	Jahandar Shah . .	Do. .	..	2	..	..	2	
Do. .	Farrukhsiyar . . .	Do. .	..	11	..	..	11	
Do. .	Muhammad Shah . .	Do. .	..	1	..	..	1	
Do. .	Alamgir II . . .	Do. .	..	1	..	..	1	
Do. .	Shah Alam II . .	Do. .	..	4	..	..	4	
Do. .	Muhammad Ali Shah .	Nawab of Oudh.	..	1	..	..	1	
Do. .	Wajid Ali Shah . .	Do. .	..	2	..	..	2	
	Total purchased .	..	4	32	..	..	36	
	Grand Total .	..	13	270	131	24	438	

List of exhibits received in the Taj Museum, Agra.

(Presented.)

1. A picture of the Taj Mahal presented by the Right Hon'ble Marquis Curzon of Kedleston, P.C., etc.
2. An image of a Jaina Tirthankara found some 15 years ago in a stone quarry near Baiju-ki-Barahdari at Fatehpur Sikri.

APPENDIX C.

List of antiquities found at Nalanda in 1921-22.

SITE No. I.

Serial No.	Class.	Description of finds.	Find spot.	Depth.	Measure.	REMARKS.
538	Stone .	A group of three Buddhas standing side by side on a lotus pedestal. with three small Buddhas standing to left of each and a small elephant kneeling to left of the centre one.	H 25 *b4*	7′ 9″ below the upper verandah level.	7½″ height	More than half of the centre one and head of the right one gone.
539	Terracotta	One votive terracotta plaque with Buddha seated on lotus throne in Bhumisparsa Mudra, surrounded by many votive stupas. Three lines of inscription occur under the lotus throne.	L 27 *b2*	16′ 3″	4¼″ „	
540	Stone .	Standing Buddha on lotus, an attendant standing to right with a votive stupa to left, probably a portion of a larger statue.	J 26 *d3*	17′ 2″	3½″ „	Left hand broken.
541	„ .	One stone pedestal with one male and one female figure lying under the feet of a standing figure. May be Trailokyavijaya.	K 26 *d4*	18′ 0″	2″ „	Standing figure is missing.
542	„ .	One three-headed figure seated on a lion throne in a preaching attitude, has ushnisha, like a Buddha. Inscription on back.	W 24 *c1*	12′ 7″	6¾″ „	
543	Metal .	One iron lock, one ring, five nails and two pieces of iron.	P 24 *a1*	17′ 0″	..	
544	Stone .	Seated Avalokitesvara on a lotus throne. Left hand resting on the head of an attendant and right arm lying on his knee ; a votive stupa to left, and a monkey kneeling to right side on pedestal. Inscription on back.	J 24 *d2*	16′ 9″	8¾″ „	Broken in two pieces.
545	„ .	Small Buddha seated on a lotus throne under the Bodhi tree in Bhumisparsa Mudra.	L 24 *d4*	14′ 7″	4½″ „	
546	„ .	Seated figure on a lotus throne with two attendants on each side standing on a lotus, and two other smaller attendants, one kneeling to right and one standing to left. Two lines of inscription on back.	J 25 *a1*	14′ 3″	7¾″ „	Upper half is missing.
547	Terracotta	One double-faced round seal. One face with the Sarnath emblems. Dharmachakra and deer, with two lines of inscription. The other with Siva seated on bull holding Trisula, with one line of inscription.	K 26 *a1*	18′ 3″	1½″ round both.	
548	Stone .	Lower portion of a small standing figure	I 25 *c2*	18′ 4″	1½″ height	Upper portion missing.

NOTE :—All depths recorded as below the upper verandah level.

APPENDIX C—*concld.*

Serial No.	Class.	Description of finds.	Find spot.	Depth.	Measure.	REMARKS.
549	Terracotta	Votive terracotta plaque similar to No. 539.	I 25 *b*2	17′ 6″	..	Lower portion with a line of inscription gone.
550	„ .	Fragment of a votive terracotta plaque similar to No. 539.	I 25 *b*4	17′ 9″	..	
551	Stone .	Pedestal of a seated figure on lotus throne, one line of inscription at bottom.	K 25 *b*2	17′ 9″	3¾″ height	Right half missing.
552	„ .	Fragment of a halo back-ground, a votive stupa to right and a portion of inscription.	K 25 *b*4	18′ 0″	4½″ „	
553	„ .	Fragment with a standing female figure holding a chowri in her arm.	J 26 *b*2	18′ 3″	7½″ „	
554	Seal .	One Nalanda Seal	J 24 *b*4	16′ 0″	..	
555	„ .	One small head, very rudely carved .	J 24 *b*1	15′ 3″	..	
556	Metal .	Seated Buddha in Bhumisparsa Mudra, in 2 pieces.	O 27 *a*4	16′ 0″	10″ height	
557	Stone .	One votive stupa	N 26 *d*1	13′ 3″	10″ „	
558	Pottery .	One earthen chiragh	I 24 *d*4	16′ 0″	..	
559	„ .	One small jar	I 24 *d*4	16′ 0″	1¼″ height	

NOTE:—All depths recorded as below the upper verandah level.

M1DGofA—18.8.24—50C—GIPS.

(a) DALANS EAST OF SIRHI DARWAZA, AS RESTORED, TAJ, AGRA.

(b) KOTLA FIROZ SHAH; ENTRANCE GATEWAY OF THE MOSQUE FROM INSIDE THE MOSQUE, DELHI.

Photo-engraved & printed at the Offices of the Survey of India, Calcutta,

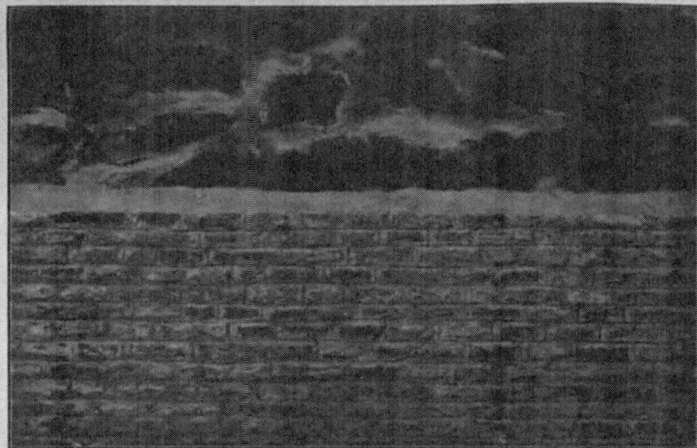

(a) Akbar's Tomb; External face of compound wall near south-west corner Burj (1) Wide flush pointing in rubble masonry (2) Rod or rule pointing in brickwork, as done previously. Sikandra, Agra.

(b) Akbar's Tomb; External face of compound wall south-west corner Burj, as raked out. Sikandra, Agra.

(c) Akbar's Tomb; External face of compound wall near south-west corner Burj (1) Wide flush pointing in rubble masonry (2) Rod or rule pointing in brick-work, as repointed. Sikandra, Agra.

(d) Akbar's Horse; Before removal, taken from north-west. Sikandra, Agra.

(a) TUGHLAQ'S FORT; BREACH IN BASTION AFTER REPAIR. TUGHLAQABAD, DELHI.

(b) TUGHLAQ'S FORT: SECOND GATEWAY SHOWING CHABUTRA AND GATE AFTER REPAIR AND CLEARANCE. TUGHLAQABAD, DELHI.

(c) WEST GATE OF QADAM SHARIF, QADAM SHARIF, DELHI.

(d) SOUTH-WEST WALL OF QADAM SHARIF UNDER REPAIR. QADAM SHARIF, DELHI.

(a) CHHATRI OVER ASOKA PILLAR AT SARNATH, AFTER COMPLETION.

(b) STUPAS TO NORTH-WEST OF MAIN SHRINE, SARNATH, AFTER CONSERVATION.

Photo-engraved & printed at the Offices of the Survey of India, Calcutta, [illegible].

(a) JAULIAN MONASTERY. WEST WALL BEFORE CONSERVATION.

(b) JAULIAN MONASTERY. WEST WALL AFTER CONSERVATION.

Photo-engraved & printed at the Offices of the Survey of India, Calcutta, [illegible]

(a) NALANDA. MONASTERY NO. 1. SHOWING ORIGINAL STAIR DESCENT UNDER RECONSTRUCTION AND RUINED ENCLOSURE WALLS REPAIRED.

(b) NALANDA. MONASTERY NO. 1. INTERIOR QUADRANGLE. CHABUTRA ON EAST SIDE, AS EXCAVATED.

Photo-engraved & printed at the Offices of the Survey of India, Calcutta,

(a) NALANDA. MONASTERY NO. 1. SCULPTURED SLAB IN LOW CHABUTRA EXPOSED ON SOUTH SIDE OF QUADRANGLE.

(b) NALANDA. MONASTERY NO. 1. MAIN WESTERN GATEWAY BEFORE REPAIR.

Photo-engraved & printed at the Offices of the Survey of India, Calcutta, 1924.

(a) NALANDA. MONASTERY NO. 1. MAIN WEST ENTRANCE. NORTH WALL OF VESTIBULE UNDER REPAIR.

(b) NALANDA. MONASTERY NO. 1A. WEST WALL OF QUADRANGLE SHOWING RUINED STYLOBATE PARAPET RECONSTRUCTED.

Photo-engraved & printed at the Offices of the Survey of India, Calcutta,

(a) TEMPLE OF ANANDESWAR, FROM NORTH, AT LASUR, DISTRICT AMRAOTI, C.P.: SHOWING NEW FACING OF EASTERN SHRINE.

(b) JAMI MASJID, ASIRGARH, NIMAR DISTRICT, C.P.: EXTERIOR FROM S.E. SHOWING CONSERVATION WORK IN PROGRESS ON MINAR, ETC.

Photo.-engraved & printed at the Offices of the Survey of India, Calcutta.

(a) BARA DARWAZA, AT CHIKALDA, DISTRICT AMRAOTI, C.P., SHOWING KANGURAS REBUILT TO THE OLD SHAPE.

[illegible] TOMB OF NADIR SHAH, BURHANPUR, C.P. SHOWING REPAIR OF FACING IN PROGRESS, AND RECONSTRUCTED CHABUTRA.

PLATE XI.

(a) STONE PILLAR AT KOSAM AFTER EXCAVATION; DISTRICT ALLAHABAD.

(b) MATH AT RAJBARI, DACCA, FROM NORTH-EAST.

Photo-engraved & printed at the Offices of the Survey of India, Calcutta, 1924.

(a) CAVES NOS. II, III AND IV ELEPHANTA. AFTER EXCAVATION.

(b) CAVE NO. V. ELEPHANTA. BEFORE EXCAVATION.

(c) VISHNU AND DURGA FOUND IN CAVE NO. III ELEPHANTA.

(d) CAVE NO. V. ELEPHANTA. AFTER EXCAVATION.

(a) FRONT OF DELHI GATE, SHANWARWADA, POONA. BEFORE CONSERVATION.

(b) FRONT OF DELHI GATE, SHANWARWADA, POONA. AFTER CONSERVATION.

(a) FIRST COURT, SHANWARWADA, POONA. BEFORE DEMOLITION OF MODERN STRUCTURES AND EXCAVATION.

(b) FIRST COURT, SHANWARWADA, POONA. AFTER EXCAVATION.

Photo.-engraved & printed at the Offices of the Survey of India, Calcutta, 1924

(*a*) CHALUKYAN TEMPLE IN SHOLAPUR FORT. BEFORE EXCAVATION.

(*b*) CHALUKYAN TEMPLE IN SHOLAPUR FORT. AFTER EXCAVATION.

Photo-engraved & printed at the Offices of the Survey of India, Calcutta, [illegible].

(a) ST. FRANCIS CHURCH. BRITISH COCHIN.

(b) VIRABHADRA TEMPLE, EAST VIEW, MOTUPALLE, GUNTUR.

Photo-engraved & printed at the offices of the Survey of India, Calcutta, 1915.

Plate XVII

(a) Dutch Tombstone of R. Van Harn in St. Francis church.

(b) Old Belfry outside the Port and Customs Office.

(c) Dutch Tombstone of G.W.S. Van Gollenesse and two children in St. Francis Church.

Plate XVIII.

(a) Royal tombs in the Fort at Mandalay.

(b) Fort Dufferin, Mandalay.

Photo-engraved & printed at the Offices of the Survey of India, Calcutta,

(a) MIN-O-CHANTHA PAGODA, PAGAN.

(b) RATANAMANAUNG PAGODA, MYOHAUNG, AKYAB DISTRICT.

Photo-engraved & printed at the Offices of the Survey of India, Calcutta, [illegible]

(a) SARNATH. EXCAVATIONS IN OPEN FORECOURT OF MAIN SHRINE.

(b) STUPA No. 136. DETAIL OF N.E. CORNER.

Photo-engraved & printed at the Offices of the Survey of India, Calcutta, 1908.

(a) SARNATH. HEAD OF AVALOKITESVARA.

(b) SARNATH. FEMALE CHAURI-BEARER CARVED IN THE ROUND. BACK.

(c) KURUKSHETRA. A PITCHER.

(d) SARNATH. YAKSHA FIGURE (SUNGA PERIOD) FOUND IN THE EXCAVATION AROUND THE PILLAR AT KOSAM.

(a) KURUKSHETRA. TRENCH B-C FROM S.W.

(b) KURUKSHETRA. TRENCH D FROM S.W.

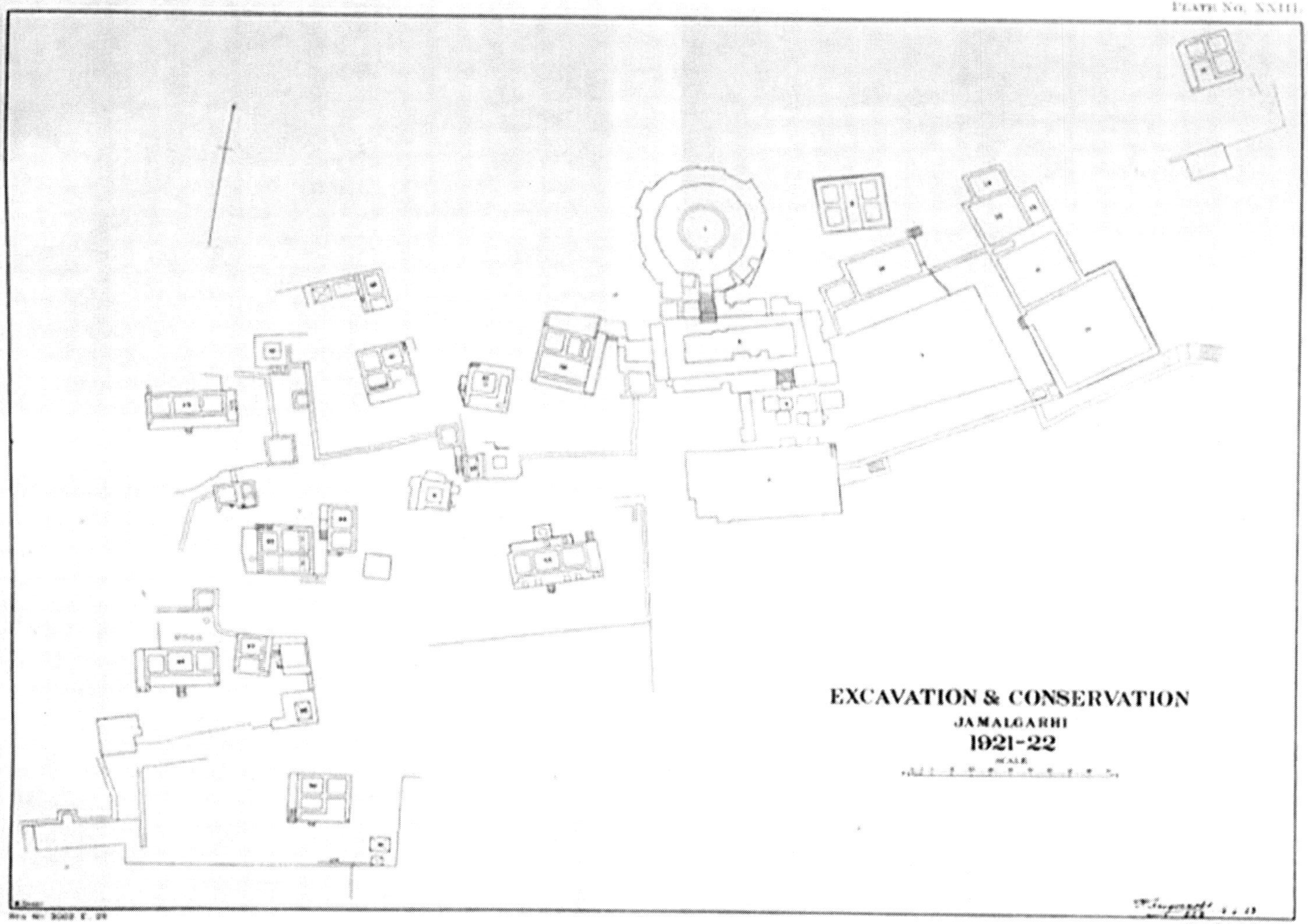
EXCAVATION & CONSERVATION
JAMALGARHI
1921-22
SCALE

PLATE XXIV

(a) JAMALGARHI. FOUR SUNK WATER POTS AND SMALL MASONRY PIT

(b) THE TEMPTATION BY MARA AND HIS THREE DAUGHTERS.

(c) RELIEF. THE APPROACH TO THE BODHI TREE

(d) RELIEF. THE NURSING OF THE DEAD WOMAN

[illegible] SEATED BUDDHA WITH FLAMES ON THE SHOULDERS.

[illegible] BUDDHA UNDER THE BODHI TREE. MARA AND HIS DAUGHTER TO LEFT.

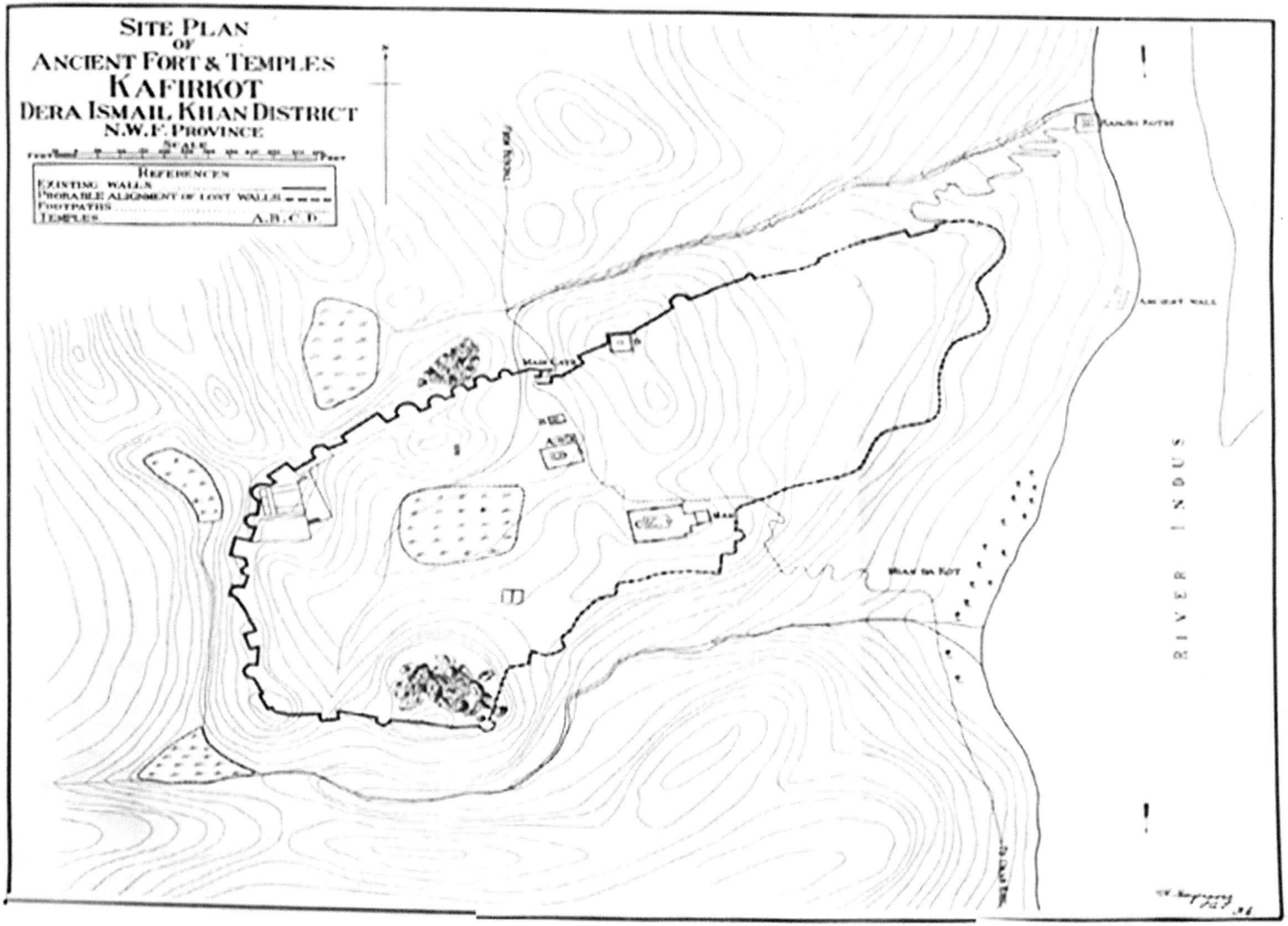

SITE PLAN
OF
ANCIENT FORT & TEMPLES
KAFIRKOT
DERA ISMAIL KHAN DISTRICT
N.W.F. PROVINCE
SCALE
REFERENCES
EXISTING WALLS
PROBABLE ALIGNMENT OF LOST WALLS
FOOTPATHS
TEMPLES A.B.C.D.
MAIN GATE
ANCIENT WALL
RIVER INDUS

(a) DETAILS OF THE MATH AT KODLAH FROM NORTH, KHULNA

(b) BHANDISVAR SIVA TEMPLE FROM EAST, AT BHANDIRVAN, BIRBHUM

(a) PILLAR WITH INSCRIPTION OF THE CHEDI PRINCE KARA, AT NARAYANCHATVARA, PAIKORE, BIRBHUM.

(b) BROKEN PILLAR WITH INSCRIPTION OF VIJAYASENA AT PAIKORE, BIRBHUM.

(c) IMAGE OF MANASA AT BHADISVAR, BIRBHUM.

(d) IMAGE OF NARASIMHA, AT NARAYANCHATVARA, PAIKORE, BIRBHUM.

(d) Image of Parsvanath in the temple of Siddhesvar, at Bahulara, Bankura

(b) Terracotta head from Sihari at Devkot, Dinajpur

(c) Chaturmukha linga on the right bank of the Unakoti stream at Unakoti, Tripura State

(e) Stele representing Buddha with scenes from his life at Si[illegible] village, Khulna

Plate XXX

(a) Group of colossal Ganesa and other figures in the bed of the Unakoti stream at Unakoti, Tripura State

(b) Colossal rock-cut head of Siva after jungle-clearance at Unakoti, Tripura State

(a) SARAI AT KARI; REAR WALL.

(b) EARLY CAVES, MANGYA TUNGYA, NASIK DISTRICT. IMAGE IN SHRINE OF CAVE NO. I.

Photo-engraved & printed at the Offices of the Survey of India, Calcutta,

(a) EARLY CAVES MAUNGYA TUNGYA, NASIK DISTRICT. SCULPTURES IN VERANDAH OF CAVE NO. I.

(b) MAUNGYA PEAK, NASIK DISTRICT; STELE IN CAVE NO. II.

(a) Holkar's palace at Chandor. Façade.

(b) Holkar's palace at Chandor. Interior.

(a) Two fresco slabs packed into bundle as brought from Chinese Turkestan

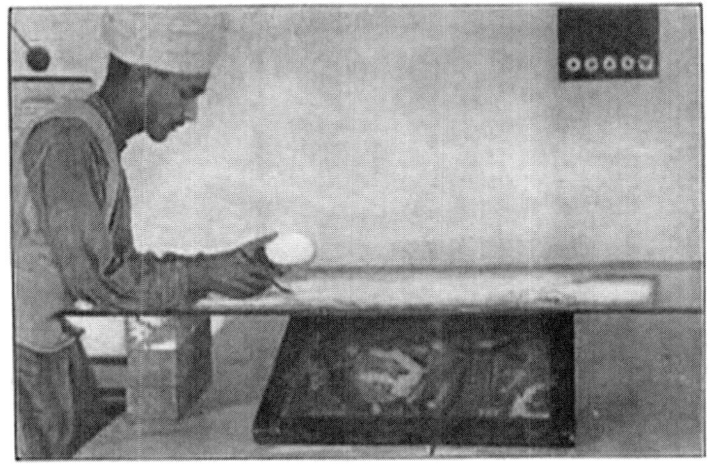

(c) Applying the first backing of plaster, mirror below

(b) A bundle of fresco slabs being lifted from their box

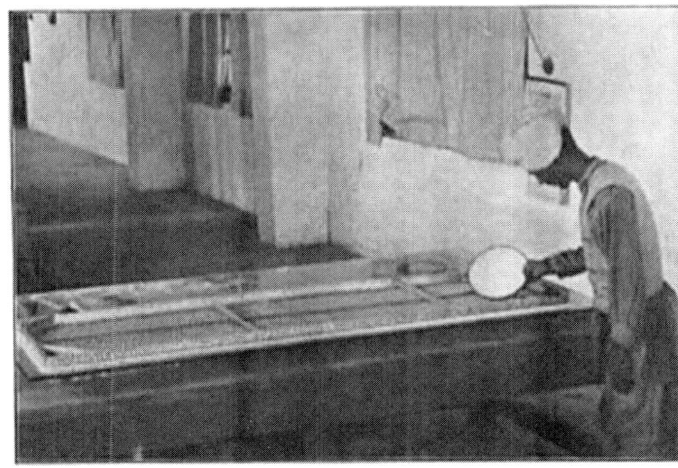

(d) Putting final plaster coat after back has been placed in position

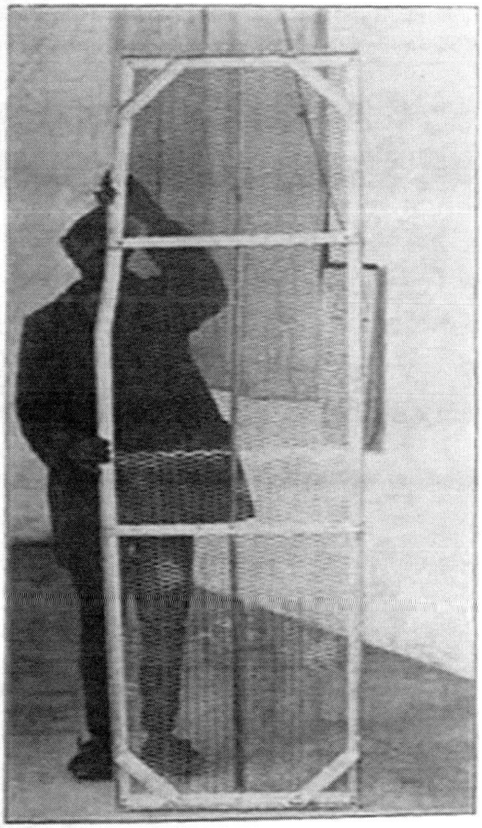

(a) ALUMINIUM FRAME USED IN MOUNTING SECTION OF FRESCO SHOWN IN FIG. 6.

(b) SECTION OF FRESCO MOUNTED ON ITS ALUMINIUM FRAME.

(c) WALL PAINTING FROM SHRINE XII, BEZEKLIK, TURFĀN, AFTER BACKING AND MOUNTING.

a

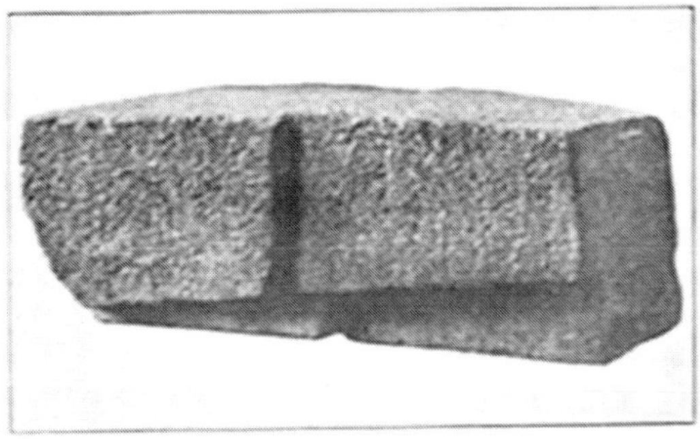

b

c

d

e

f

FRESH ACQUISITIONS IN THE INDIAN MUSEUM.

a

b

c

d

BRONZE IMAGES ACQUIRED FOR THE INDIAN MUSEUM.

Photo-engraved & printed at the Offices of the Survey of India, Calcutta.

PLATE XXXIX.

VASE FOUND NEAR BAGHDAD.

PLATE XI.

(a) KURUKSHETRA: BRONZE OBJECT.

(b) BRONZE IMAGE OF BUDDHA AT KALI TEMPLE, DHARMAGHAR (SYLHET).

(c) MASON'S MARKS ON ARCH-STONE FROM PATALIPUTRA.

(d) INSCRIBED FILTER VESSEL OF THE EMPEROR AURANGZEB.

(e) VISVANTARA JATAKA.